THE ART OF
MOTIVATION
FOR SPORTS

THE ART OF MOTIVATION FOR SPORTS

JIM HINKSON

GSPH

GENERAL STORE PUBLISHING HOUSE INC.
499 O'Brien Road, Renfrew, Ontario, Canada K7V 3Z3
Telephone 1.613.599.2064 or 1.800.465.6072

http://www.gsph.com

ISBN 978-1-77123-046-9

Copyright © Jim Hinkson 2014

Cover art, design: Magdalene Carson
Photos: All photos from Dreamstime.com, except for cover, bottom centre photo on
cover (and page 71), Courtesy of Christian Bonin (www.tsgphoto.com)

Printed by Image Digital Printing Ltd.
dba The IDP Group, Renfrew, Ontario
Printed and bound in Canada

Library and Archives Canada Cataloguing in Publication
Hinkson, Jim, author
The art of motivation for sports / Jim Hinkson.
Issued in print and electronic formats.
ISBN 978-1-77123-046-9 (pbk.).--ISBN 978-1-77123-124-4 (epub).
-- ISBN 978-1-77123-125-1 (mobi).--ISBN 978-1-77123-126-8 (pdf)
1. Sports--Psychological aspects. 2. Coaching (Athletics). I. Title.
GV706.4.H55 2013   796.01'9   C2013-905150-3   C2013-905151-1

To the Hinkson clan

Thanks for the great journey

My wife, Cynndy
Jeff and Maggie and daughters Sophie and Elyse Webb
Chris and Kate, daughter Tesa St. John, and their dog Kawi
James and Sarah and baby James Hinkson

CONTENTS

FOREWORD

As a former NCAA Division 1 coach for fourteen years as well as having coached at the high school and grade school levels prior to that, I have read more than my share of books on coaching philosophy. Jim Hinkson's comprehensive look at all the aspects of the profession is both detail-oriented and, more important, quite insightful. He provides wonderful food for thought for coaches of all ages and levels. I thoroughly enjoyed it and found it to be dead-on for what is important for success in coaching.

I've heard it said many times: "It's not the X's and O's but the Jimmys and the Joes." We're in the people business, and Jim Hinkson's book gives you the kinds of concepts that you need to consider as you deal with the endless challenges that face coaches today in the twenty-first century. The playbook is important—without doubt—but this book will help make you that much more of an effective leader, communicator, role model, and coach; and that's what makes the difference.

Jack Armstrong
TV analyst for the Toronto Raptors of the NBA
Former head coach of the Niagara University Purple Eagles

ACKNOWLEDGEMENTS

I would like to thank Les Bartley, former coach of the Toronto Rock of the NLL, for his time when we talked about lacrosse in his home in St. Catharines, Ontario.

Thanks to W.T. Westhead, who was head of the Stephen Leacock English department, for editing my rough copy. This is the third book he has helped me with.

I would like to thank Jack Armstrong, former NCAA coach and now a colour analyst for the Toronto Raptors, for taking the time to write the Foreword to this book.

I would like to thank Ron Pither, former Canadian National Rugby Team coach and teacher, for his input. His knowledge was invaluable to the book. He dissected the book the way he coached—down to the last detail.

I would like to thank Mike Keenan (former NHL coach and now a TV colour analyst) and Joe Nieuwendyk (former player and general manager of the NHL) for their endorsements of the book.

I would also like to thank Guilio Giordani, former coach of the University of Toronto Football team, Canadian Champions, for his time when we talked about coaching. His expertise, his ideas, and his coaching strategies helped me a great deal.

I would especially like to thank Jane Karchmar of General Store Publishing House, who did a magnificent job of editing my book. As well, I thank the other GSPH staff for their help and involvement in this project: publisher Tim Gordon, designer Magdalene Carson, and publicist Andrea McCormick.

PREFACE

Trying to write a coaching manual for all sports is not an easy task; due to different personalities and different philosophies, no two coaches have exactly the same approach. But there are certain leadership skills one must have to be successful, such as how to motivate, how to organize, how to run practices, how to make good decisions, and how to set goals. It took me thirty-eight years of coaching basketball and lacrosse to put these coaching ideas into a book. I am definitely not saying I have all the right answers on "how to coach"—I don't think anybody does—but I have given it my best shot. Like parents, coaches tend to coach the way they have been coached. But this way might sometimes be the wrong way, so we need to expose ourselves to different methods and points of view.

I hope you as a coach will find useful ideas here or reinforce old ideas that you are using now. One of the main differences between coaching teams and coaching individuals, of course, is that in team-coaching, team cohesiveness, team chemistry, and team building are extremely important.

Team building is one of the major keys to becoming successful in a team sport. Being a cohesive unit will definitely give you the edge over other teams, as players have to be unselfish, get along with one another, and co-operate with one another. Having this solid, team-oriented philosophy, which comes from the coach, is the glue that binds all the players together.

I realize that most coaches don't want to read through page after page of theory. Here, I intend to give you the practical answers right away from my experience and the trials and tribulations of coaching teams over a long season.

If you are new to coaching, you will learn about all aspects of coaching—selecting players, planning the season, running practices, coaching during high-pressure game situations, and helping players become the best team they can be. If you are an experienced coach, this book will give you some food for thought about your current coaching practices, as well as ways of handling situations you may have found challenging.

I have been lucky enough to have played under a great lacrosse coach, Jim Bishop; I have attended hundreds of basketball coaching clinics throughout the United States and Canada; I have worked at numerous basketball camps; read tons of books on coaching and motivation; and talked with some of the best coaches in the coaching business. So if some ideas sound familiar, it is probably because they are. I thank those who have contributed to my development as a coach.

The "New School" of Coaching

The way we coach today is different from the way it was done in the past, when coaching and training followed an almost militaristic model. The coach was the general, the assistants were the lieutenants, team captains were, well, captains, and the players the foot soldiers. There was a strict hierarchy, and all participants were expected to follow their superiors unquestioningly. The team's fate rested in the coach's hands. Games were battles in which the coach's commands had to be obeyed without question, and mistakes were harshly punished.

While some remnants of the old command-and-control coaching style still persist today, it has generally fallen by the wayside because it doesn't reflect the social realities of the modern athlete. As most young people no longer have to engage in compulsory military service, they do not understand this hierarchical model anymore.

In addition, our society puts greater emphasis on individual freedom and choice than ever before. Young people have been taught to question authority. The school system is generally less structured, and students are invited to participate in devising lessons. They are used to being asked for more of their input and opinions than ever before. The speeded-up Internet/video game world they inhabit has shortened their attention span. Coaches have to take this into consideration when teaching.

Another reality is the diversity of our society. Athletes today come from a wide variety of social classes, cultures, and religions, leading to great variation in values.

Girls are participating in sport in greater numbers than ever before, and many coaches have found that they, like their male counterparts, do not respond so well to the traditional command-and-control coaching methods.

And finally, more and more children are growing up in homes where parental control is lax or non-existent. It's not that these kids have no respect for authority—they don't even grasp the concept.

All of these changes mean that the authoritarian style of coaching is no longer very effective. In fact, no single coaching method will work with every team, given our great social diversity.

Coaches today cannot be rigid with just one type of coaching style. To be successful they have to be prepared to adapt their styles to their teams' needs.

This book is about a "new school" of coaching that meshes with these new social realities and makes effective use of them to build successful teams. The basis of my approach is that the coach retains control of the team, laterally rather than vertically, by involving the players in making team decisions, such as setting the team's long-term goals. I have found this to be the most effective way of motivating today's athlete—and motivation is one of the coach's greatest challenges.

The Key to Successful Coaching

Another difference in today's coaching methods described here lies in how "success" is defined. I do not equate success with winning. Winning is a pleasant by-product of success.

Winning a game or a series or a championship might not be under a team's control. No matter how hard a team plays, there can be another team that is simply more talented that can defeat them. In these situations, if a team has set winning as its only objective, when it loses, the effect could be devastating.

However, if a team comes up with its own definition of success through setting its own long-term and short-term goals, it is in control of its destiny and can succeed whether a game is won or lost.

Goal-setting is a major topic of this book, for it is possibly the most effective motivational tool for today's teams. Success in this book lies in setting challenging goals and doing what is necessary to achieve them. This comes from my belief that the coach's job is not only to create successful teams, but also to develop successful individuals who will excel both on and off the playing field.

The Goals

There are four major goals that I use in coaching, and they will appear again and again in the pages of this book.

Outcome Goals

These long-term season goals give players a target to aim for—of where they want their team to end up. It could be winning a championship, of making the playoffs, of being in a certain position in the standings, or of improving their play. Once the team has a vision, it must follow it up with a plan. *A plan refers to the specifics, a step-by-step process, a series of smaller, short-term goals of how it is going to achieve the vision.*

Behaviour Goals

These goals give players a clear vision of how they should behave on the playing floor/field. *If a coach wants his team to play like champions, they have to know how champions play.* These short-term goals give the team guidelines and order on how to behave, act, and play to be successful based on values, principles, and character. The twelve team behaviour goals—such as to play hard, to play with enthusiasm, to play with intensity, to play smart, and to play with discipline—are the foundation and the fundamental building blocks of a successful team.

Performance Goals

These short-term goals are part of the overall plan to give players a clear vision of what they want their team to accomplish in every game—other than winning. If a team wants to improve its playing ability, it has to measure and evaluate its performance; and the coach has to constantly give feedback to the team from these statistics. *Team performance goals based on thorough and accurate statistics are the building blocks for the team's motivational system!*

Team or Team Cohesion Goals

These short-term goals give players a clear vision of how they should treat their teammates and each other. The four team cohesive goals are: being *committed* to the team, *playing together* and depending on each other, *trusting* each other, and *encouraging and supporting each other*. These goals are very important in building and creating a culture of team unity and teamwork. When a team follows these four cohesive goals, they stand a much better chance of achieving their other three major goals and truly becoming a "team" rather than just a group of individuals.

■ HOW TO USE THIS BOOK

The book is divided into five parts. You can read it straight through from start to finish, or you can browse to find topics that interest you.

Part I:
The Art of Motivation through Leadership

This section should get you thinking about what your approach to coaching will be. This is about the foundation of coaching. These chapters will help you figure out your coaching philosophy, one that meshes with your personality. Along with the theory presented, there are practical suggestions for making important coaching decisions, such as choosing players for the team. Even if you have been coaching for a while, you should review this section, for one of the hallmarks of successful coaches is never thinking they know it all.

Finally, I conclude this section with a discussion of the importance of continuing to develop as a coach, for by now you will have realized that successful coaches never stand still.

Part II:
The Art of Motivation through Setting Goals and Team Rules

The focus of this section is motivation—external and internal. Although the book's main focus is on external motivation by the coach, I talk about how the coach can influence a player toward self-motivation. Coach gains the team's commitment by working with them to set team goals and team rules—outcome goals, performance goals, behaviour goals, cohesive goals, and team rules. As you will see, the process of devising the goals and rules is just as important as the goals and rules themselves.

Part III:
The Art of Motivation
through Planning and Teaching Strategies

Here, I provide solid techniques for handling the practical aspects of running a team—planning the season, teaching skills, running practices efficiently, and putting together a playing system.

Part IV:
The Art of Motivation by Working with Individual Players

This covers another important component of successful coaching: communicating with players, building a trusting relationship between player and coach, and building self-esteem. Coaches cannot expect automatic obedience and respect from today's athletes; they must work to achieve trust, respect, commitment, and support from communication and relationships. This section shows you how to do that.

Part V:
The Art of Motivation
through Pre- and Post-game Speeches and Game Coaching

This unit deals with the practical elements of preparing for a game with pre-game talks and post-game talks, especially after a loss; how successful coaches coach during a game; how successful coaches make a comeback; and their approach to the big game.

INTRODUCTION

▪ THE PURPOSE OF SPORTS

> ❯ Sports provides the discipline and structured environment that players often lack elsewhere in their lives. You can teach many values important to building character and, if players practise these values, they will have a good chance of being successful. Sports also teaches the importance of attitudes in forming success: that championships and winning seasons do not measure success; striving to be as good as you can be is success.

> ❯ The purpose of sports is to develop positive character traits, such as self-discipline, self-control, self-confidence, sacrifice, and a work ethic. Sports teaches that players should have firm principles and values to live by and learn not to bend them even if everyone else is doing it.

> ❯ Character is built much more quickly in sport than in life because of pressure in the former. Sports reveals character, especially in a crisis, but it doesn't necessarily build character on its own. Through the vehicle of sports, you as the coach are capable of building character by reinforcing the way players react.

> ❯ The purpose of sports is to give young people an environment in which to grow. Sports is like life. It is to prepare players for the day when they can stand alone. You should not develop a player who is dependent on you, but one who becomes independent. Good coaches believe in developing the physical, mental, psychological, and moral character of players. You must believe in developing not only the players' talent, but also their character. Talent will get them through the first period of the game, but character will get them through to the end of the game.

> ❯ Sports teaches players how to motivate themselves. They must find something they love and then fill their life with it. If a player doesn't love or have a passion for playing the sport, it will always be work. Motivation is result of loving what you do. Motivation comes from chasing a dream by setting goals. Coaches get across the idea that real motivation comes from within. If coaches have to motivate players, they motivate them for the game. If coaches teach players how to motivate themselves, they motivate them for the season and for the rest of their lives.

> Sports is about learning the lessons of life and building good citizens who will contribute to society; in other words, it makes "men out of boys."

> Purpose of sports is to teach players how to be successful. Sports gives players values that are essential to a successful life. Self-motivation, preparation, self-discipline, and dedication are very important ingredients for winners in any endeavour. The values learned through sports, especially hard work and determination, become an investment that will pay off in meeting the demands of life.

> Purpose of sports is to get healthy and fit.

> Purpose of sports is for physical activity to carry over into life and to find a game to enjoy for life!

> Purpose of sports is to receive enjoyment and recreation.

SPORTS PARTICIPATION IS LIFE PREPARATION

■ THE VALUES TAUGHT BY SPORTS

Sports teaches one how to be successful and to become a good citizen. The many other benefits of sports include teaching young people:

> *The value of hard work.* The bottom line is that sports teaches players that to be successful, they have to have a good work ethic. Everything of value in life requires hard work. Sports teaches that natural talent is not enough, just as intelligence is not enough. A player must be willing to pay the price of hard work if he wants to be successful. It hurts to run one more lap; it hurts to do one more rep; but that's exactly the kind of effort that makes a player stronger and better. Why not get the most out of life; why not do it 100 percent right, rather than merely "going through the motions"? Players get satisfaction by knowing they are putting out a 100 percent effort.

> *Perseverance.* Perseverance is never giving up, especially in the face of adversity; and to come back from defeat. The road to success is not easy. Every player faces difficult times, but successful players find a way to cope with them and overcome the obstacles.

> *Co-operation and teamwork.* Sports teaches players to compete, yet promotes co-operation. Players compete to make the team; then they compete to get playing time. But they must co-operate with their teammates to accomplish the goals that they have set together.

> *How to sacrifice.* To be good players, they have to sacrifice good times. They have to get a good night's sleep; eat good food; avoid drugs, alcohol, and cigarettes; be considerate of others; and be on time.

> ❯ **Unselfishness.** A player does not become whole until he becomes part of something greater than himself. Team sport teaches players that they are part of something greater than themselves. By being part of a team, a player becomes better than he could be alone. To be the best that one can be, a player has to depend on his teammates. Sport is a good setting to learn to care for others. Sport brings the Golden Rule to life: "Treat others the way you want to be treated." Players learn to sacrifice for the team; they learn that to play on a team, they must sacrifice their individuality; they learn to put the team before themselves.

> ❯ **Self-discipline and self-control.** Discipline is controlling one's emotions, controlling one's thoughts, controlling how one plays, and controlling how one behaves. Disciplined players obey rules, are punctual, do as they are told, behave as they are expected to, and check their anger and other negative emotions. Disciplined players get up for a game when they don't want to; they run when they don't want to; they ignore pain when they want to quit; and they play within the rules even when they want to hit somebody dirty.

> ❯ **Mental toughness.** Players learn through sports the value of mental toughness to deal with failures, defeats, and pain. Players learn how to deal with pressure and how to perform under pressure.

> ❯ **How to cope with pain.** Players learn to play with pain, to tolerate pain, to overcome fears of injury, and to push themselves to come back from injuries.

> ❯ **How to handle success and failure.** Players learn how to handle success and failure, disappointments, and losses. They learn not to be afraid to make mistakes and to learn from them. They learn to handle success with humility, and that even with failure, there will always be another day.

> ❯ **How to accept responsibility.** Sports teaches players to be responsible for their actions, their behaviour, and their mistakes rather than looking for excuses or blaming referees or teammates.

> ❯ **Sportsmanship.** Players learn to compete fairly. They develop sportsmanship. Players should treat their teammates the same way they would treat their own family.

> ❯ **The value of respect.** Players learn to respect adults and authority figures, especially referees, by accepting their decisions even if they are wrong or they disagree. Players learn to respect their opponents by being humble in victory and proud in defeat, by being good sports, win or lose. They learn to respect the history of their sport.

> ❯ **How to respect the rules of the game.** Rules are there to prevent cheating and to make everything equal. Players learn to respect the rules of the game and to play within those rules. The rules of the game are like the rules of life. Playing fair in the game of life is more important than cheating or playing dirty and winning.

◼ THINGS TO THINK ABOUT WHEN YOU ARE A NEW COACH

> ❭ The first thing you have to do, as a new coach, is find out how the other coach ran the team and what he or she did. Even ask the trainer and equipment guy questions about last year's team.

> ❭ The next thing is to contact the players individually before the season starts to let them know what you are all about. You have to send out your own message to the team during the off-season: "We're going to bust our butts this year and you're going to be accountable for how you play."

> ❭ Then find out what the players and veterans are all about just by talking to them, asking them questions about how the team can improve, and about the past season. Create an informal and relaxed conversation with the players and listen twice as much as you talk to find out what they know.

> ❭ Then your job is to get the assistant coaches to reflect their philosophy; and together, you and they have to get the players to be a reflection of that philosophy.

> ❭ Players will want to know what you, the new coach, have to offer. If you have no tradition or reputation, and few players know what you can offer, you will have to sell yourself and your program on the very first day; but you can't just come in and immediately say, "This is how it's going to be done." As a new coach, you are trying to sell yourself, your ideas, and your system to players and coaches whose love and loyalties might still belong to the coach you are replacing. So it's important to ask the players to share your vision and then get them to participate in the planning, as this gives them a sense of ownership. Players will support your plan if they have helped to have a hand in it. A plan forced upon players whose input was not asked for will probably run into resistance.

> ❭ Players want to see if you, the new coach, know what you are talking about. You have to earn their respect over a period of time, not in fifteen to twenty minutes. You have to remind the players that it is not the system chosen, but *their belief* in the system chosen, that matters. "Our system is best for this team because it is based on hard work and commitment."

> ❭ Last, in your pre-season talk you congratulate last year's coach for doing such a great job, but now it's your job, as the new coach, to finish the hard work that the former coach and the players have done to put themselves on the brink of a great team. "I want you to give me a chance; I need you guys to believe and trust in my program that we are going to implement here; and I need the veteran players' (name some) help; I am going to ask a lot from you guys."

> ❭ *Note:* If the new coach is an older coach, he has to sell himself to show he still has his passion, his desire, and his energy for the game, because his advantage is definitely his wisdom and experience.

PART ONE

THE ART OF MOTIVATION
THROUGH LEADERSHIP

1 WHAT IT TAKES TO BE A SUCCESSFUL MOTIVATING COACH

If you have ever been a coach or in a leadership position or you have ever been coached or led by someone else, you know that good coaching and leadership do make a difference. Simply throwing together a group of people and telling them or bossing them around to accomplish something as a team does not work, no matter how skilled or talented the individual team members may be. A successful team needs a coach or leader who knows how to select players, how to organize them, how to put them into a playing system, how to help them hone their skills, and how to get them to play together—in other words, lead them. Above all, they need a leader who can motivate them to do their best and dedicate themselves to achieving excellence together. Players want to be coached, to be taught, to be pushed, and to be disciplined for one reason: they know their success as players and a group depends on these qualities.

If a coach or leader can eliminate the guessing, the mistakes, the trial and error, and the misdirection one learns from the school of hard knocks and substitute proven techniques and approaches of coaching and leadership, he or she will be much further ahead, and hopefully, this is what this book will do. The coach and leader by understanding what works and what doesn't work can develop players' skills and knowledge much faster, which in turn will help produce a successful team more quickly. What matters the most is what a coach or leader does day after day over the long haul. He or she, along with the team or group, must keep on getting a little bit better every day.

The New Definition of Leadership

A leader is:

> A person who motivates, influences, monitors, guides, leads, persuades, excites, unites, teaches, organizes, evaluates, empowers, and inspires a group of people to achieve common goals

> A person who has the ability to influence others to play and work to their maximum performance to accomplish a goal

> A person who has "the knack or the art" of getting people to do the impossible

The old definition of leadership would go something like this: A person who has total control over his team or group. In this command-and-control style, a coach would tell his players to do something and they would either do it or not play. In this old leadership style, the leader led by position or title. But as we will see, bossing people around is not leadership; and being in a position of command or power does not qualify one as a "true" leader. A position of authority identifies the leadership role, but the degree to which one *appropriately* influences others truly identifies the leader.

Leadership ability is the most important characteristic of a coach. Leadership is not about telling people what to do; it is about inspiring people to do their best for the team.

Is Leadership "Art" or "Science"?
Are Leaders Made or Born?
How Do Leaders Become Leaders?

Being in a leadership position or being handed the title "leader or coach" doesn't automatically make you a good leader. Nor is leadership managing or bossing people around.

Are leaders born or made? They are both. Certainly there are great natural leaders who are born with a special gift, leadership qualities, or some characteristics of great leaders. And they lead with no formal training, but just use the natural qualities they were born with. We all know of people who have shown leadership quality from a very early age. This is the "art" of leadership.

But generally speaking, leaders are taught or self-made, not born with the ability. Even the gifted leaders or "true" leaders have to work at learning to lead. They have to train themselves to become better leaders through paying their dues by working, learning, and developing their leadership skills; this is the "science" of leadership.

So leadership is both an "art" because one can be born with a special gift; and a "science," as there are certain skills of leadership one needs, such as the ability to analyze, motivate, strategize, teach, team-build, make decisions, coach games, and understand strategy. And the better their leadership ability is, the greater their influence is on the team. If the leadership is strong, the standards or goals for the team are high.

Those of us who lack this "inborn natural quality" can still learn to be great leaders. We can do this by training ourselves through coaching clinics or courses, by asking questions, observing great leaders, and by reading books like this one. To find out about motivation, coaches should always be looking for models of success, such as businesses and companies that are successful.

Leadership Skills a Successful Motivating Coach Needs

Winning alone cannot be the measure of a successful team. Whether a team wins or not might be beyond their control. Besides, every team will eventually meet a team that can defeat them, no matter how hard they try or how well they play. On the other hand, a team is bound to encounter teams they can beat without even trying very hard. So, merely winning or losing is not an accurate way to measure a team's ability or to show the results of their hard work.

Successful teams will handle either of these situations, winning or losing, with humility, because winning or losing is not really what matters to them. Playing to their potential and improving is what really matters to them, and to build this type of team philosophy, the coach needs the following solid, effective leadership skills and qualities to motivate his or her players. He or she:

> ❯ Must have a good character, based on principles and values, to serve as a role model
> ❯ Has to have a clear coaching philosophy
> ❯ Must know how to motivate his/her players
> ❯ Makes good decisions
> ❯ Recruits the right people
> ❯ Needs to have expert knowledge of the game
> ❯ Must be very good at teaching fundamentals, values, and team play
> ❯ Can put together a playing system
> ❯ Must be "the right kind" of disciplinarian
> ❯ Must be a good "game coach"
> ❯ Must be a good "practice coach"

The Roles of a Successful Motivating Coach

Coach sets the vision of excellence for every player to play to the best of his or her ability and to "help" or push the players to become "the best they can be."

The coach does this by teaching players:

> ❯ The skills of the game and to get them battle-ready
> ❯ How to play, perform, and work as members of a team (team building)
> ❯ How to make good decisions
> ❯ How to be successful as players and as people
> ❯ To do the best job they can
> ❯ Not to be afraid to fail
> ❯ Character values

> ❭ How to be good leaders
> ❭ How to compete and to push themselves to their limits

Coach develops a healthy philosophy of success

One purpose of the coach is to build (selection, philosophy), prepare (game plan, practices), and focus his or her team on being successful by first attaining performance goals and displaying behaviour goals with the end result of obtaining the game outcome goal of winning. You have to do whatever it takes to get your players to be "battle-ready" and perform well on their journey to success.

Coach builds life skills

Another role or purpose of the coach is to help players become good citizens so they can contribute to society. *The coach develops not just good players, but good people.* He or she encourages players to live right by helping them stay out of trouble; by making sure they go to class and get an education and that they improve their behaviour. Coach uses sports as a medium or platform to teach young people life lessons and how to stay on the straight and narrow. The journey to success involves teaching the players how to take care of themselves physically, nutritionally, morally, academically, and socially. As a coach, knowing you have made a difference in your players' lives is a very fulfilling experience.

Coach builds relationships

To lead effectively means getting the commitment of the team. The leader gets this commitment by earning the trust and respect of the team through integrity; by earning loyalty from his or her players who are challenged and recognized for their efforts; and by building relationships with his players. As a result of this relationship, the team will work together and perform consistently over time. It is important that the leader form relationships or partnerships with his or her players rather than the old command-and-control hierarchy of leader and servant.

Coach builds leaders

Part of a coach's responsibility is developing each player to become a leader; to build men and women of character. Leadership is not something you own and keep for yourself. A coach must provide core players the opportunity to take charge and exhibit their abilities, where you have "players inspiring players." There is no better way to develop confidence and leadership than delegating responsibility to players for making decisions for the team. A coach should aim at everyone's being a leader on his or her team.

Note that the leadership legacy is when a former leader has had a great influence on you, and you, as a leader, are now expected to do the same for others.

You must train players to lead; or develop a possible successor to take your place. No one makes it to the top without a mentor.

Coach is service-oriented

The main characteristic of being a good coach is being other-oriented: having the ability and desire to serve, to help, and to support the players. This new coaching style is called "servant-leader"; that is, someone who is willing to accept the position as a follower now and then, comfortable "to let go of his power" and give power to his players, allowing them to lead and make decisions. By stepping back and delegating responsibility to his players to make decisions about the team or group, he ends up empowering them. But when it is again appropriate for him to step forward and lead from the front, he does so without hesitation.

Coach builds and motivates the team

Players are willing to follow a successful coach because they want to, not because she makes them. Leadership is about getting people to follow you by buying into your goals and systems. A leader's ability to attract followers is also based on who she is: her character, not on her title or position.

A coach can't get the job done alone; she has to rely on her players. The greatest coach does not necessarily do the greatest thing; she gets her players to do the greatest thing. It's her job to convey the message, the vision, the inspiration, and the direction to help drive the team. True leadership is about empowering, motivating, and inspiring players to achieve; it is about helping the team's performance to improve; it is about making the team better and taking it to the next level. The bottom line of coaching is to form, build, and mould a winning team. To do this, Coach has to:

> Teach the team fundamental skills

> Get players to pull together as a team; get them to believe in the power of the players' working together toward a common goal

> Help change their behaviours to being team-oriented

> Help players believe in themselves by giving them confidence

> Be a good role model through the "asking" method of leadership rather than the "telling" method.

> Get commitment from the players to their team by empowering them

You can take a team of horses to water, but you can't make them drink. Proper leadership gets them to drink.

Coach is a problem-solver

There are going to be problems every day, so a coach has to expect them and be ready to deal with them. He or she has to identify the problem and then offer solutions. For example, one way of solving a lack of effort problem by the team in a game is to tell the players you expect to see more effort, more concentration, and more discipline when it comes to playing the game—or there will be consequences.

Wrong Reasons for Coaching

Some coaches fail because they choose to become coaches for the wrong reasons.

> ❯ For power: Some people become coaches just so that they can control others and fulfill a fantasy of power. But this is not what coaching is about.

> ❯ For trophies: Another fantasy many would-be coaches have is that of winning the big championship, enjoying the adulation of fans, and being in the limelight. While this is certainly an enjoyable aspect of coaching, it can't be the sole purpose of it. Obviously, not everyone can win every time, and most teams must go on after a big loss. Therefore, there has to be more to the desire to coach than winning or winning trophies.

> ❯ To fulfill their own agenda: Unfortunately, some people take up coaching in hopes of getting their child on the team or getting their child more playing time. It is great to take on the task of coaching your child's team, but to do so in order to fulfill your own private agenda is a recipe for disaster.

Right Reasons for Coaching

Here are valid reasons for choosing to be a coach that will lead to success.

> ❯ For the enjoyment of teaching players to play better and helping them to develop physically, mentally, emotionally, morally, and socially. You have to love helping kids become better people; to grow, mature, and develop. You enjoy teaching young players proper values to be successful, such as discipline, hard work, conquering their fears, and establishing reachable goals. You have to be in coaching for the right reasons, and liking young people has to be number one. As a coach, you must become less task-oriented and more human-oriented.

> ❯ To help young athletes have fun

> ❯ To be part of the game—for love of the sport

> ❯ For the challenge of taking a group of individuals and moulding them into a cohesive unit

> ❯ To pass on knowledge

> ❯ For the thrill and excitement of the sport

> ❭ Because your own children have gotten involved with the sport and you want to share the experience with them

As you can see from this list, there are many reasons to coach, but none of them has to do with winning prizes or controlling others.

One other reason people become coaches is that they really do not have a choice. You may have taken on a coaching job because nobody else wanted to do it, as is often the case with children's teams. This is both a right and a wrong reason to coach: right because the team might not go on without a coach, and the kids will miss out; wrong because having no choice in the matter may lead you to do the task half-heartedly. Obviously, this will not generate a very satisfactory result. If this is your situation, we suggest you take another look at the "Right Reasons for Coaching" list. You should be able to find at least one reason to make your coaching experience worthwhile and thereby generate some enthusiasm for your task. Nothing kills a team's spirit faster than an apathetic coach. Whatever the circumstances of your appointment as a coach, you must keep in mind that successful coaches set aside their own wants and focus on meeting their team's requirements.

What Motivates Successful Coaches?

Coaches motivated solely by the desire to win and to gratify their own ego will never be truly successful, even if they do get to hold a trophy in their hands. Nor will those who take up coaching to satisfy a need to have power over others. Successful coaches usually have a number of different motivators:

> ❭ A love of coaching
> ❭ A sheer love of the game
> ❭ The fear of failure—ironically, one of the secret ingredients of success
> ❭ The need to prove to people that they are good at coaching or just to prove something
> ❭ A love of competition—the chance to compete where there will definitely be a winner and a loser
> ❭ The challenge itself
> ❭ The great highs and the "rush" of winning

The greatest experience in a coach's life is when he feels fulfilled and satisfied within because he knows he did his best.

The Realities of Coaching

When you become a coach, you have to be prepared to rid yourself of some of your preconceived ideas about coaching. Many people become coaches assuming that 1) all players will be skilled; 2) all players will be of good character, with no behavioural problems; and 3) all players will be good athletes. In other words, they anticipate dealing with the ideal athlete. This is very seldom the case. The reality of coaching is far different: every coach will have to work with players of different skill levels, of varying athletic abilities, with attitude problems . . . You have to teach the skills and get the players into great shape, moulding them into team members who play with discipline and heart.

Successful coaches seem to know how to work with the modern athlete. They understand that the title of "coach" does not automatically command respect and obedience from players as in the old days. They know they must earn their players' trust and respect. They know there are two sides to coaching: a teaching side, to prepare players to play and to improve performance; and a leadership side, to build character.

You may find that you will do most of your coaching—and probably your best coaching—when you have little talent on your team. Here, especially, you will understand that good coaching does make a difference. You can take a mediocre team and make it good. But when you do have more talented players on your team, you can ease up a bit and give these players more freedom and creativity to bring out their natural abilities. Knowing when to give your team a lot of direction and when to ease up is an important coaching skill.

Remember: Great players make great coaches! So when you do have great players, you need to appreciate them that much more.

2 USING YOUR OWN COACHING STYLE AND PERSONALITY TO MOTIVATE

■ YOUR COACHING STYLE

When you watch coaches, you will definitely see a variety of coaching styles and personalities. No one style or personality seems to account for success or lack of it. No one style or personality is better or worse than others. The coach may be strong in one style; or use a combination of all the different styles; or use one or the other in certain situations.

But whether a coach uses one leadership style or a combination, he or she must coach with strong character and substance, guided by firm principles, to build a competent team. In fact, you will see the principles of integrity and consistency in behaviour at the core of the different styles and personalities of successful coaches.

As you develop as a coach, you should strive for consistency in your style and personality—so be aware of what kind of response your style or personality will provoke in your players. If you tend to have a more controlling style, you will want your players to adhere strictly to practice plans, systems, game plans, schedules, etc. (See the modern task-oriented coaching style.) If you have a more relaxed approach, you will expect your players to be creative and take the initiative in games and practices. (See the player-oriented coaching style.) If you have a freer style, in which you want more participation from the players in planning games or practices, you have to be prepared to give up some of your direct control as a coach (see the modern power-oriented coaching style). In reality, your coaching style might not be strictly one or the other. Good coaches adapt their styles to their team's particular needs, depending on the age and experience of the players and the particular situation. Some teams need strong control and direction; others will respond better when they are permitted some freedom to develop their own playing style.

Most of us develop a particular approach or style to coaching that we tend to use all the time. But we need to be aware that sometimes our usual approach may not be effective. In these cases we can "borrow" from other coaching styles to make our own coaching more effective. Some coaches fail because they adhere too rigidly to one coaching style. Some coaches have to reinvent or change themselves as leaders to be successful.

A successful coach uses a coaching style in which he can get his players to want to play for him because of his high standards, his vision, his personality, his philosophy, and his principles. He wants his players to enjoy the journey and be satisfied with nothing less than doing their best.

Five Types of Successful Coaching Styles

> Modern task-oriented (uses a controlling style of telling, yelling, teaching)

> Modern power-oriented (gives up power and empowers players by asking instead of telling)

> Player-oriented (serves players by building relationships)

> Goal-oriented (inspires by setting dreams and goals)

> Principle-oriented (builds trust through character and honesty)

Modern Task-Oriented Coaching Style

This type of coaching is similar to—but not in the extreme form of—the old autocratic, dictatorial, or authoritarian style. Because this style focuses on performance, the modern task-oriented approach works on getting good results. This is the "teaching side" of coaching; it is also sometimes considered the "tough side" of coaching. The modern task-oriented coach says, "Do as I say" to keep the team organized in the drills, practices, and systems. This type of coach knows the game inside out, the technical side, and uses his know-how to improve the performance of the team.

Yelling at a player

This modern task-oriented coach gives feedback by sometimes screaming and yelling in practice to let players know he means business. He may not be a screamer by nature, but he might yell when a player or unit constantly repeats the same mistake. A coach can be patient for only so long. Players don't like coaches who yell and scream all the time, but for some coaches the only way to be heard is by yelling. They're not yelling because they're angry; they're yelling because this is the only way that they can be heard and get their point across to a team/player. It seems with this type of coach you can never make him happy. Sometimes, players feel that the coach picks on them because he doesn't like them. But the reason he challenges them all the time is that he cares about them and wants to make them better. It's when he ignores you by not yelling at you that you should be worried.

Telling players what to do

The coach tells the players what position they are playing on his team, tells them what they have to do in the game strategy, no matter what their talent is, tells them what to do during the game, and tells players what their roles are on the team. They follow whether they like it or not—just so they can play. Telling players what to do works best in large group settings, where everything can be kept under control, and where there may not be time for a lot of one-on-one discussion, and where it may be impractical to consult with team members on all major team and game decisions.

Note: Telling somebody to do something is quick and easy and it provides the coach with a feeling of being in control. But the problem is that players resent being told what to do and do not learn as quickly, because their recall declines when they are simply told something without discussion or explanation.

The Modern Power-Oriented Coaching Style

The title of "coach" gives those who hold it the *power of position*, which gives one a tremendous amount of power to control others. These coaches can build or destroy a player; praise or punish a player; make a player's stay with the team a good time or a miserable one; play or bench a player; and keep a player or remove him or her from the team.

Empowerment

But the modern power-oriented coach motivates by giving some of his power away; this is called "empowerment." Although coaches have power, they shouldn't abuse or take advantage of it. They should not overuse their power to control the team, even though they need control over it to get the team to play the way they want. True power today does not come from the title "coach"; true power does not come from a physical posture; and true power does not come from using interpersonal charm. The key for today's power-oriented coach is in knowing how to use power correctly: by empowering his/her players. The coach keeps the main control of the team, but gives some power or control away by encouraging players to provide input into team decisions. The relationship now becomes a *partnership* between the coach and the players. The successful modern coach realizes that by giving up some power, he is actually enhancing his ability to control his team.

The modern power-oriented coach uses subtle ways to get her players committed through empowerment by asking players to "think about" or "consider" something rather than telling them they "must" or "should" do it; by involving players in decisions and consulting them about their opinion; by asking players for their input about the team and goal-setting; by giving players decision-making power through formal or informal team meetings; by giving players responsibilities and roles; by holding players to a higher standard because she has given them power; and by giving players suggestions rather than bossing them around. Bossing players around is not leadership.

Building independent leaders

You develop players into leaders by encouraging them to step forth and assume a leadership role. To build leaders, you have to make the players independent so they can play with freedom and make good decisions without you around. To do this, you must again give some of your power away to your players by letting them decide how the team is going to play and act. This may make it appear that the players are running the team, but that is not so in reality.

Mixing control and freedom

Although good coaches need control of their team, they can't have too many rules or controls, as this creates a counterforce. The more a coach tries to control or manipulate his players, the more they will reject him, as they want some freedom to use their creativity in a game. Even though a team may be very talented, they still have to play with freedom, passion, and creativity within the controlled and disciplined systems set up by the coach. Players today become internally motivated and committed if they have some freedom rather than being under total dictatorial control, having rigid performance standards, and fear-based motivation. So the power-oriented coach has to resist the temptation to totally control his players.

Two destructive needs of a coach's ego are the need for approval and the need to control others. A coach should just ask, "Are the actions I'm about to take aimed at either the need for approval or control?" If the answer is yes, take a deep breath and let the need go.

The modern power-control coach presents a tough, demanding, coaching style and coaches through some fear and intimidation. He doesn't coach "friendly" in the group setting. He feels there must be a modicum of intimidation in what he does. He feels that to be effective, he should be someone players fear slightly, but follow out of respect because he treats them fairly. He treats everybody alike, from the star to the little guy. He neither plays favourites nor applies double standards. He sets up consistent and fair rules.

One way a coach uses his power comes from controlling playing time. If players do what they are supposed to do—that is, play with discipline and play hard—they earn their playing time. If players do not follow orders and do not play hard, they are punished by losing playing time. This coaching style should not be confused with the old-fashioned command-and-control style, where players obey just out of fear, not out of respect.

> ## COACHING IS A BALANCING ACT BETWEEN TOUGHNESS AND TENDERNESS. THE TRICK IS KNOWING WHICH TO USE AND WHEN.

The Old-Fashioned Command-and-Control Style

The old-fashioned command-and-control style tried to influence by intimidation. Since the coach was at the top of the hierarchy, he told or even ordered players what to do and seldom listened to anybody. He made decisions without getting valuable input from his players, as he did not recognize the value of involving players in the communication and decision-making process. This type of coaching was many times ineffective and stifling for the players. Although the old-fashioned control-oriented coach had the power, he didn't have the most important thing: total commitment and respect of the players.

The old-fashioned "command-and-control" coach likes to use "my way or the highway" philosophy, where he tells, gives orders, and lectures his players, but it has been proven players do not learn effectively in this situation. In a chain-of-command organization, players don't do anything until they are told to do it.

The Player-Oriented Coaching Style

The democratic player-oriented style coach focuses on the individual player, getting to know him so he can understand him as an individual. He connects with his team members as people, as well as players, so that he can recognize their needs and their personal strengths and weaknesses much better. He understands what makes them move, what motivates them, what pleases them, and what makes them happy. The player-oriented coach doesn't coach "a sport"—he coaches young people who play a sport.

Most players expect task-oriented, autocratic, or power-oriented leadership, so they might be surprised, or even confused, by a coach who presents himself on a very participative note. A few players might even imagine this leader to be weak or unsure of him/herself. So, on the first day of practice, coach should describe his servant-coaching style and invite questions about it.

A "people business"

The modern servant-coach now uses a more player-oriented style than was typical in the past. The player-oriented style coach is similar to, but not the extreme of, a humanitarian, democratic leader, or a laissez-faire leader.

The player-oriented coach presents a warm and motivating coaching style, which can be very energizing to players. He or she uses a "friendly" coaching style, treating players like family or a partner in running the team. This softer approach in coaching gets every player on the team involved and encourages the players to motivate themselves.

The player-oriented coach has a "people side" of coaching style to motivate the players. She is in the "people business": by treating the players fairly and honestly with the result of gaining their trust; by helping players learn from their mistakes in her observation of their mistakes and in her patience in dealing with mistakes; by knowing how to constructively criticize players; by being more sensitive when pointing out mistakes; and by providing positive encouragement to maintain the self-esteem of the players. The player-oriented coach rarely yells and seems more interested in building good teams than worrying about her own win-loss record.

Focusing on relationships

This coach does a lot of one-on-one communication to give his players a chance to interact with him and build relationships. By focusing on interpersonal relationships, he builds high team morale. Because it is fun to play for a player-oriented coach, everybody looks forward to going to practices and games. This coach knows the team can become successful through these relationships with his players; that is why he uses this player-first philosophy. You must be aware that if you show any favouritism, this can poison team morale.

The player-oriented coach believes he is there for the players so he stops trying to control them and instead tries to serve them. Since he is not self-centred, he looks to serve his followers instead of having his followers serve him. He does not come across as a know-it-all and he is not afraid to ask for help from his players. He strives to get his players to become independent thinkers rather than relying on him to make their decisions for them. It appears almost as if the coach is working for the players.

He follows the philosophy that the more he gives, the more he gets. This philosophy is really the opposite approach to the typical "command-and-control" form of leadership. To the player-oriented coach, leadership is less about the position and more about the players. The coach is always asking, "How can I help you?" In return, players reciprocate by giving the coach their full commitment.

Building self-esteem

The player-oriented coach builds his players' self-esteem, because he knows that when players do not feel valued, they tend to do just enough to get by. The coach builds self-belief in his players and makes them feel like winners by believing in them, by encouraging them, by being positive, and by treating them as equals. And certainly a coach's belief in his players has a direct impact on their performance for the better. To get the best out of his players, a coach has to believe in them to make their own choices and decisions.

"Asking questions" to get commitment

The player-oriented coach asks instead of orders players so they will take on more ownership and commitment. The task-oriented coach says, "Do as I say," while the player-oriented coach asks, "Why are we doing these things this way?"

In a player-oriented coaching style, the coach might ask individual players how they see their role on the team and tries to build his team or game strategy around the talents of each player.

Coach gives empowerment to the players by asking questions; by involving the players in team decision-making power; by asking them for their input; by consulting with them; by giving them responsibilities; and by giving them suggestions rather than bossing them around.

> ## COACH KNOWS THAT ORDINARY PLAYERS WILL DO EXTRAORDINARY THINGS WHEN THEY ARE COMMITTED.

The Goal-Oriented Coaching Style

Coaching is not about being popular; it's not about having power over others because of one's superior knowledge; and it's not about someone having "position-power" or the title of "coach." Coaching is inspiring people to follow you by giving them a purpose, a dream, a vision—an "Outcome Goal"—and then acting upon it by giving the team a realistic and workable plan to follow. This is what gives a coach "true" power.

So, if one of the chief responsibilities as a coach is to motivate your players to follow you, how do you give them this motivation? You set long-term outcome goals and short-term performance and behaviour goals, and then help the players to work toward achieving them. This results in self-motivation. We will discuss these different types of goals in more detail in future chapters.

The coach who uses the "goals-oriented" style has to be passionate about this future long-term outcome goal and to show this passion by constantly talking about this vision. He or she may be able to run well-organized practices and put a well-disciplined team with superior systems together, but unless he/she can get his/her players to be motivated and committed, little will get done because there will be no passion, no "feeling" in what they do. And hard work without passion is hard work.

A goals-oriented coaching style encourages participation by the players in the decision-making of these goals because coach knows that in return she will get this motivation and commitment from her players. Coaching is not *forcing* players to work hard toward these goals—it is having the ability to convince players to *like* working hard toward these goals. The best way to do this is by conducting team meetings and working with the players on a one-on-one basis in setting up all these team goals. The modern goals-oriented coach knows the main way to motivate his/her players is through goals, not through fear, manipulation, trickery, or misuse of power.

The Principle-Oriented Coaching Style

The successful modern coach also uses a "principle-oriented" coaching style and is better known as a "character coach" whose character is based on deeply rooted and proven principles. It is not exactly what you do, but who you are.

If a coach has knowledge, but lacks character, there will be no trust in the relationship with the players. In other words, if his actions as a coach are inconsistent with his words, he will be distrusted no matter how much he knows, and his team might underachieve. If a coach has character, but lacks knowledge, his team still might underachieve because of his inexperience. A good leader is someone with both character and knowledge.

Good character is a coach's greatest ally

Character does matter, especially for people in positions of power. They must have "character" based on strong values and principles. What are the principles of the "principle-oriented" coach? They are a set of beliefs that guide how he should conduct himself. These principles are the foundation of leadership and can be learned.

Once players trust their coach, they will believe in his or her goals. But before an ordinary coach becomes a great coach, he must be a person of substance. A good coach stands for something worth playing for, and players will follow him because of what he stands for. The type of person he "is" is important. He should have ethically grounded principles built upon things like morality, ethics, and decency, and his words and actions should reflect these principles. A "principle-oriented" coach has a set of core principles and values that won't waver under pressure and that he uses as a guide for his decisions to inspire and motivate his players. The principles and values are also guidelines for players on how they should act and play the game in a manner that is desirable and positive for the team.

Being a good role model

You have probably had a coach as a role model who inspired you; now it is your turn as a coach to lift others up. Coaching is the ability to get players to perform above what they are capable of performing. A coach gets this credibility because of his or her skill in leading by example and by being a good role model.

The principle-centred coaching style works best when the coach displays the proper behaviour characteristics. She chooses her response to situations based upon her principles. Her actions, behaviour, and attitude will definitely affect the team, and the team will become a mirror of the coach.

A coach is either a good role model or a bad one; his example is either helpful or harmful; he either builds the lives of others or destroys them; his behaviour inspires or demotivates his players. He should never forget that his players are always looking at him, judging him by his behaviour—on and off the floor/field.

He doesn't push or drag his players into doing what he wants them to do; he inspires his players to follow him by watching him take the lead in how he wants them to behave. He leads the way and the players will follow of their own accord.

Being honest, building trust

Honesty is the core of the principle-oriented coaching style. Honesty solves 90 percent of team problems. Since trust is the foundation for effective coaching, the coach has to build a trusting relationship with his players by being honest with them.

Trust is one of the most important and most powerful requirements for having a good performance by players: players must trust the coach; the coach must trust his players in what they say and the way they play; and players must trust each other to do their job. You have to build trust and respect in your players through integrity. You have to earn respect; and you earn respect only by proving yourself as an honest leader.

Without truth, there can be no trust; and without trust, there can be no relationship; and without a relationship, the chances of achieving success are very low. You must realize that it takes time to perfect the right blend of integrity and partnership, and that you have to earn the respect and trust of your team on a daily basis.

The climate within the team comes from the coach's keeping his promises, doing what he says he is going to do, doing the right thing, making the right decision (even though it may be unpopular), having an open-door policy where he is truly accessible to the players, leading by example, and challenging his players.

In moving toward an environment of integrity, you must build guidelines of trust and respect.

Coach earns trust and respect by:

> *Being honest.* To build a trusting environment, you need to have a set of operating values that guide players' behaviours at all times,

especially during a game. Players have to know that the coach can be trusted to act with integrity. Players don't want to play for someone they don't trust, and they certainly won't follow a coach they don't trust.

> ***Backing up his or her words with actions.*** Coach earns trust by doing the little things: by keeping promises; by telling the truth; by always doing what he says he is going to do; and by treating players in a fair and honest manner. Integrity is keeping promises made to the players, so the successful coach has to be careful of not making promises to players about being in the starting line, about their playing time, or about being on specialty teams unless he can back it up. Players have to earn these things.

> ***Telling the truth.*** When something is wrong, you must tell your players it is wrong; when something is right, you tell them it is right; players must be tough-skinned enough to accept the truth and be able to handle it, even when it hurts. The bottom line is if a coach wants his players to trust him, he must tell the truth. If you give someone your word that something will get done, you'd better make sure it gets done.

> ***Following the Golden Rule.*** Treat others the way you want to be treated. You treat players as equals, with respect and honesty; you treat them fairly, but you do not necessarily treat all players the same.

> ***Building player loyalty.*** Player loyalty rests on the coach's doing what he says he will do, when he says he will do it; in other words, his words and actions are the same. Player loyalty also rests on the coach's being loyal by standing up for his players.

> ***Supporting players during the good times as well as in adversity.*** If a coach wants to earn his players' trust, he has got to be there when they hit that bump in the road; he has got to be there when things get tough; and he has got to support them and help bring them back up during the rough times.

> ***Actively listening.*** You want to show your players you care about them by involving them in decision-making and listening to their opinions.

Projecting self-confidence

> ***Coach projects his or her self-confidence by looking the part.*** You should dress like a coach by wearing coaching gear. You have one opportunity to make a great first impression, so your appearance is important. How you dress as a coach is motivational, as it sends a message that you take coaching seriously.

> ***Coach displays his or her self-confidence through body language***. A self-confident coach gives the appearance of being completely unfazed, thoroughly relaxed and at ease, but alert both in mind and body. The attitude of the body communicates confidence by the way the coach stands, walks, smiles, and speaks.

You must learn to display a posture of confidence at all times—head up, back straight, chest up, shoulders back, and looking straight ahead. This posture gives you an appearance of being thoroughly confident, positive, relaxed, at ease, and in control of the situation even if you are not.

When the coach walks into the dressing room before a meeting or pre-game speech, he should pause for a split second to announce, "I'm here." The pause is important because it gives him a chance for a slow, deep breath before he opens his mouth, so his words will come out right.

The way a coach sounds and what he says when he opens his mouth is important. So slow down and think before you speak. Slowing down just means doing things purposefully—it means patience. In the pre-game or between-period talk, Coach should speak more slowly than he normally would. When a person slows down, it buys him time and he can think things through, it makes him appear calm and confident. When a coach appears calm and confident, players think he knows what he is doing; and when he has a relaxed manner, he gets the best results. You shouldn't forget to let your players wait a bit by throwing in a dramatic pause between key points for emphasis.

Note: Here is a strategy to relax: Take a deep breath through your nose, fill your lungs, pause, then exhale and say the word "relax" to yourself.

> ***Coach displays his self-confidence by acting "as if" he is confident.***
> During the season, a coach has good times and bad times, good days and bad days; and to get through the bad times, it takes "acting"—that is, acting a certain way even when he doesn't feel like it. The players are constantly watching and feeding off Coach's moods to see if he is up or down. He could be projecting optimism or pessimism and not know it.
> *Note:* By acting calm, you'll end up feeling calm; by acting energetic, you'll get energized. In fact you should "act" happy, calm, enthusiastic, relaxed, energetic, in control, and pleasant no matter how you are feeling—and eventually you will legitimately feel that way.

THE MORE CONFIDENCE A LEADER HAS, THE MORE OPEN HE IS TO ACCEPTING OTHER PEOPLE'S IDEAS

Self-confidence and leadership are interconnected, as good leaders can't have "presence" if they aren't confident in themselves. A confident coach has to be a tough coach; he has to be hard and demanding, stretching players past their limits; he doesn't let players slack off or get lazy; and he demands the work to be done his way and in his time frame. A self-confident coach inspires confidence in others; he has a positive attitude toward the future of the team; he sets high standards of performance; he is driven by excellence; and he holds himself accountable for the team.

How does Coach develop his/her self-confidence?

> *By acting quickly and decisively.* Trust your intuition and gut feelings. You must dominate the crisis or it will dominate you. You cannot ignore any problem or crisis, but face it head-on. After a time, this will build self-confidence.
>   *Note:* Failing to make a decision is also a decision. It is a decision to leave everything to chance or to the initiative of others.

> *By taking bold action.* A "true coach" doesn't wilt under pressure—she welcomes pressure. Fear causes hesitancy and procrastination. She gets the job done regardless of her personal fears. It's one thing to have fear and act; it's another to have fear, but not act. Growth comes from going beyond your comfort zone, which in turn builds confidence.

> *By little successes.* A coach develops his own self-confidence by achieving small goals, then more difficult goals. In other words, success breeds success. The more competent a coach becomes, the more confident he becomes. If a coach has been successful in the past, he has a better chance of being successful in the future.

> *By becoming a leader in another area of her life.* In everyday life, no one wants to take on the responsibility for volunteering to do whatever needs to be done. But this becomes an opportunity for the coach to take the lead. She should seek out and accept leadership jobs outside her normal responsibilities.

> *By teaching and helping others.* Give up some of your time and energy to teach the younger kids in other areas than sport.

> *By developing expertise.* You have to research your sport in depth. You also get confidence from the total concentration and energy you put into your game preparation.

> *By practising positive mental imagery.* Visualize yourself being successful. The secret is first to relax and then give yourself positive images. The result gained by seeing a favourable outcome over and over has a dramatic effect.

> *By acting "as if" you are confident.* If you pretend long enough, it eventually becomes real.

OUR GREATEST FREEDOM IS THE FREEDOM TO CHOOSE OUR ATTITUDE AND RESPONSE

Displaying self-control

You have to act with self-control. Coach and players can't always control circumstances, but they can control their response to the situation. The first person a coach has to lead is himself. He must make decisions based upon the principle of self-control rather than on his emotions. He has the choice of getting upset or of doing nothing—which is, most times, the best response.

Although a coach's emotions might run up and down like a roller coaster, she must have the ability to look comfortable, cool, and collected even when she is actually not. By Coach's displaying consistent behaviour all the time, the players feel comfortable and know what to expect from her.

It is important for you to set an example of self-control around your team, as players look to you as their role model. If Coach panics, then everybody panics.

Here are three strategies for controlling your emotions:

1. Counting to ten slowly while taking three deep breaths
2. Showing a sense of humour
3. Waiting ten seconds before reacting or speaking. Coach has to catch or "check" himself and correct his thinking and actions about one hundred times a game.

Note: You can get excited yet still be under control. Getting excited is one way to motivate your team.

Demanding discipline and hard work

A successful coach starts with this premise: in general, people would rather do something that's easy than something that's hard. In order to get around this, a coach has to be very demanding with his team. He always gets more out of his players when he demands more and has a high standard of performance. A strong and intense personality helps because it is this forceful trait that helps his team to play with higher intensity and discipline.

Coach also has to display a good work ethic to provide a model to his players; he has to be energetic and hungry; in fact he has to put his whole mind, body, and soul into coaching. He has to be a great example to his players so that hard work by them is the expected norm. He has to be willing to do the extras by staying later with individual players, by always being prepared with a good game plan, and by running a good practice. It will be a coach's actions more than his words that will influence his players' behaviour.

Tough love

Good coaching is a balancing act between coaching with fear and coaching friendly. It is like a "tough-love" approach: tough on one side and caring on the other; it is discipline mixed with love. The coach is like a friendly boss whom the players fear but respect.

It is more important for a coach that his players become good players rather than they become his good friends. A coach should not become too close to his players because he needs room to be objective enough to make clear decisions. He is not "one of the boys"—he is their leader, their coach. But when dealing with individual players, the coach must be kind, thoughtful, friendly, and considerate. If the players know the coach cares about them, they will be more willing to go into the game and battle for him.

Taking full responsibility

Coach earns credibility by not making excuses; by not blaming; by not criticizing; and by not getting angry when things go wrong. She is the one in charge of everything and the one who makes all final decisions and takes responsibility for everything that happens. In other words, she takes the blame for everything. She gives credit to the players and assistant coaches in victories and takes full responsibility for losses; in fact, she takes full responsibility for everything the team does.

Notes: You delegate responsibilities to your assistant coaches, then trust their judgments to make the right decisions. You encourage your assistants to be independent thinkers. "I coach the coaches and they coach the players." But Coach retains the veto power over the final decision.

Summary of Coaching Styles

Coaching is a balancing act between being tough and demanding with control; or being tender and building relationships. As you can see, the modern type of leadership is highly situational.

"Is the coach dealing with an individual player or the team as a group?" Task-oriented and power-oriented coaching styles work best in team situations, and player-oriented and principle-oriented coaching styles work best in one-on-one situations. "Is the coach dealing with an experienced team or a young, inexperienced team?" The player-oriented style works better with an experienced team, and the task-oriented style works better with a young, inexperienced team. The secret is knowing when to use one or the other at the right time. In today's new information age, it is important for a coach to listen to the players' ideas and opinions. The good coach knows that using different types of leadership, especially task-oriented and player-oriented, will produce both high team morale and good team performance and a balance between control (discipline) and freedom (allowing them to express themselves athletically).

"Is the coach dealing with young players or experienced players?" The player-oriented style of coaching makes it easier to deal with different types of players. It allows coaches to be flexible with different players in different situations. For example, a coach deals with a young player differently than he would with an experienced player. With rookies, a coach may use the "task-oriented style" by telling them what to do and by being actively involved with them, which makes them feel secure. With senior or experienced players, a coach should not insult their intelligence and expertise by telling them what to do and ordering them around; in fact, he should use the "player-oriented style" by asking for their input and their leadership to gain their support.

IT TAKES DIFFERENT COACHING STYLES FOR DIFFERENT SITUATIONS

Developing your coaching style is an ongoing process that never really ends.

While your style has to mesh with your personality, successful coaching involves putting your ego aside and focusing on the needs of the team. Most of your personality traits have positive and negative aspects. You have to develop a coaching style that puts your positive personality traits to good use. For instance, the task-oriented type of coach is usually someone with very strong organizational skills. He needs to learn to direct those skills positively—by keeping precise statistics and organizing season schedules and practices—and to tone down their need to control in other areas, for example, when setting team goals.

While coaches need a solid core of principles to guide them, they must also be prepared to learn and adapt to their team's needs. Also, during the season, a coach can start out with an autocratic or power-oriented style of coaching and then tone down as the season progresses to a democratic or player-oriented style of coaching. In other words, a coach may start the season being firm and demanding and then gradually let control move into the hands of the players as they get used to how things are done on the team.

■ YOUR PERSONALITY

What motivates a team to play for or follow a coach?
Is it his vision or dream; his good character; involving
his players in team decisions; or his personality?

There are coaches who know nothing about styles or how to motivate players but are successful because of their personality. Players just like them. They are friendly, positive, and enthusiastic. Your coaching personality is how you act, how you coach, and how you present yourself. You could be a tough guy, an easygoing guy, or a soft guy. Some players want to be led by "nice guys" and some by "tough guys." The tough guy approach is sometimes hard to play for, but is successful; the soft guy approach might be easier to play for, but can also be successful. Being yourself is extremely important for connections with your players; having a positive outlook on life and being enthusiastic definitely energizes players; and being friendly and approachable helps to build this relationship.

Being Humble

Humility is the ability to put others first; it is being understanding and compassionate. If you actually want to serve and have an impact, you can do it only with a humble attitude. A great coach does not let his ego get in the way by bragging and taking credit when his team is successful; he is quick to give the credit to his players and assistant coaches for the team's successes; and is willing to take the flack when things aren't going well.

For some coaches, being wrong is a sign of weakness. But actually, admitting a mistake is a sign of strength, maturity, and fairness. It shows that one is a human being who can make a mistake.

A humble coach is open to new ideas from players and is willing to ask them questions when he doesn't know something. He is willing to seek solutions to problems from players.

A humble coach does not put on airs; she is not a phony; she doesn't take herself too seriously; she doesn't try to be someone else; she is "real." If you are a vocal, fired-up kind of person, then you must be that kind of coach. If you are a quiet, low-key type of person, then you must be that kind of coach, while being careful not to seem aloof. Your style of communication should be based on what kind of person you are. Be aware that players can spot a phony as soon as she walks into the team dressing room.

Having a Positive Attitude

A positive coach teaches players to see the good in every situation because he knows positive thoughts are a "self-fulfilling prophecy"—it results in positive things happening. So you must maintain a positive attitude and pass it on to your players, especially in the bad times. If you are a positive, enthusiastic, and upbeat person, it's hard for the players not to be that way themselves, and it is even harder for them to be pessimistic in that type of environment. A team's positive outlook toward the game is one of the most important basic principles and prerequisites for success.

Players want a coach who makes them feel important, makes them feel good, one who compliments them for their good effort, as well as their good results. Players want to hear how great everything is and how excited the coach is about the game and the team. A team does not want to be around a coach who is negative, who runs teammates down, who is dull, a gossiper, and a complainer.

How does Coach remain positive?

> *By having high self-esteem.* Coach needs to feel good about himself. He needs a strong sense of self, so he can stand the test of time and survive adversity.

> *By controlling his attitude.* Coach's mind must be under control because once he has thought something it can't be un-thought. He chooses the bright side of life as opposed to the dark side; he chooses a constructive outlook as opposed to a destructive perspective; and he chooses to take the bad experiences in his life and turn them into positive motivation. The great successes in sports are built on taking the negatives and turning them around; even after a loss, a coach must look for the positives.

> *By using self-talk.* Coach needs to control his thoughts and thereby his attitude by emptying his mind of negative, non-productive, and destructive thoughts and talking to himself positively and productively. Thinking and saying good things to yourself doesn't necessarily make them immediately true, but it makes for a happier outlook in the meantime.

> *By keeping a determined outlook to remain positive.* Anything worth striving for requires effort, commitment, and tenacity over the long haul. No matter how far back the team slips, how hard it falls down, or how bad it is losing, the coach through his spirit of optimism always keep the team up and never lets it give up.

Being Enthusiastic and Passionate

The two things that are great energizers in a coach's life are the love of coaching and the love of working with people. The successful coach fills players with a true passion and love of the sport. If the coach is excited and enthusiastic, then the players will be excited and enthusiastic. Enthusiasm is caught, not taught; it is contagious, it is infectious. A classroom teacher with passion can make his subject exciting; a dull teacher can make his subject boring. So do not forget the importance of passion; it is one of the major factors in a team's success, because usually a team takes on the personality of its coach.

COACHING STARTS WITH THE HEART AND ENDS WITH THE HEART

How does Coach show his passion?

> *Through his love of coaching and his personality.* If he has a passion for coaching, it will show in his enthusiasm, his work ethic, and his attitude. The players will see it every day—they will see that he loves

working with players, that he knows how to motivate them, that he knows how to get along with them. And they will see how he gets excited about the game. These qualities will create a good learning environment for the team. And perhaps no other leadership quality or principle is more important to building a team than true enthusiasm.

You want to be enthusiastic most of the time, but there will be times when you just don't feel like it. So how can you be enthusiastic when you are not? That is the time you have to be a great actor and act enthusiastic where the players want to be around you. Nobody will know whether your enthusiasm is acting or real.

> *Through his love for the game.* The true coach has a passion for the sport and loves to coach. He thinks, eats, sleeps, and breathes his sport twenty-four hours a day. If a coach loves what he is doing, if he loves the preparation, the practices, the pressure, and the games, then the players will love it, too. The coach sets the example. He must have a passion for the game in order to be able to "fire up" his team. Those around a passionate coach sense his enthusiasm for the sport almost immediately, through his physical vibrancy, whether it is the bounce in his step or the brightness of his eyes.

> *Through his voice.* In his pre-game speeches, Coach looks for ways to get players excited, as they perform better when they are excited about what they are going to do. Coach appeals to their competitive spirit; he appeals to their pride; he challenges them; he appeals to their past accomplishments. He meets regularly with his players to remind them how valuable their work is and to give them information on what is happening to the team. If the coach cannot verbally get the team excited then he looks to his core player-leaders, that is, players who are excitable and respected by their peers. Coach needs help to lead. He can't do it alone. He must rely on others to give the team some "juice" or energy.

> *Note:* He meets regularly with his players to remind them of how valuable their work is and to give them information on what is happening with the team.

Being Friendly and Humorous

Because a coach has tremendous power, she can make players shake in their boots or she can make them relax by calling them by their first name, extending her hand first, smiling first, and asking questions first. In a tense and serious situation, she can interject humour by telling a story to relax herself and the team. She has to learn to make players laugh, to have fun with them, to joke with them, and to lighten them up by laughing at herself. Remember, most laughter has nothing to do with jokes.

A smile is good body language as it makes the coach look good-natured, friendly, younger, and cheerful. It is important for the coach to always look like she is having fun by smiling and putting on a happy face, even when she doesn't feel like it. If she acts happy, she will become happier. Her cheerfulness, friendliness, and good humour spells confidence. Smiling has probably served leaders better than any other technique.

Being Approachable

Coach starts to build relationships with an open-door policy and an open line of communication whereby players can visit with him in his office. But players will sometimes be afraid to approach him, so he must get around and visit and talk with every player. He must see and be seen; and he must keep his eyes and ears open. The coach needs to be available when the players need him.

3 MOTIVATION THROUGH YOUR COACHING PHILOSOPHY

Players want to know up front what your coaching philosophy is—what you believe in, what your vision is, what your principles are, what you expect from your players, and what the team stands for. You must provide this philosophy with clarity.

There is a difference between philosophy and style. Your philosophy is your own set of high standards, beliefs, and principles that you coach by; your style is the way you present your philosophy and what kind of response it will provoke in your players.

Your coaching philosophy is your own set of principles, beliefs, guidelines, or script that guides your approach to coaching and keeps you on track. It is a list of statements or team affirmations reflecting what you believe in that will help you make good team decisions, set high standards, and accept nothing less than excellence. When applied, these beliefs or principles will make the team successful. An identity the team can build on usually comes from your coaching philosophy. The coaching philosophy is the foundation of the organization; it helps keep the team together, it helps players improve, and it gives everyone a common direction.

It is important to know exactly what your coaching philosophy is so that you will be consistent and yet flexible in tricky situations. What will you do when you are pressured by parents or administrators to win at any cost? How will you deal with the talented player who is disruptive? What will you do with the player who has no talent but who brings character and heart to the team? By giving thought to your beliefs or principles as a coach and a person—by building a sound coaching philosophy and, in turn, keeping your players connected to it—you will be ready for these and other dilemmas that are bound to arise in any coach's career.

Your coaching philosophy is the basis of your team's behaviour goals (chapter 10) and defines how you expect your team to behave. Do not confuse what I call your playing-system philosophy (chapter 16) and your coaching philosophy. The coaching philosophy I am presenting here is personal and may be different from what you believe in. Hopefully it will get you thinking about your own coaching philosophy.

Here are some of my coaching philosophy beliefs to motivate my players:

> You have to have a vision or team goals
> Your players have to know what success is (and it is not winning)
> You have to be a positive role model
> You must strive for excellence, not winning
> You have to have a positive attitude toward mistakes
> You have to have the attitude that playing is an opportunity for success
> You have to have the attitude that your players are ready to face their fears
> You must have an attitude that opponents are partners

■ HAVING A VISION OR TEAM GOALS

Successful coaches believe in setting outcome goals, behaviour goals, and performance goals as a major part of building a successful team that is motivated, empowered, and committed and then stating them as team affirmations.

A team affirmation is a positive statement about what you think the future holds, how you want your team to act and become, how you want your team to perform, and what you want to achieve to be the best. These team affirmations are powerful tools to get the best possible performance out of players. The first step in creating a successful program is affirming the belief that great things are possible; this is called a "self-fulfilling prophecy": what you expect to happen is usually what happens.

Examples of team affirmations:

> Anything worth doing is difficult.
> We are a physical, hard-working, and aggressive team.

To have a coaching philosophy, it is important to have a vision regarding your outcome goal, performance goals, behaviour goals, and team cohesion goals. A successful coach believes:

> A team needs a clear idea or vision of where it is going for the season (chapter 8, outcome goals).
> A team needs a clear idea of what it is expected to do in a game (chapter 9, performance goals and chapter 16, playing systems).
> A team needs knowledge, information, and feedback from game statistics to motivate them (chapter 9, performance goals).
> A team needs a clear idea of how it is expected to act during the game (chapter 10, behaviour goals).

■ KNOWING WHAT SUCCESS IS

What is success? Most definitions of success in sports are measured in terms of championships, win-loss records, personal statistics, or the game outcome goal of just winning. Here are some other definitions of success to think about:

> Success is attaining and improving on a team's performance goals (chapter 9).

> Success is giving it your best effort.

> Success is defeating your opponent—yourself.

> Success is displaying the team's behaviour characteristics (chapter 10).

These definitions are the ones you should focus on—not winning!

Attaining and Improving a Team's Performance Goals

Success occurs when a team aims for a goal and is constantly improving on it as it reaches for its objective. By trying to achieve their performance goals, players are always trying to improve their fundamental skills and team playing systems. The team never accepts where it is now because no team stays the same—it is either getting better or getting worse.

The team has to be striving to make small steps toward performing better. Sometimes it's more important that players learn and improve than it is to beat a team that isn't very good. Anytime the team stops striving to get better or going forward, it is bound to get worse or go backwards. It can always improve on "something," and it is up to you to find that "something" to improve on. And it's this process of constantly meeting and raising the standard bar that makes a team play to its potential.

The question before the season begins is: "How can I know whether this team is going to be a successful team?" Sometimes you know you are going to be successful just by the players you have but usually you don't know where you stand with the other teams; so you just have to go into the season focusing your attention on yourself, determining that you are going to improve and get better.

Success is setting some standards—performance goals—and trying to perform to those standards. Players need to have gauges by which they can experience success other than winning, such as statistical measures of some of the team's top performance goals. Even if the team loses a game, you can emphasize specific things that the team did that were successful in the game.

The team sets realistic performance goals so that the players will always have something to play for over a long season; otherwise, every game becomes the same. If the team attains its performance goals, it stands a good chance of meeting its outcome goal for the game: winning. Achieving the team's performance goals now becomes the primary objective, while winning becomes the secondary objective.

One result of this healthy successful philosophy is that the team focuses on competing against itself in trying to attain its performance goals rather than focusing on beating their opponent or winning. This puts success entirely in control of the team's hands. You want your team to compare its team performance with its own performance goals.

A limited-talent team that is going to have a losing season

If you end up with an inexperienced team of limited talent that you know is going to lose almost every game, it is more important than ever to find a way to make the season enjoyable, fun, and successful anyway. The main criterion definitely has to be chasing team performance goals and the steady improvement and growth of the team, game-by-game, over the season, because this limited-talent team is going to lose lots of games, and winning cannot be an objective.

> ## IN YOUTH SPORTS, THE EMPHASIS SHOULD ALWAYS BE ON HAVING FUN RATHER THAN ON WINNING

Giving It Your Best Effort

You have to realize that the only thing your team can control is attaining its performance goals, and it does that by playing to its ability and giving it their best effort; in return, winning will often take care of itself.

You must explain to the team the difference between winning and being successful. If the team wins the game, but played poorly, the team will feel it has underachieved and will not feel good because it did not reach the high standards it set for itself. But if the team loses the game but felt it played hard and put out a pretty good effort, the team will feel pretty good even though they lost. So a team's performance is measured qualitatively by attaining its performance goals and subjectively answering the question, "Were we the best we can be?" But what is a team's "best"? It is attaining or improving on its performance goals.

> ## IT'S THE TRYING THAT MAKES THE DIFFERENCE

Being successful is hard. That is why only a few teams are successful. One can go through school, through life, through lots of things, putting in a half-effort and still be successful. But one can't put in half-effort at being successful in sports.

Success Is Defeating Your Opponent—Yourself

Because the team can control its own performance, it should compare its performance with itself rather than comparing itself with opposing teams. In this way, the team feels it has more control over the way it plays; it can control these performance goals, but it cannot control the outcome of the game. The outcome is influenced by many factors, such as the strength of the opponent, how the opponent plays, the referee's calls, or just plain luck. If the team competes against itself, the performance goals become the main objective for the game instead of the outcome goal of winning.

The battle within

The traditional definition of a battle or competition requires having an opponent, and the objective of a battle is to beat your opponent. But by our definition of success, the true battle is about competing against yourself. In fact, players know their real opponent is within themselves and the true battle for players has less to do with external events than with internal battles against conquering their enemies: thinking negatively, losing control of their emotions, fear of their opponent, losing their concentration, experiencing fatigue, pain, and injury, playing lazily, the fear of making mistakes or failing, being selfish, trying too hard, and wanting to quit. We know that the real purpose of playing sports is about the struggle with ourselves. In a game, you have a hundred struggles every time you go on the floor to test your limits.

Players win the battle within themselves by staying focused, staying positive, controlling their thoughts, controlling their emotions, ignoring mistakes, relaxing, fighting fatigue, pain, and injury, and never giving up. The opponent within a player's head is far more difficult than the player on the floor/field—and the competition with yourself is never finished.

Displaying the Team's Behaviour Characteristics

Success is a process toward a long-term season outcome goal, but only by meeting and surpassing short-term behaviour goals and performance goals. With the pressure of worrying about always winning being removed, a team can now enjoy the journey—playing for the moment, having fun, playing relaxed and confident, and playing the game for the sheer enjoyment of it while striving to be the best it can be.

Success Is Attaining the Team's Outcome Goal

The team has to start the season with the end in mind. Once a team has defined its long-term outcome goal for the season, its dream for the season, it has defined what "success" means to the players. Success now becomes attaining their long-term goal, such as winning a national championship, making the playoffs, ending up in fourth place, and so on. Teams that set season outcome goals never accept where they are now. Because they know where they are going, they are always striving to get better so as to reach their long-term goal. When a team thinks about the future, they motivate themselves.

The Problem of Focusing Strictly on Winning

The supposedly real definition of success in sports, especially in the pros, is winning, and too many coaches do emphasize winning—the "winning is every-thing" attitude or "winning at all costs"—rather than looking at other definitions of success, such as effort and improvement. They perceive their win-loss record as a measurement of success, and the only objective is to beat their opponent. They believe that winning and beating their opponent is what drives their team to become better. But this is not always true.

An overemphasis on winning can exact undue pressure on players. When a team has to win, it increases its anxiety and stress because it has no control over the outcome on the scoreboard and performance suffers. The saying "if you focus on winning, you are more likely to win" is wrong and counter-productive. When winning on the scoreboard means everything, players begin to worry about whether they will win or lose. And when they are nervous, they tend to make more mistakes; and as they make more mistakes, they play more tenta-tively and are more timid.

The problem with coaches who stress winning is: If the team wins, the play-ers look at themselves as successful, competent, and worthwhile human beings, but if they lose, they look at themselves as failures, incompetent, or unworthy human beings, with the result that the players' confidence fades and so does their performance. You don't want your players to confuse their self-worth with their performance and winning or losing. You should stress winning as a result of the team's effort and execution, and if it loses, the players can simply blame it on their lack of effort or execution.

Another problem with coaches who stress winning is that they compare their team with others to determine their value as a team. But perhaps a team loses because it has been outscored by an opponent with superior ability, and it doesn't seem to matter that they had played their hearts out or had improved markedly—even though they lost.

Results of a Healthy Philosophy of Success

Players today are conditioned to view success as something that can only be measured on the scoreboard. But you want to show your players that there are many other ways to be successful. If you put winning into perspective, a team can lose and still be successful and play great.

Players with a healthy philosophy of success look at the game as a test of themselves. The result is they try harder, enjoy playing more, and look forward to the challenge of the game. The real success of coaches should be gauged by how much fun the team has along the way. This philosophy of success takes the worry out of the game; now all players have to do is "let it happen" and just concentrate on playing to the best of their ability.

DOING YOUR BEST LASTS A LIFETIME

■ BEING A POSITIVE ROLE MODEL

Building the Right Positive Environment

The successful coach has a special personality of creating a good positive and enthusiastic learning environment for his team, where players really enjoy practising and playing. You want to create a positive, high-performance learning environment of high trust, support, teamwork, hard work, enjoyment of playing, and a commitment to excellence.

You build this right environment through your positive encouragement and support; by ensuring that players know what success is; by rewarding learning and improvement; by striving for excellence; and by your attitude toward mistakes, fears, your opponent, and playing.

When you create a supportive environment, the players will play with more confidence, enthusiasm, positive emotion, and passion and will really enjoy what they are doing. This motivational climate is fostered by everything you do—your attitude, verbal messages, and non-verbal actions; these will have a deep impact on moving the players to a higher level.

Having the Right Attitude

Coach's attitude is critical to the team's success. Attitude is a state of mind. It is a choice. What you think you can do, whether positive or negative, will most likely happen. Because your personality and thinking affects everything you do, you must control your attitude and how you feel. So, focus on the positive, laugh a lot, and uplift the team's atmosphere by playing tricks and pranks on your players.

Belief is at the heart of everything—players must believe in themselves, in their teammates, in the system, and in the coach. So, as a coach, you must believe. If you constantly tell your players, "You can do it!" and they believe they can, they will then prepare themselves by working hard and doing the extras.

IF YOU CAN BELIEVE IT, YOU CAN ACHIEVE IT

You have to encourage all your players to speak and think only in the affirmative, because what you think, you become. If you think a negative thought, it attracts negative results, whereas if you think a positive thought, this creates the power of positive possibilities. A good strategy when a negative thought enters a player's mind is for him or her to say, "Cancel that thought!" and replace it with a positive one or just say a positive affirmation out loud.

Praise the Players

Coach must let players know how they are doing. You definitely need to praise and recognize players in front of the team because you want everyone on the team to know about the player's accomplishment, no matter how small. Praise as soon as possible.

One of the toughest things for a coach is to look for players' doing things right, because as coaches, we are conditioned to look for mistakes. It has been proven that players will repeat the performance for which they get praise, so every time they do something right, give them praise. Make it a habit to focus on what the team can do (positive) rather than on what it can't do (negative).

Recognition is one of the most powerful human motivators there is and the desire by players for recognition is one of the most valuable assets in leading people. It is the second highest on Maslow's list of human needs (see chapter 6, Motivation). You make players feel important and appreciated by supporting, rewarding, and recognizing them for their hard work and effort, and not just for scoring goals.

No one likes to be told she has done something wrong, so when you criticize, be careful. This criticism must be done in a special way called the "sandwich technique": you say two good things or give two compliments about the player on what she did right before and after the criticism. Criticize in private because if you tell a player in front of others that she has done something wrong, you might embarrass her.

Handling a Crisis in a Positive Way

It is wise to expect problems every day and to expect three to four major crises every season, so that when they do happen, you won't overreact, but remain calm, positive, and confident. By reacting positively to a crisis, you can bring the team together. By reacting negatively, you can destroy the team. You can explain to the team that dealing with losses and bad breaks is simply part of the game, and teams have to overcome this adversity to become successful. You look at these problems and crises as chances for the team to grow and to test its character. You turn these negative situations into positives, especially when things are falling apart, such as when you are on a losing streak, or when the game becomes chaotic. You have to encourage the players to see the good in every crisis and problem; and they must rebound from it quickly.

■ STRIVING FOR EXCELLENCE, NOT WINNING

What Does Excellence Mean?

Here are some definitions of excellence:

> When you perform a skill the correct way or when you execute a play the right way

> When you are proud of what you do

> When you are the best you can be

> When you are striving to play to your full potential

> When you strive for and attain the performance goals

Finally, the best definition is: *When you play your very best every time you play.*

Coach's outlook toward playing and practising sports is that excellence, high standards, or quality work is expected; good is commonplace; mediocre or fair is not tolerated; and sloppiness is simply not an option. This means you have got to be totally dedicated, totally committed, willing to sacrifice, and be self-disciplined to attain excellence.

Setting Excellence as a Standard, Not Perfection

Doing it the right way

Successful teams don't play just "good enough," or go through the motions—they know the only way to play is the right way. Some teams are content to stay where they are and feel that playing just "good enough to get by" is okay. This thinking is the enemy of excellence. When you strive for excellence, it is a process of players' always striving to get better, always trying to improve, never being satisfied, and playing to the best of their ability.

WHEN YOU ATTAIN EXCELLENCE, THE BY-PRODUCT IS WINNING

Perfection

But be aware that you should strive for excellence, not perfection. There is no way to do everything perfectly. "It's okay to shoot for the moon; if you fall short, you'll still be one of the stars." Perfection is unattainable and it is futile to search for it. We live in a world where even the greatest athletes are imperfect, and the plays in even the best games are many times not executed correctly. Players need the freedom of knowing it is okay to make mistakes.

Setting high expectations is one of the most powerful tools a coach has. If you set them high, your team will strive for those expectations. The highest standard is the standard of excellence, which is being the best you can be and doing the best you can. Excellence is the difference between throwing a pass in the general area of the stick's pocket versus hitting the pocket "dead-on"; or jogging down the floor versus running all-out.

Building Pride

You have to develop pride among your players, because pride will give them a feeling of satisfaction for doing something really well.

How do you instill pride? One way a team develops pride is by feeling they are "the very best" at doing something. To get this feeling, players will say they are a good defensive team, but the coach says no, they're not—they're the *best* defensive team. Feeling they are the "best" builds a bond that is stronger than superglue. But a team has to have a *valid reason* for believing that they are the best. They have to have something that can be measured—statistics—as proof. *For example*, if the team wants to be the best defensive team in the league, they must take pride in playing defence. The coach instills this pride by making sure the team works hard at defence in practices and games; by making the players feel they are better than anyone else at defence; by taking the time, patience, and dedication to develop the "best" defensive team; and by telling the team you expect them to be the best defensive team every night.

You can stress team affirmations to reinforce pride, such as, "We are the best defensive team." And you can instill pride by creating an environment that makes players feel good; and by praising things players do to make them feel special. You should not forget to praise the little things to make players feel proud of something they might have taken for granted.

Encouraging Constant Improvement

You must expect your team not to worry or even think about winning or beating the other teams. All they need to think about is this commitment to excellence, "being the best they can be" through improving or attaining their performance goals. In other words, you do not focus your attention on beating the other team; you focus on yourself. The philosophy that "you can always do better" guards against overconfidence. Complacency is a team's biggest enemy, especially if they are winning. But with excellence, there is always a gap between where we are and where we want to get to.

Teams have to know what they are the best at. You use statistics to make "quality," "excellence," or "best" specific. Quality means meeting your performance goals of shooting 20 percent, of getting 60 percent loose balls, etc. You use real numbers and set real goals, not make general statements such as, "we have to shoot well" or "we have to be the best shooting team in the league." The team needs quality feedback from the statistics and meaningful acknowledgement (praise or criticism) from you.

After every game, you can reward everybody on the team for a good performance; for example, if the team attains its defensive shooting percentage. If you want to stress "the team," reward the team. If you want to make role players feel good and important, reward them. If you want to reward the star players, reward them (see chapter 15, "Running a Good Practice"). Or, you can practise over and over again the fundamentals or the playing system that caused a bad performance.

Paying Attention to Detail

Achieving a standard of excellence or execution is about taking care of the smallest details; focusing on fundamentals; and making sure things are done the right way. It is not always the big things, the big play that trips you up or guarantees you success or excellence in a game, but rather a combination of small details. In pursuing the path of excellence it's a combination of the little things over the course of the game that makes the difference. So, if you want excellence, do the ordinary things right and better than anyone else.

Excellence means players have to give up something. Players who do the extra little things will enjoy an edge over the opponent who is unwilling to make sacrifices.

Being Demanding

Another difference between an average team and a great team is a demanding coach. Usually when you demand more, you get more. You always expect more because you know your team can never play the perfect game. You should show disfavour over poor execution because you expect good execution every game.

You expect and demand your players to do it correctly all the time. Players must realize it's not so much what they do, but how they do it. When players play for a demanding coach who does not accept mediocre play they play at a level higher than they ever realized they could reach. Players appreciate coaches who push them and demand more from them than they believe they can achieve. The true competitor wants to be associated with coaches who set and maintain high standards. Excellence requires many things, but discipline above all is the most important; without discipline, nothing else matters.

If a player is struggling with his game, you have to change what the player is doing by getting him to put in extra effort and time to work on his game by taking extra sprints, extra shots, etc., and by getting into the arena early and staying late.

You must also demand high intensity. Many players will take shortcuts or take an easy way out if they can get away with it rather than work hard. You must demand that your players practise and play with high intensity. Coach should be concerned over two areas. The first area is where players are not trying hard, not going all-out, only going "through the motions" or giving half an effort. It has been stated that only 20 percent of the players work at doing things right all the time; the other 80 percent look for the easy way out by taking shortcuts. The high standard of working hard must be the norm. If players want excellence, they must work for it.

The other area is lack of concentration. Players have a tendency to fall asleep as the drill or game goes on which results in a poorly run, sloppy play. You expect your players to concentrate all the time in practice and games to attain this excellence.

Quality Players, not Skill, Make the Difference

The most important component of an excellent playing system is the players; the more unstable, irrational, and unpredictable the players are, the more unstable the system will be. Therefore, anything you can do to stabilize the performance of your players will improve their playing system. The behaviour goals empower the players to become more consistent and predictable in their performance: more stable, rational, disciplined, and unselfish in their play. Quality players make a difference to your team by creating cohesiveness and chemistry.

Emphasizing Fundamental Skills

However, if you want excellence, you have to do the *ordinary fundamentals* better than anyone else, because it is not what you do as a team, your formations and systems, but how you do it, playing fast, hard, and being fundamentally sound, that makes you successful.

Note: In the big game, all we had to do was run a certain play and we would win. If we couldn't do it, it was because we got sloppy.

Coach Asks Players for Their Input in Decisions

How do you get this high standard of excellence? By involving and giving players power in making team decisions; by getting players to contribute ideas on how to improve the team; and by encouraging them to ask "why." In fact, you should constantly be asking your players how to improve the team in problem areas, such as how to get the loose balls percentage higher.

Your asking for help is evidence of strength, not weakness. By asking questions, you invite the players to give input that will improve their performance; by players' giving answers, they take on responsibility and ownership, which will bring their performance up to a higher standard.

Note: If you force your players to do something they don't want to do, you might win the battle, but you will lose the war of player commitment and involvement.

Coach Demonstrates Consistent, Patient Behaviour

A team also reaches excellence through the proper behaviour of the coach. You have to be consistent in your behaviour all the time, so that players know what you are going to do.

You coach by the principle of patience because the pursuit of "real" excellence takes a long time. A certain price has to be paid in terms of practice, sacrifice, patience, and persistence. If you set high standards, you must have the patience to coach the players through their growing pains. Excellence doesn't happen overnight. A player has to work at it day after day.

> ## EXCELLENCE IS A MARATHON RACE, NOT A SPRINT

Review of Excellence

Here is a quick review of how a coach can get his players to play at a higher performance or excellence:

> Convince your players that they are "the best" and that they should take pride in that.

> Demand good execution and high intensity.

> Be patient and have a consistent behaviour when teaching.

> Pay attention to detail.

> Set excellence as the standard.

> Ask your players questions to find out their point of view and to get them involved in team decisions.

> Give your players freedom in practices to pursue excellence.

> Stress constant improvement and correction in performance goals and statistics.

> Give your players meaningful feedback and information from statistics on their playing ability.

> Realize that quality players, not skill, make the difference.

> Encourage your players to try new fundamental skills.

> Remind your players that what "they believe in or think will shape what they want to achieve".

> Remind your players that to become excellent requires effort, "grit," discipline, and passion over a long period of time.

■ POSITIVE ATTITUDE TOWARD MISTAKES

Why Mistakes Occur

> Player has poor timing. Player's mind and body are totally out of sync.

> Player has poor concentration. He lets distractions get to him.

> Player didn't understand the instructions; misunderstood the instructions; or forgot the instructions.

> Player is too nervous to play well.

> Player overreacts rather than anticipates a play. He tries too hard.

> Player does not try hard enough. He plays lackadaisically.

> Player is afraid to make a mistake. He worries about making mistakes and ends up playing cautiously.

> Player hurries a play rather than playing with poise. He panics.

> Player shows off in front of fans; tries to impress people; plays too fancy.

Be Positive

You have to have a philosophy of creating a risk-free environment if you want your players to learn the game, where it is okay to make mistakes, and if something doesn't work, it is not a major problem. You have to let your players know that they are allowed to take some risks and that failure and mistakes are nothing more than learning how to be successful. In other words, you give your players power and freedom by giving them permission to fail.

You have to find a way to change mistakes and errors into something positive, and the first rule of being positive is to eliminate the negative. You have to help players correct their mistakes by building them up, not tearing them down. You cannot expect to have a positive effect on players tomorrow if you criticize or antagonize them today. You have to see mistakes as temporary errors in judgment, not permanent flaws in character. Players can't learn something complicated if they are afraid to make a mistake. You must make it explicitly clear that it is okay to make mistakes. You want doers on your team, because doers make things happen—but they also make mistakes.

If a player makes a mistake, in a split second you make the choice between yelling at the player or helping her learn from her mistake. Supporting her helps her to build character and is a stepping stone to greater performance. It is your attitude that creates this latter positive environment where players are given the chance to fail and learn from their mistakes. The difference is what you choose to do about it. It is in those few seconds that you can have the most impact.

A major motivator for players is when you don't get on your players' backs or get upset if they make a mistake. You free your players' minds by having them play without worrying about making mistakes. You allow this freedom for failure, as failure is nothing more than learning how to do something right. This freedom gives players the courage to try even harder and even try new things. So when players make mistakes, you should just explain to them what they did wrong and ask them, "What should you do when such-and-such happens again?" Of course, you should give supportive communication regarding both mistakes and well-executed plays.

Note: When players play in fear of making mistakes, they end up playing tentatively "not to lose," instead of playing aggressively, "to win."

IT IS OKAY TO MAKE MISTAKES

Getting Players' Commitment

The best way to avoid the fear of mistakes is to get a commitment from players by getting the players' input into the team's outcome, performance, and behaviour goals. When players know and understand and are committed to the team's goals, they are willing to take risks and are not afraid to fail in order to be successful. And when players take risks, there is a high chance of making mistakes. Commitment also means not holding anything back when playing a game. If players are going to succeed, they can't hold back.

Learning from Mistakes

To be a successful coach, you have to have a philosophy that believes mistakes are a necessary part of learning; mistakes are great teachers and are stepping stones to improvement; mistakes help players become better. "The shot that hits the open spot is the result of a thousand misses." You realize players perfect their game through overcoming mistakes and failure. In fact, players will learn far more lessons when mistakes are made than when success comes easily.

Players have to believe that each mistake puts them one step closer to success. They shouldn't fear mistakes; they should learn from them. It seems players learn a great deal more from what doesn't work than from what does. And the main thing players learn from a mistake is not to repeat it, but to learn from it.

If you criticize and punish failure and mistakes, and only reward and praise successes, players will be afraid to fail. If players make technical or playing mistakes, you must accept responsibility by teaching the skill and the system better. If you get upset every time players make a technical mistake, you will put undue pressure on them, and they will end up playing tight. Your reaction to mistakes will tell how players will do in a game. You are there to encourage and build confidence.

Note: But any mistakes caused by a lack of effort (no effort for loose balls, not sprinting the floor, not fighting for position) or lack of focus (falling asleep on the floor) should be unacceptable to the player and the coach. This is when the coach should get upset.

If a player makes a mistake, it would be a good idea for you and the player to analyze the problem and discover why it happened. You can even ask the player to explain what happened.

MISTAKES ARE PART OF THE GAME

You have to have the attitude that mistakes are inevitable, they are part of the game, and that each mistake is one step toward success. You look at mistakes as character lessons. Successful players view mistakes as an opportunity to learn; unsuccessful players view mistakes as failure. You should realize that you will never see a perfect game played. Mistakes and sports are synonymous. The greatest players and teams have failed many times. You must reinforce to players that during a game there are going to be a lot of mistakes, errors, miscalls, and misjudgments, but they must play on.

How to Cope with Mistakes

Focusing on the next play

You must stress to players that for them to be successful they must be able to handle mistakes by understanding that mistakes will happen; that they can learn from them; that they don't dwell on them; that they forget about them immediately; and that they refocus quickly on thoughts of the next play. Thinking about the next play keeps the great players "on the job at hand" and keeps them from playing cautiously. They don't try to analyze what happened right then; they don't try to think it through; they don't even think about it one second more. They stay in the present moment, forget about the last play, and get on with the next one.

Every successful player faces disappointments. It's how he or she handles them that makes the difference. Players must find a way to cope with adversity and overcome obstacles. You teach strategies for handling mistakes to your players because you know success is the result of how a player handles his or her mistakes.

Note: Players' steps to learning: admit the mistake, analyze what went wrong, learn the lesson, then forget it and move on.

How the coach handles mistakes

Another strategy of teaching players how to cope with mistakes is being a good role model on how to react to them. In fact, success of the team depends on how you react to mistakes. In all crises, it is your response that decides whether or not the crisis will escalate. Players will suffer setbacks, mistakes, frustrations, failures, and bad calls during the course of any game, but the outcome is determined by how you and the team handle them.

Keeping a positive outlook toward mistakes

You have to make sure your players approach the game with a great outlook; have your players approach the game:

> Knowing that there are no perfect games; there are no perfect plays; and there are no perfect players. When players understand that if one plays sports, one will make mistakes and will have to live with them and work through them, the game becomes easier.

> Knowing that mistakes won't lead to punishment or criticism. With this positive atmosphere created by the coach, they will play with freedom.

> With the attitude that when a mistake happens, "what's done is done"

> Always looking for the "silver lining" in all mistakes. They should see opportunity instead of disaster in a difficult situation.

> ❭   Looking forward to facing any challenge rather than fearing it

> ❭   Knowing they are going to make mistakes, but they have a plan
>   for them. Coach must prepare his team for as many setbacks as
>   possible that they might encounter in a game situation.

Benching a player or pulling her off the floor for making mistakes makes her
feel inadequate and not good enough and she will stop taking risks. If players
are afraid to make mistakes, and play on "eggshells" or "pins-and-needles," they
will end up playing not to make mistakes and usually end up playing tight and
cautiously, thereby making mistakes anyway. Usually, players who worry about
making mistakes have already made one. One of the hardest challenges for you
as a coach is to resist the impulse to respond to a mistake in a negative way; your
job as a coach is to build confidence.

IF YOU THINK YOU WILL FAIL, YOU WILL FAIL

■ HAVING THE ATTITUDE THAT PLAYING IS AN OPPORTUNITY FOR SUCCESS

Attitude Is a State of Mind

Having the proper playing philosophy and mental approach toward a game makes
all the difference in the world. The first and most important step toward success is
the feeling that you are going to succeed. The whole game is about one's attitude
or how one thinks—how players approach the game; how players view the game;
how players think about the game: It is a choice between thinking positively or
negatively. It is crucial that they have an awareness of their attitude because they
have to know that their attitude affects their behaviour and performance. Players build these positive attitudes from their habits of positive thoughts, and they
build positive thoughts from their positive self-talk. The successful player's mindset will determine whether he actually becomes successful.

THINK POSITIVELY TO ACHIEVE THE IMPOSSIBLE

Players can choose how they view or think about the pressure of the game.
They must understand that this pressure comes from how they look at the game

and what they say to themselves. Through their outlook, they either put pressure on themselves or not.

Attitude of Top Teams Compared to Average Teams

Usually there is only a thin line between teams in most leagues. Therefore, the separation between the talented teams and the also-ran teams comes from their attitude, their mental aspect of the game, and their approach to the game.

In fact, there is always a different attitude between the top teams and the average teams.

The top teams exude an aura of confidence that separates them from others, and from this confidence, they not only expect to win—they know they are going to win. This is the most powerful state of mind for a team to have. In fact, there is so much cockiness that it's mind-blowing! In fact, the elite teams will even win some games where they didn't play well and should have lost.

The average or lower-level teams are convinced they are going to lose. They might have a few players who believe they are going to win, but the majority of the players, deep down in their subconscious, have the negative thought: "Are we going to win this game?" And with this attitude, they will just go through the motions and lose. The weaker teams don't fully believe in themselves and will end up losing games a lot of people thought they should have won.

Note: The challenge of the century was War Admiral versus Man O'War. War Admiral was a small horse; Man O'War, who was purebreed, was a big horse (an all-star). But if you look War Admiral in the eye, it tells you he has spirit and heart. War Admiral beat Man O'War not with his legs but with his heart.[1]

Important to Have a Plan

Your entire philosophy or game plan created for the team is based on the conviction that motivation is ignited by a vision or long-term season outcome goal and is carried forward through attitudes and beliefs that generate success. Then, you must have a process or plan for attaining this long-term goal by players' demonstrating behaviour goals and attaining performance goals. Finally, you must continually communicate the season outcome goal by reinforcing and reminding players of this vision.

Team Made Up of a "Bunch of Fighters"

Your philosophy is that your team might not be the most talented one in the league but you want it to be the most "mentally strong" team. You want it to reach a playing level where there is no panic and certainly no quitting; you

---

1   From the movie *Seabiscuit*.

want it to toughen as the season progresses; you want it to be prepared to handle anything that might occur on the floor; you want it to play with a sense of urgency and hunger, with the team never being satisfied with *almost* getting there; and you want your team to fight and thrive on competition to the end.

It is important for success that you create a team attitude before every game where players are mentally prepared for the worst. "Character players" are prepared to face whatever is presented to them on the way to attaining their performance goals and to do whatever is required to achieve their goal. They will succeed because they know the game is not going to be easy, that challenges will have to be dealt with and they will be overcome. You want your players to get excited about competing; not scared, not nervous, but exhilarated.

You can tell stories to illustrate "what was once thought impossible turned out to be possible," to inspire, encourage, inform, and educate your players. There are tons of stories of magnificent human achievement that no one believed possible until it happened. You can talk about how at one time it was believed impossible to climb Mount Everest; to run the mile under four minutes; or to high-jump seven feet; but these myths of impossibility were shattered. You can ask your team: "Do you believe in the impossible?"

■ PLAYERS HAVE TO BE READY TO FACE THEIR FEARS

Causes of Fear

Even the great players have fears; fear can be a player's greatest enemy. The greatest barrier to a high performance is fear. Players can be afraid of almost anything, but their main fears are among the following:

> Fear that they are not prepared

> Fear of playing against a good team and that they are in over their heads

> Fear of playing against an intimidating team that is bigger, stronger, and more physical

> Fear of losing a game or failing

> Fear of the unknown and uncertainty. The player's looking too far ahead in a game causes anxiety and fear.

> Fear caused by putting pressure on themselves: "I've got to get a goal"; "I've got to win"

> Fear of making mistakes, fear of not playing well, fear of not being able to succeed, and fear of not scoring

> Fear of the coach's negatively reacting after every mistake players make all the time. Fear of being punished; of being criticized; of being ridiculed; of being yelled at; and of being embarrassed by the coach

Good Results from Fear

Although fear can inhibit players, it can also be a great short-term motivator. Players should not fear losing because it is one of the secret ingredients of success. The fear of losing has driven a lot of teams to success. Fear can be looked upon as something positive because it gets players ready to play, makes them alert, and gives them a "fight or flight" response. Thus, players can use the short-term energy fear creates in a good way by acting on it in the right way.

You must welcome adversity and losses because you know a team needs hardship and needs to be battle-tested to grow, and this is the first step in the success process. Why do teams fear adversity and losing when they know it is the only way to truly get better?

Fear of the coach is also a powerful motivator for success. Coach has to use some form of fear or threat along with some sort of reprimand to motivate. However, it is short-term motivation because if the fear is taken away, the motivation is gone as well. Fear is not so good as a long-term motivator, since eventually it either becomes ineffective or drains confidence in players.

Bad Results from Fear

Fear causes stress, panic, and anxiety, which tighten players' muscles, causing them to play poorly. It prevents players from keeping their minds free from distraction while playing. It fills players' heads with worry—worry about the outcome of the game.

Fear also causes a lack of confidence—it takes away players' nerve. Players end up not playing with the risk-taking attitude they need to play the game, but playing safe, tentatively, cautiously, hesitantly, and playing not to lose.

Players end up taking a "posture of defeat" with their body language: the way they look, the way they walk with their heads down, the way they slope their shoulders, the way they talk, and the way they look as if being "half-asleep."

> ## IF YOU FEAR MAKING A MISTAKE, CHANCES ARE YOU WILL MAKE A MISTAKE

Coach Can Help Players Handle Their Fears

You can help your players overcome their fear by helping them understand their fears and teaching them techniques and strategies to not only manage their fears, but to master them.

Fear is normal

You can tell players that being scared is normal, and fear is part of any challenge. They must understand that even the best players feel afraid at times, due to pain and fatigue, to go to the next level. Fear helps players to grow; they have to go beyond their comfort zone and attack and defeat their fears. They cannot let fear take over or they won't achieve success.

Going right into fear's face

Courage is not the absence of fear, it's confronting and defeating fear; it's having the strength to face personal danger; having the power to do something in spite of the difficulties and challenges; it's being afraid but playing against one's opponent anyway. You can remind players that fear or playing scared is just part of playing sports, and the best way to approach fear or intimidation is to have the courage to simply face it and attack it aggressively.

Everyone's afraid of something; fear is just part of the challenge. Players have to decide to make a commitment to stop being afraid and face their fear.

It seems that all great performances are the result of courage in some form of pain, adversity, sacrifice, and suffering.

Some suggestions for handling fears

Tell your players:

> Take deep breaths so as to relax.

> Avoid self-talk about the future, as this increases fear.

> Think about or visualize past successes, which are far more real than the failures you might fear in the future.

> Think about all the things you can do rather than thinking of all the things you can't do.

Breaking the game into small segments

You can reduce fear for your players by breaking the game into small segments, such as attaining their performance goals rather than looking at the end result of winning. This approach makes your players more confident, as it brings their attention back to things they can control.

■ OPPONENTS ARE PARTNERS

You should present your philosophy to your players that they should look at their opponent not as the enemy or bad guy, but as a partner in helping them to reach their full potential by making them play their best and pushing them to greater heights. So, rather than being nervous about playing against their opponent, players should accept the opportunity and challenge to test how far they can go. In fact, the tougher the opponent, the more it offers the players an opportunity to live up to their full potential and be the best competitors they can be.

Without their opponent giving their greatest effort, players would never discover what they are truly capable of doing; so players should appreciate their opponent. With this philosophy, players no longer fear their opponent; they view their opponent not as a threat, but instead as a way to help them bring out more of their talent, energy, and determination.

4 MAKING IMPORTANT DECISIONS AND TEAM SELECTIONS

■ DECISION-MAKING

Coaching is a thinking game, so you have to work on becoming a better thinker. You must always be thinking about the future and about how to improve your team. This is the context within which all decisions must be made.

Decision-making involves making clear, smart decisions about where and how you spend your time. It is about making lists, prioritizing them, and then attending to the top priorities on that list, which will help you to manage your time. By choosing one thing on the list at a time, a coach can put his total energy into that one thing.

Decision-making is a basic part of coaching, as there are problems every day and successful coaches expect them and are ready to deal with them. Coaching is not about being popular with the players; it's about making tough, honest, and sometimes unpopular decisions that are best for the team.

Who Decides?

There are three basic ways to make a decision in coaching: you can make the decision on your own; you can make the decision together with your team; or you can just let the team decide on the solution. There are advantages and disadvantages to each approach.

Coach makes decisions alone

Decisiveness is one of the most important characteristics of leadership. There are always going to be problems along the way, difficult decisions that must be made, and situations that, if not handled properly, can lead to dissension in the ranks and a split in team unity. It's normal to have problems every day, so you have to expect them and be ready to head them off right away. Whether the decision is right or wrong is immaterial. What is important is that you have the courage to follow through with what you think is the right course of action and make the tough decision. If you are going to be wrong, be wrong decisively. You will look ridiculous if you are indecisive, uncertain, or reluctant to make difficult decisions. It is even better sometimes to be wrong than indecisive.

MAKING TOUGH DECISIONS IS THE ESSENCE OF LEADERSHIP

A coach has to take responsibility for everything that happens on his team so he has to act quickly and decisively, trust his intuition and gut feelings, live with his decision and not second-guess it, and not allow a problem or tough decision to become a major distraction. Sometimes you have to become a salesman and explain your reasons why you made the decision. If you just tell the players that they have to do it your way and don't give them a reason, the chances are they might resent it and play halfheartedly.

Note: Failing to make a decision is also a decision. It is a decision to leave everything to chance or to the initiative of others. People procrastinate out of fear and therefore they feel much safer not doing anything.

Coach makes decisions when game coaching

During a game, you must make quick decisions on your own, because there usually isn't time to get everyone's input, or to debate, or talk about it; timing is everything when making a decision. During a game, you often have only a split second to decide what to do. So you just tell the players what to do or give them an order or command with no discussion.

However, note that making a decision on one's own may seem faster and less complicated in the beginning, but this approach actually can end up taking more of your time, because you will have to do all the thinking all the time for your players throughout the season.

Because you make a lot of tough decisions quickly every game, some could be wrong. When you make a mistake or a bad decision you just have to admit it and try not to defend it. You must cut your losses and move on, just as you would expect your players to do. If you make a controversial decision during a game or other situation where you can't pause to discuss it with others, take the time later to talk it over with the team.

Remember: When you make decisions, you must take responsibility for the results.

Coach makes decisions quietly

The best coaches are often those you hardly notice. They stay quiet until they know what they are talking about; they have an organized and logical approach to decision-making and they quietly do what is necessary when it is necessary. They find solutions that no one else thinks of. They seem to penetrate to the heart of the problem and do things that make bad situations better. The best coaches seem to have a knack for knowing just what needs to be done and said in a tense moment.

Coach works with the team to make decisions

Another way of making decisions is working with your team. If you want to get your team's input before making a decision, it should be because you sincerely want to hear from the players and team staff. While at times it may be more efficient to make your own decisions, there are still good reasons to consult with your team.

If you involve players in team decisions, you might not end up with the best decisions, but the players will be more committed because of their involvement.

They will be more enthusiastic about carrying out decisions when they have participated in making them. In fact, it's a good idea to establish as many ways as possible for your players to be accountable for their own actions to empower them.

There are two basic ways of consulting with the team on decisions. You can gather input from players and assistant coaches and then make a decision that may or may not comply with everyone's wishes; or you can get input from all the players, then develop a solution to the problem based on the team's opinions, which may or may not be in line with your own wishes.

Most times when there is a problem, you should present it to the team and tell them exactly what has happened. You can then get information from all the players by asking for their opinion and develop a solution to the problem based on the players' information. You can then make your decision based on their information. In a team meeting situation, for instance, you could sometimes actually hold a vote and make the decision democratically.

You can also seek input by discussing the issue with small groups of veteran players. It is a good idea before a major decision that you should discuss the problem with your core of player-leaders personally and individually to see what they have to say. Whenever there is a major problem, you have to let the veteran players step up and talk about the problem.

TEAM INPUT INTO DECISIONS BUILDS TEAM SPIRIT

Another good reason for consulting with your players is to develop their decision-making skills. Players will take on ownership and accept accountability and responsibility to the team. There will be many times, especially in a game, when players will have to make decisions on their own, and good coaches will have their players prepared for these situations. You do not want to become the team's problem-solver. You want to create players with independence.

And you will want your players' input so as to learn from them. A good coach is a good teacher, and the best teachers are those who recognize that they still have much to learn. If you listen with an open mind, you might be surprised at what you can learn from your players and the useful contributions they can make toward a decision.

Team makes decision alone

Some coaches feel that if they have a problem, they should just let the players work it out by themselves. This may take time, but it could become an "airing-out" for the team, and good things might come from this situation. In this "laissez-faire" approach of decision-making, it involves only the players, and they basically decide on what they want. Sometimes, of course, the players make poor decisions due to lack of experience and a lack of awareness of what to do in certain situations. This decision-making style takes a lot of time, and the result may end up with no decisions, but putting the decisions in the players' hands to decide their own fate may make them more committed.

Guidelines for Making Good Coaching Decisions

Good judgment is a difficult thing to teach and to learn. There are no set rules to follow that will lead you to make the right decision every time. But there are some guidelines you can follow, such as your coaching philosophy, your principles, and behaviour goals that will help ensure that your decisions are fair.

Coaching decisions based on what is best for the team

Your philosophy of a team should be, "The team is always more important than any individual, including the coach." As a coach, you have to make tough, unpopular decisions; you have to push players beyond their limits; and you have to discipline players—benching them for missing curfew; not dressing them for a game for not working hard or missing a practice; or making them run sprints for being late for practice or for playing badly. So players may sometimes end up being angry with you.

You must have the courage and discipline to make tough yet good decisions; tough decisions can often be unpopular ones, but if made for the right reason, you can't go wrong. If you have to make an unpopular decision, it is important that you take the time at some point to explain the reasons for your decision to the player and sometimes to the team. The player might still be unhappy, but at least with time she will come to understand why you did what you did, and her resentment will subside. Further, if you are fair and consistent in your decision-making, resentment will be kept to a minimum. When there is a trusting relationship between a coach and his players, the players will be more likely to go along with tough decisions even when they don't like them.

Making decisions as a coach is not about being popular, being liked, or enjoying the power of telling people what to do; it is about gaining respect. You get respect by sacrificing being popular for doing the right thing and doing what you believe is in the best interest of the team. You cannot please everybody. Therefore, you must keep your "professional distance" from the players, because there will be times when you must go against their wishes, yet still build relationships—which is tough to do. You must lead everyone equally and fairly, and to accomplish this, you cannot show favouritism, bias, or allegiance to a few individuals.

You will find that the most difficult decisions involve conflicting priorities of short-term goals versus long-term goals. You should never make any short-term decision that could jeopardize the team's long-term success. For instance, you could coach for the present moment by making all game-decisions for the players, or you can coach for the future by letting players make their own game decisions.

Coaching decisions based on doing the right thing

You should not try to make quick decisions, but most of the decisions you make have to be made quickly. You do not have the luxury of saying, "Wait, I need more time." So when knowledge of the problem is lacking you have to act with integrity. When you don't know the answer, the surest course is to do what you believe is right, even though it may be unpopular. In any moment of decision, the best thing you can do is the right thing; the next best thing is the wrong thing; and the worst thing you can do is nothing. There is no such thing as a bad decision; there are many different decisions you can make, and whichever one you make is the right one—that is, if you are committed to it.

It's also easy to make decisions when you know what your values and principles are. To do the right thing, you and your team must follow your philosophy based upon sound principles—and sometimes common sense and sometimes tradition—to guide them in making good decisions. The decisions you make as a coach are backed by a broader set of coaching principles and philosophy. Players respect a coach who acts with a good reason, and they will follow you because they trust you to do the right thing. So just ask yourself: "Is this the right thing to do?"

INTEGRITY IS ALL ABOUT DOING THE RIGHT THING NO MATTER WHAT THE CONSEQUENCES

Coaching decisions
based on "art" or intuition

Sometimes you won't be able to explain why you decide on certain things, only that you feel it is the right thing to do. Your judgment or decision may be based on your gut feeling, your intuition, your instincts, your conscience, or common sense. This is where coaching becomes an "art"—where you don't make decisions by the book. You can't explain it; you just know your decision is right. You must trust your instincts; and since your instincts are your conscience, let them be your guide.

A good coach has a "feel" for the game and knows exactly what is going on and exactly what to do. You will find the decisions based on your instincts are right more often than they are wrong. You acquire this experience or "feel" for the game from your past playing experience, from your past coaching experience, from being in the trenches, from getting beaten, from making mistakes and learning from them, from winning tight games, and definitely from winning national championships. From this experience, you learn that there are certain things that work better than others in certain situations. The more high-pressure situations you are in, the more you learn about the game and being successful. You become better at making decisions by learning from winning (what worked) and from losing (what didn't work). Your intuition develops with experience, knowledge of the game, and knowledge of your players. When you make decisions based on intuition, the team has to trust them as much as you do.

Consequently, you have to earn the trust of your team before you can make intuitive decisions, because you won't be able to explain your rationale to the team—they will just have to take it on faith that you are acting in their best interest.

Note: You can get a "feel" of how the players feel in a pressure situation by looking them in the eye and reading their body language. Are they ready to play or are they questioning themselves? Is it a "posture of defeat"— shoulders stooping, head down, sleepy eyes expressing lack of confidence? Or is it a "posture of confidence"—standing straight, head up, shoulders back, eyes alive and expressing confidence?

Coaching decisions
based on "science" or percentages

There are certain situations where coaching or decision-making is scientific. These decisions are made from real knowledge based on facts rather than from just pure chance or luck. Here, you play the percentages to make your decision based on the laws of averages and facts from game statistics, from experience, and from using your coaching skills. You think the decision through from all your data and if you believe the advantage of doing it one way outweighs the risk of doing it another way, then you go for it. Knowing the percentages doesn't necessarily predict what will happen every play, but over the long haul of the season, it seems to work the majority of times.

Decisions based on science is knowing the probabilities and making adjustments to put your team in a position to be successful. You can't control the outcome of a game, but you can increase the odds of being successful. You cannot be indecisive; you have to decide. If the odds are in your favour, then you have to be aggressive and "go for the kill." But if the odds are not in your favour, it is time to play a bit more conservatively and wait for the right moment to strike.

Again, experience and knowledge of the game help you make better decisions, even in cases where you are working with and evaluating from "hard" data such as statistics. Coaches who have experienced team success in their lives have the advantage of a gauge or measuring stick to compare how hard and intensely their present team is playing compared to their other successful or championship teams. This experience certainly helps in decision-making.

Coaching decisions based on both intuition and facts

Coaching is a marriage of "science" and "art." Many coaching decisions are based on a combination of facts or playing percentages, and instincts or intuition. It is best to bring both intuitive feelings and rational thought into play when making decisions. Sometimes the decision works and sometimes it doesn't. Some coaches only play the high percentages, doing their homework by gathering information, statistics, and percentages, but many times these hard facts are not enough or for some reason can't be used. Other coaches look at the statistics, go against their reasoning, throw them out the window, and go with their gut feeling.

In the end, though, coaching seems to be more "art" than "science" because the percentages of the scientific part of decision-making are constant—for example, a basketball team is trying to attain 50 percent shooting all the time—while the artistic part of decision-making changes with every coach and every situation. Coaches have got to be thinkers, but at times they also have to be gamblers and risk takers and just follow their instincts when making decisions and selecting players.

INSTINCT POINTS YOU IN A CERTAIN DIRECTION; SCIENCE CONFIRMS IT

■ SELECTION OF THE RIGHT PLAYERS

One of the first major decisions you will make when building a team, and probably your most important and difficult decision overall, is who will be on your team. It's more about the players that will make the difference. The bottom line is the best teams are successful usually because they have the best character players, the most committed players, the most competitive players who push their teammates, and the most talented players. You win with people, especially talented players. So, the selection of good character/talented players is the most basic ingredient of dictating your team's success. If you know the player has character, you can predict how he or she will respond to adversity, temptation, and success; and you know he or she is going to do all the hard work.

Selecting the "Team" Player

If you don't feel a player can be "one of the guys"—a person who can fit in with the overall team concept; or you feel a player has his own personal agenda, don't keep him. Look for individuals who want to help build the framework of your team by setting aside their self-centred desires. You know that even though there are different personalities that make up a team, everyone should have the same team agenda. The trick in selecting players is getting them to mesh, to have the same attitude about the team, about being successful, and about being part of the whole. So you look for players who love the game, who are committed to playing, who love playing, who are passionate, who are hungry to win, and who can get along with others. The secret is sometimes selecting not the best players, but the right players.

Sometimes, as with teams of young kids in house-league, you will not have a choice of selecting players, since the whole idea in house-leagues is to give everyone the same opportunity to play. In these cases, the emphasis should be on having fun, so your decisions will have to do with ensuring that everyone has a good time and does his/her best.

Another situation when you don't have a choice of selecting players is when you take on a team after the season has already begun. Where selecting, trading, or cutting players is not possible, your decisions will have to do with whom to play how often and in what roles.

But in situations where you do have to select players for a competitive team, to do a good job at evaluating talent, you should have three or four people helping you to make decisions about whom to keep. These people might include assistant coaches, trainers, equipment men, and executive members, depending on the level you are coaching at.

Releasing or Cutting a Player

The decision to cut a player is a very difficult one for a coach and players, particularly in school and community leagues. It's tough telling a young kid who is full of dreams that he or she simply doesn't have what it takes to be on the team. Or, sometimes you have to release a negative person because of the bad effect he has on the morale and spirit of the team.

When releasing a player, try to speak with the child personally, face-to-face. Find something encouraging to say to give her hope for the future; have some alternative suggestions to offer, such as playing in a less competitive house-league more appropriate for her skill level; explain why she didn't make the team and what she has to work on to make the team next year; and thank her for trying out for the team. And if players are really insistent that they didn't get a fair chance, you just give them another chance.

At the end of each practice, ask all the players to see you before they leave. This way you can talk to a player face-to-face to release him or her quietly without embarrassment. Posting a list or sending out emails to players who didn't make the team is cruel, unprofessional, and could be devastating to a player.

Some Players Just Quit

But sometimes the choice will be surprisingly easy. You will find that you don't actually have to cut some players; they will quit because the practices are too hard or they just don't want to make a full commitment, or they read the "writing on the wall"—they just aren't good enough to make the team. There can, of course, be other personal reasons for quitting.

Players Who Don't Try in Training Camp and Want to Be Traded

What if a skilled player does not try hard or "dog it" in training camp because he wants to be traded? You do not want anybody "to play games" with the organization. If a player does not want to be on the team, he should be honest and just tell you. But, as you know, that doesn't always happen. You should confront any player who seems to be acting this way and demand an honest explanation for his behaviour. Players have to understand that most organizations keep everybody on their protected list, and players will stay unless a trade can be worked out. So they must work hard to make this team or perhaps not play at all.

Notes: As a coach, never stay with a pat hand from year to year. Always bring in new players to stir up competition and keep players on the edge.

The final piece in putting together the puzzle is the draft—first, look for impact players; look for players who can fill the needs of the team, that is, to strengthen the weaknesses.

■ SELECTION OF PLAYERS IN TRAINING CAMP

Picking Players at Tryouts or Training Camp

Here are some questions to ask yourself when picking players:

> Do you pick a player's attitude over athleticism? Do you focus on the player's performance rather than the player? Or do you focus on the player's attitude rather than how he performs on the floor?

> Do you pick a player's aptitude for hard work over natural ability?

> Do you pick players because they will provide energy?

> Do you pick players based on their good performance in training camp and not on their reputation? (Yes. Although past reputation is important, it is not the end-all; there are players who develop late in their career.)

> Do you pick players based on their potential and not on their poor performance in training camp?

> Do you pick players based on their past reputation, in spite of a poor performance in training camp? (Yes. You should definitely pick players who were productive in the past, such as having a reputation of being a good goal scorer.)

> Do you pick players on their performance in camp over players who look like they might have potential? (Yes. If you see potential in players who are hard workers and make intelligent plays, you have to believe they are going to improve. If in doubt, keep them and invite them back to the next practice.)

> Do you pick players who can play even though they are small? (Yes. You should always go with small players who have a good performance in camp.)

> Do you pick players who test well and look athletic? (Not necessarily. You should pick players who can play the game and who can produce and perform rather than players who test well or look good athletically. Some players test well, but can't play well while other players don't test well, but can play. Some players don't look good athletically, but they can play. "He was slow and overweight, but he was a good player who was very competitive.")

> Do you pick players who can produce and play the sport over players who look like they have potential and size? (Yes. If you are going to make a mistake on a selection, make a mistake on the side of a player's production over how a player looks. There are some players who don't have the speed or the size, but they have something more: They have great playing intelligence and the ability to focus; they play with heart and passion; and they know how to get the job done.)

> Do you pick players who fit the system?

> ❯   Do you pick players who will complement players already on the team?

Notes: If stuck making a final decision between two players, put the players side by side and let them battle it out; race them, battle for a loose ball, go one-on-one, or have a shooting competition. Also, get input from your team leaders/experienced players on the team when selecting new players, as they have a vested interest in choosing the best type of new player.

When you have decided on a player who has made the team, make sure you tell him you want him rather than just letting him assume he has made the team.

Guidelines for Picking Players

You tell the players what you're looking for

At tryouts or training camp where players are being evaluated for possible inclusion on a team, you should tell the players what you are looking for to make the team: character, athletic ability, and, of course, skill. Tell the players to show their strengths—if they have speed, show it; if they can score, show it; if they can play good defence, show it. Players should not try to play beyond their capabilities in trying to do everything to impress the coaches.

Also, be sure they understand that every player has an equal opportunity to make the team. By saying this, everybody—veterans and rookies—will work harder and smarter.

Remember: In tryouts, players want a fair chance to show what they can do. Coach should not focus on what the player can't do, but on what she can do and then figure out how she can hide her deficiencies.

You look for a range of players and skills

What are the kinds of traits you look for in a player? (Athletic, big, speedy, etc.) It is important you know the type of team you want to be and the type of systems you want to run. If you know what system you are running, then you will know what type of player and roles you want. The players' talent should complement the system. One of the keys of being a good coach is matching the right people with the right position. Also, when you put a team together, you must think of chemistry, how players complement each other. When you are evaluating the players, remember that you aren't just looking for good players; you are also looking for players with strong potential whom you will be able to develop into good players.

Remember: Teams do need "stars"—players who will carry the scoring load or whom all the others will look up to.

Guidelines for Picking Players for a Lacrosse Team

Divide your potential team into thirds. One-third of the players will be the "stars." The offensive stars will carry the team in scoring: 20 percent of the players will do 80 percent of the scoring. Usually, these are experienced players who have played for you before, or they are players who stand out in training camp. The defensive stars will be big, strong defensive-defenders and quick transition-defenders that can run and score. Build the team's style around your stars' special qualities and unique talents to get the most out of them.

Another third of the players will be those who are fundamentally solid. They will play great defence; they will get the team a goal here and there; they will do what you tell them to do; and they will do the dirty work, such as fighting for loose balls, running the floor, and screening for the scorers.

The final third of the players will be made up of "character" players who have great heart and a great work ethic, but might not have a great deal of talent. These are the toughest decisions to make.

Here are some things to think about on selecting the final third:

Speed and quickness

In most team sports, everything you stress about offence and defence is based on using speed and movement to wear down the bigger, opposing players. Most coaches believe in pressure defence and pressure offence, the fast break—so they generally look for fast, aggressive, and tenacious final-third players.

Balancing out the team

Do you need defensive or offensive players? Every team has to have its share of checkers and scorers, but it is an advantage if the scorers know how to check. Do you need big players or small, quick players? Do you need a tough, big, "enforcer-type" player? If it boils down to picking a scorer or a checker, you should pick the scorer and teach him how to play defence, because it is tougher to teach a defensive player how to score than to teach an offensive player how to check. When selecting these final-third players, you want to bring in players for specific reasons because these players will fill some of the elements in the team that are missing.

The player who complements the unit/group

Good players have to play with each other in a unit. For example, you should put the five best players together who complement each other and who have good chemistry. A unit needs some "diggers," some scorers, and some defenders in it. Sometimes the best qualification for a final-third player's making a team is being in the right place at the right time.

Experience and/or youth

Remember, experienced players have been exposed to pressure situations and usually have learned from them. These veterans can give the team their experience, their leadership, their winning kind of attitude, and their knowledge of the game. Putting a successful team together is a combination of experience and the enthusiasm and energy of youthful players.

Although rookies are great to have on a team because of their energy and enthusiasm, they might have a confidence problem, from nervousness, when trying out for the team. So the coach should be aware of this and take it into consideration when making his final decisions.

Notes: Through experience, good and bad, an experienced player is better at reading, feeling, and sensing what is happening on the floor/court. He knows the difference between a right and a wrong play and can see small openings . . . he can take advantage of things that an inexperienced player normally would not.

A problem with young people can be their inconsistency in their play—one day they look great and the next day they look terrible. They need time to mature as persons as much as players.

Players who come from a winning program

We look for players who have been winners. Select final-third players who are used to winning because they know what it takes to be successful—they have learned how to pay the price. You should always look for players who have been successful in the past because it is amazing how veteran winners always find a way to win.

Special qualities

Some players can bring useful qualities to a team:

> Players who are specialists—who can score but can't do anything else; or can just play defence; or who just fit into the playing system

> Players who are good people and who get along with everyone and never create problems

> Players of different ages—Coach may have to cut an older player to build the program with a younger player. This choice will depend on the number of graduating players and the age of the team.

■ THE DEFINITION OF A "GOOD" PLAYER

Not surprisingly, the secret to sports success is to get good players. You have to have the analytic ability to recognize potential in players. Here is what defines a "good" player:

#1 Athletic Ability

You look for players who have agility, quickness, strength, power, flexibility, endurance, speed, athleticism, the right body type for the sport, and a good fitness level. Physical talent is relatively easy to spot. With some players, technical skills with the ball/stick/puck are not a concern because of their great athletic potential. Speed, coordination, and strength are sometimes more important than fundamental skills, which can be taught. The strategy for many team sports is based on players using speed and movement to wear the opposition down, so these can be useful qualities in players.

Note: Watch for players who may have limited athletic ability and talent—do not have great size, speed, or natural ability—but are very competitive and know how to get the job done when needed.

#2 Skill or Talent

You look for fundamentally sound, skilled players who know how to play either defence, offence, or both. There is no substitute for talent. But remember that skill and talent are just the beginning of the process; competitiveness, a passion for the game, and character also help.

#3 Character

Character is what players are made of. It is the hardest thing to recognize during tryouts because most times players do not reveal their true character unless they are put into an adverse situation. A player may look great during tryouts, but could be very weak emotionally when things go wrong in a game.

You should pass on a highly skilled player with a bad attitude, as he can be destructive to the team morale, and accept a player with a bit less talent but with a good character, as he will be more coachable. You will find when the chips are down the character player is always there for you because he'll play his heart out for you. Always select attitude over skill. So you should never evaluate players by their physical appearance alone; consider what they are made of—their substance.

Traits of character players

Character is just as important as ability. Good people make good players. Look to select players with character because talent will win games but character will win championships. Besides you want to be a coach of good players rather than a maintenance guy who is constantly working with problem players.

In chapter 8, "Behaviour Goals," we expand upon the character traits:

> Commitment

> Hard work

> Teamwork
> Playing smart
> Discipline
> Confidence
> Self-control
> Focus
> Positive attitude
> Poise under pressure
> Mental toughness

Ideally, you want good players with strong character on your team. If you start with players who have the right type of character, you will have few problems later. If you choose good-quality players who want to come to practice, are unselfish, are positive, get along well with others, sacrifice for the good of the team, work hard, and are dependable and dedicated, you will have a good "character" team. The ideal player is one with both talent and character, but sometimes it is a good idea to pick a player with good character and less talent over a talented player with questionable character. Then, there are players who can perform, but are misfits or oddballs. As long as players can produce and help out the team, keep them.

Note: How players treat their parents, how they interact with their classmates, and how they contribute to their community are other things you can take into consideration when deciding on character.

#4 High Playing Intelligence

You look for smart players who understand the game, who play focused and alert, and make great decisions. They are aware of everything that is happening on the floor by playing the game with their eyes, having their head on a swivel; they anticipate well and read the floor extremely well; they almost have a sixth sense about what is going to happen before it happens; they are always thinking one, two, or three plays ahead. They have a tremendous "feel" or instinct for the game; they know exactly what to do in certain situations by being in the right place at the right time and doing the right thing. Some coaches believe intelligence—outsmarting the opposition—even outweighs speed and strength as qualities.

SUCCESSFUL TEAMS ARE MADE UP OF DIFFERENT KINDS OF PERSONALITIES

5 INCREASING YOUR KNOWLEDGE OF COACHING

The number one leadership skill you need is to become a knowledgeable person or an expert on your sport. You will always be at the centre of the decision-making process, so you'd better have extensive knowledge of, and expertise in, the game. It is important for your credibility that players believe you are competent and that they have confidence that you know what you are talking about. The "true" coach has great knowledge of not only the game but a good understanding of people. From this knowledge, you should know how to:

> Spot talent
> Work with it
> Teach skills and playing systems
> Put players in the right spots
> Put a team together
> Take players with little talent and make them "stars" in your system

Coaching is about having knowledge and putting that knowledge across to his players. Only when we absorb knowledge, digest it, understand it, learn it, and act upon it does it become beneficial to our ongoing growth as a leader.

■ HOW A COACH ACQUIRES KNOWLEDGE OF THE GAME

If you are an inexperienced coach, you have to pay your dues and work hard to find out about the game and coaching. Here are some ways you can increase your knowledge of your sport and improve your coaching.

Thirst for Knowledge

You must have this thirst for knowledge, always searching for a better way of coaching. Coaching is a lifelong pursuit. You have to be a student of the game; so do your homework and never stop learning, growing, developing yourself professionally, and getting experience. What matters most is what you do day after day over the long season. "Are you as a coach better today than you were yesterday?" You, along with your team, must get a little bit better every day, by understanding what works and what doesn't work at your level of play and by helping players develop their skills and knowledge of the game to produce a successful season.

Work with an Experienced Coach

Some novice coaches are fortunate enough to work under a successful, experienced coach, a mentor. If you are given an opportunity like this, be sure to take advantage of it. Many successful coaches came out of programs in which they were players and then became assistants under a successful coach. A key in becoming a knowledgeable coach is your willingness to listen and learn. You have to "pick their brains," ask questions of successful coaches, and learn and borrow from them. Just as important as learning from experienced coaches what to do is learning what not to do. This information can prevent you from repeating the mistakes of others, which will save you lots of time.

Stay Current by Being Willing to Make Changes

The main skill for a coach is knowledge of schemes and techniques. And it is important that you be willing to be flexible and to change with the times. You must be adaptable and open to change because there are always changes in the game. You may have to make adjustments in a game rather than staying with the old stuff; you may have to change in how you handle the new athlete; you may have to change your system because you are not staying with the times. You have to realize when it is time to change; and you have to know what to do and when to do it.

The successful coaches are always looking to improve areas of their game and are willing to admit they are not perfect. They are always asking, "Is there a better way to communicate, to motivate, to teach, and to build teams?"

A good philosophy to have is do things that you have never done before—do things unexpectedly, have surprises for your team, but do not get stuck in doing the same thing over and over again, during the season, in your practices, when playing the game, and in your pre-game talks.

Listen to Others

You should never think that you have become so knowledgeable that you don't need to have the humility and the wisdom to listen and learn from everybody. One of the biggest problems with arrogant coaches is that they think there is nothing others can teach them. Their thinking is, "Why should I listen to others when I already know it all?" This thinking is the "kiss of death." Once you think you know it all, you should quit.

Humility teaches us to be open to new ideas and new ways to improve. Do not let your ego get in the way of improving as a coach. Even experienced coaches should see themselves as "beginners" who are always receptive to new ideas and who can always learn more. You can bring in good coaches or former players to watch you in a game and a practice and then listen to their constructive criticism. You get knowledge by being open to suggestions and new ideas; by talking to other coaches; by listening to others; and by not getting defensive when people give you constructive advice.

Seek out old-timers who definitely know more than you do and ask questions. You should even ask opposition coaches who just beat your team how they did it!

Study other teams to find out the secrets of their success. You might learn that you are teaching the wrong things and measuring the wrong results. You have to know what type of system your team is going to play, but the real key is knowing how to teach and explain the system.

THE MORE GOOD COACHES KNOW, THE MORE THEY REALIZE WHAT THEY DON'T KNOW

Read books, articles, and magazines; watching videos and other media can also be very helpful. Read about the game and about successful coaches. Good coaches always seem to have a good book handy. Be sure to have a library of coaching books and seemingly unrelated books that can also yield useful advice, such as business books about management and motivation and history books about great leaders. Attend as many clinics as you can.

Observe Other Coaches at Work

One valuable way to develop your coaching skills is by observing other coaches. Asking other coaches directly for their advice or simply observing them can be helpful and effective. Sometimes there is a great difference between what we say and what we actually do. So take the time simply to watch and learn. You will soon see what works and what doesn't work. When you observe coaches in different situations—as a spectator, from the sidelines during a game, in practices (if possible)—you'll see a variety of coaching styles. You can get knowledge by bringing in good coaches, former players, or people you respect to see how they run practices.

Play the Sport

Naturally, one of the best ways of getting knowledge of a sport is to have played it, as it helps to have experienced something to really know it and to get a "feel" for the game. You must understand, though, that having played a sport will give you knowledge of the technical aspects, but not necessarily the theory of coaching.

Learn from Your Own Experience

One of the major predictors of coaching success is obtaining information from past experiences and applying it to the present moment. You obtain knowledge two primary ways: education (reading books, asking questions, watching videos) and experience (trial-and-error). Experience generally has a more meaningful effect on your level of knowledge than "book smarts." The more pressured situations you are in, the better you learn about the game and being successful. Thus, you learn from either winning (what works) or from losing (what doesn't work). You get this experience or "feel" of the game from being "in the trenches"; getting beaten; winning tight games; and definitely winning regional and national or even international championships.

You have to watch other games, not as a spectator, but as an analyzer. You watch the opposition's coaches, especially those who beat you, to see what they have been doing against you. You watch the opposition players to see how they execute their skills, and perhaps copy their technique.

There is no substitute for coaching experience. An experienced coach makes good decisions knowing when to do certain things at certain times, such as when to play key players and run special plays. If you have experienced success in your sport, you have the advantage of a "gauge" or a "measuring stick" to compare how hard and intense your present team is playing compared to your successful or championship team. You find out what works best from trial and error, sometimes winning, sometimes losing, but always learning from experience. Without this experience of paying your dues, you will never be truly a successful coach. The longer you coach, if you have love and enthusiasm for coaching, you are going to become a better coach.

Coach Evaluation

You should do a coach's evaluation by your players to rate your strengths and weaknesses. You want to know how the players see you as a coach. Even let your assistants evaluate to get feedback and knowledge about yourself to make you a better coach. An evaluation of your performance as a coach might be a bit uncomfortable reading, but the truth, good or bad, will make you a better coach.

PART TWO

www.tsgphoto.com

THE ART OF MOTIVATION
THROUGH SETTING GOALS
AND TEAM RULES

6 THE ART OF MOTIVATION

Coaching . . . it's not manipulating or tricking players into doing something, it's motivating players in a multitude of ways, and it is this accumulation that leads to their excellence. The two major types of motivation are extrinsic and intrinsic motivation. The main job of a coach is to externally motivate his or her team so that they want to reach their goals; and to help make individual players aware of internal motivation or self-motivation to play to their maximum potential and become overachievers.

There is no single factor that externally motivates all of your players all of the time. You cannot externally motivate everybody the same way. Because every player is motivated differently, you have to find the "button" that turns him or her on. Although motivation eventually begins with each individual player, you, as a coach, can do things externally to improve motivation in your players.

The great coaches are great motivators who know how to get their players ready to play at the next level, time and time again. Sometimes you spend very little time on motivating certain players and with others you spend tons of time. Motivation is the main factor that separates the successful coach from the unsuccessful coach. Everything a coach does can either motivate—"turn a player on"—or de-motivate—"turn a player off." The result of motivation is that it gives players a reason, a purpose, and a passion to do the things they love to do.

■ MOTIVATION IS:

> Getting players to do things better than they thought they could

> The main force that moves players to think and to take action to reach a specific goal

> Getting players to the next level by squeezing everything out of them

> A long-term development process of getting players to do something not just because they have to but because they want to

> The result of a coach's making players believe they can do it and believe in each other

■ EXTERNAL MOTIVATION

Coach tries to get the players to do what he wants them to do through the "carrot," or reward approach (by praise or tangible rewards); the "stick," or punishment approach (by fear, threat, intimidation, manipulation, physical exercise); and the "dream" or goal-setting approach (by generating passion).

The punishment method works on the premise that if you don't do something—for example, play hard—you're going to be punished by doing physical exercises or being benched or cut. This short-term fear approach works best for a short time as players play to avoid failure.

The reward motivation works on the opposite premise: If you play hard or are improving, Coach will give you a tangible reward, such as a candy or a prize; a verbal reward, such as praise; or a physical reward of more playing time.

When candy, pizza, or trophies are used as short-term external rewards for doing what the coach wants, the players might get a short-term boost but eventually, once the incentives are removed, this motivation wears off. Also, giving tangible rewards for performing well is a form of bribing players to do it. The message here is that players are playing to get something, rather than for the enjoyment and love of the game. In fact, the game itself should be the reward, and Coach should be challenging players to want to play to the best of their ability.

The goal-setting method gets players to set a long-term goal and then chase it. To do this, they have to have a plan for attaining it. These goals push players to work hard right to the end of the season.

You as the coach are the extrinsic motivator, so you have to find out what "buttons" you need to push to motivate the players. Some players are verbally motivated in different ways: some through praise or encouragement; some through gentle teaching; some through constant repetition; some through criticism, yelling, and harsh remarks; and some though constructive verbal feedback; others are motivated by physically rewarding them through more playing time; through a pat on the back or hug; or sometimes with a kick in the rear. There are even some players who are motivated through the "punishment" approach by giving them physical exercises (sprints, push-ups) for not performing up to their potential.

The bottom line with external motivation is that it comes from the coach and it partly entails rewards and punishments that sometimes work and sometimes don't.

Here are some of the better methods to externally motivate. Coach motivates:

> By building relationships with his players

> Through face-to-face communication skills

> Through the reward approach (by tangible rewards or by verbal praise)

> ❭   Through the punishment approach (by fear, by threat, by intimidation, by manipulation)
> ❭   Through the goal-setting approach
> ❭   By setting outcome Goals
> ❭   By setting performance Goals
>   •   Setting behaviour Goals
>   •   Setting cohesive goals for team building
>   •   By building players' self-esteem
>   •   By sharing power with players through team meetings
>   •   Through good preparation and organization
>   •   By creating a good learning environment
> ❭   Through selecting and creating team leaders
> ❭   Through pre-game and post-game speeches

Note: Two good questions for coaches are: "How would you motivate your team if you were coaching a team that you knew was going to lose almost every game?" and "What would you do in this situation to make the season fun and successful?"

■ INTERNAL OR INTRINSIC MOTIVATION

External goal-setting or motivation is set by the coach or the coach and players together—outcome goals, performance goals, behaviour goals, and team cohesion goals.

Internal goal-setting or motivation is set by the individual player, sometimes with the help of the coach—to be the best, to be an all-star, to be a starter, or to win a championship.

Here, the external motivator, the coach, is complemented by the internal motivator, the player. Besides just trying to satisfy the coach, he is now trying to also please himself. Players have to be aware that this long-term intrinsic motivation or self-motivation comes from within, so players are responsible for motivating themselves; and when a player feels good about accomplishing things himself, he becomes satisfied.

Extrinsic motivators alone, such as rewards and punishments, do not totally improve performance. Players need to supplement the existing external motivation with internal motivation. How you, as a coach, can help players become self-motivated is one of the keys to successful coaching.

The most consistent and best motivation method for players is internal motivation by human needs. "Why do you do the things you do?" Developing the players' motivation and growth should be built on understanding the basic human needs, on both a physical and emotional level.

> ## NEEDS ARE ARRANGED ACCORDING TO A SPECIFIC ORDER LIKE CLIMBING A LADDER

■ MASLOW'S HIERARCHY OF BASIC HUMAN NEEDS

A useful way of looking at human needs has been given to us by Abraham Maslow in a paper he published in 1943 titled, "A Theory of Human Motivation." Once a coach knows what a player's needs are he can help give him what he needs.

We have adapted Maslow's principles to coaching.[2]

First level — Biological Needs

These are the survival needs, the physical needs, the most basic needs, the bottom level of the ladder, such as food, oxygen, rest, and water. As a coach you must spend a great deal of time on conditioning your players because they have to be in great shape to play. You also must be aware of keeping your players fresh and energized throughout the season by giving them rest, making sure they eat properly, and drink plenty. (And don't forget your own needs!)

Second level — Safety or Sense of Security Needs

You must be aware that players are internally motivated and play better in a predictable environment where they feel safe and secure. You have to make sure your players know where they stand in the big picture so they don't worry about whether they are on the team, are going to play, or are going to be cut. You have to be aware that players become uneasy in new situations or unexpected events during the season, so your job as a coach is to prepare players for these new or unexpected situations.

Third level — Love and the Need to Belong to a Group

Players need to feel that they belong on the team and feel part of the team; that they are accepted and liked by their teammates and you; that you care about them and are on their side to help them with their internal motivation. That is why having players involved with the group is important—they need to feel

---

2   Also check out John Wooden's Pyramid of Success.

they belong. You create a friendly, caring, trusting, and supportive environment where players feel free to fail without punishment from you and where they feel free to express their feelings honestly and openly without fear of ridicule or reprimand by you. You can promote caring for the players by being kind but fair; by setting reasonable personal goals for each player; and by promoting a coach-player relationship. It is important that you define a player's role on the team early because they want to know, "What is my role?" "Where do I fit on the team?"

Fourth level — Self-esteem Needs

Players have a need for recognition — the most powerful human motivator there is — and approval from others so that they can feel important and good about themselves. You can raise their self-esteem by making sure you give them individual attention; by supporting and believing in them; by making sure they know they are appreciated; by rewarding, recognizing, and giving positive verbal feedback for their hard work; by giving them praise and recognition for doing things right; by your reaction to mistakes — that they are stepping stones to learning; and by telling them they could become the best.

Fifth level — Self-actualization Needs

Self-actualization is at the top level of the ladder. When all the basic needs on the lower levels of the ladder have been fulfilled and satisfied, this fifth level becomes important. It is a strong internal desire to fully realize one's potential. Players have this need or desire to seek purpose or meaning in their playing.

One purpose for playing should be connected to a cause larger than themselves — such as playing on a team to achieve a championship. This goal provides tremendous energy for playing and it gives players inner satisfaction and peace of mind when it is fulfilled.

■ INTRINSIC MOTIVATIONS

The love of playing

Sports teaches players how to motivate themselves. Once they find something they love to do and fill their life with it, the motivation is a result of loving what they do. If a player doesn't love or have a passion for playing the sport, it will always be work. Players feel inspired or motivated when they play with the purpose of playing because: they love the game, which is probably the single most powerful motivator; they are excited about playing the game; they love the competition itself to measure their skills against other competitors; they want to test themselves by competing against their own performance standards; and they want to win a championship. This "love of playing" motivation is important for their long-term success.

Setting a personal goal of getting better

Players become motivated to chase a dream by setting personal goals. Players get this tremendous internal drive when they have a personal goal of making the team, becoming the best at what they do, becoming an all-star, becoming a starter, or perhaps to prove people wrong. This personal goal is a powerful motivator that helps him to "light his own fire" and keeps him excited and energized. If a player wants something badly enough, it becomes a passion that will motivate him to work harder and longer on his game; he will not get bored with the purpose of getting better, which is one of the strongest and most determined desires there are. Players know it is not where they are now that counts, but the direction in which they are heading. All successful players are goal-oriented and know what they want and where they are going

During the season, a player should never let himself forget what his personal goal is by leaving reminders to himself, such as personal notes, pictures of where he is headed, and posted self-affirmation statements. A coach can usually get players to do what they want when he is there, but the real test is what players do on their own when the coach is not there. Motivated players are willing to work on their own and do not require constant supervision.

The satisfaction of the activity itself

The challenge of getting better at a certain skill is a player's own reward as he or she gets satisfaction and joy from perfecting and performing the skill itself. Players who pursue sports more for the pleasure of the activity itself than extrinsic rewards get more excited about the sport and give a much better performance.

Standing for a cause

When players have a goal or extrinsic aspiration, such as fame, trophies, and wins, if they reach those goals, sometimes they still don't feel any happier. Satisfaction depends not merely on having goals, but on having the *right* goals. Players don't reach happiness by achieving things or striving for external rewards; they get happiness from internal rewards or goals of fulfillment and satisfaction that come from playing for a cause—such as being on a team fighting for a championship; working as a group to accomplish a common cause; by doing something productive for others, such as improving the fundamental skills of other players; or serving others, such as doing charitable work and volunteering or just making a difference in people's lives.

A player does not become whole until he or she becomes part of something greater than him/herself. Team sport teaches players that they are part of something greater than themselves. By being part of a team, players become better than they could be alone. They learn to sacrifice for the team; they learn that to play on a team they must sacrifice their individuality; they learn to put the team before themselves.

Review: Players learn from the coach that the main purpose of playing is for the love of the game, which internally motivates them; another purpose of playing is to get better, which internally motivates them; another purpose of playing is to enjoy doing the activity itself, which internally motivates them; and finally, there is the purpose of making a contribution to the team, which internally motivates them to do something that matters, or gives them a cause bigger than themselves.

■ HOW COACH CAN HELP PLAYERS WITH INTERNAL MOTIVATION

You can help players move toward internal motivation: by setting up a congenial environment to pursue getting better; by giving them freedom to pursue getting better; by constantly stressing getting better; by helping them play with a purpose or goal, such as becoming an all-star, contributing to the team; and by helping them to come up with a code of ethics or conduct to play by.

Players must know what drives them; what motivates them. How do they find out what motivates them? By finding out what their individual, personal needs are and then trying to fill those needs. "Why am I playing the game?" "What do I want?" "What are my individual goals?" "What is my purpose?"

It is important for you, the coach, to know what the players want and how you can help them achieve those personal, internal goals. If players really want to perform at their best, they must be self-motivated. And a lot of times, players become more motivated by trying to satisfy their human needs; or become even hungrier when they don't get what they want.

So a player should measure her success not by statistics or championships, but by the "inner satisfaction and peace of mind that comes from knowing she did her best."

Here are some things you as a coach can do to help players become internally motivated.

> ❯ *Create an environment where players can work on their own.*
> You can help players become self-motivated by setting up a friendly, supportive practice environment to motivate these intrinsic-motivated players to pursue getting better. Rather than controlling the whole

practice, Coach can give players the opportunity to work on their own in practice so that they can direct their own training to a certain degree.

> *Give players freedom.* A break from your normal coaching can give your players the authority and freedom to make their own decisions in practice or in a game. By giving the players the power, the responsibility, the freedom to think, the freedom to play their own game, and the freedom to play as though the team belonged to them internally motivates them. Intrinsic motivation for the players is achieved by shifting the ownership, accountability, and responsibility for motivation from coach to players.

> *Generate statistics lists.* By generating statistics lists, you can definitely motivate players to move up the list. The team statistics will always be the main focus, but using individual statistics helps to generate some healthy competition among players. Post the individual statistics in the dressing room to let the players know where they stand in the team scoring and on the plus-and-minus chart. This challenges them to catch the next teammate above them. Players often want to know where they stand in the big picture in the team scoring race. This is just another way of giving players something to play for.

> *Show players how to set long-term goals.* You show your players how to become self-motivated by setting long-term personal goals—in other words, having a purpose or a dream. It is this dream that will set them apart from others. This intrinsic motivation pushes players from the inside rather than the outside.

You will find out by asking players what their goals are that most players set their goals too low, at a level they feel they can easily reach; or they aim at nothing, in which case they lack a target, a focus, a personal goal or dream, such as to be an all-star. Few players set goals because they think they are hard work; it puts pressure on them to accomplish these goals; they fear failure by being afraid they won't reach the goals; they are not sure what they want; they don't know how to set goals; or they don't have confidence. The absence of a purpose of a really meaningful goal is very draining for players because they don't have anything to play for. You have to get them to believe they can be better than they think they are.

If a coach has to motivate his players, he motivates them for the game. But if a coach teaches a player how to motivate himself, he motivates him for the season and for the rest of his life.

Note: Coaches need satisfaction, too. Winning a championship is a great goal, but you could be disappointed when you get it and end up asking yourself, "Is that all there is?" So enjoy the journey or the process, the highs and lows, the wins and losses, the good times and bad times of the season, and the positive effect you have on your players' lives, which will be just as important as the destination.

Ask yourself: "Are your players' lives better because you coached them? Did you make a difference in their lives?"

THE PROCESS OF BECOMING SUCCESSFUL IS THE REAL MOTIVATION

■ HOW DOES A PLAYER GET SATISFACTION?

Players get inner satisfaction, peace of mind, and a feeling of fulfillment from these purposes or goals: from reaching their potential and constantly improving; from achieving a difficult skill; from feeling pride in setting and obtaining their own personal goals; from playing well and knowing they did their best; and from being productive and making a difference on the team.

The richest experiences in a player's sporting life are not from coaches praising and supporting him (external reward), but when he feels fulfilled and satisfied within—when he reaches his potential and grows as a player.

SOMETIMES WINNING IS JUST NOT ENOUGH

7 SHARING POWER IN TEAM MEETINGS

One of the first things you have to do in putting a team together is to gain the loyalty and support of the players. The successful coach has the skill to motivate his team by sharing power with them through their collective verbal agreement with the behaviour goals through team meetings. As discussed in chapter 4 ("Making Decisions"), one of the most effective ways to obtain the players' support is to involve them in making decisions that affect the team. So, finding ways to empower your players to make more and more decisions is one of your jobs. Of course, there will be times, such as during games, when you can't consult with the team or a player on decisions. There may be situations, such as removing someone from the team, where it would be better for the coaching staff to make that final decision themselves. But even if you are reluctant to consult the team on all team decisions, you should find areas in which the players can give their thoughts and opinions, for this is one of the most effective ways to get commitment from the players and gain team loyalty and support.

Consulting and empowering your players takes some time, patience, and organization, but the rewards of this type of motivation—commitment and excellence—are definitely worth it. Besides, if you create the right environment within the team and give your players the opportunity to use their knowledge, their creativity, and their experience, you won't have to think up artificial ways to motivate them.

■ TEAM MEETINGS:
A LECTURE OR A TWO-WAY CONVERSATION?

It is usually best to do this consulting with the team off the playing field, at a time and in a place set up specifically for this purpose; the best forum for consulting the team is the team meeting. You can conduct a team meeting as a lecture or as a conversation. During the meeting, you might have to do some lecturing, but make sure it becomes a two-way conversation so there is give-and-take rather than just one-way communication from you. As coaches, we have a tendency to talk at our players too much. Conversation-type meetings tend to bind people together, and talk is the glue in most organizations. Besides, players love to talk to one another and they certainly do not like to be lectured. And we know for a fact that most people do not change just because someone tells them to. Players change when you hold a conversation with them and they become involved in the change.

Coach Shares Information in Team Meetings

Sharing your decision-making power with players in this information-sharing environment enhances your control of the team as coach, because they understand now why you make them work hard and play hard. They know your goals are also their goals, and that everyone, coach and player alike, is working to achieve the same objectives.

Players Learn How to Be Successful for Life from Team Meetings

Remember also that, as a coach, it is your goal not only to create a successful team, but to help players develop as successful people. Learning how to resolve disputes, get along with teammates, arrive at a consensus, set goals, and make plans to achieve them is as vital for success in life as it is for success on the playing floor/field.

Change the Team from the "Now" to the "Future"

Your job as a coach is to change the team from how they act and play now to how they should act and play in the *future*. This is based on the following list of goals and rules: team performance goals, team behaviour goals, team outcome goals, team cohesion goals, team rules, and team practice rules. To achieve these lists, you have to begin with a clear idea how you want your team to play and behave in the future. A team without the two-way conversation and sharing of information that occurs in a team meeting is just another ineffective committee.

> ## GUIDE, DON'T CONTROL

■ TEAM MEETINGS

The purpose of team meetings is to provide a quiet setting apart from the high stress of games and the hard physical work of practices where players and team staff can reflect on the team's aspirations and achievements and rationally discuss and share issues that are important to them. These meetings keep everyone headed in the right direction. They can display team strength, support, and encouragement, much like a family; and especially during difficult times reinforce the team's sticking together.

These meetings provide another means of involving the team in the decision-making process. Certainly, participation in these team meetings is important, as these meetings motivate and give players power. If a player shows he doesn't care by not getting involved, slouching in his chair, looking off in all directions, and making comments under his breath, then a word in private will be necessary.

Note: Rather than just having team meetings all the time, a coach can have smaller group meetings, such as a players/leaders group meeting, a specialty team meeting (Power Play, Man Short), an offensive group meeting, a defensive group meeting, or just a plain old bitching session in the dressing room to air everything out.

What to Discuss in Team Meetings

You should have one major, formal team meeting at the beginning of the season to discuss team goals and rules. You can also have further meetings throughout the season to assess and revise these goals as needed and any other problems that might arise or challenges that team members might encounter throughout the season. Here are some examples:

> The team talks about its vision and its team identity.

> The team reinforces team values and team goals.

> The team discusses team strategy and the team's performance in a particular game. In the excitement right after a win or the deflation after a loss, it is difficult to evaluate performance objectively. Some distance from the game can make it easier to see problems and errors and to make plans to avoid them in the future. You can let the statistics posted in the meeting tell the story of the last game, and players can see objectively for themselves where they need to improve and what they have accomplished.

> The team tries to get players involved, such as coming up with a list of suggestions on how to make the team better.

> The team tries to resolve disputes between players. If there is a confrontation or ongoing bad feelings between two players, discussing it with the whole team can bring some positive peer pressure to bear on those concerned. It will emphasize to them that their spat is affecting the whole team, and they must find a way to resolve it sensibly. Waiting until a team meeting to discuss a dispute can also provide a cooling-off period, after which those concerned may be able to look at the problem more objectively than is possible in the heat of an argument. (See chapter 17.)

What *Not* to Discuss in Team Meetings

Team meetings are not appropriate forums for discussing discipline of individual players for serious infractions or informing them they are being benched or cut from the team. This should be done individually, face-to-face, and in private.

Minor disciplinary action can be taken immediately in practices or during games. For instance, someone who is late for practice should have to do extra drills—or the team does extra drills; whatever your preference. If a player is chronically late for practices, team meetings, and games, it becomes a more serious matter and should be discussed in individual sessions.

Coach and players should not criticize, belittle, or berate individual players in team meetings. This will bring down the morale of the whole team. You want to keep team meetings positive and upbeat.

Frequency of Team Meetings

You can have a schedule of formal team meetings for the season, based on when you think the team will need them; you can have team meetings halfway in the schedule or after so many games; you can have "emergency" team meetings for special situations; or you can just meet casually as the need arises. Not all team meetings need to be as formal as described in this chapter, but you will need to have at least one of these formal meetings at the beginning of the season. At this meeting, you and the team will formulate your goals for the season. (See chapters 8–12.)

Guidelines for Conducting Team Meetings

Being invited to attend and contribute in a team meeting is very motivating to players, but time is wasted in these meetings when you arrive unprepared; when you have no clear agenda; and when you let certain players dominate the meeting. You can avoid these situations through proper preparation, organization, and facilitation of your team meetings. Here are some guidelines.

Before the meeting

> You have to be totally prepared to run the meeting properly. Have a clear idea of the purpose of the meeting and what you want to accomplish in it. You must prepare a list of objectives before the meeting.

> Write notes listing the things you wish to talk about in the meeting. Organize the agenda by priority.

> Where appropriate, get input from players and team staff about issues that need to be discussed beforehand.

> Print out a formal agenda for the meeting, headed by the date, time, and location of the meeting. Provide a contact number or email in case of questions. Post it on the bulletin board or give copies of the agenda to all players before the meeting so they can think about the topics.

> Emphasize to team members that, just like a practice, the meeting will begin and end on time.

❭ Think of any teaching tools you may need for the meeting. A chalkboard or easel with a large pad of paper that you can write on would be handy when devising lists of goals, for example. Make sure the equipment you need is available for the meeting. Don't forget to bring chalk or markers.

Beginning the meeting

❭ Get to the meeting place early to make any necessary preparations and to ensure everything is in place.

❭ Begin the meeting at the appointed time. Show the team you mean business by making sure all the players are sitting quietly and listening to and looking at you.

❭ Reiterate that the meeting will end at a specific time and you want to address all the items on the agenda within that time frame. This will help keep things moving along.

❭ State the purpose or focus of the meeting, whatever it may be: just to go over the daily business; to share information; to come up with or revise team goals; to discuss team rules; or to address any team problems and find a solution.

❭ Create a safe environment where there are no secrets; where you are reinforcing openness and honesty; and where players feel comfortable sharing ideas and talking about what is not working. In this environment, you are going to receive honest feedback from your team and sometimes you might not like what you hear. This means you have to manage your emotional reactions, such as not appearing agitated, annoyed, or angry.

During the meeting

❭ You should keep the meeting short, because the simpler the communication, the clearer it is, and the more easily it is understood. The shorter the meeting—the fewer things you and the players say—the more your players will hear and remember. Long, detailed meetings are usually autocratic or lecture oriented, while shorter meetings are more democratic, with players' input, which results in player ownership.

❭ When talking during the meeting, you should use your voice effectively—raise it, lower it, or pause to let your message sink in. When you speak, be passionate about the topic and speak with a purpose, setting goals or solving problems.

❭ When players come to the meeting, they are expected to participate.

❭ Simply ask players for their opinions to get them participating in decisions. Make sure you give everyone a chance to communicate her point of view. Encourage open discussion by inviting all players to contribute their ideas. Since you are working toward "empowerment," you want participation from the players in the meetings; for example, get players to devise their own lists and to give helpful ideas and comments.

> Some typical questions you can ask players:
>   • "What do you want to do?"
>   • "What do you think is the most important thing we need to work on?"
>   • "What can we do to make you happy?"
>   • "If you could have anything you wanted in a successful team, what would you want?"
>   • "What are three things you like about this team?"
>   • "What are three things you dislike about this team?"
>   • "What are three things we can do to improve this team?"
>   • It is always nice to start the meeting with a question, such as, "Who wants to say one good thing that we are doing?" Now the meeting starts off with successes, and you can progress on to what is not working. Asking questions rather than telling or lecturing is a great way to get players involved. The old, traditional-style coaching was the telling or lecturing approach, but the new style of coaching is the asking approach.

> By asking the players what they think, you actively involve them in finding out what they want, and in return, you are able to get the job done—finding the answer and giving empowerment.

> By hearing what's on your players' minds, you become more empathetic to what it's like for everyone in the "trenches." Getting perspectives from the "trenches" gives insight that might not have occurred to you otherwise. If you can get 50 percent of your team buying into this kind of culture, it will exert a positive peer pressure on those who are neutral or even negative.

> Some suggestions to get a quiet or shy player to contribute to the meeting or speak up are: Ask him a question, get him to make just one key point; encourage him to comment on someone else's point; get him to ask that a comment be repeated; get him to thank someone for his contribution; or just get him to give a nod if in agreement with someone's comment. It might be a good idea after the meeting to have an informal "rap session" with this smaller quiet group to give these players an avenue to vent their ideas.

> You can approach certain players before the meeting and say to them, "I need you to speak in the meeting. You can say anything you want." At least now you know that someone is going to talk in the meeting.

> You can present a list of successful team characteristics to your team for discussion, but don't just give the team the behaviour goals—let them come up with their own. Remember, simply telling them is not the best way.

> From these meetings, you can review in each practice the twelve basic behaviour goals principles. When you've run through all twelve during the season, you can start all over again.

> You should contribute and be actively involved in the meeting, but do not dominate the discussion. In these meetings, remember, everybody is equal, and you want every player's needs to be actively involved. There are no bosses.

> You have to keep the discussion on track and running smoothly. Don't allow any one player to dominate the discussion. You have to know how to reach the players and how to keep their attention, which is half the battle in meetings.

> You have to understand that when players debate and argue about ideas and then reach a final decision, this can enrich team chemistry and leave players feeling positive about the team after the meeting.

> You have to get someone to take notes during the meeting so that you can concentrate on what was said in the discussion later. If you are running out of time, make a note of points to be discussed at a later meeting. This task should be rotated so that one person does not do it all the time. A laptop would also help cut down the work involved, and the notes could be printed.

After the meeting

> You review your meeting notes and add anything else that came up during the meeting. Retain your notes from all meetings for future reference.

> It may be useful to print a report on the meeting, listing what was discussed and the resolutions, the list of goals or rules, and then distribute them or post them on the bulletin board.

> You want the players to leave the meeting feeling energized, upbeat, confident, and knowing they have played a role in making team decisions.

PLAYERS LEARN BEST BY GETTING INVOLVED

The Value of Team Meetings

Team meetings allow you to share your power with players in a meaningful way. When players have a say in setting team rules and goals, they are more motivated to follow them and achieve them. Once a team decides on what their rules and goals are, they become their own. These shared lists of goals and rules are so powerful they give a team a common direction and unity, a commitment by the players, and a focus on improving their performance and behaviour goals.

Team meetings help players feel they are in control by setting team goals

Setting goals in team meetings does take time and effort, but it is worth it. Goals are as important to the success of the team as the time and effort spent practising and training. Only unrealistic goals apply too much pressure. Realistic, attainable goals apply positive pressure and they motivate players to work hard to achieve them.

Performance goals help us stop worrying about factors that we can't control, such as winning against a more talented team. They show in a concrete way that success is possible, which will help to raise a team's confidence level.

IF A TEAM DOESN'T KNOW WHAT IT WANTS, IT WON'T ACCOMPLISH ANYTHING

Team meetings give the team common direction, expectations, focus, and unity

Through the power of lists, players know exactly how they are expected to play and act. There are no grey areas so players cannot be indecisive. Trying to achieve these performance and behaviour goals in a game helps players build team unity, a very important component for a successful team.

Team meetings create a commitment by the players

The single most powerful predictor of success in the long run is commitment from the heart. Goals are reached through a commitment to them. Commitment is what players show when you are not around between games and practices. What players do off the floor is as important as what they do on the floor.

Commitment is achieved with input from players and their being involved in the coach's decision-making process to form those lists of shared team goals and rules that will govern and guide them. The contribution and active involvement by the players in the discussion in team meetings is the most critical determinant in creating a team's dedication, loyalty, and commitment because it gives players a feeling of ownership. Players are more willing to follow the list of team goals and team rules because they want to, not because they have to, as they are *their* goals and rules and not the coach's.

You cannot dictate, order, or "will" commitment and co-operation to a team. The one thing you know as a coach is that what separates the winner from the also-ran is commitment from the players. So the question is: Are your players committed? Because once a player decides to commit to his team, he will absolutely refuse to let his teammates down. It now becomes a matter of not wanting to disappoint his teammates.

These team meetings help to get players thinking how their team should play and act and are, therefore, a very powerful motivator.

Note: If Coach tries to force goals and rules on players, they will resist. They will just go through the motions of playing, as their hearts will not be in it!

Team meetings help the team focus on improving their performance and behaviour goals

The team focuses first on improving their performance goals and then on winning. The team has defined what the most important things are on these lists of performance goals. You will look at the priorities on the list and see if, after a game, the team reached the important ones. These lists of performance goals give you and the team something concrete to measure against through the statistical feedback.

The prioritized list of behaviour goals is also important, because they put everything in order and give the team direction in a game and over the season, especially when things get chaotic. These lists of behaviour goals also give the team something to measure against, and, through proper verbal feedback, will help it grow.

On a team with these successful team behaviour goals, players know exactly how to act—or at least know what is expected of them—on the floor or field and they will try to act accordingly. Hopefully, players' behaviour or decisions in a game will be based on the team's behaviour principles, to which they have committed rather than to their own selfish motivations.

Team meetings help create self-control and self-discipline

Of course, a team is a lot easier to coach if players are working with you rather than against you. You need a commitment from the players that they will "govern" or "police" themselves regarding goals and rules. This approach to team meetings, where players have input into team goals and rules, places the responsibility where it belongs—on the players themselves. You don't control the players; they control themselves. If the players have helped develop the goals and rules, then they know exactly what is expected of them, and you, in return, will have fewer discipline problems.

When you empower your players by giving them power in decision-making for the team, you no longer have to control them; they control themselves. The players now share the power with you, versus your having total control and telling them what to do.

The control is still there, but it is not the coach's control—it is self-control. Control of the team is still important to you, but it doesn't necessarily have to be used as a "club." You now draw your power from the team. You still have the power, but you must not take advantage of it. You keep the main control of the team, but give power away in subtle ways: by giving the team decision-making power through team meetings, by giving players responsibilities and roles, and by giving players suggestions rather than bossing them around.

■ THE PROCESS OF COMING UP WITH LISTS OF TEAM GOALS

Setting team goals is not complicated. It can be challenging to try to reach a team consensus, but the process itself is valuable in building team cohesion and commitment— important factors in any team's success. Your goal as a coach is to get everybody to agree to work with you. Different types of goals are needed:

> Long-term goals or season outcome goals help players focus on the future.

> Shorter-term or performance goals help focus on the present moment and can measure progress on the way to reaching the long-term goal.

> Team behaviour and team cohesion goals also help the team work together toward outcome and performance goals.

Along with the team rules and practice rules, these sets of goals help make the playing experience enjoyable and satisfying for all players.

Coach Presents a List of Successful Team Goals

You help guide or influence some of the team goals and rules by handing out a list of successful team characteristics, goals, and rules. You talk about certain characteristics that previous teams and successful teams have in common. These prepared lists outline how successful teams act and play. Teams have to know what the successful teams do, how they play and behave to have a standard to which to compare. These successful team characteristics separate an overachieving team from an underachieving team.

Coach Involves Players in Devising Lists

How the team produces its own lists in these team meetings is as important as the lists themselves, because the process involves a commitment from all players. One reason teams are successful today is because the modern coach allows players to provide input into the goal-setting process, thus increasing the players' commitment to goal achievement. It now becomes the players' team, not the coach's team.

The modern coach knows that "knowledge is power" and he wants his players empowered with information and knowing what is going on with the team. The successful coach knows he can't do it alone so he gets input from the players, which creates empowerment and commitment. When the players understand the vision, the goals, and the system, they don't need the coach always telling them what to do—they take on ownership and figure it out for themselves.

How you as a coach want to go about creating sets of team goals and rules will have to do with your personality and coaching style. Getting the team's input on goals and rules can mean either listening to them and then making the final list yourself, or leaving it entirely to the players to set their own goals, with you acting as an advisor. Whichever method you choose, it is important that players feel they are being heard and their opinions are being taken seriously. Otherwise, it is all a pointless exercise.

From shared ownership comes peer pressure

Players need to talk about and discuss every decision related to the team from team rules, team goals, and team problems. In fact, a coach's responsibility should be to involve your players in setting the lists of team goals and rules. The amount of involvement a player has in setting the goals and rules will affect her motivation and commitment. By empowering players and getting them included in the process of making decisions, they take on shared ownership and become more committed. From this shared ownership comes peer pressure, where all the players motivate each other, watch out for each other, and support each other.

Players tend to cling to old habits, and these habits are hard to change. To help players make new habits or break old ones takes great commitment, which comes from involvement. Once players have input and are involved in team decisions, you have got commitment, and the players are empowered to take control of their lives.

PEER PRESSURE IS A GREAT MOTIVATOR

Players' making decisions independently leads to commitment

For most coaches, collaborating with the team to create team rules and goals is very rewarding. If players are going to be 100 percent committed to the team, they have to be in charge of their own destiny, and therefore you have to make sure the players have a say in how they're going to play and act. When the players make a verbal agreement in front of the team to follow the team's goals and rules, they take on ownership of these and become more committed to following them.

The goals are now the team's, not the coach's

By providing input, players not only make the goals, rules, principles, and guidelines their own, but they create a clear standard that belongs to this particular team and to which the players will be totally committed. Now they know what they are expected to do, and there is a sense of responsibility and ownership felt by everyone, with the result of a closer and more energized team.

If you want to motivate your players, you must involve them in the process of making most team decisions where you and the team can work out the solution together. Plus, once the group of individuals devises and accepts the goals and rules, they become united with a single-minded purpose.

Coach Reinforces These Team Lists before Games and in Practices

You now can talk about these prioritized lists of team goals and rules during games, during practices, in pre-game talks, and in post-game talks. You reinforce to the team that this is what they said they wanted. You can post the written prioritized lists of team goals and rules in the dressing room where they can be seen every day to remind players what their team is all about—and to what they've committed themselves. These goals will define the character of your team: "This is who we are!"

■ GENERAL GUIDELINES FOR SETTING PERFORMANCE, OUTCOME, AND BEHAVIOUR GOALS

It is important before the season starts that you begin with the end in mind. Goals motivate and inspire your team to achieve them. Your team has to know where it is headed. It is important to set short-term goals, performance and behaviour goals, to achieve your long-term outcome goal.

While there are different types of team goals, there are some general principles that can be followed when formulating all of them and following through on them. You have to keep in mind that the process of setting goals is as important as the goals themselves.

All Players Must Have Input in Setting Goals

By getting everyone to work together on setting the goals, you send the signal that every player is valued and equally important to the team. When they have input in the defining of goals and publicly agree on them in the team meetings, players are making a commitment to follow them. When the team defines its goals, those goals belong to this particular team alone. The team then owns the goals. This sense of ownership builds team cohesion and spirit. The process of having all players contribute their opinions about what the team's goals should be is also an opportunity for you to get to know the players and find out what motivates them.

Note: There are winning teams that have great players, but not the characteristics that are associated with successful teams. They win only because they have better players than everybody else in the league.

Goals Should Be Challenging, Yet Realistic

You have to make sure the goals are not only challenging, but attainable. Goals that are set high and hard, yet realistic and attainable, and slightly above what you think you can achieve, produce better performance than easy goals. For example, reaching the playoffs or the finals of a national championship may be as challenging as the goal of going undefeated for the season, but the former goals are more realistic. What happens if the team is defeated during the season? That goal has to be thrown out altogether.

It might be difficult to arrive at a realistic goal, particularly when you are working with a new team at the beginning of the season.

If the performance goals are too difficult, the players will become overwhelmed and frustrated trying to reach them and become discouraged. On the other hand, if the goals are too easy, there is little challenge, and players become bored and lose motivation. The team ends up putting out little effort, and that is when upsets occur. This is another reason to consult the team when setting team goals. The players probably have a better idea than you of what they're capable of doing. With your guidance, the players can usually do a good job of setting realistic goals for themselves.

Revise Goals When Necessary

As a coach, you should have high expectations. When the team has set its goals, you must do what's necessary to ensure those goals are reached, but you also must be ready to change the goals if necessary to give your players time to grow. You should review the statistics after every game and determine whether the original goals must be revised. When goals are achieved you have to get the team together to establish newer, more challenging ones or just keep the same ones.

Goals Should Be Specific and Concrete

Setting long-term realistic and specific outcome goals, such as "winning a national championship" or "getting to third place in the standings" are more effective goals in improving performance than general goals such as "let's have a good season" or an unrealistic goal such as going undefeated for the season. General goals as motivational tools are limited, because there are no particular criteria for determining when or if they've been reached.

Setting specific goals is like finding your destination on a map. Once you know where you want to get to, you can work out the best routes for getting there, and you can plot your progress along the way. And then you can celebrate when you reach your destination.

Make Goals Measurable

Where possible, encourage your team to set performance goals that are measurable so that progress toward them can be evaluated. "I want to shoot 20 percent" versus "I want to shoot better." Specific, measured goals are effective in improving performance because they allow the players to know exactly where they are and see where they want to get to. Goals that can be measured in statistics, such as number of shots on net, can be reinforced through verbal feedback from you and visually through graphs or charts that show progress toward the goal.

It is best to state these goals in positive terms. Keep statistics on "number of balls caught" versus "number of balls dropped," or "number of scoring chances" versus "number of missed scoring chances," to emphasize achievements rather than failures. When players are feeling despondent, perhaps after a loss, they can look at achievements of the past, to show that, though they may have lost a game, they have won the battle against themselves to achieve some of their goals. This is what success is really about.

Write Goals Down and Post Them Prominently

Goals become serious when they are formally written down and posted where everyone can see them and be reminded of them. Once goals have been written down and posted, they cannot be casually altered, ignored, or disputed.

Devise a Written Plan for Accomplishing Goals

Once long-term goals are set, the team must put together an action plan for accomplishing them. For long-term goals, the team can work backwards and start with simple, prioritized short-term goals that are specific and achievable to help contribute to the realization of the long-term goal. Again, the plan must be made solid by being put in written form.

Set a Specific Time Frame for Achievement of Goals

The long-term goal should be accomplished within a reasonable time, e.g., in first quarter of season, by end of season, by week 12, and so on. This puts some healthy pressure on the players to work hard in practices. Having the players themselves set the time frames for goals gets their commitment and limits disputes with you. They themselves have set their schedule, so they can't complain to you about it.

Recognize Achievement of Goals

Once the team reaches a performance goal, celebrate it by giving extrinsic rewards, such as candy, a night off, a pizza party in the dressing room, or a fun practice. These rewards can motivate the whole team. These rewards remind them that they are on their way to their long-term goals. These achievements should also be noted and recognized at team meetings.

Prioritize Goals

When a set of performance goals has been compiled, the team should then list them in order of priority to give some order to what is important in becoming a good team. The players have to know which goals are more important in being successful so they can focus their energy and attention on them. The more important the goal, the more effort it will demand. In return these prioritized lists motivate the team, and help you get organized and manage practice time better.

8 SETTING THE TEAM'S SEASON OUTCOME GOAL

You cannot dictate, order, nor "will" commitment and co-operation from players. So how does a coach get commitment from his players? The best way to get commitment is to convince your players to buy into a set of common team goals.

If players have no goals, no plans, they have no commitment. So you have to get them to help set team goals. Goals or dreams put players back in charge of their lives. Goals or dreams allow your players to focus on what's most important to them and how much time they will give to them. Goals or dreams will drive your players.

Players must have a clear vision of the future:

4. Where they want their team to end up (season outcome goal)
5. How they want their team to play (playing systems)
6. How they want their team to behave on the floor (behaviour goals)
7. What they want their team to accomplish every game (performance goals)
8. How they want their teammates to treat each other (team-building or cohesive goals)

IF YOU CAN THINK IT, IT WILL HAPPEN

■ THE SEASON OUTCOME GOAL

A true motivator leads his players from the present into the future, and the season outcome goal is where the team wants to end up at the end of the season. Most teams set the championship as their main season outcome goal, but the goal doesn't have to be that high. The goal could be making the playoffs or ending up in third place. If a team knows its long-term season outcome goal, it will never be indecisive. But goals don't just happen, and success is not the result of chance.

Success comes from successful coaches using their skill of setting a long-term season outcome goal, a vision; then creating a step-by-step plan for achieving it, which includes specific, short-term performance goals and constantly giving feedback from these statistics; having a daily outlook of always getting better; and never letting their players forget the season outcome goal. This is the process of how a team turns its dreams into reality.

Gets Everybody Thinking the Same Way

One of the main reasons to have a common outcome goal, a common dream, or a common vision is that it gets everybody thinking the same way, working in the same direction, having a shared interest, and focusing on what they want, such as obtaining a championship.

An outcome goal helps the players function as a unit rather than as a group of individuals with conflicting agendas. Teams do not win championships if their players have different agendas; everybody has to have a unity of vision and work together, and it is this process of working together that helps them attain their specific goal. Your job then is to keep the team focused on the long-term season outcome goal.

Generates Self-motivation

The strength of a motivated team is awesome. Losing teams lack this unified focus and are usually composed of individuals who act only on their own behalf. Players playing for themselves (personal agenda) are not as committed as players who play for the team (team agenda).

Players' setting a long-term season outcome goal is what motivates them to practise and play hard to make it come true. And once the confidence starts to kick in from the players' effort, you will see amazing things happen.

Self-motivation is a passion; a result of loving what you do; or a result of chasing after your dreams. Players must have a passion or love for playing the game, otherwise playing will only be hard work. How do players get this passion or love? Some are born with it; others get it by setting a long-term season outcome goal either personally or team oriented. Once a team has a season outcome goal, it helps players "light their own fire" and it generates the passion to achieve it.

Gets a Team through the Rough Spots

The team vision nourishes a team's spirit and fuels its enthusiasm; it keeps the team going, especially when the season gets tough. The season outcome goal is the "light at the end of the tunnel" that keeps the team going and provides the extra spark no matter what happens. Often, the biggest difference between teams who succeed and those who do not is not talent, but persistence. Successful teams do not quit. They get up one more time than they have fallen down. Most of today's players want success right away. They want things quickly and without much effort. Then, when things get tough, they want to quit. Becoming a successful team can be slow, monotonous, and difficult.

Helps a Team Anticipate Problems

Once you have a season outcome goal, you can foresee problems before they occur and help deal with failures, frustrations, setbacks, mistakes, obstacles, and losses. Goal-oriented teams know they must maintain a positive attitude and remain confident and persistent in the pursuit of their season outcome goal, no matter what happens, right to the end of the season.

When you can anticipate difficulties, you can make plans to deal with them so that when they arise, they do not become insurmountable. Again, it's like planning a trip: if you know you are going to have to travel some rough roads to get to your destination, you make sure you have the equipment you need: map (or GPS), tools, a spare tire, and so on—so you will be prepared to handle any problems that come up. You will be far better off than the person who sets off on a trip without a map or any special precautions.

So when you have a season outcome goal, and you make a plan for getting to it, you become very resilient. You work out your own system for measuring your progress, so what other people might find discouraging, you simply expect and deal with. Once a team has established the goal it wants and the price it's willing to pay for success, it can ignore the minor hurts, the opponents' pressure, and the temporary failures and frustrations.

Note: When teams fail, it is not because they aim too high, but because they aim at nothing; they lack a target, a focus, and a direction. Few teams set goals because: they think it is hard work; it puts pressure on them to accomplish these goals; they fear failure because they are afraid they won't reach their goals; they are not sure what they want; they don't know how to set goals; or they don't have confidence.

> ## IF YOU FEAR PURSUING YOUR DREAM,
> ## YOU WILL NEVER EVEN GET STARTED ON THE JOURNEY

Future-oriented

Unless a team is dreaming about something, it doesn't have anything to shoot for. The season outcome goal commits players and coaches to the work, the time, the pain, and whatever else it takes to achieve this dream. A team must have a clear vision of where it wants to end up. Players need a target to aim at, because they can't hit what they can't see. By having a clear long-term vision, players always know exactly where they are headed.

Defines the Team's Feedback

By having a season outcome goal, a team defines its own feedback—in this case, wins and losses. Feedback from you gives players motivation to reach their season outcome goal. In fact, feedback by you is as important in motivation as setting the goal.

Teams who set a season outcome goal never accept where they are—they are always striving to get better. In setting a season outcome goal, you can compare where the team is right now with where it wants to be. The team might not be happy or might be dissatisfied with its position in the standings right now but it will definitely try to do something about it.

The season outcome goal not only gives a target to aim at; it also provides a gauge for measuring progress toward it. Feedback keeps a team going. Feedback tells a team whether they are headed toward their goal or are off track. If the team's goal is to reach a certain level in the standings, seeing its name move up the standings provides further motivation to work toward the ultimate goal. If the team is in third place, it can fight to get to second. You must have reminders of the team's long-term goal on the dressing room wall where the players can see it on a daily basis.

Creates Positive Pressure

By stating its season outcome goal, a team creates positive pressure to go after it. It is this pressure that motivates a team to push itself and demand more. If there is no pressure to go after something, there is no motivation.

Note: "We want the pressure of winning a championship!"

■ HOW TO SET THE TEAM'S SEASON OUTCOME GOAL

We have already stated that it is your job to establish a direction for the team; to get everybody motivated; to get everybody thinking the same way; and to get everybody passionate about playing for the team. And the season outcome goal is an extremely important tool for doing this job. In fact, it's impossible for players to really get motivated without it. And here are a few steps for you and your team to follow for goal-setting.

Realistic Long-term Season Outcome Goal

A team has to decide what's important to them for the season by setting goals. One of the main questions of goal-setting is asking your players what to set for the team's season outcome goal. Could this long-term *goal be to win the championship*? Yes! For the top organizations or great sports programs, the season outcome goal is to always win a championship almost every year. The coaches believe they have to aim high if they expect to reach the pinnacle of success. The good programs get to the championship so often because the coaches demand it, expect it, and say it out loud from the first day of training camp.

But if yours is a middle-of-the-road program, you can also set a reasonable long-term goal of coming in first place in their league, of winding up in the top ten in the standings, of winning twenty games this season, of aiming for a certain position in the standings, or even to just make the playoffs. Your chances of achieving one of these long-term goals may seem a whole lot better and more realistic than going for the top, so your players will be more inclined to work for this goal.

Even coaches who take on last-place teams know it might be unrealistic to talk about even making the playoffs; so they talk in general terms about how the players can improve and get better as a team.

Avoiding unrealistic season outcome goals

For some teams, setting a long-term goal of winning a championship can seem intimidating, too far away, unrealistic, impossible, and even ridiculous. So you must help the team set realistic long-term season outcome goals. Taking on too much can be quite intimidating, can create undue pressure, does not give the team a chance to enjoy the smaller accomplishments along the journey, and can be a morale-breaker, making the team frustrated and setting it up for failure.

In the team meetings, you might try to influence the discussion in such a way that the players arrive at this season outcome goal decision themselves, rather than imposing your ideas on them. When they set their own goals, players feel better about them than they do about goals set by someone else.

Think big, focus small

In the good programs, from the very beginning, they think big—they expect to make the playoffs or win the championship—but they focus small by focusing their attention on small, ordinary details and continuous daily improvement as keys to achieving the greater accomplishment, such as focusing on their fundamentals, team execution, performance goals, and behaviour goals. These short-term goals are what separate them from everyone else. When you want to win a championship, you don't focus on winning—you focus on improving the small performance tasks you have to do every day and every game in order to win!

Note: Setting a long-term goal to motivate players for the season is important, but during the season, players need to focus on the next opponent through their performance goals.

Set Specific and Concrete Season Outcome Goals

The team has to make its long-term season outcome goals specific and concrete so players know exactly what they have to do to attain them. Specific goals, such as "winning a national championship," are more effective in improving performance than general goals, such as "let's have a good season" or "let's get better as a team." It seems general or vague goals do not inspire a team as much as specific goals.

Intermediate Goals

A team can have a long-term outcome goal to achieve by the end of the season, and several intermediate goals to achieve throughout the season or at logical breaks in the schedule. A single monumental goal may seem overwhelming for some players, so having intermediate goals may be more manageable for them, such as being in third place at the quarter mark of the season. But be careful when setting more than one outcome goal; if you have too many goals, they may lose their power as team motivators, because individual players may focus on different ones, and forget about the main one. It is your job to keep the team focused on the main season outcome goal. You can mention that to get to the season outcome goal, the team has to achieve its intermediate goal, which might be winning the division or the league.

Being in a Certain Position in League Standings

Rather than setting a championship as their long-term goal, the players could set a certain position they want to finish in the standings. You can then motivate your team by posting league "standings" in the dressing room so they know how hard they have to work to catch the next team ahead of them. By comparing the team's progress to the league "standings" the players will then come to know how important certain games are without your saying anything. The team has to play for something over a long season to stay energized, or every game becomes the same.

Note: Coach can also accumulate individual statistics throughout the season and use them to motivate players. The team statistics will always be the main focus, but using individual statistics helps to generate some healthy competition among players. Post the individual statistics in the dressing room to let the players know where they stand in the team scoring and on the plus-and-minus chart. This challenges them to catch the next teammate above them. Players often want to know where they stand in the big picture in the team scoring race. This is another way of giving players something to play for.

Team Meetings

To set the season outcome goal and the other goals, you must have a formal team meeting at the beginning of the season. At the team meeting, have the players sit down, discuss thoroughly, and agree on the season outcome goal so that everybody on the team knows exactly what it is. Encourage all players to participate. Everybody must get the feeling that their contribution, however small, is important; this involvement by the players also gives them "empowerment." The players now feel that they work for themselves, not the coach.

The key to getting the whole team committed to these goals is to work with the players to set them in team meetings. By having them set their own team goals, you show them that it is their choice to be successful or not. They choose whether or not to work for their goals. A well-defined season outcome goal, shared with others and sparked with enthusiasm, will draw energy and forces that cannot be measured.

Note: Some coaches ask those players who want to win a championship to stand up and say they want to win a championship—to show their commitment.

None of these types of goals—season outcome goal, behaviour goals, performance goals, cohesive goals—will produce success on their own, but together they are all essential. Each of these types of goals works with the other goals to help a team become successful.

The season outcome goal is based on results—wins and losses. All successful teams are goal oriented and know what they want and where they are going. If you have no vision of where you want to go, no one will follow you. You have to have a goal or dream if your team is ever going to achieve anything.

Once the season outcome goal has been agreed upon by the whole team, write the goal as a positive statement or affirmation or as a contract on paper, and write down the deadline or date for attaining it. It is important to have a deadline so you can check on whether you are on schedule for reaching your target.

Here are some examples of team affirmations for season outcome goals:

> ❯ We are going to win the championship.
> ❯ We are going to win our division or league.
> ❯ We are going to finish first [second, third] in the league.
> ❯ We are going to make the playoffs.
> ❯ We are going to win [so-many] games in the season.
> ❯ We are going to win [so-many games] in our mini-season games of five game segments.

VISION AND ATTITUDE DRIVE RESULTS

Reinforce and Remind Players Constantly

Once the season outcome goal is in place, one of your major tasks is to review it, reinforce it, and remind the players of it constantly. You cannot let the players forget or lose sight of the dream as the season progresses; you must provide direction. As well as posting the written season outcome goal and putting up a picture of the championship site or of the trophy prominently in the dressing room, you should also reiterate it verbally in team meetings, at practices, and at games. The season outcome goal is a bit like the background music in a movie. It is always there during the day-to-day operation of practices and games so the players never lose the clarity of the big picture.

Note: The power of reinforcing a team's outcome goal by team affirmations is incredibly strong!

Share the Season Outcome Goal with Others

For older and more experienced teams, having parents, fans, administrators, and anyone else interested in the team know what its dream goal is for the season puts the team under maximum positive pressure to accomplish what they've set out to achieve. By saying it out loud—"We expect to win the championship"—they are motivated to attain it.

Note: With younger teams, let parents know what the team's game outcome goal is so they can help their children work toward it. For example, winning the game is not the team's game outcome goal—the goal is to have fun and improve—and parents should be made aware of this so that they don't focus on winning and put undue pressure on the kids or the coach.

Use Visualization

To use this technique for a season outcome goal, have the players sit quietly, shut their eyes, and picture themselves overcoming obstacles and achieving their goal. You can help them visualize the whole season as though it were a movie and they were writing the script. They see themselves doing everything correctly, working together smoothly, displaying positive behaviour, and receiving their championship trophy.

Imagining or visualizing goals gives players direction and motivation to help make the dream come true. It's a bit like a controlled daydream. The team can take some quiet time during a practice, in a team meeting, or before a game for visualization sessions. Visualization is a powerful psychological technique for building confidence in players.

Reward Achievements

Celebrate when the team reaches a milestone—one-quarter of the way along in the season—in its pursuit of the season outcome goal. You can have a party, give out awards, or give the team a special treat of some kind. This reinforces the idea that they are on their way to the goal and re-energizes them to keep on working toward it.

■ A PLAN FOR THE SEASON OUTCOME GOAL

You have to make the vision of what the team wants crystal clear to everybody. Once you and the team have come up with the vision, you must follow it up with a plan—a specific, step-by-step process—a series of smaller, short-term goals of how you are going to achieve the vision. If you have a vision, but no plan, you'll have a lot of players thinking that it's just a "snow job." But with the right plan, hard work, good decision-making, and strong communication skills to sell the vision, there is no reason why the team cannot achieve it.

The difference between a wish and a dream (or outcome goal) is a written plan to make it happen. A season outcome goal is vital to a team's success but is not enough on its own to keep the players motivated and working hard; there has to be a definite plan.

Here are some ways you can achieve the vision:

> Work harder than any other organization

> Create a winning attitude from the top down

> Make good decisions in recruiting a franchise player, a "star"

> Make good decisions by selecting or recruiting character players who are intelligent, tough, and better conditioned than the players you compete against

> Know your team's style of play and playing systems

> Pay attention to details (a sign of a well-prepared game plan)

> Know how you want your team to behave on the floor and set behaviour goals

> Know how you want your players to treat each other and set cohesive goals

> Know what you want your team to accomplish every game and set performance goals

> Build a positive environment by stressing the positive and noticing all the good things the players do

A PLAN FOR THE GAME OUTCOME GOAL

Once a team has established its team season outcome goal, it must now devise a plan or have a process for what it needs to do to attain that goal. A major part of this plan or process will be improving certain physical team skills during a game—called performance goals—that a team needs to do well in order to achieve their game outcome goal. Performance goals are short-term goals that come into play by knowing what you want your team to accomplish in each and every game.

Note: Teams play the game at three different levels: the disciplined level, the casual level, or the sloppy level. Coach wants his players to play at a highly disciplined level, so they must be highly trained. To play at this high level, Coach must establish a clear vision, provide a plan, and present a simple and practical playing system.

A PLAN FOR THE INTERMEDIATE OUTCOME GOALS

The intermediate outcome goals should be accomplished within a reasonable time (at quarter-points of the season). Players should set deadlines for achieving certain goals; for example, by halfway into the season the team should be in third place.

You should have a plan for setting up the season into mini-seasons; the big picture could be to win the championship, but because the season is so long, you have to break it down by creating a series of games to strive for—such as a shorter schedule of five-game segments—to get an edge and to get re-energized.

> ## TO MAKE THE IMPOSSIBLE POSSIBLE, GO IN LITTLE STEPS

ABOUT WINNING GAMES

Although the game outcome goal is to win, it is secondary. The main focus should be on the primary objectives of performance goals and behaviour goals.

By focusing on the game outcome goal of winning or beating an opponent, the problem is that the team tends to lose its "present focus" on what it has to do! Game outcome goals are natural to have—everybody wants to win, everybody wants to beat their opponent. But never take a game outcome goal into a game, because to win when it counts the most, a team can't think about winning (the future), it has to think about its performance and behaviour goals (the present moment). This becomes an oxymoron: let go of the need to win in order to win.

You should never talk about winning the upcoming game, but talk about the things that lead up to winning. Playing for the sake of winning alone creates worry, tension, and pressure for players. When the team's performance and behaviour goals become the framework for playing, acting, and behaving in a game, the team enjoys the moment-by-moment playing much more than just winning.

Focus on What We Can Control: Performance Goals

Another problem with a game outcome goal that has to do with winning is that a team does not have complete control over what happens in a game. The team could play its best game ever and still lose because the other team played better or is better. A team has more control over how it plays by trying to attain its performance goals than it does over winning. A team can think about its long-term season outcome goal—the dream of a championship—throughout the season, but when it comes time to play an individual game, it has to focus on the present moment; that is, attaining its performance goals.

9 SETTING THE TEAM'S PERFORMANCE GOALS

As I have mentioned, when you want to win a game, you don't focus totally on winning. A team needs something other than winning to give it some direction on how it plays or how to measure success—it needs performance goals.

To derive performance goals, you must first make a list of performance characteristics (see below), and you then make these characteristics into team performance goals on how to perform. Then, focus on these small, short-term goals in order to win. The team can now judge itself as having succeeded or failed, based not on whether it won or lost the game, but on whether it achieved its performance goals. If a team focuses on its performance goals rather than on defeating its opponents, the result—winning—will take care of itself.

Players have to know what successful teams do, and performance goals, with their priority lists, give a team some order of what is important in becoming a good team.

■ WHAT ARE TEAM PERFORMANCE GOALS?

Team performance goals are expressed in short-range, realistic numbers or percentages that focus on immediate game accomplishments; they are one way you can measure the team's performance and thereby their success. You set high team performance standards or goals for your team to accomplish each game because these goals define what is and is not acceptable. These short-term objectives are part of a motivational system based on game statistics, and are another significant factor in a team's success.

If the team is dissatisfied with where it is in its play, it needs to know specifically what it has to do to get better, or it will never improve. By stating its performance goals—how it wants to perform—a team will be motivated to demand more from itself. You can never stop checking and reviewing the team's performance, because there is always something your team can aim for or get better at.

Note: The coach must consistently keep his team in touch with the performance goals. He can leave simple reminders for the players by leaving notes, posting statistics in the change room, and talking to them personally about how they are playing. These reminders are very powerful.

■ WHAT ARE THE BENEFITS OF PERFORMANCE GOALS?

They build confidence

A team might not always win, but it is always capable of achieving some of its short-term performance goals, which will build confidence, keep the team motivated and enthusiastic, and lessen the team's fear of the overwhelming game outcome goal of winning. In fact, winning should never be a goal; winning is a by-product of the performance goals.

They get everybody going in the same direction

As with season outcome goals, performance goals get all players thinking the same way and playing the same way in a game rather than doing things on their own. They let the players know what is important and what is expected of them. Setting performance goals gets the team focused on the things it should do to be successful.

They make a team feel it has direct control over its performance

Most teams set game outcome goals that are focused on winning or beating an opponent. The problem with goals like these is that teams have no direct control over them.

With performance goals, the team feels more motivated, as it has control over what it will do. Its success will be based entirely on what the team can control in every game, such as its own hard work, performance, and attitude, and not on what the other team does, since they have no control over what their opponents do.

They lessen the emphasis on winning

The more the team talks about its performance goals, the more it improves its chances of attaining them. If the team's energy is directed solely toward winning, i.e., focusing on the results, everybody will try to force things to happen and worry. Yet if the team focuses on the process of getting there—the playing systems, the performance and behaviour goals—everybody will let things happen and feel relaxed, as they feel they are in control. Performance goals are the keys to victory and help the players to focus on the present moment and what they have to do to get the job done—not on how they are playing or the thought of winning.

They provide statistics as one of the keys to motivation

Team performance goals based on thorough and accurate statistics are the building blocks for the team's motivational system! Players have to know what a successful team's top performance is, and these performance goals state how your team wants to perform physically. By achieving these goals or improving on them frequently, the team will build confidence, motivation, and commitment. The key is that the team is competing against itself. It competes against its own performance standards, set by itself, no matter whom they are playing. Also, playing a long season can become boring, where every game has a tendency to be the same as the last one unless you do something to break the monotony. Setting a number of short-term performance goals to gauge their performance will offset the boredom of a long season.

They provide focus

Focusing is the ability to put everything out of your mind except what you are doing; it is the ability to control your thoughts so they don't interfere with your performance; it is when you and your performance become one. The performance goals help with this.

Doing the same things over and over again, players tend to get mentally lazy and lose their concentration. Players' minds will always wander, regardless of how hard they try to focus. Performance goals help to keep players focused and prevent their minds from wandering and falling asleep during the game. Many mistakes in a game come from this lack of concentration where a player's mind was not on the game.

It is okay to dream about winning before the game, because it motivates the team, but the key to enjoying each individual game is to focus on the present moment. Specific performance goals during the game help to take the players' attention away from worrying about winning the game and encourage them to focus on what they are doing right now. When you let your thoughts drift to the future or the past, you take your concentration with you.

> ## PREOCCUPATION WITH WINNING MAKES ONE MINDLESS

They provide small successes in a game, even if the team loses

If a team loses a game, you can emphasize specific things through the performance goals that they did successfully during the process of the game. Players need to have gauges by which they can experience success other than winning, such as little things that they are improving on even if the scoreboard indicates otherwise. The bottom line for evaluating performance is not wins and losses, but how the team performed on game day.

Setting realistic team performance goals will ensure that the team achieves a certain degree of success in every game. Attaining some of the performance goals will help maintain players' confidence and prevent them from being discouraged if the team loses the game. These small successes can help the team feel good about itself no matter what happens.

Performance goals create "games-within-a-game," and usually if a team wins the little battles and skirmishes, it will win the war—the game.

They give the coach objective information for evaluating performance

How do you evaluate the team's performance? You now have measurable post-game feedback, performance goals, and statistics, which help you make objective measures of performance, instead of subjective measures, about how the game was played. The objective information helps you assign your time and attention in your practices; and the objective information gives you exact and specific information on your appraisal of the game for your talk between periods and in practices.

Performance goals give clear and honest evaluation, replacing judging and blame. You measure and compare the team's performance against its previous performances, whether you are winning or losing, and you will learn from the results.

Once the team has set reachable performance goals for the game, Coach sets up a reward-and-penalty system. He takes something away or punishes the team if it doesn't reach certain goals; or, for achieving certain goals, he gives rewards, day off, fun practice, or the opportunity to play another sport in practice. Example: Let's say the performance goal for the team for a particular game is to cut down on its turnovers. If they meet the objective, they get a reward, such as playing a fun game at the end of practice. If they don't meet the objective, they will work on passing-and-catching or running at the end of the practice.

Note: Here is another form of evaluation using statistics. The coach, at the beginning of the season, asks the players to list their top individual performance goals. The players fill out the "report cards" or self-evaluation of their performance after a few games. Then one-quarter of the way into the season, Coach asks the players to evaluate their playing performance again on their report card. Where did they succeed? Where did they fail? Next, the coach performs the same evaluation of the player on her playing ability. Then the two compare their grades and have a conversation about where the grades agree and where they disagree. This report card is a way of offering players useful feedback on their progress.

■ HOW TO SET THE TEAM'S PERFORMANCE GOALS

How many coaches do you know who use statistics to break the game down?

Using Statistics to Devise Performance Goals

Coming up with a season outcome goal is usually fairly straightforward, and players can often decide on a suitable one with a little help from you. Team performance goals are a little more complicated. A team usually needs a large number of these goals, and players might not have the knowledge needed to work out the details, but you should still consult with the team about these goals. You could just let the players come up with some team performance goals on their own; or, to help with the process, you could list the team performance goals or statistics of your present team, of former successful teams, or of successful teams in the league for a general idea and then let the players decide on their own realistic goals.

Here are some suggestions:

> Check the league statistics to see the standards or average numbers for the league and the statistics for the top teams.

> Check your own team's statistics and find out if there is an underlying pattern of statistics that are high when the team wins and ones that are low when the team loses.

> Compare your team's statistics with the league's average standards and the top team's statistics to come up with a realistic standard for your team to be successful. For example, if the average league statistics for shooting is 18 percent and the top teams shoot over 20 percent, then a realistic statistic for your team might be 19 percent shooting for every game.

> Of course, you might have to make your performance goals higher or lower, depending on the type of team you have, as the statistics should be realistically attainable.

> To figure out which statistics are the important ones for your team to concentrate on: When looking at the league statistics, certain ones will stand out more for teams that win all the time. These become the top statistics that will help your team become successful.

Tailor the Number of Performance Goals to the Needs of the Team

The number of performance goals your team will need depends on its experience level and the sport. Some sports have more statistical measures than others. For lacrosse, you might get an older, experienced team to come up with about thirty game objectives, whereas with a youth team, you might come up with about eight objectives.

Revise Performance Goals Periodically

Since performance goals are based on statistics, they are relatively easy to measure and to change when it becomes clear that they are too easy or too hard to achieve.

Performance goals too easy

If the performance goals are too easy, the result is boredom and very little challenge. The problem of goal setting is not aiming too high and falling short, but in aiming too low and achieving its mark. The team might have to put in too little effort to obtain the objective, and this is when upsets occur in sports. If a team can easily and consistently attain a performance goal, you have to change it to make it harder and more challenging.

Performance goals too hard

Sometimes the team sets performance goals that are too difficult—for example, setting too high a percentage of obtaining loose balls, a goal that the team will never reach. If the team sets its performance goals too high, it is setting itself up for failure, and the players will become overwhelmed, anxious, and frustrated trying to attain them and become discouraged by never attaining them. You have to lower these high performance goals to make them more realistic to achieve.

Set performance goals high and hard, yet realistic and challenging

You should be constantly setting the bar high for performance goals because there is always room for improvement in performance. You can periodically change the performance goals up or down, to set more realistic and challenging goals—just a notch above the team's ability—so that the team has to put in a greater effort to reach them, giving them a feeling of success and confidence. Attaining performance goals does not happen overnight; it takes time; you need patience and hard work to get there. You should set high standards but make sure you give players time to grow. By setting a team's expectations high, it raises the focus and intensity in practices and games, and gets everyone excited about the sport.

Games are now looked upon as challenges along the way toward achieving the team performance goals, not as the end result of winning a game or defeating an opponent. Players get into the "zone" by making an ordinary game into a challenge by trying to achieve these performance goals. You must review the statistics after every game with the result of re-evaluating the original goals. Once the team consistently achieves performance goals, you might have to establish newer, more challenging ones; or keep them the same. You should never be satisfied.

IMPROVEMENT TAKES TIME

Set Specific, Measurable Statistical Benchmarks

It is important to set short-term performance goals that are as specific as possible and are measurable so they can be evaluated. Such goals are effective in improving performance because the team can be evaluated and the players know exactly what they have to do to reach their standards and in return be accountable. You have to supply the feedback or knowledge of results of the game through a method of measurement about the team's progress. This statistical record keeps the team aware of where it stands.

Feedback tells a team where it is now and how far it has to go to reach its performance goal. If you want something to happen, you need to attach a specific number to it. You have to make the goal measurable, such as "wanting to shoot 20 percent as a team," or "wanting no more than 24 turnovers," or "wanting to get 60 percent of loose balls as a team." Specific, short-term performance goals are more effective in improving performance than vague ones, such as "trying to do our best," "improve our shooting," "handle the ball better," "increase loose balls possession," or "decrease turnovers." These general goals won't do as much because they give no direction and they are impossible to evaluate. They start out as good intentions but are seldom fulfilled.

Trying versus Succeeding

What you focus on usually gets better. But in the beginning of the season when the players are still "trying" to obtain the performance goals, you can be a little lax about the results. As you measure and report the numbers, hopefully as they get better they will eventually achieve their objectives. But if you keep rewarding the "trying" or "effort" all the time, you might be sending the wrong message to the players—that the trying is okay even though they never attain their objective. Eventually you have to hold your players accountable for their results and not just for how hard they are trying.

State Performance Goals Positively

After consultation with the players, you write down what you think should be the team performance goals. You make these goals as positive statements or team affirmations to help the team focus on success rather than failure; for example, "We will catch ten passes" versus "We will not drop the ball"; or, keep statistics of "number of balls caught" versus "number of balls dropped"; or "number of scoring chances" versus "number of missed scoring chances."

Prioritize

After listing the team's performance goals, you and the team should then prioritize them to focus their attention on the most important performance goals. It is important to identify the most important goals for success so you and your players can devote the most attention to them and get the greatest payoff in a game. As you and the team prioritize the performance goals, you can follow the 20/80 rule, which states that "20 percent of the performance goals give 80 percent good results." You will have statistics in all areas of the game, but you must know what the important statistics are and it is this 20/80 rule that reminds you to focus on what really matters.

Now you spend your time working on the performance goals that bring the highest rewards. Certainly the more important the goal, the more effort it will demand. In return, these prioritized lists motivate the team to do better and help you stay organized and to manage your time better in practices.

Regardless of the team you are working with, the top 20 percent of objectives in a specific sport are almost always the same, although the order of the priorities might be different. The most important thing about these short-term goals is that they allow the players to see immediate improvements in performance and thereby enhance motivation. If you tell the team they had a good game, it is subjective. It is much better if you can be specific and objective—and that is what the performance goals do; they give you a concrete breakdown of the game.

■ BOX/INDOOR LACROSSE PRIORITIZED PERFORMANCE LIST

Here is an example of a prioritized list that emphasizes the top 20 percent—or top eight—performance goals in lacrosse. Although these were drawn up for a lacrosse team, the concept should work for almost any team sport.

Offensive and Defensive Performance Goal No. 1
We will obtain 60 percent of loose balls and faceoffs.

This first performance goal reinforces what you want your team to be known as, a great loose-ball team, and thereby forces it to work at being the best. Basically the team wants to obtain more loose balls than the opposition. It wants 60 percent or more of all loose balls in a game. Faceoffs can be included in this statistic. You must stress the idea that "who wants it, gets it!" On offence, you want offensive loose balls from rebounds off the boards and off the goalie. On defence, you want defensive loose balls by urging players to hustle, battle, and attack all loose balls rather than waiting for the ball to come to them. You must stress boxing-out or cross-checking your offensive check on a shot to stop him from going after a loose ball. You want your players to be aggressive, show perseverance, be physical, and get in front of their opponent or between their opponent and the ball. This statistic is extremely important in controlling the game, because if you don't have the ball, you can't control the tempo.

Offensive Performance Goal No. 2
We will have 20 percent shooting.

The next top performance statistic is high shooting percentage. It is one of the most important and the hardest statistic to achieve. You want your team to shoot over 20 percent; i.e., one out of five shots goes in the net. This statistic is important because it makes players aware of taking good shots.

Defensive Performance Goal No. 3
We will keep opposition shooting under 20 percent.

The best indicator of a solid defence is how well the opposition shoots. The team wants to force the opposition into low shooting percentage. This statistic tells you that the defence and goaltender are doing a good job. Look to see if your team is playing aggressively and hard on defence with constant pressure on the ball carrier and shooter. The team attains opposition low percentage shooting by tough defence and helping each other.

Offensive Performance Goal No. 4
We will keep turnovers under twenty-four.

The team's objective is to have fewer turnovers than the opposition, i.e., twenty-four or fewer turnovers, by protecting the ball and making good passes. Players should know the difference between a low-percentage pass that has a low chance of being caught, such as a spectacular play, a risky pass, a pass to a player who is covered, a passer throwing the ball away under defensive pressure versus a high-percentage pass that has a high chance of being caught, such as a low-risk pass, a good-decision pass, an unforced pass, a receiver who is wide open, an accurate pass.

Defensive Performance Goal No. 5
We will force opposition over twenty-four turnovers.

The team wants to force the opposition into more turnovers than itself, i.e., twenty-four or more. This statistic happens through aggressive defensive pressure. This is one of the team's most important statistics, because if it is a defensive-oriented team, it looks to pressure, force turnovers and fumbles, strip the ball, and looks for steals and interceptions.

Offensive Performance Goal No. 6
We will score one-third of our goals from breakouts or from fast breaks.

The team wants to play hard and fast, and to run at every opportunity, even if there is not an odd-man situation. The team wants to get the so-called "easy goals" by running all out and wear the opposition down. It wants one-third of its goals per game from breakouts.

Performance Goal No. 7
Power play goals/chance will be 57 percent (4 goals / 7 penalties).

Performance Goal No. 8
Man short will limit opponents 50 percent or under goals/chance (3 goals /6 penalties).

Other Box/Indoor Lacrosse Performance Goals to Think About

> You want more possession-time of the ball than the opposition (55–60 percent).
>
> You want to keep your penalty minutes down under twenty-five minutes every game.
>
> You want to score (so-many) breakout goals a game running the ball up the floor or passing to a player coming off the bench.
>
> You want to keep the opposition under (so-many) fastbreak goals a game.
>
> You want to get more transition goals than you give up.

You want to make twenty defensive stops in a game.

You want to set (so-many) "picks" on offense in a game.

You want to make (so-many) "cuts" on offense in a game.

You want to make (so-many) passes caught in a game.

You do not want to be scored upon in the first possession or the last possession of a period/quarter.

You want to make a big play or stop a big play from a simple routine play.

Remember: Statistics is the key to success. Teams are motivated through the list of performance goals. It thinks it can do better by moving up on the list.

■ HOW TO USE STATISTICS FEEDBACK

There is a saying that "anything worth doing is worth measuring," and it seems what you measure usually gets accomplished by the team as it realizes what is important for success.

One of your tasks as a coach is to let the team know three things from the statistics:

1. What is expected of it; in other words, the performance goals

2. How it is currently performing, as demonstrated by the statistical feedback from a particular game

3. Steps it can take—improving fundamentals and team execution through practice—to meet the performance objectives

Statistics are a powerful method of motivating a team, especially when the excitement or motivation starts to fade during the long season. The more you measure team performance goals, the more motivated your players will be to attain these goals and to improve on them. The feedback from the team statistics are the building blocks for this motivational system. You have to constantly measure, review, analyze, and revise the statistics.

Some Ways to Put Statistics to Work

Break the game down or assess the game performance

You measure performance goals because they help you break down the game into steps. Statistics gives you a beginning. From these statistics, you can use this information to analyze and dissect the game. Statistics help you figure out why your team won or lost; tell you where you should focus your energy to improve the team; tell you where you should focus your attention when planning the next practice and game; let you know what is working and what is not; tell you where your team's weaknesses and strengths lay in that particular game; and tell you how to plan your next pre-game talk from this information.

Note: When evaluating a game leave no stone unturned—know what the team did right, what the team did wrong, what the team hadn't done enough of, and what the team could have done more of.

Review the performance goals before the pre-game talk

You should reinforce the prioritized performance goals before the next game, focusing the team's efforts on two or three of the highest or weakest priorities. Players are most effective when they focus on a maximum of three goals at a time. Talk about the specific numbers regarding the performance goals in your pre-game talk, whether you are getting better or not.

Use charts to give visual feedback

Supply statistics feedback and past game results to the team through charts. These visual records of team performance goals keep the team aware of where it stands and whether it is progressing toward its objective. You can post the statistics after every game so the players can read them and know where the team is being successful and where the team has to improve. When you post the team statistics for performance goals, plus the league standings and the individual players' stats, you will be motivating your players to do better. You should give rewards to everybody on the team if they achieve a specific team goal that they had set at the beginning of the game, such as attaining its defensive shooting percentage, or keeping the opposition under 20 percent . . . everybody gets a reward: pizza, candy, pop.

Aim at improvement

You should celebrate small successes, especially when the team is getting close to some of the performance goals. This performance appraisal method is aimed at performance improvement, not punishment. If the team accomplishes a few of the performance goals, it knows it has done a good job; if not, you can use this negative feedback from the statistics to improve or correct the team's performance by having them practise harder and correcting their mistakes rather than criticizing or punishing them.

> ## IF YOU DON'T EXPECT MUCH FROM YOUR PLAYERS, YOU WON'T GET MUCH

Keep it real

Statistics can correct players' misconceptions because they are clear, hard, indisputable facts. For example, players may think they got fourteen loose balls during the game, whereas the statistics state they got only ten. Statistics help avoid wishful or subjective thinking and keep players objective about their performance. If the team got 50 percent of loose balls in a game, it can strive to get 55 percent in the next game. If your good passing team completes thirty passes, it can become a better passing team by completing forty passes in the next game. You can constantly challenge your team to always do better and always improve. The team is always playing against itself.

Post-game talk

The in-depth, post-game talk is usually at the next practice. You should prepare these post-game talks with a lot of thought. You can look at the statistics to give some objective information right after the game, but usually it's done later. Following the game, or at the next practice, you can discuss their performance goals and compare them with the statistics from the last game. Players can also contribute ideas on how the team can improve certain statistics. This participation empowers players and keeps them committed to the team's goals. The post-game analysis of statistics also helps you plan the next practice. If the team is weak in a certain area, it becomes one of the drills to improve that statistic for the next game.

Give Verbal Feedback from Statistics

Performance goals help players who are bad shooters, poor defenders, lazy loose ball players, joggers, and poor passers and catchers to improve in all those areas by constantly reminding them of "how they performed." These goals get your team to focus on its own performance. The team now becomes aware of taking better shots, going after every loose ball, and concentrating on their passes so they do not have a high turnover rate, and working on their defence to keep the opposition shooting low. Throughout the season, successful coaches motivate their team by constantly stressing and reinforcing these performance goals by talking about them in practice, in pre-game speeches, in between-period talks, and by posting them in the dressing room.

Verbal feedback is immediate information from you that tells a team how it is doing, whether its performance is good or bad. This verbal feedback is believable because it is reinforced by measurement and statistics. Receiving a constant stream of verbal feedback from you on how a team is doing is one of the best ways a team can learn the correct performance.

Do a careful analysis

First, you have to analyze the cause of the poor performance. For example, if a team shoots below its shooting objective, you have to find out the reason for it. Was it bad shooting technique, bad positioning, forced shooting, telegraphing the shot, lack of concentration, or not being able to hit the open spot? Then, you correct the players by explaining to them what they did wrong; explaining why it was bad shooting; or just reminding them to take better shots. You have to correct or immediately point out the problem so it won't happen again. The goal is to get the players to shoot a certain percent while building their confidence, not destroying it.

PRAISE IS A POWERFUL MOTIVATOR

Use Positive Comments and Praise

Players learn more quickly in a positive environment. You should therefore use more positive comments, more encouraging, more praising, and less criticism. In fact, you should praise three times as much as you criticize. Positive feedback can motivate players to attain the team's performance goals, so you should get into the habit of praising players whenever they make good plays.

We often get into the bad habit of giving feedback to our players only when they do something wrong. Of course, you have to look for what is wrong, as you have to correct poor performance, but you also have to look for good plays to praise so the players feel good and will do them again.

However, you should praise only when players deserve it, such as when they make an outstanding play in a crucial situation. Do not praise or pat a player on the back for doing the ordinary things or what is expected every time; but if a player has been struggling in a certain area, you should praise him or her when you see small improvements.

You should praise players in front of the team and make it personal by calling out their first name. You shouldn't forget to recognize and praise effort and improvement, and not just good performance.

Use Negative Feedback or Criticism Sparingly

Criticizing to correct a team's bad performance really makes an impact when done periodically. Continual negative feedback over a long period of time, however, decreases the motivation of the team and destroys its confidence. The periodic-negative approach is used to try to stop a bad performance from being repeated. It consists of mainly negative verbal feedback, such as criticizing, yelling, scolding, threatening, warning, and appearing to be upset. Keep in mind that this periodic criticism should focus on the performance, not the players.

Give Verbal Feedback Accurately

You should be aware of how you are giving your feedback. For instance, coaches can give the wrong feedback by patting a player on the back to console him or her for making a bad play: if this is misconstrued, it can hurt the learning process by giving players false confidence that they are doing better than they are. Coaches who give no feedback or say nothing about a good or a bad play also hurt the learning process. Players may not know where they stand unless you tell them. Coaches who give too much feedback—"paralysis by analysis"—also hurt the players' ability to learn by overloading their thinking processes.

10 SETTING THE TEAM'S BEHAVIOUR GOALS

Setting season outcome and performance goals will do a lot to achieve success on the playing floor / field. But these goals alone will not ensure a team to be truly successful. If players do not enjoy the process of accomplishing these goals and if they do not become better people—not just better players—as a result, their on-floor/field success will ultimately mean very little. Coaching is not just teaching individual physical skills and team systems; it is also changing players' behaviour so that they can become the best that they can be. To address this important aspect of the team sport experience, coaches and their teams must have a third set of objectives based on values and character that contribute to team success: team behaviour goals. Before players can become successful, they must master the characteristics and values that will help them get there. So team behaviour goals are the building blocks that help define who they are as a team.

For a team to be successful, a coach must again use his skill of defining and creating the team's behaviour characteristics to motivate his players. Again, these characteristics, like the performance goals, give the team guidelines based on values and character and impose order on how to behave and play to be successful. This is another priority list to give a team some idea of what is important in becoming good at what they do. Team behaviour characteristics also get everyone working in the same direction rather than individually.

Note: You have to prevent these "poisons" from contaminating your team's attitude: lack of commitment, laziness, selfishness, bad decisions, lack of confidence, lack of self-control, poor concentration, negative emotions, lack of poise, lack of toughness, and a poor playing attitude.

■ FOCUSING ON THE JOURNEY; THE PROCESS OF BECOMING A CHAMPION

The season is about the journey, and on this journey of success, you begin with having a dream, turning it into a goal, writing it down, having a plan step-by-step process or plan of getting better and attaining the goal, and then getting down to work.

We use team behaviour goals as our characteristics, our guidelines, and our values to play like champions. But to become a great team or a champion does not come easily—it is a process that takes time and patience to strengthen these characteristics. Everybody wants to win a championship. That's the destination, but the journey is way more important. The journey, playing the season, and how a team gets to the destination, or gets to the long-term goal you set, should be emphasized over the outcome or the destination.

Sport is not just about winning or beating an opponent — it is about enjoying the process and playing to the best of your ability. For you to unleash the power of the "championship team," your major focus should not be just on what you want your team to do (team's season outcome goal), but it should also be on building the process, or the plan on how to get it done (team's performance goals) and what it takes to get there (team's behaviour goals).

The season outcome goal will get a team started and keep it going to a certain degree, but if the journey — the season — is not enjoyable, the players will quit inwardly; if the journey is enjoyable, the players will continue to pursue the season outcome goal. It's important the coach makes the journey his focal point — getting there through their efforts, their joys, their successes, their triumphs, as well as their hardships, their adversities, and the struggles of the journey.

Your team may or may not win, but you want it to play like champions by demonstrating the team behaviour goals in games. Remember, all you want your team to worry about is what it can control, the process and the plan, and as long as it is improving and getting better in its behaviour, performance, fundamentals, and systems — getting better is one of the major definitions of success — it will be successful.

Notes: Coach should ask, "Have we made a difference in the players' lives?" and "Did our players enjoy the journey?"

■ DEFINING THE TEAM'S BEHAVIOUR GOALS

It seems all championship teams stand for something; they have the same values, the same principles, the same behaviour, and believe in giving back to society. So defining your core values, your team behaviour goals, will help build a successful team. Team behaviour goals will put into words how the team should act and behave on the floor in a manner that upholds their values and principles. These are statements, a set of commandments, a basic set of rules, a blueprint, a set of principles, or expectations that specify what the players should and should not do to be successful. These team behaviour goals are sound, proven principles that guide and govern high-performing teams; they are the core of successful teams; they are the tools a team needs to get the job done; and they are something players can always depend on.

Team behaviour goals work with the season team outcome and team performance goals to build a fully successful team. The twelve team behaviour goals are the foundation and the fundamental building blocks of a successful team. In fact, they are part of a coach's philosophy—to play hard, to play with enthusiasm, to play with intensity, to play smart, to play with great effort, and to play with discipline. These principles represent the kind of team the players want theirs to be or who they are as a team. You want your team to play like champions! How do champions play? What does it take to become champions? The team behaviour goals help to answer these questions.

A Sample List of the Twelve Team Behaviour Goals:

1. Be committed
2. Play hard
3. Play with persistence
4. Play together
5. Play smart
6. Play with discipline
7. Play with confidence
8. Play with self-control
9. Play focused
10. Play with positive emotions
11. Play with poise
12. Play with mental and physical toughness

■ REASONS FOR SETTING TEAM BEHAVIOUR GOALS

Guide Players' Behaviour

Your players likely come from diverse backgrounds with a wide range of values and beliefs. You cannot assume that all your players have the same understanding of correct behaviour as you and some of their teammates. It is necessary to spell it out for them as precisely as possible. Championship teams act a certain way, prepare a certain way, and play a certain way. The team behaviour goals are their own road map to give them direction in decision-making and to guide them in behaving like champions during a game. These code-of-conduct goals help shape the character of the team and define exactly what successful behaviour is to players: what is expected of them; how they should act and play on the playing floor; who they are; and the decisions they should make. Your job is to help your players behave properly and to make the right choices.

Help Players Stay in Control

For most players, emotions dictate their actions. With the players' input into these team behaviour goals, you empower the players to govern themselves; the players' actions or reactions are now dictated or governed by these principles, not by their own selfish emotions. You want your players to control what they can control and forget about everything else. And the things players can control are what is inside them—not what is outside them. When players worry about things they cannot control, they lose their grip; the purpose of these team behaviour goals is to put the players' actions totally within their control. If a team focuses on their team behaviour and performance goals, the game will take care of itself.

When a coach has problems on the team, he or she must follow the 90/10 rule and understand that most problems are technical and playing-system problems (90 percent) versus some problems with players' attitudes (10 percent), but by correcting the players' problems, it corrects the majority of the technical and playing-system problems. Are we outworking, out-running, and out-hitting our opponents? Are we playing smart? Are we playing together? These are things we can control.

Remember: Team behaviour goals are important, but coaches still must constantly think about and reinforce the long-term season outcome goal, such as winning a championship.

Help Coaches Improve Players' Behaviour

It seems the more you nag your players to change, the more they stay the same. The solution to this is to find out what the players want through team input. Although you have to sell your vision to the team of how you want it to behave, eventually it has to be the players who decide which behaviours are acceptable and which are not. They should also determine the consequences for unacceptable behaviour. Then, it is up to the players themselves to abide by their team behaviour goals. Now you should no longer have to nag them to get them to comply. Without team behaviour goals, players often begin to operate selfishly, in a system that really needs co-operative work, with the result of the team's falling apart.

Notes: Giving players team behaviour goals helps make them live better lives both on and off the playing field/floor.

Even if a team does not end up achieving its season outcome goal, such as winning a championship, it should still feel successful because of the way it played, such as playing hard, with enthusiasm, and with intensity; playing smart, and playing with discipline.

Create Positive Pressure to Improve

A team may be dissatisfied with its behaviour, and part of what motivates human action is a sense of dissatisfaction. By stating its team behaviour goals—how it wants to act—a team creates pressure to play that way. If there is no pressure to go after something, there is no motivation. For example, even when a player doesn't feel like acting with self-control, he or she is more likely to when there are clear team behaviour goals to follow. Discipline is following a code of conduct. And making the right decisions takes discipline. If players know the expected behaviour and display it, it is because they have developed self-discipline. To be successful, players have to prove they have self-discipline for playing in high-pressure situations.

Foster Team Unity

Team behaviour goals get everyone behaving the same way as part of a team working for a common purpose rather than going on their own; players know what is expected of them in terms of proper behaviour. To be successful, a team needs to operate with the same thinking and the same principles.

However, these team behaviour goals do not mean anything until they are tested in a game. Players can't acquire characteristics, such as self-discipline, self-control, and a work ethic until they are given a chance to prove themselves.

■ HOW TO SET TEAM BEHAVIOUR GOALS

Teams have to know what the successful teams do, how they play and behave to have a standard with which to compare themselves. These successful team characteristics separate an overachieving team from an underachieving team and set a behaviour standard to compare to.

Team Meeting to Discuss the Behaviour Goals

As with other goals, Coach helps to create team behaviour goals by consulting with his players in a team meeting to devise a list of their own goals. You can start the team meeting by discussing what makes a team successful. The team can use the sample list of the twelve team behaviour goals given above as a basis for discussion. Players can talk about what previous successful teams that they played on have done. You can invite the players to suggest other characteristics to add to the above general list. You definitely can't go in the dressing room and say, "I want you to be like this." Rather you have to ask the players for their feedback: "What are the intangibles of a championship team?" "How do you see yourselves as a team?" "What characteristics would make you extremely hard to play against?" Let the vision of the team behaviour goals, championship habits, come from the players.

When the players discuss and understand the guidelines, everyone gets on the same page, everyone starts to build these championship habits and become committed to the guidelines. You should introduce these guidelines early in the season and refer to them often throughout the season.

Note: In the team meetings, encourage the players to write down words or phrases that describe its characteristics as a team.

WORK HARD, PLAY TOGETHER, PLAY SMART

Prioritize the Team Behaviour Goals

Once the team has decided on its list, it should prioritize its team behaviour goals. We use the 20/80 rule, which states that 80 percent of the correct behaviour in a game comes from the top 20 percent of the team behaviour goals. So if we have twelve behaviour goals, the top 20 percent or the top three team behaviour goals are: *working hard, playing together, and playing smart*. If players can display these top three goals, they will be in great shape during the game.

■ HOW COACH GETS HIS PLAYERS TO DISPLAY THE TEAM BEHAVIOUR GOALS

It Takes Time and Patience

Good coaches tell players what they have to do to be a good team, but great coaches take it one step further by taking the time to explain how to do it, such as how to develop a good work ethic, how to become a team that plays together, etc. Wouldn't it be nice if you could simply tell your players to do something or act a certain way and they would just do it? But the reality is that most players do not do as they are told. Anybody can coach perfect players, but there aren't any perfect players.

You can't merely tell players to be disciplined or self-controlled and expect everybody to be that way immediately, especially if they have been undisciplined and lacked self-control all their lives. Changing behaviour is a challenging process because when the pressure is on, players revert back to old habits.

To ensure that a player behaves properly, he needs guidelines on how to play and behave and he needs reinforcement or feedback on his behaviour. It takes a good deal of time and patience, because nothing of value is developed quickly.

Note: The best way you can get your players to display the behaviour goals is by coming up with a deal or a verbal agreement with them in a team meeting. Now you provide the support for the behaviours that reflect this agreement and the consequences for actions that go against this agreement.

NOTHING OF VALUE IS DEVELOPED QUICKLY

Constantly Teach, Stress, and Reinforce Proper Behaviour Goals

If it were easy to act properly, all teams would act the right way. But it is not an easy task. Learning the proper behaviour is a repetitive learning experience. Teams can be motivated by their team behaviour goals, but it is the salesmanship and feedback from you that keeps the team always striving to get better. Successful coaches instill proper behaviour or change bad behaviour by talking, reminding, stressing, reinforcing, repeating, preaching, and focusing on behaviour goals on a daily basis throughout the season until the desired behaviour is present.

Quotations on the wall

You can post short, motivating quotations or team affirmations on the wall or bulletin board inside the locker room and put up simple slogans that promote the team and remind them what they stand for, such as togetherness, hard work, etc. You can talk about proper behaviour during practice and in pre-game speeches. During a game, you can point out players—even opponents—who are displaying the proper behaviour.

Tell stories to reinforce behaviour goals

You can also help players understand the team behaviour goals by explaining the meaning and by telling stories from your own personal experience to inspire, to inform, to reinforce, to make a point, to entertain, or to accomplish whatever proper behaviour is needed at that moment. You can tell stories to illustrate that many teams before them have faced the same problems they have now and overcame them. You could teach a lesson every day on team behaviour goals with quotes to prepare your players to be successful in life.

Visualize the behaviour goal

Finally, get the players to picture or visualize themselves doing a certain behaviour goal, such as playing with passion, striving for excellence, playing with poise, etc. The more the team talks about team behaviour goals, the higher the probability that they will be attained.

Being a Good Role Model

You have to start with your own behaviour. The main role of the modern coach is to help players reach their potential, and one way of doing this is by modelling the team behaviour goals you want. Players will watch you to see which behaviours are acceptable and which are not. So it is important that you live the principles or characteristics that you want in your players—"walk the talk."

Here are a few examples of what you might do:

> Demonstrate hard work by working hard in practice and working hard off the floor.

> Work with the players and treat them like partners.

> Make good decisions based on the right reasons and based on the philosophy that "the team comes first."

> Discipline yourself to display self-control, consistency, and patience, especially during games.

> Focus on what is happening in the game. You cannot become "a spectator" by just watching the game.

> Show passion for the sport and for coaching.

> Show poise and confidence, especially during adversity.

> Display a positive attitude or outlook about playing, success, mistakes, and losing.

WORDS MOTIVATE, ACTIONS INSPIRE

Give Verbal Feedback

Verbal feedback is saying something to a player when he does something good or bad. Receiving continuous feedback is one of the best ways for a team to learn proper behaviour. Feedback refers to anything you do to increase the chance of the player's repeating the proper behaviour or decreasing the chance of the player's repeating the improper behaviour.

If you fail to tell the player of an improper behaviour, he will likely do it again. Plus, it also will send a message to the rest of the team that as a coach you do not care, that any unacceptable conduct is acceptable.

To change or correct bad behaviour or reinforce good behaviour, you have to make it clear what the expectations are. You have to make sure the team prioritizes the list of team behaviour goals, and then you have to make sure you give more positive feedback (90 percent) when players are meeting these expectations than negative feedback (10 percent) when they are not.

Ninety percent of feedback is positive and it should break down this way:

Sixty percent of positive feedback is correction or instruction feedback (what to do, how to do it). You use energizing words to stress the behaviour goals (Run! Work! Hustle! Relax!). Thirty percent of positive feedback is praise (compliments, encouragement, smiles, pats, and jokes).

The other 10 percent of feedback is negative and comes in the form of constructive criticism, scolding, statements of displeasure, and body language of displeasure such as shaking your head.

Note: Coaches should correct twice as much (60 percent) as they praise (30 percent) and they should praise (30 percent) three times more than they criticize (10 percent).

Verbal praise to reward proper behaviour

Praise is the most powerful way to develop and strengthen desired behaviours. When players display the proper behaviour, you should give verbal praise, encouragement, and compliments such as, "Way to go!" "Excellent job!" and use non-verbal body language, such as smiles, thumbs-up, pats on the back, hugs, fists, and high fives. What you are really saying is, "You are appreciated" and "Your contribution makes a difference." Simple verbal recognition for displaying the correct behaviour is a powerful motivator. These positive responses not only reinforce correct behaviour but also make the players feel good, which increases the intensity of their play, especially when they are flat or not ready to play. A gentle word or warm smile will do more good than any verbal criticism.

It seems coaches many times notice players when they behave badly and then try to correct it, while failing to notice examples of good behaviour. Since you cannot just give negative feedback all the time when players display bad behaviour, the best way to shape behaviour is to catch players behaving the *right* way and rewarding it. Positive reinforcement of the desired behaviour works much faster and is much more permanent than criticizing poor behaviour.

Note: Coaches should be aware of how they deal with misbehaviour because it can either reinforce or undercut their team's atmosphere. When players display unwanted or improper behaviour for attention, too often coaches focus their attention on these players, giving them exactly what they want: attention. Coaches should sometimes just ignore the behaviour they don't want.

• *Praise a good effort*

You must also praise players for displaying good effort: even if players work hard to fight for a loose ball and lose it; even if players run hard to get back on defence to stop an opponent, but get beat; even if players run hard on the fast-break, but don't score; praise them for having *tried* so hard. You should recognize not just results, but the character, effort, and attitude with which a player competes, as it will eventually pay dividends. When players are rewarded for good effort they feel good. You can hand out the "Mr. Hustle Award" to help shape the behaviour you want.

• *Give praise only when it is deserved*

You should not continually praise players for normal or expected behaviour, for acting the way they should, or doing what they should do. Rather, you should praise players when they deserve it or when they show improvement. If you praise too much, it will appear as though you don't mean it, and it will lose its effectiveness. If you praise too little, however, it means you are criticizing too much. The best ratio between praise and criticism is three to one: You should praise three times as often as you criticize. Just don't overuse either one of them.

• *Praise players in front of their teammates*

You should praise players in front of the team to make them feel special.

Verbal correction to change improper behaviour

It is critical to stress here that what you say and how you say it is important. Players have higher self-esteem when you respond to improper behaviour by being supportive and giving correction feedback, rather than when you use verbal criticism or physical punishment. You can shape the desired behaviour characteristics faster with correction feedback by pointing out what they did wrong.

When giving correction feedback, you should use the "sandwich" approach, which means that you first compliment the player on something: "I like the way you are hustling"; then you tell her what she is doing wrong: "I feel you are losing your focus during the game. Do you know how you can get your focus better?" Then you give her another compliment, such as, "I like your attitude."

Verbal criticism to change improper behaviour

Criticism is the most common means of trying to change unwanted behaviour, but it is usually the least effective. You must realize that yelling, screaming, criticizing, scolding, lecturing, threatening, and getting upset at players all the time does not change their behaviour. Besides, negative criticism can cause negative thoughts, which create fear.

However, if a player displays bad behaviour, you have to tell him immediately and decisively that he was wrong. And remember that what you say and how you say it is very important.

If you allow a player to act inappropriately and you do not do anything about it, the players may lose respect and stop following you. Behaviour decisions are "tough people calls" and should be made immediately as behaviour-problem players could become a cancer on the team.

Note: Know the difference between criticism and correction. It's what you say and how you say it.

Use criticism and negative feedback only periodically

When you use negative feedback only periodically (10 percent of the time) to prevent undesirable behaviour being repeated, it makes an impact. This fear of being yelled at periodically becomes a motivating factor for not displaying proper behaviour. You should use criticism as a last resort after other approaches have failed to get the point across. But excessive negative feedback over a long period of time decreases the motivation of players and destroys their confidence, and consequently their performance suffers.

• *Yelling as a "wake-up" call*

Yelling at your players shows a lack of control and is really no way to coach. But sometimes you do have to "wake the team up." If you yell at players, you must make it clear that you are upset with their behaviour, not with them. You have to explain you are not attacking them personally, so they should not take the yelling personally.

• *Separate the person from the behaviour*

You must separate the player from the improper behaviour. Explain that you are measuring the player's behaviour against the team's behaviour standards and principles. Instead of attacking players as being stupid, selfish, or lazy, tell them how the team expects them to act in accordance with the behaviour goals.

• *Do not criticize players in front of their teammates*

If you get upset with a player, you have to bite your tongue and wait to talk to the player privately. If you single out a player for poor performance in front of the team, you might make the player feel inadequate or bad and thereby demotivate him or destroy his confidence. There is nothing to be gained from embarrassing the player in front of his or her teammates.

• *Display annoyance when players are lazy and fall asleep in a game*

The times you can really express annoyance the most is when players are not putting out an effort or lose their concentration in a game. These behaviours are not acceptable and are the fault of the player. But you should not get upset over technical mistakes, as this type of mistake is partly the fault of Coach, who has to teach the skill better.

Other Methods by which Coach Can Change Improper Behaviour

Handing out physical punishment

You must hold the players accountable for their actions, and the players must suffer consequences if they continue to display bad behaviour. One of these consequences is physical exercises. Physical punishment is still a very common method for punishing inappropriate behaviour, such as suicides, sprints, and push-ups.

Some coaches believe that physical punishment for the sake of punishment only temporarily changes behaviour so it really accomplishes nothing and just makes the player suffer pain. These coaches have stopped using punitive discipline, like running, for bad behaviour or poor attitude.

Notes: An alternative to physical punishment for bad behaviour, such as a player always arriving late, is to find a way to reward those players who come on time.

Testing the team behaviour goals is one way players can determine whether the coach really means what he says and whether these goals are going to be enforced or the limits can be stretched.

Taking away playing time

If players display inappropriate behaviour, you can talk to them once or twice and periodically criticize them. But if players continue to display certain inappropriate behaviour patterns, they must be dealt with differently. The most effective consequence for changing a player's behaviour is simply taking away a privilege; this works better than physical punishment or criticism. Most players want to play; therefore, they must suffer the consequences for wrong behaviour by not dressing for a game, by having their playing time taken away, or by being benched for a shift, a period, or even a whole game, until you think the player has gotten the point. Certainly the best "hammer" you have is benching players—it becomes a learning experience rather than a punishment.

Here are some good reasons for taking away playing time: continually taking a retaliatory, bad, or stupid penalty; constantly yelling at or arguing with the referee; continually displaying negative emotions such as pouting, whining, pointing fingers, dropping their heads, losing their temper, displaying negative body language, yelling, swearing, or making gestures at the opposition; for not hustling; continually "falling asleep" on the field/floor and not staying alert; and for showing off to the crowd.

Players rate themselves on their own behaviour

You just get the players to rate themselves on a scale from one to five on the behaviour goals—one being the lowest and five the highest. Remember, self-assessment is one of the most productive forms of assessment.

Mental preparation

You can teach mental preparation techniques for instilling proper behaviour, such as positive self-talk and visualization. You can even make a list of "what if" situations for the players—things that could go wrong, and the positive way to react to them.

Use statistics

Unlike performance goals, which are easy to measure objectively, most team behaviour goals can be measured only by subjective evaluation. But there are some statistics that can be used to measure these goals objectively—for example, number of loose balls reveals hard work; a low number of penalty minutes reveals discipline; and a high number of team assists in a game reveals unselfishness.

Use video to reveal improper behaviour

You can make a video of a player to correct unacceptable or negative behaviour to get across to him how he is misbehaving on the floor. Privately show the player the video of him pouting, whining, pointing his finger, dropping his head, and losing his temper. Many players do not have any idea of how they are acting or playing until they actually see themselves.

Note: Coaches can make up a video of good behaviours, too, and show it to the player to pick him up when he doesn't feel confident. Remember, a video is worth a thousand words.

■ BEHAVIOUR GOAL #1: COMMITMENT

Commitment is the primary building block upon which all the other behaviour goals are based, because without commitment, players will not likely follow the behaviour goals totally.

What separates the winning team from the also-rans is total commitment from every player. If players are committed, especially to excellence, they will have no patience for sub-par performance and they will give everything they've got to the team. Plus, if a coach has committed players, he won't have to worry about them when they leave the playing floor/arena. Committed players will do what is right in conducting their lives away from the arena/gym/field.

Uncommitted players are the biggest problems for team failure. One uncommitted player can negatively affect the performance of the whole team.

You either have to get these players to "buy in" to the program or get them off the team altogether. Commitment on the part of players is essential for a team's success. The question is how do you get commitment from your players?

How Coach Gets His Players Committed

Committed players think about their long-term outcome goal and are hungry all the time in their relentless pursuit of this goal—despite the difficulties, the adversities, and the decisions that might discourage them—as they know they just can't turn "hunger" on and off. Committed players do what they say they will do. If they commit to the team, they will never quit. They will just keep plugging away. The strength of a player's commitment determines the staying power of his persistence in overcoming struggles and adversity. The stronger his commitment, the more self-discipline and willpower he will have to draw from.

Commitment means paying the price and being willing to do whatever it takes to achieve the long-term outcome goal; and it means continuous improvement in the pursuit of this goal. It also means being willing to sacrifice for the sport; it means making the sport a priority in a player's life; it means putting in extra time without being asked. Commitment, discipline, and hard work are the difference between "going through the motions" and getting the job done.

There is a saying that goes, "What you do in the dark will come to light." In other words, what a player does when nobody is watching will surface when someone is watching, whether it is good or bad. The result of being committed is what players do when a coach is not around between games and practices.

If players are committed, these are things they will do: they will drink to stay hydrated; eat properly; get plenty of sleep; stretch before all games and practices; get better as the season goes on; pay total attention to the coach when he talks; know what they have to do in the systems; be on time for all meetings, bus trips, and games; and be on time for all classes, attend all classes, and pass all classes.

Coach helps to set the long-term outcome goal for the team

We have already stated that you cannot dictate, order, nor "will" commitment and co-operation from players. One of the best ways to get commitment from the players is for you to convince them to provide input into a set of common team goals—season outcome goals, performance goals, behaviour goals, and cohesive goals. But to be successful as a team, there has to be a commitment by every player to a single purpose: the long-term outcome goal. A good coach provides direction or a vision to get every player on the same page, because once everyone is on the same page they have something to work with, and it brings the players closer together as the season progresses. Once a player makes a decision to commit to the vision and to the team performance goals and behaviour goals, he is making a choice for himself and for his team.

So, you can help set a vision that is a dream with a plan and this in return will help players with this process of commitment. With a dream or a long-term goal, players become motivated and committed from within and then are willing to put in the time, effort, and energy it takes to pursue the long-term goal.

A TEAM WITH A DREAM WILL SET ITSELF APART FROM OTHERS

Coach gets players to make the decision to commit from the heart

So, the first thing you do is to ask players if they are committed. If they say they are committed—knowing all the expectations—then this is the first step of building trust. Commitment is the power of committing to the process or plan and not just the end result. Until a player is committed, there is always hesitancy, the chance to draw back. But the moment he definitely commits himself verbally, then, luck or fate moves in. Players make decisions with their brains, but they make commitments with their hearts. That is why commitments are longer-lasting and harder to break. If players make a commitment as a team that they want to win a championship, they make this commitment with their hearts, not with their heads.

The next thing you do is give the players more responsibility; the more responsibility they have, the more committed they will become, because more responsibility means taking on more ownership of the team.

Coach asks players questions to promote commitment

The job of a coach is not only to get the job done, but to develop his players. The very act of asking someone a question shows you value her and her answer. If you simply tell players what to do, there is no exchange, no development. When you ask questions, it encourages ownership and commitment by the player along with self-esteem and self-motivation. But make sure that when you ask players for their opinions, you listen to their answers.

Note: The coach asks the question, "How bad do you want it?" to remind players that this game is going to be like a marathon race—the ending is based on who wants it badly enough. Most wars are won on willpower! Willpower refuses to give up.

Coach establishes a stable environment

Heartfelt commitment is a process that can only occur in a stable environment where a close-knit team shares the values of trust, loyalty, and respect.

This extrinsic motivation, a stable environment created by the coach, makes players feel safe and committed to the team.

Note: When you make a commitment and then you fail, it hurts deeply. If you make no commitment, then failure doesn't affect you as much.

■ BEHAVIOUR GOAL #2: PLAY HARD

One of the key ingredients to being a successful team is working harder and playing harder than anybody else; because when you work hard, good things happen. Coaches know it is not easy to become a good team. There are no quick fixes, no magic formulas, no trick plays, and no unusual systems for being successful. Success is a by-product of hard work and playing hard. To be a good team takes daily, monotonous, hard work. One of the main characteristics of championship teams is having a great work ethic. Victory comes at a price and it has to be earned.

How Coach Gets His Players to Play Hard

Hard-working players are very aggressive and competitive; they are fierce competitors and play with a "killer instinct"; and they come to play every night, as they hate to lose. They have a "true warrior" attitude. They're the players who bring energy and excitement to the team. They play every game as though it were their last.

If a player displays a below-standard performance, the coach has to talk to him about the behaviour goal of hard work. Coach can say something like, "This type of performance is not acceptable because this is not who we are. Who we are is a hard-working team."

Your best players and senior leaders should be your hardest workers.

Note: A competitive player told his coach: "You can yell and scream at me as much as you like—just don't take me out of the game."

Coach verbally reinforces the attitude of hard work

This major behaviour goal is to "compete and play hard all the time," yet the toughest thing is to get teams to play hard. You must verbally stress, reinforce, and challenge your team to play hard right from the beginning to the end of the game and expect nobody to outwork your team. You believe if your team plays hard, good things will happen to it, especially in the third period/fourth quarter. There is no substitute for working hard to get the job done. Without hard work, you won't go anywhere. Coach wants his team to have the mentality of a bunch of lunch-pail labourers who show up ready for work, no matter how they feel.

Notes: You might not have the best team in your league, but you want the hardest-working team. Players have to bring physical energy to the team.

Coach stresses the importance of having "role players" or "foot soldiers," who will take pride in doing the dirty work in a game, such as fighting for loose balls and playing aggressive defence. You can't have enough of these "role players."

ANYTHING WORTH HAVING IS WORTH WORKING HARD FOR

Coach compares hard work with talent

You can tell your players that they can make up for what they might lack in talent by outworking everyone else. If their opponents are more skillful, then they have got to make up for their lack of skill by making their "will" stronger than that of any opponents they are playing against. Sometimes a team does not have enough talent to win on talent alone, so Coach's team of common players has to be a team of *uncommon* players. And it seems most players have a better chance to be uncommon by their work ethic than by natural ability or God-given talent. To be uncommon, a player has to play at an uncomfortable pace, where his body has to do something it doesn't want to do — to fight through pain and fatigue.

A team should be upset after a win if they won the game on just talent alone, as a team's focus is to get better every game. Getting by on talent alone is not acceptable because this means the players have coasted during the game. If a team relies on its talent alone to win games, when they play a team that has *more* talent, they might be in trouble.

We never fear a more talented team because we know we will make up the difference in talent with our hard work, our playing together, and our ability to make good decisions. When playing against weaker teams, superior teams, or evenly matched teams, the goal is not just to win, but to work harder and to outplay that team.

Note: The common or average players feel that if the pain, hard work, exhaustion, and commitment are what it takes to win every week, then they don't feel it is worth it.

Remember: Successful or uncommon players do what unsuccessful or common players don't do. They practise all the time, even when everyone else is partying or resting.

Coach expects and demands hard work

You have to expect hard work every day. Hard work has to become a habit. The bottom line is: teams are successful because everyone is working and playing hard all the time. Players can't just turn it on and off. There is no such thing as a game-player who doesn't put out in practice, but thinks when the game is on he can then turn it around and go all-out.

NO ONE IS ABOVE HARD WORK

Most average teams are in the middle of the pack because some of the players are just "going through the motions." If players are putting out half-effort on a team, you have to chew them out. Half-hearted play is like a disease that infects the whole team. Other players will look at the other players "going through the motions" and think, "If they aren't working hard, why should we?" You expect everyone to practise hard and play hard. If you don't get "second effort" from your players, it's because you are not being demanding enough. "Second effort, third effort, etc." is coachable and can be disciplined.

Coach runs hard practices

You have to run hard practices so that your team will play hard, run hard, and fight hard every play of every game. Especially after a poor-effort game, you have to have a punishing workout to send a clear message that poor effort will not be accepted. Players have to be mentally tough by going the extra mile and working harder than their opponents in every game.

You want to create conditions in practice that are harder than any game so that when they play the actual game it will be easier. By having hard, intense practices, the players will feel physically stronger and mentally tougher; they will become used to pressure; they will have more confidence; and they will get comfortable playing at an "uncomfortable pace."

THE WAY A TEAM PRACTISES IS THE WAY A TEAM PLAYS

Coach is hard on his players

When you yell at a player in practice, sometimes he thinks that you are "picking on him" or that you don't like him. That is the exact opposite. You have to make it clear to the player that you are hard on him because you care about him; you see potential in him; you are trying to make him better; and you will count on him to perform at his best in the game. You bark at your players to challenge them every way you can to get the most out of them, to push them to their limits, to make them better players, and to develop mental toughness. When you don't yell at players, that is the time when they should worry.

You must demand that players function by your standards and principles during practices. You set the tone by pushing players to their maximum, demanding they do everything right, and demanding they play unselfishly. You should be always challenging your players to get better.

Player understands he controls how hard his team works

Players can't control a lot of things in a game, especially outcomes (winning and losing), but they can affect them. A player can control hard work: he can control how hard he works by outworking and out-hustling his opponent. Working hard gives the players a chance to be successful; besides, if they don't work hard, they are going to get their butts kicked. Coach has to stress that nobody is going to work harder, prepare better, or sacrifice more than this team. If a team really wants something, it has to work for it. Hard work is definitely not an easy way to play, but you have to make the other team play at an "uncomfortable pace" by forcing them to work hard.

Note: Coach challenges his team during a game by asking a player, "How long are you going to get your butt kicked?" Everyone knows he is really asking the whole team the same question. Now the question goes from a personal evaluation to a collective one. Now everyone feels accountable for not playing as hard as they can.

Coach plays the hard-working players

You tell your players you don't coach effort—you expect it. If players don't play hard with effort, then they will not play. You can talk all you want about playing hard, but the best way to sell your players on working hard is simply by playing the players who work hard. If a player works hard, he will be rewarded by getting playing time. If players do not work hard, they do not play. This philosophy will get the message across. The ideal player is a player with the right attitude who competes every night.

Is working 99.9 percent good enough?

Coach asks, "Is it too much to give 100 percent or is 99.9 percent good enough?" Consider if 99.9 percent were good enough in other fields: the U.S. Postal Service would lose 400,000 letters each day; pharmacists would fill 3,700 prescriptions incorrectly every day; eighteen airplanes would crash every day; and doctors would drop ten babies during delivery each day.

"GOOD ENOUGH" IS NOT GOOD ENOUGH

Coach gives tangible rewards for hard work

You motivate your team to play hard by giving individual awards after the game for hard work, such as "The Mr. Hustle Award." This award is presented to the hardest-working player in the last game with a symbolic old glove, old running shoe, old jock strap, or a used stick. Even in practices, you can give out a symbolic award, such as a stuffed animal, to the player who practices the hardest. This award gives the team something to compete for.

Note: Coach teaches players to play physically hard versus physically trying to hurt someone. Coach teaches his players to respect the rules and the game. He doesn't want players to do things intentionally to hurt opponents, but an opponent could get hurt simply from the result of their competitive and aggressive nature of playing hard. He wants his entire team to play tough, physical, and hard every shift and every game, but play legally within the rules.

Coach reinforces examples of playing hard

If on the bench or in the dressing room, you say, "You have to play hard," what does this mean? You have to give your team examples of what you mean by playing hard.

Playing hard is:

> Breaking quickly and running all-out to the other end of the floor, creating an odd-man situation

> Hustling back on defence or to the bench

> Working hard on defence by putting defensive pressure on the ball carrier to stop him from going to the net

> Putting defensive pressure on the ball carrier to force every shot

> Helping out a teammate on defence and then recovering back to his own check

> Cutting hard through the middle of the floor, looking for a pass

> Setting a solid, full-body pick or screen for a teammate

> Running hard to the bench and off the bench on a line change

> Fighting for possession of every loose ball and going after every rebound off the boards or off the goalie

Remember, jogging does not pass for running hard.

■ BEHAVIOUR GOAL #3: PLAY WITH PERSISTENCE

How Coach Gets His Players to Play with Persistence

Persistent players never quit; they never give up; they have tremendous staying power, never giving in to mental or physical fatigue; they persevere and work hard all the time; they have tremendous willpower; they give a little extra when it is important and second effort is a natural thing; they have a fighting spirit, especially against impossible odds. Even when they are tired and have pain, they still keep on going.

Talent versus persistence and tenacity

Teams who achieve the highest level of success have an unbelievable work ethic and determination. And as long as players decide to keep playing the game no matter what happens, they control one of the other most important ingredients in obtaining success: their determination to never quit. You have to constantly talk about "being determined" as one of the most important abilities a team possesses. And once you see that your team never quits and has the drive to overcome adversity, you will know it has a chance to be successful.

In any great journey or game, there is always a point in time when everyone is tempted to give up because they are so disappointed and exhausted from running into obstacles, setbacks, and disappointments. That's the exact point in time in which they need to redouble their efforts to see things through. Many people stop only inches away from victory; if they could have just intensified their determination and perseverance a little bit more, they would have succeeded. You point out to the team that the difference between winning and losing is usually one or two goals/points. That means to be successful, you have to be a team that is willing to battle the whole way, has the grit to hang in there, that refuses to give up, and a team ready to make one to two more plays than the other guy.

There are two types of players: those who have learned how to work through their frustration, and those who wished they had. Tenacity is as important as talent. There are plenty of talented players who give up when the going gets tough, and there are also players who have persevered and triumphed despite incredible adversity. These are the players who are willing to go the extra mile to be successful.

So you tell them: Don't be one of those teams whose reputation is defined by one event, usually a bad loss. Every failure or setback presents an opportunity to never give up—to persist in pursuing their performance goals.

Note: "If you saw Walter Payton (NFL) play, you never knew whether he was winning or losing—he played the same all the time."

PERSISTENCE IS CRITICAL TO SUCCESS

The power of one more

Players have to learn to do one thing more than their opponent does. If they want to be the best, they have to do one more lap, one extra shot in practice. That little extra makes the difference. When the work is the most difficult, it is also the most rewarding—you should never fear giving your players too much hard work, because they will rise to the challenge.

Note: Of the top twenty-five golfers on the pro tour, the twenty-fifth-ranked golfer made $25,000 with an average score of 70.1; the top-ranked golfer made $625,000 with an average score of 69.2. The difference was 0.9 of one stroke.

Overcoming the "impossible"

You ask your players: "Do you believe in the impossible?"

Greece was 80–1 odds on winning the Euro Cup in 2004, but they won; everybody said Mount Everest could not be climbed, but it was climbed; everybody said the four-minute mile would never be broken, but it was broken; everybody said nobody could jump seven feet, but somebody did. As a team, if you question the impossible, the possible will happen.

■ BEHAVIOUR GOAL #4: PLAY TOGETHER

A team is not just a group of people; it is a group of individuals with shared goals and values working together to accomplish these common goals and values. If there are no common behaviour goals, such as the goal of teamwork, the team is just a collection of players with no overachieving common cause.

How to Get Your Players to Play Together

Players who are team oriented have a "team comes first" attitude and are very loyal to the team. They form meaningful relationships and get along well with their teammates; they have the ability to work with others; and they care for teammates by encouraging them, especially after a mistake. They take pride in making the players around them better.

Stress "team first" philosophy

You must emphasize a "team first" philosophy; that the players are like a family and they must stick together no matter what happens. You stress that the team is bigger than any individual on it, and that everyone works best when everyone puts the team ahead of themselves and does what is best for the team.

You stress "team over talent" or "collective ego over individual ego." On your team everyone is working together because ordinary or average players that play together as a team can beat talented or all-star players that play as individuals. Superstars don't win games—they might win individual scoring awards, but it's the team that plays together that wins. So when talking to great players, explain that they have a choice of hanging onto the ball and winning an all-star award or sharing the ball and winning a championship.

Notes: Coach has to be aware of cliques and rivalries on a team.

Players can have personal goals for internal motivation, such as wanting to play in the pros or wanting to be the best or an all-star, and still be tremendous team players.

Reinforce and stress team play

The team with "the players who work and play together as one" is the one that is successful. The one thing successful teams have in common is this team play. Players have to have a natural feeling of being together and playing together, where they care about one another and enjoy being together.

Having an individual ego is a good thing as long as the player has a team ego that is greater than her individual ego. Players must realize that by being a part of a group and putting the needs of someone else before themselves, they become better individuals; they will accomplish something that they could never have done alone. By being part of a cohesive team, players become better, stronger, more energized, and more confident than they would have playing on a team of individuals.

Co-operation between the great players and the average players to reach the team performance goals will determine whether the team will be successful. Teams become close-knit because everyone plays together; everyone works together; and everyone co-operates to build team cohesion. A together-team plays for things larger than themselves, such as for the quest of excellence; the love of the game; and the love of their teammates and coaches.

Note: Coach talks about five players being like a fist, with five players playing as one, rather than five outstretched fingers, with the five players playing individually. The fist is stronger than the individual fingers.

Talk about the "disease of me"

You must talk about the "disease of me," or selfish players, which is the cause of most teams falling apart. A selfish player cares only about his own personal feelings and personal statistics; he wants the credit when the team wins and blames others when the team loses. Of course, blaming someone else for something going wrong is the easiest thing in the world to do and is usually wrong—usually the player who points the finger is the one to blame. Players with personal agendas definitely cripple the team concept. On a cohesive team, the lone wolf, the ball hog, or the selfish player might score lower, but the team would score more. The selfish player becomes a "full-out" team-player when he lets go of his own ego and selfish interests for the good of the team.

Ask questions such as,

> "Are you a team player or do you run teammates down when they're not around?"
>
> "Do you feel as if you have to criticize others to make yourself feel better?"
>
> "Are you always building yourself up at the expense of teammates?"
>
> "Do you always have to be the one in the spotlight?"
>
> "Do you pass the praise on to your teammates?"

On a team, the question is: "Does everybody have their own agenda first or the team's agenda first?" Players must understand there are "me" and "we" players, but a team can only be successful when "me" becomes "we." When a player sacrifices his ego and personal agenda for the team's ego and agenda, the team has a better chance of being successful.

A truly unselfish team player does not care who gets the credit; he doesn't want to let his team down; he doesn't complain about playing time; he doesn't want to hurt his team by taking bad penalties and making bad decisions; he is willing to make the extra pass; he doesn't say anything negative about his teammates; and he doesn't blame anybody for a loss—will even take the blame himself—when things don't go right. The most important thing to an unselfish player is that the team is successful.

Passing is one of the biggest factors in developing good team play in most team sports. Because you know players have to be unselfish to give up the ball/puck, you have to stress passing unconsciously. This relieves game pressure because players will not take the time to question whether or not to pass; whether or not their teammate can catch; whether or not their teammate can score; or who takes the shot. If a teammate is in a better position to take a good shot, the ball carrier must automatically pass to him.

You definitely do not want to have a competition on the team to see who has ball possession the longest. You know that a "one pass, shoot the ball offence" is not only a bad offence, but also destroys team morale. Usually, selfish or greedy players will make a half-hearted pass in desperation to an open teammate if all other options are exhausted; they can't get their shot off; or they are in trouble.

It is a known fact that ordinary players who play together as a team can beat players with superior talent that play more as individuals. A player usually scores because of a teammate's screen or pass. Success is not measured in who scores, but in terms of players working together as one—which means members of a team have to depend on one another.

TO GET A GOOD SHOT ON NET, PLAYER MUST GIVE UP THE BALL

Note: Question: "Who are you playing for?" Answer: "The other twenty guys on the team dressed like me."

Make sure you thank your players

You have to stroke and thank players for their sacrifices. Unselfish players give up something for the team by putting the interest of the team over their own interests. So, as a coach you have to let players know you are aware of their personal sacrifice by putting them in the spotlight by thanking them in front of their teammates for what they have given up for the team. Remember, most times you are always putting the spotlight on the team, not the individual players, and you are always reinforcing that no player is more important than the team.

Talk about "team skills"

By combining individual skills, you create a whole new skill called "team skills," which are measured and compared to the performance goals. To play with maximum effort, a team must be committed to improving or getting better in a team concept.

Players who don't want to put in the effort to play with others never develop their skills into talent. Talent is putting individual skill into productive "team skill" use. Having the skill does not make a player great, but developing his skill into team play does. So, the willingness of the team's top players to share the ball is extremely important in being successful.

Note: A skilled player must be able to play with the Three I's:

> Intelligence—making sound decisions on his feet
> Immediacy—getting the job done at the moment of truth
> Intensity—bringing passion to his game

SKILL ALONE DOES NOT EQUATE TO TALENT

Talk about trust

Players might believe in their teammates, but do they trust them? On a team, players have to rely on others; they cannot rely on just themselves. Trust means putting your own success in your teammate's hands.

Talk about "the final play of the game"

In a game where somebody wins and somebody loses on the final play of the game, you must stress that the outcome isn't really decided by that final play, because of someone's action or inaction, it is simply a result of the many plays that have happened in the game before that final moment. Each possession of the ball should be considered the play that can make or break the game. In fact, if a game comes down to a last-second play in which one person decides it all, the team accepts the fact that even if someone makes the shot, he didn't win the game by himself; the team put him in a position to hit the shot that wins the game. Even if someone doesn't make the shot, the team doesn't point fingers but accepts the responsibility. After all, the team should have made sure throughout the game that it wouldn't be in the position to rely on a last-second shot. You have to stress that a single individual does not win or lose a game; the team wins together and loses together.

Results of Teamwork — Synergy

What is synergy? "Synergy" is the result of players co-operating and working together, and the team skills become more than the sum of individual skills. Synergy is "the total effect being greater than the sum of the effects taken independently." That means twenty players working together will always produce better results than twenty individuals working alone. A team that plays together creates this synergy.

It is fun coming to work in a winning environment where everyone is happy; where players care enough about the team that they put their selfish desires aside and do whatever it takes to help others.

Without co-operation or team skills, there can be no "synergy"—and the result of synergy is that ordinary players can achieve extraordinary performances.

■ BEHAVIOUR GOAL #5: PLAY SMART AND MAKE GOOD DECISIONS

How to Get Your Player to Play Intelligently

Intelligent players understand the game, play focused and alert, and make great decisions. They are aware of everything that is happening on the floor; they anticipate well and read the floor extremely well; they almost have a sixth sense about what is going to happen before it happens; and they are always thinking one, two, or three plays ahead. They have a tremendous "feel" or instinct for the game by being in the right place at the right time and knowing exactly what to do in these situations. They play the game with their eyes by having their head on a swivel. Some coaches believe intelligence and outsmarting the opposition outweigh even speed and strength as winning qualities.

Build independent players so they play smart

Your job is to develop independently thinking players who make their own game decisions with and without the ball. You do not want players who are like robots or little children who need to be told what to do all the time and have all their decisions made for them. You motivate your team to play smart by giving players independence to make game decisions. During a game, you can sometimes tell your players to figure it out themselves. By your "letting go," your players will play better and learn to make those split-second decisions that will make or break a game or a season. You basically want to get every player to think and act like a coach on the floor. If you create the right environment within the team and give the players the opportunity to use their knowledge, their creativity, and their experience, you will not have to think up artificial ways to motivate them.

Empower your players by having them make their own decisions

If you make yourself the most important person on the team, you are not doing your job as coach. Most great coaches do not do all the work themselves, but get results through their players. The role of the coach is to challenge her players to think; to train them to be autonomous; to empower them to make decisions on their own and thereby become independent. The essence of good coaching is giving the game to the players by giving them more responsibility and the power to do what they want.

Some coaches say, "I can do it better myself," but this is wrong. Motivated players don't just happen, they must be developed; and the main way to motivate players is by giving them input and control over the decisions affecting their play and the team. The true coach creates an entire team of leaders whose talents and energy are in turn multiplied many times over.

You can make your players happy by giving them the authority to make their own decisions, which is a break from the norm. You give the players the power, the responsibility, and the freedom to think, the freedom to play their own game, and the freedom of playing as though the team belongs to them. You praise them when they make the right game decisions or the right plays on their own and correct them when they make bad ones.

Note: Playing sports is made up of the legs, the heart, and the head. Players have to learn to play more with their hearts and make better decisions with their heads; their legs will follow orders.

Encourage players to ask questions to help them make good decisions

You should be encouraging your players to ask questions all the time. To ask for help is a strength, not a weakness: so replace "I think . . ." with "What do you think?" When players learn to think through and solve their own problems, they learn faster.

Note: As a coach, assess whether you are training players to be dependent or independent.

Let players try new things

You have to let players try new things and try new skills, knowing they might fall down. You must reinforce the concept that failure is nothing more than learning how to do it right.

■ BEHAVIOUR GOAL #6: PLAY DISCIPLINED

How to Get Your Players to Play with Discipline

In the old days, discipline was associated with rules and punishment, where players were disciplined or punished if they did not follow the rules, if they did something wrong, or were disobedient.

Discipline in this day and age does not necessarily mean just rules and punishment. Discipline is "doing what you are supposed to do when you have to do it whether or not you feel like it." You can use sports as a tool for players to learn self-discipline. Self-discipline comes in many forms, such as players playing within the guidelines of the team's playing system; following the team's rules; following the behaviour goals, such as being patient, self-controlled, enthusiastic, and energized; listening to you and understanding what they have to do; doing fundamentals or executing plays correctly; and doing what they are told to do or supposed to do.

If you ask a self-disciplined player to do something, you know it will be done, whereas if you ask an undisciplined player to do something, it will never get done. You have to know whom you can put on the floor in pressure situations and will remain controlled, poised, and disciplined.

Self-discipline is when players "police themselves" or display self-control. Self-disciplined players are like machines—they just go out and play; they take anything thrown at them; they "walk away" from any confrontation; they get the job done even if they don't want to do it; and they do not let anybody or anything throw them off their game.

Discipline comes into play when things are chaotic; when a team is losing; when a player feels fatigued and frustrated; when a player has to practise and he doesn't feel like it, but he does it anyway. A player can't become good if he plays and practises only on the days when he feels like doing it.

Discipline is the hardest thing to acquire, yet the most important thing to have if a team wants to be successful. Players may rebel against rules because they don't want to give up some of their freedom, yet they know they need discipline to be successful.

Note: Many teams do not have discipline, since it does not come easily. That is why there are not a lot of good teams around.

WOULD YOU BE WILLING TO TAKE A DIRTY HIT – NO RETALIATION – TO WIN A CHAMPIONSHIP?

The goal of discipline is not to administer punishment, humiliate, or dismiss a troubled or weak-skilled player; it is to teach self-discipline, correct poor behaviour and encourage proper behaviour, and create good habits of fundamentals and good team execution in the playing system. To achieve high standards of discipline, "doing what you are supposed to do" is a tough job and takes time to accomplish. You teach discipline simply by reinforcing it over and over again and by being a good role model yourself.

For a coach, discipline should be proactive: First, uncover the problem by talking to your players to find out what is going on with the team; then head the problem off by coming up with a solution, rather than giving out punishment immediately and ending up in a bad situation.

Some players don't want discipline; some don't have discipline; and some don't know what discipline is, so they might fight you all the way. To be successful, your players must play with discipline.

Discipline is doing what you are supposed to do—every time

Demand discipline

Coach has to explain to his players that it takes self-discipline to do all the boring, monotonous things that it takes to be good on a daily basis. Players must do what they are supposed to do every day to be successful. It is the coach's external motivation that helps to discipline them, drive them, and make them practise when they don't want to, to build good playing habits; although there will be some intrinsically motivated players who will do this themselves. You have to explain to players that to be good at something, they have to pay attention to detail, which takes time, patience, and discipline. When conditioning your team, if you tell your players to run lines or suicides, you must make sure the players touch the lines or they must do it over again. You stress to your players that if they only get close to the line, they only get close to success. Be aware that some players will do only what they can get away with. You get your players to do what you tell them to do by proving you mean what you say. They must understand that if they do not do what they are told to do, there will be consequences.

> **Deliver discipline calmly**
>
> Discipline must be delivered by you calmly, firmly, and with self-control so the message is not lost in the messenger. Words shouted in the heat of the moment can sometimes destroy weeks and months of careful nurturing.
>
> **Note:** A coach should not be afraid to discipline someone—it shows that he cares.

> **Get discipline by taking away a privilege**
>
> Discipline is not punishment but an attempt to change a player's behaviour or poor performance. You want to discipline your players so they act and play properly all the time; and the best consequence to change a player's behaviour or performance is simply taking away a privilege. Since most players want to play, therefore, the consequence for wrong actions is not dressing for a game, taking away playing time, or being "benched." You have to hold players accountable for their actions by giving them a consequence.

> **Get discipline by giving physical punishment**
>
> The most common and fastest way of getting discipline is to punish the player or players for being late or not performing with effort by doing physical exercises, such as push-ups or sprints, to remind them this behaviour is not tolerated.

Some coaches feel you should not use physical exercise to correct bad behaviour, poor attitude, or poor performance, as it is a negative consequence. They feel physical punishment does not motivate a player to change wrong behaviour or performance—it just makes the player suffer pain. Punishment for the sake of punishment accomplishes nothing.

Other coaches feel that if a player is always late, the coach should find a way to reward those who make it on time rather than punish the one who is late.

You sometimes just have to tell your players that they are just a normal, average team, because they lack the most important ingredient to being successful: discipline. Some players would rather take bad, lazy, selfish penalties to satisfy their own personal needs rather than thinking of the team. This type of team becomes a group of individuals who care only about their own selfish, personal desires.

■ BEHAVIOUR GOAL #7: PLAY WITH CONFIDENCE

Confidence has to do with a player's belief that she "feels good" about herself and knows she can "do it"; she feels she can do anything; she feels like a winner; she believes in her ability; she believes she is the best; she can handle unexpected situations well (in fact she knows what she is going to do before it happens); and she brings a swagger to the team.

Confidence is one of the most important assets for a player to be successful. It is 60 percent of the game, and as we know, confidence is a very fragile quality. The process of building confidence for a player is always the number one priority for a coach, and it does take time. Therefore, building confidence becomes a very delicate situation for a coach. Even a coach's words and actions have the ability to either build their players' confidence or destroy it. A confident attitude is the greatest factor in a team's success, while the lack of confidence is the greatest factor in its failure. With high confidence players focus more effectively on what they have to do—their performance, the ball, the open spot, stopping their opponent—than what they can't do.

The question is: "What comes first, confidence or success?" There's a vicious circle about confidence: a player needs confidence or a belief in himself to be successful; but he also has to have a successful performance to produce confidence.

To bring out their confidence, a coach must first express his own confidence in his players by giving praise, recognition, and encouragement; then they will start coming through with better performances. A coach should not wait until the player has a great performance to start praising him.

Another good question about confidence is: "Does a coach give players confidence, or do players already have the confidence?" The answer is both. Some players arrive with tons of confidence, and others arrive with little confidence and are more fragile. Even during the course of a game, players might be confident one minute and then, after the next play, they have lost their confidence.

Players that lack confidence play *not to lose* rather than playing to win, and they are constantly looking over their shoulders, playing cautiously and safely because they fear they may make mistakes.

Note: You can watch the body language of your players to get evidence of confidence or lack of it. Body language that reveals lack of confidence is the "posture of defeat": walking with head down, banging stick on the boards, shaking head sideways, and dropping their shoulders. Whereas the "posture of confidence" is: head up, looking people in the eye, back straight, and walking tall with a little swagger.

Confidence Comes from Hard Work and Physical Preparation

We have stated that confidence comes from success, but what if your players are not experiencing success? What can you do as a coach to strengthen the feeling of confidence? You motivate your players to play with confidence by letting them know where confidence comes from. Confidence is developed from hard work and physical preparation. And it is the preparation that is the key to success: Players who practise long hours to develop their physical skills through repetition; who work at their game; who have success in the drills; who know their roles and responsibilities in the system; who work out with weights to build up their strength; and who work on their physical conditioning to get into better shape will feel better about themselves, play better, and have more confidence.

There is no instant success in sport. Working hard is boring, dirty, painful, and sweaty; it hurts; it's exhausting; it's very lonely; it requires sacrifice; it requires time; but it is a necessity to be successful and confident. Players who have worked hard feel they deserve to be successful because they have earned it. Working hard and deserving success go hand-in-hand. If a player is physically prepared, then she will be supremely confident and have the best chance to perform up to her potential to get the job done.

Note: You have to figure out if the player is underachieving because of lack of motivation, lack of confidence, lack of courage, fear of injury, laziness, lack of conditioning; or just plain lack of talent.

CONFIDENCE IS 90 PERCENT OF THE GAME

Confidence Is Built from Small Successes

Besides hard work, confidence comes from past successes and winning. So, you should set up players early for success by experiencing small successes, small victories, and winning; this will inspire players to get to the next level, which should make them feel more confident. You instill confidence by putting players in situations where they can succeed and grow, such as putting a struggling player with a good player, giving them attainable assignments that enable them to achieve some level of success, and by creating special drills where they will succeed and thereby build up their confidence.

By putting players in situations that they're not ready for can make it difficult for them to develop their own self-confidence. Confidence is built one step at a time through small, successful experiences. Once players experience success, or at least once their performance starts to improve, you can acknowledge and celebrate these successes, and their confidence starts to rise.

If you have a young, inexperienced team, it is important for you to make sure the team has successes early in the pre-season to build confidence; therefore, you should not seek out top-level competition for this team. So in setting up pre-season games, make sure the team plays teams that it can beat or be competitive with, and set realistic performance goals for these games to build confidence. Eventually, once they have had some success, they are more ready to play some tough league games, but the easy games are more important early on, because usually the players are still learning the system and the skills, and their confidence could still be very fragile.

How to Get Your Players to Play with Confidence

Players' personal strengths build confidence

You build confidence by focusing on players' personal strengths and accentuating those strengths. You want to build on their strengths and worry about their weaknesses later on. By focusing on what they are good at, you will turn good players into great players.

For players to improve or get better, they need to be in a good mood. When they think about what they are good at, their energy will pick up. If players focus on what's wrong with them—their weaknesses—this puts them in a bad mood and their energy drops.

Believe in your players

If you believe in your players, you will build confidence, especially when things aren't going well. If you treat them as if they are "special," they will become special. You make your players believe they are going to be the best in the league by being positive with them; by giving them constructive feedback; and by supporting them.

Help players to feel good about themselves

It is important that you catch players doing things right and praise them publicly for it. Your players often depend on your positive reinforcement—compliments and encouragement—to help them to feel good about themselves, which raises their self-esteem, which in turn helps them to play at a higher level and with more confidence. If you put positive thoughts in your players' minds, you will have a better chance of getting positive results.

> ## EXTRAORDINARY SELF-ESTEEM PRODUCES
> ## EXTRAORDINARY PERFORMANCE

Tolerance of mistakes

Coach's positive, constructive outlook and approach to mistakes can also help to build confidence. (We have discussed mistakes earlier in the book.) You want your players to look at mistakes as a learning experience, not as failure. Mistakes are not only the best teachers, but are natural steps on the path to success.

When working with a player who is having problems understanding a skill, you can make it a "we" project by saying to a player, "We need to work on this together." And you can definitely inspire and provide confidence by supporting the player.

You want your players to take risks in a game, and one way of doing this is by letting players play through mistakes where possible. The quickest way to create a fear of failure in players is to punish them when they make mistakes. You have to create an environment where players can make mistakes without worrying about it.

COACH STANDS BESIDE HIS PLAYERS IN TOUGH TIMES AND IN GOOD TIMES

Encourage players to do positive self-talk

Positive self-talk will instill self-confidence, whereas negative self-talk will create fear, anxiety, self-doubt, and negative thoughts that will hinder performance. So Coach must get players to reverse their negative thoughts and state positive words in their minds. Through the power of positive thinking by saying, for example, "I can do it!" players will find hidden energy reserves. Players have to consciously work on this "mind control" by talking positively to themselves a hundred times a game to build and maintain confidence. To help players focus on the positive, post in the locker room team affirmations with phrases such as, "We can do this" and "We are going to work hard."

Another method to build confidence is for players to write a positive, descriptive self-statement of how he wants to play, such as, "I am a strong player. I take care of the ball. I pressure the ball. I am unselfish." When his confidence is low, he can repeat the statement to himself.

Have players revisit past successes

If a player finds he is nervous before the start of a game, he has to find a way to relax and regain his confidence while he waits. One way of getting back his confidence or to maintain it is to visualize one of his better games from the past as if it were happening all over again. The player in turn will begin to feel the same emotions as in the actual game. He will feel strong and there will be a resurgence of his confidence.

Coach can also boost confidence by finding videos of the player's past successes and showing them to her. When a player loses a bit of her confidence, you have to build it. So make a video—nice goal, nice defensive play—to build on the positive.

Give players simple roles

You have to give certain players simple roles and specific assignments until their confidence grows. Coach can make a change in their playing position, give them a different and easier role, or put them with better players.

Quiz players about their playing ability

Coach can just ask a player, "Why are you not playing up to your potential? Is it because of a girlfriend, a family problem, a medical problem, or an injury problem?" Coach should always take a positive approach because of the delicacy of the situation. Coach can challenge him by asking him, "Do you think you are playing up to your potential?"

Finally, to get your players to play with confidence, just tell them: "I know that you have worked really hard in your training, you are experiencing some success in your games, and you are starting to become competent players, and, in return, you are starting to project confidence and play with more risks. It is this confidence you have that shows you know you have the skill, the energy, and the enthusiasm to face any challenge you will see in any future games."

What Makes Players Feel Confident about Their Team?

Players are confident because:

> They have earned the right to be confident through their hard work and successes as a team

> They know they have great talent on the team; they have players who are committed and dedicated, who want to be successful, who have bought into the system, and who believe in each other

> They know they have good coaching and they know that good coaching does make a difference. A good, experienced coach knows how to be successful and how to teach players how to be successful; he knows how to teach skills; he knows different playing systems; he knows how to deal with people; and he knows how to motivate a team.

> They know they have great player-leaders (captains and seniors) who understand what leadership is all about. Their player-leaders lead by example, are the hardest-working players on the team, and help to develop good team chemistry and team character. They know their

best players are their hardest workers; and when the great players work hard, the rest follow.

> They know they are fundamentally sound. They know that how a team executes is more important than what type of system it plays.

> They know their team has the ingredients to be successful. They know their team is totally prepared (emotionally, mentally, physically, and strategically); they know they have a good game plan for every game (statistics from previous games and from scouting reports), and therefore they are convinced they are going to be successful.

> They know everybody will play within the behaviour goals: play hard, play smart, play together, play with discipline, and play with poise

> They know everybody has an enthusiastic and a positive attitude about playing

> They apply the "as if" theory: They know by projecting, acting, looking, and thinking like winners and confident players, they will eventually believe they are winners. If they want to be a championship team, they have to think and act "as if" they are a championship team.

■ BEHAVIOUR GOAL #8: PLAY WITH EMOTIONAL SELF-CONTROL

Self-control is a form of self-discipline; it is the ability to control or manage one's emotions, feelings, and attitude so one's performance is not hurt; it is the ability to remain poised when everybody else is losing their control; it is the ability to play the same way all the time game after game, whether ahead or behind, whether the situation is critical or meaningless; it is the ability to stay on an even keel no matter what happens. Players who manage their feelings and emotions have an advantage in sports because players' emotions must be under control for them to perform at their best—your mind controls your body. Emotional highs and lows are the real enemies, as they get in the way of great performances. Anxious feelings erode confidence, while positive feelings bolster confidence. Mentally tough players control their emotions by focusing on their performance and behaviour goals.

Getting Angry

Anger is the enemy. If a player makes a mistake and gets upset and angry, he is setting himself up to be more likely to make another mistake. When a player gets angry in a game, he becomes totally useless. He could end up concentrating on the thing that got him upset and not on his performance.

Some causes of getting a player upset would be things like making a mistake, receiving a bad call, or receiving a dirty hit. Players have to be aware that getting upset can hurt their performance because negative emotions, overreacting, and anger weaken their decision-making ability. The key here is they have to be ready for bad calls, dirty hits, and mistakes and to know how to control their response.

You can also show players how to consciously focus on taking a dangerous emotion like anger and using it to be productive. One way of using anger to a player's advantage is to channel the resulting adrenalin back into the game by making a play or "taking it out" on their opponents legally. Anger energizes players and can intensify their concentration, but only for a few seconds.

Remember: Allow players to express their anger after a mistake, but only for a few seconds.

Why Controlling Emotions Is Important

High levels of emotions come into play when the game is close or chaotic, or when players are so frustrated that they are on the verge of "losing it" with the result of a drop in focus. Obviously, a player's self-control will not be tested when everything is going right. Players have to know they can't compete well when they are angry and that when emotions take over, bad things generally happen, because they are not controlling the situation.

Players know that controlling their emotions is a constant battle, and they have to learn to "check" their emotions to be disciplined. You teach players to control only what they can and let the rest go. And what players have control over is how they play and react in frustrating situations. They have no control over their opponents or the referee.

The key is to stay relaxed, yet focused. Players have to maintain their focus and control their frustration and anger on the floor. After getting upset, it is hard to get back into the game.

Players need to establish a routine, a strategy, or have a plan for staying in total control of their emotions whenever they find themselves getting frustrated or angry. They need to know what to do if they get upset.

Strategies for Getting Players to Play with Self-control

Keeping on an even keel

You help players realize that they will make mistakes and that they will have a tendency to get upset during a game. But you must remind players that the great players have the same feelings as everyone else but they have learned how to handle them effectively; they don't put their emotions on display; they work at being patient and keeping their cool; they work at the strategy of keeping an emotional balance; they become stone-faced and try to show no negative emotion; and they work at balancing the highs and lows in a game. Great players "will" themselves to hold their focus and not get upset. As a team, you should never want it to get devastated by its losses or overexcited by its wins. You have to talk of being constantly balanced as opposed to being enslaved by emotional highs and lows.

- *Visualize solutions to problems before they happen*
  One of the best ways to deal with anger is to be prepared for it. So you have the players make a list of all the situations that get them upset, where they lose control. The players then have to visualize how they should react or deal with these situations. They should see themselves getting hit from behind, then recovering by taking a deep breath and refocusing on the next play. They should see themselves responding the way they want to: with poise and composure.

- *Staying focused in the present moment*
  You can help players handle mistakes by using the self-control strategy of always staying focused in the present moment. To perform effectively, players must focus on what they are doing right now, this very moment. After making a mistake, players should not focus on the past—their mistake—but learn from it, forget it, and refocus on the present moment.

- *Use a cue word*
  Players need to have a refocusing plan to get back on track in case they are distracted by negative emotions during the game. They can immediately think of what they have to do on the next play; or they can say a refocusing cue word, such as "Next," "Enjoy," "Stop," "Stay cool," "Let it go," "Forget it," or "Fun" to get them back under control; or they just shift their attention from what made them upset in the first place. Mistakes happen, but more mistakes happen when players lose focus.

- *Pause before responding*
  You can teach players to control their emotional outburst by stopping or pausing for a few seconds to get control of their emotions before they react or get back into play, rather than overreacting right away. A blind response based on negative feelings is almost always a bad response.

- *Take a deep breath and do muscle relaxation*
  You can suggest to players that they take some deep breaths and do muscle relaxation to help themselves calm down. This calming effect generates positive feelings of confidence.

- *Walk away from a confrontation*
  You tell your players that they have to play disciplined in their games because many of their opponents might play dirty and do a lot of hitting after the play is finished. If your team shows a lack of discipline, their opponents will know they can get them upset by giving them little cheap shots; and they will do it more if they know they can throw them off their game.

Even when the opposition "trash-talk," knowing they can get under your players' skin, you must teach your players not to get sucked into reciprocating, but just let the others talk themselves out. Your team will simply walk away and focus on playing the game. Good players should be aware of this tactical device often employed by the opposition and know that it is better to ignore it.

• *Keep a "posture of confidence"*

You encourage your players to commit to themselves before the game starts to remain positive and keep a "posture of confidence" (standing tall, keeping head up, shoulders back, and looking opponent in the eye) all the time during the game. They must promise themselves not to show any negative emotions, which coaches feel is a sign of weakness, and to never take a "posture of defeat" (chin down, head dropped, shoulders slumped, arms hung limply).

Coach Is the Role Model for Self-control

The single most important ingredient of teaching self-control is leading by example. You have to take the responsibility for being an example of self-control. When you respond to a difficult situation with calm assurance and faith in your players, the chances your team will rise to the occasion are a whole lot better.

■ BEHAVIOUR GOAL #9: PLAY TOTALLY FOCUSED

Focusing is one of the secrets to sports. Focus is the ability to devote all your attention to your performance, tuning out all distractions; focus is when your thoughts and performance are one; when your mind and body are one; when you are able to put everything else out of your mind.

The ability to focus is among the most important characteristics a player can have. In fact a lack of focus is one of the primary reasons for mental errors and mistakes. She has to focus to avoid the intrusion of self-defeating thoughts (worry, low confidence, doubt, fear) and to enter the game with her own thoughts, feelings and beliefs. She has to prepare for and minimize as many distractions as possible and focus on her mental preparation and on her upcoming performance. A player gets positive feelings from her positive thoughts, which give her energy and enthusiasm.

How to Get Your Players to Play Totally Focused

Never take a "routine play" for granted

Great players never take a routine play for granted by playing it casually. They focus all their attention on performing their best in order to play to their ability. In fact, they are prepared to concentrate for the whole game, because letting their minds wander for a split second could cause a major mistake. Great players do not worry about the past (mistakes), do not worry about the future (winning), do not let fans bother them, do not worry about how they are playing, and do not worry about the competition; they worry only about themselves. They concentrate on the doing rather than on the results, such as winning or scoring a goal. If they focus just on winning, they will try to force things to happen rather than execute their skills in a relaxed manner, which is what they need to do to be successful. Great players control their thoughts by thinking only of one thing: what they have to do.

Have players focus on what they can control

Players must make up their minds to stay focused during the game and to concentrate on the things that are under their control, such as their emotions; their performance; doing their best; on their execution, such as having a good shift; their specific skills, such as throwing the ball well; playing aggressive defence; running hard; executing on offence; making every shot a good one; seeing the opening in the net; staying with the shot all the way; knowing the goalie and the opposition players. Players do their best when they forget about the things they cannot control, such as how they are doing, making a mistake, what the opposition might do, the referee, and bad calls, which are both useless distractions and a waste of energy. The only thing players should worry about is focusing on their own game and competing. You teach your players to think of one thing at a time and block out everything and anything that might take their mind off that one thing. Players have to stop their minds from wandering or drifting off, that is, focusing on something else; from having concentration lapses ("falling asleep") on the playing floor; and from letting distractions, such as bad calls, fans, referees, opponents, noise, and worry, anxiety, or anger interfere with their concentration and get back on track of playing the game.

The key is that players must be able to separate the important stuff, things they can control, from the unimportant stuff, the clutter, things they can't control. By minimizing the distractions, it maximizes a player's focus.

Note: Mental lapses or losing one's focus causes: penalties, missed checks, not calling out one's check, or losing one's checks.

THINKING OF WINNING IS PROBABLY THE GREATEST BARRIER TO FOCUSING

Use a cue word to refocus

If players lose their concentration, they need a refocusing plan to get back on track. To refocus their concentration, they think of what they have to do next; or, as in the previous section, they can say a cue word, such as "Enjoy," "Relax," "Focus," or "Forget it," to help shift their attention from what caused them to lose focus in the first place; or they do a performance cue, such as gripping their stick or punching their hand to refocus their concentration.

Players must stay in the present moment

You can't afford to waste time thinking about a mistake (the past) or thinking about winning (the future), because these thoughts are distracting and leave you unprepared for the next play. Playing sports is not about mistakes that just happened or the good plays that just happened—it is about what's going to happen in the next play.

You expect your players to stay focused in the present moment throughout the whole game by blocking out all distractions that might take their mind off the game. It is very easy for players to get distracted. Playing "one shift at a time" in the "now" is a very important concept because it focuses on the present moment, not the past (mistakes) or the future (winning).

Great players have short-term memories: they forget bad calls and bad mistakes and just concentrate on playing "one shift" at a time, one play at a time, and one game at a time. They feel what's done is done. This approach is the only way to play the game.

The tendency is to "drift away" or let "the mind wander" from time to time during the game, and this is when they must shift or "will" themselves to hold their focus to the present moment; to concentrate on what's happening right now. When players are having a great performance, they're totally focused on the present moment. Getting into the "zone" is brought on by nothing more than intense concentration.

For players to stay focused in the present moment, they cannot be concerned with the game's outcome. They have to shift their focus from the "outcome" winning, which creates fear, to a focus of one of the following: playing for the enjoyment of the competition, giving it their best effort, playing hard, and playing to challenge themselves.

Players focus on "enjoying the moment"

Successful performances in sport are the natural by-product of moment-by-moment enjoyment. Encourage players to focus not on how they are playing or the thought of winning, but on the sheer joy of playing for the competition itself.

This philosophy really motivates players. Players have to remind themselves to have fun and enjoy the moment when they are playing a game because they compete best when they are loose and relaxed.

Play one game at a time

The good teams are focused on one game at a time. Teams can get distracted very easily by looking down the road and talking about what teams they can beat and what teams will give them problems. It is a major mistake to look past the game at hand.

> # RESPECT EVERYBODY
> # AND FEAR NO ONE

Always focus on the positive

Players' good performances come from thinking about what they want or have to do rather than what they don't want to do. Great players avoid concentration lapses by focusing on positive performance cues to keep their thoughts positive. Going toward a behaviour goal produces much better results than trying to avoid certain behaviours. When players tell themselves not to make a mistake or try to avoid making mistakes, or play not to get angry or nervous, they actually end up making the mistake they wanted to avoid, or end up in these negative emotional states. This is called a "self-fulfilling prophecy," when things that they're trying to avoid come true.

Take a break from focusing

Players get tired of thinking and tired of focusing, since it is hard work. When players start to feel they are losing their focus, they must take a short break to give their mind a rest—for example, when there is no action in the game or when they are on the bench or the sidelines.

■ BEHAVIOUR GOAL #10: PLAY WITH POSITIVE EMOTIONS, PASSION, AND FUN

You can teach players how to check, you can teach them how to run, you can teach them how to play the game, but you can't teach them passion: how *hard* to check or how *fast* to run has to come from inside them. Without passion, the game will always be hard.

Passion comes from making a commitment to a cause or goal. We all have something that motivates us, that pushes us when we don't want to be pushed, that sparks a fire to go beyond what is necessary—and that's what goals do. Passionate players have heart; they hustle all the time; they just love to play; they get excited about playing; they have fun playing; and they make things happen.

As a coach, you want to find out early who has passion and who does not, because enthusiasm and passion are the basic factors necessary for achieving anything. These types of players make a difference to your team by contributing energy and chemistry. So, if you surround yourself with positive, enthusiastic, upbeat players, the team will have a hard time staying pessimistic. You certainly do not want your players to play with a negative or a neutral attitude. Neutral is not good. Players with a neutral outlook are complacent, non-committed, and unenthusiastic about playing.

A player who has talent but no heart or passion will not be successful. So don't be in a hurry to judge a player on talent alone; the great players are the ones who better their skills with real inner determination and passion that turns talent into greatness.

Note: The things a coach can't measure right away are attitude, passion, and commitment.

HARD WORK WITHOUT PASSION IS REALLY HARD WORK

How to Get Your Players to Play with Positive Emotions, Passion, and Fun

Stress having fun

A team that has fun is easier to coach, as it brings energy to practices and games every day. So you should build a positive, fun environment to deliver a dose of energy to the team. Encourage the players to have fun playing and make sure there are smiles, teasing, humour, and laughter; players on the team can joke around and even play pranks on one another.

Because game pressure breeds team pressure, players may seem nervous and uptight before a game, unless you find a way for them to let off some of the steam. The best way for you to loosen up your players is by instilling a little fun. When players have fun, they become relaxed and enjoy the moment, reducing the pressure of worrying about winning or making mistakes. If a team goes into the game having had some fun first, it has a better chance of doing its best and thereby being successful. (Remember that to have fun, a coach must have a good sense of humour.)

Be enthusiastic about the game

If you like what you are doing, do it passionately—you coach because you love to coach and you love the game—because this type of atmosphere will be fun for the players. You should fill the players with a passion and love of the sport. If you are excited about the game, then your players will be excited. Enthusiasm is contagious and infectious. A coach who is low key, uninterested, and complacent creates a boring, unenthused team atmosphere. The coach's energy and passion will make the difference between a dynamic team and an ordinary team. His enthusiasm and energy is one of the most important things a coach can bring to his team. So keep in mind to smile more, show a sense of humour, and joke around with your players.

In the bad times, when there's not much to be excited about, the players especially need the excitement and enthusiasm of the coach. Even when a team has nothing to play for, the coach has to be the energy provider by telling his team that they have to play this game "like it's going to be their best game of the season," or they have to play this game "like it's going to be their last game of the season."

Note: Even doctors can make mistakes because of complacency.

Stay positive

You should explain to your players that staying positive is also a part of discipline. You encourage your players to force themselves to have positive thoughts, a positive outlook, a positive attitude, and a positive approach to the game. Players must understand that they can program themselves to be positive: A good attitude and a bad attitude are just two different ways of looking at the same situation.

Players must understand that positive thoughts are also a powerful "self-fulfilling prophecy." If a team thinks it is going to be successful, it will be successful. A team having a positive outlook on the game is one of the most important prerequisites to having a successful game. So you should stress to your players how important and powerful it is to control their attitude or self-talk.

Notes: We need players to bring physical energy (hard work) and emotional energy (enthusiasm, positive attitude) to the team. If players do not bring energy, ask them, "What do you have a passion for?" When you are passionate, you love playing and love pursuing your destination of winning a championship, being an all-star, etc.

Coach can teach skills, he can teach players how to think in a game to make good decisions, but he can't teach positive attitude. He can only provide the right environment.

IF YOU THINK GOOD THOUGHTS, GOOD THINGS WILL HAPPEN

"It's only a game"

You do not need to coach a game like it's a do-or-die situation all the time, getting into shouting matches with your players, the referee, the opposition players, or the opposition coach. You can coach with intensity and enthusiasm but you must stay under control and focus only on the game. It is, after all, only a game.

■ BEHAVIOUR GOAL #11: PLAY WITH POISE UNDER PRESSURE

Game pressure can do one of two things: it can inhibit players or it can excite them.

You can explain to the players that poise is keeping your composure; making the right decision under pressure. The real greatness of a player always occurs in response to intense pressure. There is nothing more important than having poise under pressure and learning how to perform well when the pressure is on. This is the ultimate challenge.

Great players have the attitude of loving the big game because they are in the limelight. It seems when ordinary players are nervous, the great players are smiling; when ordinary players are cautious about playing, the great players can't wait to play and be aggressive.

Poised players "come through" in close or big games; they make the big play when needed; they perform under pressure and maintain their focus in pressure situations; they have a tremendous ability to think under pressure; and they do not panic. The truest test of players is pressure.

How to Get Your Players to Play with Poise under Pressure

Approach every game the same way

The way your players approach the game helps with composure. Since every game is played the same way, then every game, whether it's a regular game or a playoff game, should be approached the same way. Players get composure by approaching every game with the attitude that it is a challenge, an opportunity for success, rather than a threat or a risk of failure.

Remind players to prepare the same way every time

The sameness of the preparation by your players will help to control and stabilize the nervousness and "butterflies" that precede a game. You should get your players to do such things as muscle relaxation, self-talk, visualization, and deep breathing to mentally prepare to play.

Good Pressure versus Bad Pressure

It might appear that pressure is a bad thing, but pressure is necessary for players to play their best. Gordie Howe (NHL) experienced "butterflies" right up to the age of fifty-one. How a team plays under pressure is the real question. Some teams rise to the occasion and others do not. A team gets its reputation on how it handles those few decisive seconds when it is a critical moment, such as in the last minute of play in a tied game. It seems games are won and lost in just a few seconds rather than sixty minutes.

"Good pressure" (some stress) occurs when a team is prepared to play. Good pressure is what players feel when they know what to expect and what to do without hesitation. They are prepared, and preparation reduces pressure because it builds confidence and one feels loose.

"Bad pressure" (extreme stress) is something a team feels when it is not prepared to play. Bad pressure is what players feel when they don't know what to expect, they fear the unknown, they know they are unprepared, and they are hesitant about what to do. Bad pressure tightens up the muscles, erodes confidence, and causes players to worry.

■ BEHAVIOUR GOAL #12: PLAY WITH MENTAL AND PHYSICAL TOUGHNESS

Mental Toughness

Aside from pure athletic ability, talent, and skill, mental toughness is the greatest attribute that any player can have. Mental toughness, which is far more important than physical toughness, is the ability to keep problems of all kinds from affecting a player's attitude and performance, such as rebounding quickly from mistakes, setbacks, and bad breaks in a game.

Mentally tough players have the ability to handle all kinds of stress (physical, mental, and emotional) and not let it bother them. Nobody can intimidate mentally tough players because they are not afraid of anyone. Coach knows mentally tough players will keep going when things get difficult.

It seems parents and adults do everything for kids today. Kids are soft and spoiled, and it is your job as a coach to make them tougher. Every kid should be forced to do something he doesn't like to do, so he can learn toughness.

You want every one of your players to have tremendous toughness. Mental toughness is something players can develop, and it is your job to make them so tough on the floor/court that they will show no weakness.

How to Train Your Players to Be Mentally Tough

Resist the temptation to quit

You reinforce and stress to your players that a mentally tough player has the ability to resist the temptation to quit. Mental toughness is the ability to keep playing after a player's energy has deserted him. He plays hard even when he doesn't feel like playing. Players know that they have a reservoir of strength—"mind over matter"; that there is always a little bit more left in the tank; that the body will give out before the mind if they force themselves. There is a specific time in the game to suck it up and play harder, called "gut check" time. Great players are successful because they are tougher mentally than the opposition. If they are winning, they never quit; if they are losing, they never quit, if they are hurt, they never quit, if they are fatigued, they never quit.

Withstand mental and emotional punishment

Your job as a coach is to develop mentally "tough" players who can overcome anything. They can handle mental and emotional punishment (fear, bad calls, problems, mental pain) as well as physical punishment (getting hit, physical pain, fatigue, and injuries). Nothing bothers them; they just grit their teeth and play, ignoring screaming fans, bad refereeing, bad calls against them, or taking a dirty hit. They don't sulk or mouth off; they just cheer their team on. They can accept blame and receive strong criticism from the coach without feeling hurt.

Good teams with mentally tough players cannot be intimidated. Mentally tough players can deal with physical and emotional pain in a game because they have put themselves through pain in the off-season games and practices to prepare for the season. In fact, they are so focused on doing their job in a game that pain never enters their minds. They condition their minds for pain as well as their bodies.

Physical punishment

Most physical sports are like a war where people want to physically attack you. And as a coach, you certainly don't want your players to be afraid to get hit.

Some players enjoy the physical aspect and others don't, and they are the ones who have to work to overcome the fear of contact. Opponents may try to bully teams, to intimidate them, but the players of good teams have physical courage.

These mentally tough players are in the action all the time because they are not afraid to hit or be hit; they have physical courage to go into corners to take a hit, to fight the battles along the boards, and the courage to go inside the defence, where they are going to be banged around. It is the "soft" players who won't hit, are afraid to be hit, and won't compete against physical teams, as they are not willing to pay the price. You are measured as a player when you get hit by your opponent as hard as he can. How you react by either going after the guy or putting your tail between your legs will determine your character or reputation.

Play the same all the time

You explain that mentally tough players play when they are hurt, when they have pain, when they are tired. They do not get down on themselves after being scored upon or after being beaten defensively. They have this great ability to bounce back from adversity. All the players have a job to do, regardless of the situation or how they feel—to perform to the best of their ability.

The one thing a team does not want to be known as is a "front-running" team: a team that looks good when ahead or when the game is close, but falls apart when it gets behind. Remember, if the mentally tough team is winning, it plays the same; if the mentally tough team is losing, it plays the same; if the mentally tough team is hurting and beat up, it plays the same.

For a player, mental toughness is not letting anything bother him; never showing his opponent a weakness through his words, facial expression, or body language. The opposition can never get "under his skin," get him upset by giving him cheap shots, or "yakking at him." They can never throw him off his game.

Forget mistakes

You motivate your team to play with mental toughness by preaching how players view failure. You have to make players aware that making mistakes is an important part of learning and there should be no fear of making mistakes. Players should "play like they have nothing to lose." Mistakes become a thing of the past and should be forgotten.

Be hard on players in practice

You are hard on your players so that you know when the pressure of a game is on, the players will react correctly and with discipline. In a tight game, you have to know that nobody can rattle your players because of all the crap they have put up with from you.

What can a player who is slow, not athletic, and not talented do to improve? He can become mentally stronger and tougher. How do you as a coach help him to do that?

You have to be tough on all your players. You have to push them to their maximum to test their character, physically and mentally, especially at tryouts. First, you have to find out every player's limits and playing ability, and to do that, you have to challenge and push them all the time to find out if they can take the stress and pressure of you yelling at them. Then you have to find out how they are going to react under game pressure.

You give certain players a hard time because you know you will have to depend on them in crucial times in the game and you want to make sure they can handle the pressure. You give them a tough time pushing them to their physical limit to see if they will quit or become mentally stronger. Good players take it because they know it will help them become better players. The competitive players want to play for tough coaches because they want to be pushed to their maximum. They know that the more players are pushed to exhaustion, the greater their mental toughness will be.

Coach "picks on them" to make them tougher

But sometimes when you are hard on players to make them better, they will ask, "Why is the coach picking on us?" They feel they can't do anything right because you are yelling at them or criticizing them for every little thing. You can tell these players you "pick" on them because you care about them and you want to make them better players. You see potential in them and know down the road they will help the team a great deal. Players have to understand that you are not the enemy.

You also explain to a player that if you get on her case for something, she should not mope or pout like it is the end of the world. A good player has to have the confidence and "thick" skin to take it. Some kids take it, and some say, "I quit!"

Having competitive players

It is important that you have a few competitive players who are always trying to beat up on other players and who are always verbally fighting over calls, over the score, over fouls, over everything in scrimmages. These types of players will instill an incredible amount of toughness in your team.

Note: During a game, you still keep coaching and yelling at your players when they are up by a big score. You do this to remind them to stay mentally tough no matter what the score.

IF YOU WANT TO BE CHAMPIONS, YOU HAVE TO BEAT CHAMPIONS

How to Get Your Players to Be Physically Tough

Coach explains that physically tough players are hard-nosed competitors who are not afraid to get hit and are not afraid to hit anyone; they are physically gifted, intimidating, and very competitive and aggressive. They play with reckless abandon, laying it on the line every game; they don't hold back, they are never out-fought or out-hustled. They are just a little bit tougher than the next guy—they are totally into the physical part of playing.

Let players know they are going to hit or get hit

Players have to play physical in most sports, knowing they are going to get hit while going after a loose ball or cutting into the middle of the floor. You explain to your players that they can't play most sports and not expect to get hit or hit somebody. Players with physical toughness are not afraid to go into corners knowing they might have to hit someone or get hit. Physically tough players are always in the action; they are always going after the ball, after their check, or heading toward the net.

Because you want your team to be physically tough, the players have to understand that when they make physical contact with an opponent, they have to be the instigator. Either the opponent will do it to them or they will do it to the opponent. So your players must take it to them first. Players have to be totally into the physical part of playing sports. One of the key team affirmations is: *We are the most physical team in the league.*

Get players to play all-out and be aggressive

When your players come off the floor, you want them to be totally exhausted; you want them to leave everything on the floor; you want them to battle for everything, out-fighting and out-hustling their opponent. You also want them to play aggressively; you do not want them to be afraid to hit an opponent hard enough that it will upset, irritate, or "tick him off"; and you want hard-nosed competitors who play with a chip on their shoulder yet are mentally tough enough to play composed.

Physically tough players never want anybody to question their heart or character. They approach the game with the thought of starting by hitting people or getting hit to get themselves into the game. They want the opposition to know that this is the kind of game they are going to be in—a very physical game. "When opponents play against us, they know they are going to be in for a war, as we play harder than anyone. We play every game like it is going to be our last game."

If you want to be a championship team, you have to play when hurt, play when fatigued, and keep on playing when you get hit dirty. Great teams play tired and hurt because they want to play; they run the hardest when they feel the worst. So, if you feel your players are not getting beat up, hit, bumped, cut, and tired, then they are not doing their job.

Note: You want your team to have physically smart toughness (physically controlled aggression within the rules) versus physically stupid toughness (out-of-control, reckless aggression, hitting from behind; stupid penalties).

11 BUILDING TEAM UNITY; TEAM COHESION GOALS

Along with outcome, performance, and behaviour goals, there is a final set of goals a team needs: to get players to work together in a respectful manner. These are called team cohesion goals, and they are very important in building and creating a culture of team unity and teamwork. One of the most important abilities in coaching is teaching "teamwork"—that is, the ability to get the players to perform as members of a team, where their personal goals and the team goals are one and the same.

There is no quick solution to building a team; it takes time and patience, and is a process in an age where everybody wants instant success. You can select players, but you cannot select a whole team. Over time, and with reinforcement of the cohesion goals, players will develop and evolve into a team. You, as a coach, are naturally one of the key factors in developing this team cohesion; therefore, you should have a vision of how a sports team should be built, along with your ability to work with your key player leaders.

To Be Successful, a Team Must Have a Code of Conduct

A "team" is a cohesive group of people who combine their talents to accomplish a specific goal or a series of goals. Putting a group of diverse players together to work co-operatively and to think and act as one to achieve team success is the main challenge of coaching. How do you get team members on the same page?

One way is by establishing team values and a code of team conduct that the players have to follow. These team cohesion goals are part motivation by you, and part team building by the players. This list of successful characteristics of a cohesive team states how the players should treat each other and these characteristics should be based on strong, sound family values.

Here is the list of the cohesive goals:

> Everyone has to be committed to the team.

> Everyone has to play together.

> Everyone has to demonstrate trust.

> Everyone has to encourage and support each other.

Team Cohesion Goals Get Players Working Together

These principles create a team of individuals working together who can accomplish much more than a group of individuals working alone. But it's amazing how ordinary players who play together can accomplish extraordinary performances. Cohesiveness adds strength to the team because "none of us is as good as all of us together." The individual team members now realize they have a common purpose and a common plan for achieving that purpose. Whatever their individual differences may have been, they now all have something that they can agree upon and that is an important step in team building.

Team Meetings

In a team meeting, you and the players together establish the principles that create this team cohesion. Having lists of goals and rules that the whole team has agreed to is an important step in creating team unity. In fact, the process of creating its own lists of team rules and goals through team meetings in itself does a lot to build a unified team.

Coach "Sells" Team Cohesion Goals to the Players

Coaching is getting the players to "buy into" your philosophy, your systems, and your goals. You must sell your ideas so everyone will want to accept them. It is very difficult to build team cohesion, but teams are built one step at a time, one idea at a time, one practice at a time, and one small success at a time.

Your responsibility as a coach is to develop the players to grow as a team that consistently produces high-quality outcomes. So, you need to use your people skills to get players to work as a team; to get players to treat each other properly; and to get players to play their best and not settle for anything less than the best. In building a team, you are constantly making small corrections and adjustments all the time when players get off the path. You have to work every day at building your team.

Players Must Set Aside Their Own Interests

These cohesion goals are often the most difficult to achieve, because they require individuals to put the interests of the team and their teammates ahead of their own. So you have to take additional steps to sell players on the importance of overcoming individual interests.

Individuals are used to having many choices and having their individual needs fulfilled. They are used to immediate personal gratification so they tend to focus on the short-term benefits rather than the long-term ones. So, it takes a great effort by you to overcome these individual habits of thought and expectation.

One of the major cohesion goals of a successful team is teamwork, co-operation, and togetherness. The cohesion goal of togetherness has to be firmly reinforced because players often behave selfishly in a system where co-operation is critical. Is the team a collection of individuals? The true coach understands the importance of natural team chemistry, which is the main ingredient of any successful team. In this chapter, we will give you simple, practical methods for addressing this problem. The methods are mostly ways of persuading players to put aside their own agendas and work together as a unified, cohesive unit to achieve a greater goal than they could on their own.

Four Team Cohesion Goals

You work with your team to build team unity by setting cohesion goals. Setting out the goals specifically, posting them in the team room, and reminding the team of them when problems between players arise sets the tone for the whole team and reinforces appropriate team behaviour. When teams follow these four cohesion goals, they stand a much better chance of achieving their outcome goals, performance goals, and behaviour goals, and truly becoming a "team" rather than a group of individuals. Knowing what the team cohesion goals are is a big step toward unifying a team—but actually achieving them requires some effort by you.

Here is the sample list again:

> Everyone has to be committed to the team. All are unselfish.
> Everyone has to play together, co-operate, and count on each other.
> Everyone has to demonstrate trust by getting to know each other and talking to each other honestly.
> Everyone has to encourage and care for each other; support each other; look out for each other; help each other; respect each other; and believe in each other.

Everyone Has to Be Committed to the Team

We make decisions with our brains, but we make commitments with our hearts. That is why commitments are longer lasting and harder to break. If players truly make a commitment that they want to win a championship, they will make this commitment with their hearts.

Note: Coach must create an atmosphere where players all feel secure and feel like part of the team before he can talk about commitment.

Having regular team meetings to discuss "lists" and problems

To get all the players pulling together toward a shared or common goal, you build verbal agreements with them for team rules, team outcome goals, team performance goals, team behaviour goals, and now team cohesion goals through discussion and input from your players during regular team meetings. As a coach, you must let your players in on the action, giving them "empowerment."

You must welcome involvement, discussion, and input from all of your players. In fact, you should make players partners in the running of the team. It is amazing to see how motivated and committed players can be when they know their contribution is valued. The more responsibility players are given, the more committed they will become. With this responsibility comes a sense of ownership and peer pressure, which is the most powerful weapon a team can ever have. The payoff from this involvement with these decisions is that players take a share in the ownership. When you give your players ownership, they feel much different toward the team than if you had made the lists of goals yourself. Individual players' agendas are now replaced by team agendas.

You have now created a cohesive atmosphere where players feel connected because you really listened, and everyone played an important role and had input into the team decisions, not just the "stars." If a coach keeps his focus on just a select few, he will build barriers rather than bridges. Coach should show no favouritism to the "stars"; the average players should feel just as important as the stars. It is important that whenever the coach talks with the team, he use the first person plural of "we" and "us," to stress team togetherness.

Notes: Besides the commitment formed from team meetings, players build relationships while discussing goals and rules.

Team meetings + empowerment = commitment

Create a "team comes first" attitude

It is a real challenge for a coach to work with players who don't subscribe to "team skills and needs" and are more interested in their own needs. You have to get the players to focus more on the team and less on themselves. You do this by talking about the "team comes first" attitude through team meetings and individual talks with players. Coaches are always hearing "Me, Me," rather than "We, We"!

What is teamwork?

The definition of "team" is a group of players working together to achieve a long-term common goal.

"Teamwork" means working together; it means giving more than taking; it means relying on one another; it means a "me" player is replaced by a "we" player. "We" becomes the most important word in our vocabulary because it invites players to take on ownership.

"Teamwork" is where the team wins and loses together as a unit; where players share and stick together in the bad times along with the good times;

where everyone is willing to trade self or selfishness for the team; where players focus on success of the team rather than on their own success; where players put the team's interest over their own personal interests; and where players have to think of the "team first" rather than of themselves. Players on success-ful teams believe that the relationship and bonding they go through as a team exceeds those of other teams.

The team's success is the most important thing

You have to stress that "the team is bigger than any individual player," and "a team can do great things if the players don't care who gets the credit." You ask the players to "check their egos" at the dressing room door if they are committed to the team and to being successful. Some teams have very talented players, but can't win because of the selfishness of the various players who are interested only in their own stats. Players become "all-out" team-players when they let go of their own egos and selfish interests for the good of the team. They must understand that when the team does well, individual goals will be taken care of. By dropping their selfishness, by sacrificing for the team, by sacrificing their personal agenda to serve the team's agenda, by giving themselves up for the team, and by doing their best for the team, players will always be rewarded in the end.

Note: When you have a few outstanding players, you have to ask them, "What would you rather have: an all-star season or a national championship?" Because to be successful, these outstanding players will have to learn to play together and give up the ball.

Players have to think both selfishly and unselfishly

One of the most important characteristics of a championship team is unselfishness. There is a fine line between selfishness and unselfishness. The contradiction is that you want your players to be unselfish by playing within the team system, yet selfish in that they have to do what makes them great. You still need the players to think "team first," but you don't want them to forget about their talent or gift for scoring or playing great defence. Players must real-ize that their personal success is important for the team's success. But they must also understand that the team's success is even more important than their own personal success. If players don't care about their own individual stats and are more concerned about the team stats, great things will happen. In other words, if you have a team full of unselfish players, you will be able to accomplish extraordinary things together.

You try to get the players to focus on what they can *do* for their team (unself-ish) rather than on what they can get from their team (selfish). The team that has a "get-all-you-can" attitude has little or no morale. The team that has a "give-all-you-can" attitude has a feeling of confidence and positive spirit.

Talk about the team as a "family"

To be a team, you have to be a family first. Of course you want everybody getting along, working together, and not fighting, bickering, complaining, or criticizing. Players are either committed to the "team concept," where they treat each other like family, or they are not. You can talk about the team as a family environment because families always have to get along, and in a family-support system, a person never feels alone, as the players can count on each other. This family environment gives a player a sense of belonging, and a player feels she can always achieve more by being part of a group. In this family setting, a player feels through communication she can share problems and receive help, emotional support, love, understanding, and encouragement in solving them. Players support their teammates not because of what they do or can do for each other, but just because they are part of the family and they feel more responsibility to each other. You can stress that they are "special" players playing on a "special" team, a team of destiny; and to be successful, they have to make a total commitment to the team.

TEAM CHEMISTRY IS IMPORTANT FOR A TEAM TO BE SUCCESSFUL

Everyone Has to Play Together

The key to winning the battle of unity of purpose is the team's season outcome goal. This long-term season outcome goal made by the group creates an atmosphere of a shared goal that is now owned by the team, and to reach it, they have to work together. The season outcome goal gives the team a clear sense of purpose; it "fires them up"; it gives a reason to be successful . . . a reason for being together. If there is no common goal, the team is just a collection of players with no overachieving common cause. At the root of team cohesion is unselfishness, so it is your job to see that the team goal is greater than the goal of any one player.

The goal of togetherness is the ability to get along with each other. You build team unity and cohesion by stressing and reinforcing the characteristics of a cohesive team; by encouraging positive peer pressure for the players to replace blaming and finger-pointing. So if a player is seen as acting in a selfish way, the players as a group have to address it immediately. This type of action develops a strong "team ego" versus individual egos.

Note: How a coach gets the team to work together in a game to achieve positive results is by having short-term game performance goals. These short-term game goals focus on team success, not individual performance.

Be positive

> When you communicate with your players, try to always be positive.

> You build players' self-esteem by giving praise.

> When players display proper behaviour on the floor, you reinforce it through praise.

> You give feedback of praise when performance goals are attained or improved.

> You give praise when a player's skill is improved.

> You give praise on good execution or improvement within the system.

> You must always expect positive results.

> You have a principle of "always being positive" by controlling your own emotions in difficult situations and remaining positive with difficult players.

Give recognition to groups who deserve it

You celebrate everything related to the game. You develop teamwork by ensuring that some players get some sort of recognition after every game such as the Power Play Group, the Man Short Group, the Faceoff Group, the Defensive Group, or the Offensive Group.

Be aware of what's going on

If you want high morale, you must constantly monitor what is going on with your team. You must keep your eyes and ears open, look for trends, and, most important, get around to visit and talk with your players every day.

Select good player-leaders who will help build togetherness

Besides the coach, player-leaders have a great impact on developing and creating team unity and togetherness more than anything else. Great team leaders, seniors, and captains, make a big difference in setting the tone for team spirit, cohesion, and chemistry on the team. Player-leaders keep everything together by reinforcing the cohesion goals. They encourage and root for the shy players, the new players, the extras to take an active part with the team. The core leaders invite all players, including the shy or new players, along if the team is going out or just hanging out, to make them feel part of the team. Good team leaders get rid of any pecking order or cliques.

You put the responsibility of building teamwork on the seniors, experienced players, or captains to get rid of the disease of selfishness: loners, jealousy, greed, and laziness. The motivation for a coach is to get the older, more experienced players to think team oriented, as opposed to focusing on themselves; that's not as hard as it sounds, as most players want to be on a good, cohesive team.

Note: A team that is happy has fun together. Look for certain players who help to create a light atmosphere by keeping everybody laughing.

A true team must "take ownership" through empowerment

To build a team, the coach has to involve the team players in the decision-making process.

Today's coaches are willing to follow rather than lead when it is called for. You follow by asking for players' input and allowing the players to have a say in how things are done. Empowering the players strengthens the team's foundation. When players set out the goals for the team, the most important thing is not the specific goals they set, but the fact that they are setting the goals, not you. The most effective teams are those in which all the players have a say in the direction of the team by taking on ownership and accountability: They help create and enforce rules; they contribute ideas; they put positive peer pressure on their teammates; and they help set goals.

Note: Coach presents a vision and then "sells" it to his followers; then allows those same followers to control their own destinies.

Reinforce statistics of togetherness

Some statistics that reinforce togetherness are: number of passes completed, number of screens set, number of assists, number of times players helped out a teammate on defence. If these team performance goals are attained or improved upon, the players receive some sort of reward, such as a party, candy, pop, and so on. Having these team incentives helps build teamwork.

Use quotations and team affirmations

To reinforce the behaviour goal of togetherness every day to your players, you should use a good story, so be a collector of stories, analogies, quotes, and sayings. Some coaches even give books and articles to players to read and bring in special speakers from business, former players, or anybody else who would have a positive effect on the players. Team affirmations can have the powerful effect of drawing the players together into a unit.

Create a feeling of "we are the best"

If you make players feel they are the best, the result is that the team develops a feeling of pride that it really is the best. How do you convince your team that it is the best? It actually has to be the best at something, and the key here is to focus on some element that is the team's strength and that will help make the team successful. It helps that whatever the team selects to be its greatest strength has to be measured through statistics, because the team must have a valid reason for believing it is the best. For example, the best defensive team would be reflected in its low goals against average or forcing the opposition into a low shooting percentage; or the best loose ball team in the league would be reflected in obtaining 60 percent loose balls or obtaining more loose balls than its opponent.

You can also reinforce your talks with team affirmations, such as: "We are the best defensive team in the league." In other words, you make the players feel they are better than anyone else—the best. You can also focus on the team being great and not just good, because great means being the best.

The game itself can bring players together

The game itself brings the players together through wins and losses, and through sweat and tears. By learning to win together, the players develop relationships with one another and build an energized and cohesive unit. Their togetherness pushes them to play above and beyond the call of duty. "We win together, we lose together."

Team-building exercises and devices help players get to know each other

The purpose of these team-building exercises and slogans, etc., is to foster friendship and build team solidarity by allowing time for personal connections. Anything that brings more camaraderie to the team is essential in team building and worth doing.

> Pre-game stretch—stretching together, calling out the number of stretches in unison

> Team dress code—dressing exactly the same on the floor and off the floor

> The same team uniform for everyone—shirts tucked in at all times, no names on the back, socks the same length, and no headbands or wristbands

> A team bulletin board to display newspaper clippings of other teams, the league, Internet sayings. Half of the write-ups can be real and the other half made up for motivation; post team sayings.

> Team slogan, team theme song, team outcome goal for the season, team cheer, team nickname, team fight song

> Teammates spending time together socializing and having fun outside of practices and games. Socialization as a group is important so that the players feel they are part of something special, helps to bring players closer together, such as buffet meals or family picnics, team parties, going to a movie that represents togetherness and teamwork (such as *Hoosiers* or *Remember the Titans*) or theatrical plays, on the road having team breakfast together, visiting a hospital, pre-game meals together; fun activities such as golf, driving range, miniature golf, water polo, go-carts, bowling, tug-of-war, dodge ball, other sports.

Coach wants players to have fun together, as this is a great way to build team spirit and cheerfulness, which has a great effect on team morale. Having "characters" on a team who are funny and play tricks on teammates is a great thing to keep a team loose.

> Team T-shirts or jackets with team logo or a special saying on them

> Team newsletter to keep everybody informed

> Players interview teammates to present to the team so the players get to know each other. They can talk about their sport, their personal goals, their school, their career, their family background, their hobbies, their likes and dislikes, and why they want to play for this team. They can bring in pictures of their family and talk about them; they can tell stories of their life experiences.

> Team-building games

> Give a card to each player with a picture of the championship trophy, championship ring, or championship medallion on it.

> A Winner's Circle. Just because players are on the team doesn't really mean they are on "the team." Players have to earn their place to be in the core group of players called the Winner's Circle. Players on the team are not treated equally, but are rewarded for how they contribute to the team. This Winner's Circle is proactive and is based on trust by the players' showing obedience to team rules and putting forth a high degree of effort in the classroom and on the court/floor. This is a way to motivate players to work harder by rewarding them for doing things right rather than doling out punishment for doing things wrong or not at all. By being committed to the team, players are rewarded with T-shirts, sweat tops, pizza, given special privileges, or any other ideas players can come up with.

How do players make their way into the Winner's Circle? Players are rewarded for: being a good person/student and working hard in the classroom, being on time for every class, attending the study hall and working in the library; working the hardest on the court/floor; working the hardest in the weight room; attending all practices; dressing appropriately; and getting plenty of rest and eating right.

Nicknames and slogans create a team identity

A team needs something to give it an identity or style of play, such as being known as a tough defensive team, a running team, or a patient offensive team. You could ask the team what image they want to project by means of a nickname, such as the "Broad Street Bullies," the "No-Name Team," "Teamwork and Togetherness," and so on.

Here are a few examples of slogans to stress what the team stands for: "You've got to believe!"; "Unfinished business"; "The last stand"; "We mean business"; "No excuses"; "Until there is one left standing"; "Take no prisoners"; "Whatever it takes"; "Us against the world"; "We'll find a way!"; "One heartbeat"; "One for all and all for one"; "We need each other"; "In serving each other we become strong"; "No passengers."

Physical symbols to represent the team

A lunch pail could represent the blue-collar worker; a chain link would represent togetherness; a hammer, a tough or hard-working team; and so on.

Team theme songs

Examples:
> "Everything's Gonna Be All Right" (Bob Marley)
> Theme songs from movies such as *Rocky* and *Chariots of Fire*
> Play the favourite song of each player during a stoppage of play in the game or after they score.

Team traditions and history of past teams

You should find out about the tradition and history of your organization. Traditions are usually established by former teams, and the present players feel a form of responsibility to live up to those traditions. The more you can find to promote past teams, the better. What if you don't have a tradition? Start one. This will give players a feeling of belonging, a feeling that it is *their* team.

So, let the players decide on: type of music in the change room; type of game clothes they want to wear; type of game bags; what order of leaving the dressing room; any routine before leaving; special handshakes or gestures for the team; joining hands before they go on the floor to create team unity; and a team cheer at the beginning and end of every practice and game.

Notes: Along the hallway or in some conspicuous spot, post action photos of players playing great, plus former team pictures.

Have a team signing, where every player on the team signs his name in a special place in the arena/field as defenders of their home court.

Make sure everybody feels like they are part of the team's success

To create togetherness, you have to make everybody feel like part of the team. You, along with the experienced players, welcome the newcomers to the team with open arms. You sometimes have a "buddy system" whereby the seniors mentor or teach the rookies.

Encourage players to tell their own personal stories

One way of team building is to get players to tell stories in front of the team about a team they were on or about themselves; to talk about the history of great players and the game; how they prepare themselves to play, etc.

Make the dressing room a showplace

You can make sure the dressing room is comfortable, with carpeting, names above stalls, positive sayings and posters, towels in the bin, and anything else that gives it a professional appearance and a feeling of pride.

You want the environment in the dressing room to be upbeat, enthusiastic, and positive. And you definitely do not want any complaining or negative comments in the change room.

The locker room is the players' room and the heart of the team. Players should take ownership of the dressing room by keeping it neat and clean. Usually, it is the leaders, the seniors, and experienced players who create a positive environment in the dressing room. There is no question that the dressing room environment influences team success by promoting togetherness and better communication among the players—which will extend to the field/floor.

Everyone Has to Demonstrate Trust

Players have to depend on each other; trusting that one's teammates will get the job done is what teamwork is all about, which is important for a team game. Trust is the glue to being successful; and you build trust by everybody communicating honestly with each other, by believing in each other, hanging out together, spending time together, having a common team goal, and working together toward this goal.

When players realize that you, as a coach, don't "play games" and won't allow gossiping, complaining, bad-mouthing, or criticism of teammates, the level of trust goes up and the negative behaviour decreases. When players communicate with each other openly, honestly, and positively, an atmosphere of trust and respect is created. When you and the players are honest with each other, they know they can speak the truth, they feel they can share their point of view, they can tell each other and you what they really think and feel regardless of the consequences. That can take your relationship with them a long way. Successful coaches know that players have to depend on one another in a game, and when trust is high among players, they have a feeling of confidence, knowing they are not alone and that someone has their back. The result is that they can do a lot more together.

To build teamwork and trust, make sure you and the players never air your problems or grievances in public; you never humiliate or embarrass a player in front of others; and you argue or talk in private.

Honest communication

> ❭   How do we talk to each other? We talk to each other honestly and positively.

> Where do we look when we talk to each other? We look each other directly in the eyes. This sends the message that we are telling the truth.

> What do we call each other? We call each other by our first name.

> How do we listen to each other? We actively listen to the other person.

Notes: If a coach respects, understands, and listens to his players, he won't lose power or control; he'll gain it.

As a coach, you have to do what you say you are going to do. You must demonstrate integrity by saying what you mean and meaning what you say. You can tell players straight up how you feel: "You are playing great." "You are not working hard enough."

Everyone Has to Encourage and Care for Each Other

Another cohesion goal successful teams have in common is an absolute caring for each other more than themselves. A cohesive team creates these types of environments: a family environment, a warm, caring, positive, supportive, safe, trusting, encouraging, happy, and co-operative environment.

Stress "not letting your buddy down"

One of the key factors in building team spirit is a genuine consideration for others; playing for the guy beside you. The main motivation for a player to play hard is a sense of psychological unity with other members of his team, "not letting your buddy down." A cohesive team is about being on a team where team members truly care for one another, and nothing is more powerful than the responsibility for, and accountability to, another person.

"Who are you playing for?" The answer is, "The other twenty guys on the team dressed like me." How a coach gets players to play "better than they are" is by getting them not to play just for themselves, but to play for their teammates, which makes them play better than they are.

Note: When a player does not get along with his teammates and has antagonistic feelings toward them, this can become cancerous within the team, gradually eating away its joy, energy, and peace of mind.

Encourage players to look out for each other

You want teammates to physically stick up and protect each other in a game where they have each other's back. If an opponent gives one of their team-mates a dirty hit, everybody must automatically come to his aid. Coach must also verbally fight for her players by sticking up for them with referees and opponents.

Make sure players get to know each other

You encourage players to get to know each other by having them talk about themselves in front of the team or with a teammate. When players know each other, they can then care about each other, and teamwork will improve. During training camp, it is a tradition that each player stands up and talks about herself in front of the whole team for one minute. In this way, players get to know each other a little bit more. Players can talk about the sport; their personal goals; school and career; their family; their hobbies and interests; and why they want to play for the team. The more players know about their teammates, the more they will care about and commit to them.

Encourage players to support each other, especially after a mistake

Any player can be enthusiastic when things are going well, but what about when things are going badly? When players make a mistake in a game or have a poor performance, they usually feel bad, discouraged, and disappointed. One of the most important things in building teamwork is that teammates give each other support, understanding, and positive encouragement. So, you have to always encourage teammates to encourage each other verbally or pat each other on the back for support, especially after a mistake.

When a player makes a mistake he usually knows it and could become vulnerable and fearful of making another mistake. The response from his teammates will determine how he perceives his mistake. When players support a teammate who has made a mistake or has given a bad performance, the "team" concept becomes much stronger, and the player doesn't feel like he is alone. In addition, players know it could be them next time. The feeling that teammates are supporting each other and have each other's back is a powerful force and energizes everybody.

"Treat each other the way you want to be treated!"

Respecting your teammates and the coach is essential to building teamwork and group cohesion. Players who do not respect each other do not make good team members, with the result of a divided team. Players know that building team cohesion is based on the most important people principle: "Treat each other the way you want to be treated." For example, when a goal or point is scored, make sure that players congratulate the scorer, and that the scorer searches out the passer and congratulates him for the scoring pass. How players talk to each other is another way of showing respect and can strengthen or weaken a team's cohesion.

Establish the buddy system

You can pair up or "buddy up" rookies with veteran players or players who play the same position. The veteran player "coaches" the rookie during the game and in practices. The teammates are responsible for their buddy; they build a relationship with each other; they help each other; they look out for each other; they cheer for each other in a game; and on away trips, they will telephone each other to make sure they are awake and will be on time for meetings and bus departures. The older players can also pass down to the new players the team's tradition and the proper attitude to have to be successful. In this buddy-system environment, even the talented players start spending their free time teaching and coaching those who are less talented.

Note: Some questions for team building:
"Are you committed with your heart to the team?"
"Do you trust your teammates?"
"Do you encourage and support your teammates?"
"Do you care about your teammates?"
"Do you depend on your teammates?"
"Are you a 'me' or a 'we' player?"
"What is your personal long-term goal?"

■ RESULTS OF A COHESIVE TEAM

How a Cohesive Team Feels

A cohesive team ends up with a strong team spirit, high team morale, and a good chemistry that creates fun and a relaxed environment. A cohesive team is charged with energy and enthusiasm from feeding off one another and it has a feeling of confidence that nothing will separate them and nothing will defeat them. The two by-products of building a great cohesive team are maximum performance (good execution) and good morale (players are excited about being part of the team).

On a cohesive team, players feel wanted and part of the team, they feel important; they feel that teammates and coaches care; they feel "special"; they feel a part of something special; they have a feeling of excitement and passion for playing; and they feel safe.

Synergy of a Cohesive Team

When players work together, it is called teamwork, and the end result is "synergy," which means the total becomes more than the sum of the individual parts. Through strong cohesion, a smaller, weaker team can overcome an opposition team that is larger and stronger. Twenty players working together as a team will play like thirty players and will accomplish more than the twenty opposition players working individually.

The difference between a good team and a great team is that although both good and great teams have talent, both are in good condition, and both have good fundamentals, *great teams have teamwork*—they have an unselfish attitude. On a good team or an average team, the attitude is that everybody is willing to work to just support the team ("I'll do it, but I don't really want to"). Whereas on a great team, the attitude is that everyone is eager to give their best unselfishly for the good of the team. Without co-operation, there can be no "synergy"—and the result of synergy is that each player gathers strength from the others and everyone "soars."

TEAMWORK IS WHAT MAKES COMMON PEOPLE CAPABLE OF UNCOMMON RESULTS

12 DISCIPLINE AND ENFORCING TEAM RULES

This chapter deals only with discipline regarding team and practice rules. We have already talked about discipline in other forms, such as discipline in following the team's behaviour goals—self-control and staying focused during the game—and later in the book, we are going to talk about discipline in execution of the team's playing systems. And definitely, demonstrating the team behaviour goals and executing the team's playing systems will go a long way toward building a well-disciplined team. But discipline requires more precise guidelines for off-floor and on-floor behaviour, such as following team rules and practice rules, which you can discuss with your team in team meetings to create these lists of rules. As with all your team goals, team rules are more effective when the players decide upon them themselves. Once a team has agreed on its team rules, the players can work out the more practical aspects of applying them.

A team needs discipline—law and order—right from the start of the season because it is one of the greatest assets a successful team possesses. In the old days, discipline suggested the exclusive use of following rules, with physical punishment as motivators if the rules are broken. Today, discipline means: doing what you are expected to do; doing what you are supposed to do; doing what you are told to do; and even following a set of team rules but with the main consequence of taking away playing time as a motivator. Discipline does not require Coach to administer punishment or humiliation, but to teach, correct, and improve proper behaviour or the right action. The successful coach has this tremendous skill of disciplining players to motivate them.

■ GUIDELINES FOR SETTING TEAM RULES

To be a successful team, a team needs basic team rules to get the necessary results, such as to get everybody working together; to build good team morale; and to get everybody sacrificing for the team rather than acting on their own. Teams need two sets of rules: one set of general team rules guiding behaviour in all circumstances off the floor; and a second set, practice rules, dealing more specifically with behaviour during team practices. In either case, the rules should follow these basic guidelines:

> Team rules should be written out.

> Team rules should specify what players can or cannot do off the floor. Where possible, state the rules in positive terms—"Do's" rather than "Don'ts."

> Team rules should make everything clear: "Do it or don't play." If a player breaks a rule, he will know what the consequences are. Rules give players a choice, such as, be on time or don't play.

> Team rules are brief statements, with the most important ones listed first.

> One set of team rules is the standard for every player on the team. Every player is expected to abide by the rules.

> But keep in mind that team rules cannot be absolutely cut and dried; they must be taken on an individual basis. Rules should not paint a coach into a corner—there must be some flexibility for individual cases.

> Team rules are enforceable.

> Team rules are posted in the dressing room.

■ COMING UP WITH TEAM RULES

In coming up with team rules there are three approaches: dictator, laissez-faire, and democratic.

Dictator Approach

In the old days, the coach set the rules, and the players were to follow them and obey his orders. In this tight-control style of coaching, a coach uses his power or authority in a dictatorial way to control his team. He uses fear and threats to try to motivate his players. Players did it because the coach said so. The problem with this fear-based approach is players did it only to avoid punishment; plus, in this style of coaching, players work inwardly against the coach by resisting some of the rules. A coach cannot be in conflict with his players and expect to motivate them, too. Coach should not use his power to control, but he does need some control over his team.

Laissez-faire Approach

Another extreme type of discipline is the hands-off or laissez-faire approach where a coach either has no rules, or the players set them by themselves with no guidance from the coach—in which case, things might fall apart. It seems a lot of coaches want to be liked, but to be a successful coach, you have to let go of the need to be liked by your players. These coaches would look for ways to please all their players. They would even tolerate fighting, yelling, foul language, unacceptable behaviour, and bending of the rules—just to be liked. In this environment, players could do whatever they wanted; in other words, the players were controlling the team.

Democratic Approach

There is a third type of approach to setting team rules that is a little more moderate: the democratic or player-oriented style, where the coach works with the players and gives them more and more responsibility to shape their own rules within the team concept so that they feel they own the rules. Players still need a fence—a well-defined boundary—suggested by the coach, but with enough room for them to expand and grow. Remember, the coach's role is to help the players learn to make decisions on their own by providing an environment that allows them to do so. With the democratic approach, the coach might go to a group of senior players or leaders first to find out how they feel about certain rules before presenting them to the whole team.

Note: This democratic process works when a coach has established a trusting relationship with his players.

Deciding Team Rules in Team Meetings

Coach's responsibility is also to help guide players in establishing team rules in team meetings. You can talk about what previous, successful teams' team rules were. You can even get returning players who have previously played for you to talk about those former rules. The bottom line is, you ask the team: "What rules would you like?"

If you want to succeed as a coach, you have to play by the player's rules, not your rules. You can give them a few suggestions to pick from; then, the team works together with you to establish reasonable rules that are fair and firm.

When players have a say and input into the rules, they will have a greater investment and responsibility in carrying them out. Involving the entire team in forming the team rules places the responsibility where it belongs—on the players' shoulders. The rules become "our" rules and not just the coach's rules. As with the behaviour goals, players will now "police" or "govern" themselves regarding these team rules, not because they *have* to, but because they *want* to. The good teams are those that are capable of "policing" themselves; this means that you are not cast in the role of the "heavy" all the time.

The team prioritizes the team rules

Once the team has compiled a list of rules, they should prioritize them to emphasize what is most important about team rules and practice rules. When you have a final, prioritized list, make copies to hand out to all players, and put them in large print on posters to be posted in the dressing room. You can also have the players sign the list of rules so there will be no arguments later.

The team discusses the consequences for breaking team rules

Once the team rules are established, the team then discusses the kinds of consequences that it will use for those who break the rules. You as the coach have to do most of the disciplining, but for certain consequences, you have the team leaders or senior players discipline the violating players. When players help to set and enforce the rules it gives them ownership in the team and this reduces conduct detrimental to the team.

Coach constantly stresses the team rules

You have to talk to players for continually disobeying the team rules. Getting players to be disciplined does not happen overnight. You have to work a long time with players to get the proper behaviour.

■ TYPES OF TEAM RULES

No rules

Some coaches do not impose any specific rules. They trust and expect their players to behave a certain way and be accountable for their actions; they have expectations of what is expected of the players, such as "Do not embarrass the organization," or "Do what's right and avoid what's wrong."

Having no rules or guidelines can open the door to allowing players to do whatever they want, which leads to chaos and disorder—an undisciplined team.

Simple Rules for Dealing with People

Other coaches simply ask their players to be good ambassadors on behalf of their team by acting with a lot of "class": by doing what is right; by treating people the way you want to be treated; by being polite, courteous, and treating people with respect; by saying "hello" with the person's first name; by having manners, such as saying "please" and "thank you"; by saying "yes, sir" and "no, sir"; by looking people in the eye when talking to them; by smiling when meeting someone; by giving people a solid handshake; by being honest with people; by making people feel better; by being friendly to everyone, and by not swearing. Remember, the way you talk to others reflects the kind of person you are.

A Whole List of Rules

Other coaches like to have a whole list of rules for players to make everything clear, but coaches have got to be careful that they don't become a slave to the rules. Here, it depends on the age and maturity of the group. Maybe a coach can find a middle-of-the-road approach and have just a few rules. If your team has trouble coming up with rules, show them the list of possible team rules below, which may help to inspire them. Note the use of "we" in presenting the rules; this is important in promoting team unity and conformity with the rules.

Possible team rules

> We will be at all practices.

> We will be on time! We will be on time for practices, curfews, team meetings, bus trips, home games, and away games. We will be at the arena/gym one hour before the game.

> Everybody will be dressed in uniform and ready for the pre-game talk at the appointed time.

> Everybody will go out on the field/floor together for the pre-game warm-up.

> We will be at all practices even if injured.

> We will all travel together on the team bus, unless excused by the coach.

> We will listen to music on headphones in the dressing room and team bus trips.

> Even if we do not dress for the game, we still must come to the dressing room.

> We will get plenty of rest. We will look after ourselves by getting plenty of sleep the night before the game.

> We will eat right. Breakfast is the most important meal.

> We will avoid alcohol, drugs, and smoking. The consequence for anybody who is caught smoking, using drugs, or drinking alcohol will be automatic expulsion from the team.

> It is important how a team looks, so we will dress appropriately:

> "Look like a player; dress like a player; act like a player."

> "When players look good, they feel good; and when they feel good, they play good."

> "If we look like champions and act like champions, we will play like champions."

> We will take pride in our dressing room by keeping our team room neat and clean.

> We will pursue excellence in all areas of our life. We will be the best we can be by doing our best!

Other topics for discussion in this area of team rules are: earrings, ball caps worn at practice or before games, long hair, facial hair, tattoos, and rookie hazing.

Possible team practice rules

Team practices have to be orderly. Practice time is often limited, so a team needs practice rules to make the most effective use of the time available. You and your players can come up with a similar list specific to the needs of your team.

> ❯   We will be at all practices. If we cannot get to a practice, we will phone the coach and explain why.

> ❯   We will be on time for practice, dressed and ready to play. If we are going to be late, we will phone the coach.

> ❯   We will be serious in practice and not fool around.

> ❯   We will focus, pay attention, and look at the coach when he talks.

> ❯   We will stand at all times in practice. We will not sit down, lean against the boards or walls, or use other postures that show the weakness of being out of shape.

> ❯   We will leave the field/floor only when we have permission from the coach.

> ❯   We will drink water only as a team. We will each have our own water bottle.

> ❯   In sprint drills, we will touch lines.

> ❯   If we are injured, we still come to practice.

> ❯   We will wear practice uniforms in practice.

> ❯   We will take showers after practices and games.

> ❯   When the coach calls out, "Last man," we will hustle to wherever the coach is.

> ❯   We will always come to practice with a smile!

■ HOW COACH ENFORCES THE RULES

Coach Disciplines the Violator

When you have the responsibility of handing out discipline, you have to exercise self-discipline yourself. Handing out discipline is not fun. You have to control your own angry outbursts. You must understand that yelling and screaming at players is not the best means to create discipline, although players will certainly get the idea that you are upset.

Instead of getting angry, you simply let the violator know that you are disappointed with him when he didn't follow the rules and that he has let everyone down—which might be enough to make the offender feel bad. Hopefully, the offender will feel disappointed that he has let himself, you, and the team down; and will make up for it by going the extra mile in order to please you and his teammates. This is one of the best ways to discipline and motivate: the pain and guilt a player gets from knowing he has disappointed you and his teammates becomes the discipline.

Coach Must Be Ready to Be "Tested"

If a team has rules, a coach must expect that those rules will be broken by players, and one of his primary roles will then be to enforce the rules and dish out punishment when necessary. You must be ready to "stick to your guns" to gain respect of the players. You have to show you cannot be intimidated by anyone and you have the authority to handle the offenders. Some players will test you or challenge you by seeing how far you will let them bend the rules before you step in. If a player challenges you or undermines you and you let him get away with it, you might lose your control and the respect of the team. Your credibility as coach will be based on what you decide to do about players breaking rules. If players break a rule, they must be dealt with immediately with a stiff penalty—especially the first time it occurs, to prevent any repeat offences by other players. Coach knows that in the process of players' learning self-discipline, some are going to break the rules and will have to suffer the consequences.

Coach Enforces the Rules Fairly and Firmly

To create discipline on a team, the enforcement of the rules must be consistent, fair, and firm; no player is "above the law." Because the players have helped develop the rules, they know exactly what is expected of them. So, when they break a rule, they must be prepared to face the consequences. Players follow best and learn the most when treated with respect through guidance and fair, firm rules.

Your goal should be to have the respect of your players. Coaches are not always liked when they have to enforce team rules; enforcing rules is not fun. What matters is not that you are buddy-buddy; what matters is that you try to be fair and firm when enforcing the rules; and that you hold the players accountable. If you think you can please everybody and make everybody like you all the time, you are living in a dream world.

Note: Coaching is a balancing act between being a tough, hard-nosed person and a caring one. A coach must be strict on the rules and demanding to set the tone for discipline. The more demanding a coach is, the more he gets out of his players.

How Coach Treats His Players with Regard to the Rules

You should use a democratic approach to team rules, with no double standards or bending of the rules. You don't let the "stars" run the show, but you do work closely with them to see what they think of the rules. If the "stars" violate a team rule, which would set a poor example, you discipline them immediately to let everyone else know that there are no special privileges and that no player is above the rules. This is the real test of a coach because being consistent with rule-enforcement with all your players earns you the most important ingredient with your players: respect.

You can talk all you want, but talk is cheap. Punishment or real consequences lend force to your words. You might withhold privileges, such as not playing; or establish some sort of physical punishment to hold immature players or violators accountable for their actions. In handing out punishment, you should follow the rule of "treating others as you would like to be treated." You should treat your players the same way you would treat your own children when they were young. If the same player keeps breaking the team rules over and over again, he must be disciplined. People make decisions and choices every day, and with every decision, there are consequences; some are good and some are bad.

Be Flexible at Times When Enforcing the Rules

But having said this, team rules cannot be absolutely cut-and-dried. You cannot set rules that "put your back to the wall." You must state that most times players will be treated fairly, yet will not always be treated the same, because players are different. Fair does not necessarily mean the same treatment. For example, you might treat a player who you know is totally committed to the team differently than a player you know is not yet as committed to the team or is more of a problem player. You will also treat an experienced player who has played in the league for a long time differently than a rookie who is just starting his career. So, you do have the same set of rules, but you don't have the same set of consequences for everyone on the team. You will treat the last guy on the roster fairly, but you are going to have a different set of rules and standards than from the top player. You may bench a player for a period/quarter as his punishment for breaking a rule or you may bench him for the game.

You have to use your common sense and be flexible sometimes in dealing with individual cases when team rules are broken. You cannot tell players to be disciplined and self-controlled and expect them to be that way immediately, especially if they have been undisciplined and have lacked self-control all their lives. Once you get to know your players, you should be able to gauge what sort of response will have the most effect on an individual player. What is important is that everyone has to face some sort of consequence for breaking a rule.

Team Sets the Consequences

Your role as a rule enforcer can be made less onerous when the team itself, with your guidance and approval, decides what the consequences will be for rule infractions. Once the team rules are established, the team can discuss the kinds of punishment it will impose on those who break the rules.

If you and the team establish a set of team rules and their consequences, you must "deal with" them if the team rules are broken or violated. Dealing with the rules of the team is the major crux of coaching and discipline. By doing this, you should avoid a lot of discipline problems.

If the players do not obey the rules, the surest way of instilling discipline is through consequences. Some possible consequences follow.

The team fines the player

If they are older players, the players sometimes enforce the team and practice rules through fines. One example: For breaking certain rules, players have to put money into a team fund for a year-end party.

Coach gives verbal feedback

The most basic consequence for breaking rules is verbal punishment (lecturing—not yelling and screaming, criticizing, or scolding) or warnings (threats) from you; or you can give a certain look or stare to let the violator of the rule know you are angry with him for breaking the rule; it can even be simply expressed by the tone of your voice. Or you can just go for a walk with the player and talk about the problem. You can discuss why you are upset with him and explain that when you are hard on him, it is not personal, but just a way of bringing attention to his unacceptable behaviour.

Coach gives extra physical activity to player

Another type of consequence for breaking rules is having players perform some form of punishing physical activity to discipline them. A coach in this day and age has to be careful and aware of not crossing the line—definitely no physical abuse or hitting.

Some coaches instill discipline by just punishing the violator of the rule. For example, if a player is late for practice, the violator is punished by doing physical exercises such as running suicides, sprints, or push-ups to get the point across that if you are late you will be punished. Sprints would be timed and supervised by seniors and the captain. Or if a player is slow getting to the team circle on the call "Last Man" by the coach, they do ten push-ups; and so on.

Some coaches like to use the "team concept" when instilling discipline. That is, "If one dies, we all die"; or, "We are all in this together." So, if one player is late for practice, the whole team is punished, even though the rest of the team was on time. This is the same concept that if one player blows his responsibility on the floor, we all pay the price.

Some coaches don't use physical activity for violation of rules because they feel players will learn to hate the sport. And those who usually use sprints, not as a consequence for breaking rules, but as a means of improving players' conditioning, may not want players to associate sprints with punishment.

These concerns should be discussed with the team before they decide on the types of extra physical activity they think should be used as a consequence for breaking rules, if at all. Imposing extra physical activity is perhaps the most widespread means of controlling player behaviour or punishing violators, but again might not be the best.

Coach takes away playing time

Another type of consequence for breaking a rule continually is to take away a privilege; usually this means taking away playing time by benching a player. It seems that selfish acts or decisions, lack of self-control, lack of concentration, and laziness are the main causes for the disciplinary action of benching. The only thing you really have as a weapon for discipline is "the hammer"—control of playing time. Players want to play. They don't want to be kept out of the game. Removing a privilege tends to be more effective in instilling discipline than extra physical activity or verbal criticism. If a player is benched for breaking a rule, he shouldn't take it personally, since all decisions on discipline are for the betterment of the team by teaching discipline. This way you and the players strive to have co-operation rather than confrontation.

Coach does not allow player to dress for the game

Not dressing for the next game is a little more extreme than taking away a privilege, but it has to be done for breaking rules continually or if a player misses practices continually. One of the big problems or dilemmas a coach will face is when a star player violates a team rule. The question then becomes: Do you enforce it and suspend him—which will hurt your team's chances of winning—or do you let him play? But be aware that if you sit out a good player, you are punishing the whole team, so you might consider other ways of punishing him, such as running suicides.

IF YOU DO NOT PRACTISE, YOU DO NOT PLAY

Coach removes player from the team

This is a "last-resort" measure, but it does happen. There are certain players who just don't want to do what is expected of them. It is difficult to give up on these players, because they are usually the ones who most need your guidance and help. These kinds of players often come from unstable homes and have trouble trusting people. They may try to test you to see how long you will stick with them. These individuals can really test your patience, but if you persevere and do win their trust, you can have a profoundly positive impact on their lives; and that is very gratifying. However, you must develop your own gauge for what you are willing to tolerate and for how long.

In the past, when coaches had a few hot-headed players, they would just get rid of them. Today, it is better to work with these players to try to make them into good citizens. Coaches can use sports to teach life lessons. But if a player continues to break the rules despite your best efforts, if she is having a negative effect on the rest of the team, or if she is engaging in behaviour that is harmful or dangerous to herself or other team members, you must consider this option of removing her from the team.

One bad apple spoils the whole bunch

■ DISCIPLINE

The main objective of having discipline is you want control; players function best within a structured environment. Players want clearly defined rules, guidelines, and principles to give order to the team because without rules, there is chaos and disorder. You don't discipline to show how much power you have. Discipline has more to do with control than power. You discipline to bring order to the team; you either have control over the team, or the players do.

Notes: The discipline from team rules and team practice rules does carry over into games. If a team can be disciplined off the floor, it can be disciplined on the floor.

Discipline could be called "tough love" because a coach does not discipline his players because he hates them, or because he wants to show them who the boss is; he disciplines them because he loves them and wants to make them successful.

Use Discipline to Teach

Another objective of discipline is to teach players or to get a point across. Players must suffer consequences for violation of team rules by having a privilege or playing time taken away. You never punish a player; the offender or violator chooses to be punished by his actions. For example, a player chooses not to play in a game when he chooses to arrive late for a game or practice. Discipline teaches players how to be successful in life. If the consequence for breaking a team rule will teach a valuable lesson and make the offender a better person, then a coach has properly used discipline.

Note: Discipline does not have to be, for the most part, associated with physical punishment, intimidation, or anger.

Use discipline to teach self-discipline

Another objective of rules is to help players develop self-discipline and self-control. The key to self-discipline is the ability to make the right choices, such as the ability to control an emotional outburst by stopping or delaying it.

Self-discipline involves players doing what has to be done rather than what they would like to do. Self-disciplined players develop a mental toughness to do what they have to do, even when they don't want to do it. Self-discipline gets players to practice and games on time; it drives them to practise hard when they don't want to; and it makes them finish the job when they are tired and exhausted.

Use discipline to teach the team concept

One approach to rule-breaking is if one player is late for practice, all players are punished. This idea is to teach the "team concept"; that is, "If one dies, we all die; if one is late, we all are punished." If one player blows his responsibility on the floor, we all pay the price. Players have to know that it takes a complete "team" effort from everyone to be successful.

Note: If a player is late, he is telling the rest of the team that he is more important than them. He is also saying that he is special, that he walks to his own beat, the world revolves around his schedule, and everyone else isn't important. It also reveals a lack of respect for others and a lack of discipline.

Use Discipline to Change Improper Behaviour

Changing players' improper behaviour, i.e., teaching them how to behave properly, takes time, caring, patience, and consequences. If the team creates the team rules, and you consistently enforce them, this is the foundation for building discipline. Violators must suffer the consequences if they continue breaking the rules. If a player shows up late to a meeting you have to make a decision right then and there to talk to him or discipline him for breaking a team rule. Or you may give a player one or two chances when making the same mistake, after which, you have to start disciplining him.

Note: If you have players who break the rules all the time, you have three options: 1) you can cut him; 2) you can ignore his bad behaviour and keep him by turning your head and ignoring the bad behaviour so as not to force the issue (but here the players will start to control the team rather than your controlling the team); or 3) you can keep him and work with him, which will involve a lot of frustration and work in trying to establish discipline. But this is the only approach where you can make a difference in the player's life by teaching life skills, such as self-discipline, a proper work ethic, self-control, etc., that will make him not only a good player, but a good citizen and successful in life.

PART THREE

THE ART OF MOTIVATION THROUGH PLANNING AND TEACHING STRATEGIES

13 ORGANIZING, PREPARING, AND PLANNING THE SEASON AND THE GAME PLAN

Another way a successful coach motivates his players is by using his organizational and planning skills. A good, organized plan helps you know where you are going for the entire season and also helps the players know where they are going. You must control time, or it will control you; and it seems good luck follows those who plan their time wisely.

The only way you can control time is by being organized and having a set of prioritized lists. Most coaches are list-makers, and the very act of making a list of priorities can often clarify or define a coach's plan. This helps her know what she wants to accomplish for the season, month, week, and day.

A key difference between coaches who are successful and coaches who aren't is not just talent but preparation. Preparation is the most important thing you can do. Good preparation—a good season plan, a good pre-game plan, a good practice plan, a good game plan—gives a team a quiet, confident manner.

To develop or build a winning program, you must have the ability to plan the season; you must understand that you win as an organization, not just as a team; you must be very organized down to the smallest detail; and you must evaluate everything and everybody in the organization, addressing such questions as, "How do we travel? What will our dress code be on the road and at home? Where will we eat when on the road? Is the trainer and equipment guy doing his job?"

PREPARATION IS THE MOST IMPORTANT THING YOU CAN DO

Pre-season Plan

When forming your pre-season plan, write down training camp dates, exhibition game dates, then work practices around the exhibition games. It is a good idea to know how many practice days there are before the first league game.

Personal invitation to training camp

You should never assume players will automatically try out for the team. You have to make sure you do your homework by personally getting in touch with all potential players. These potential players want to feel that they are wanted. So, you have to make sure all of them have been invited personally, face-to-face, or have been at least given a written or an email invitation.

Coaches' meeting

You have to arrange a meeting with your assistant coaches and manager. In this meeting, you challenge each other about how they teach the skills and the type of systems they want to run and you challenge their point of view to see how strong they believe in it. It is important to establish with all your assistant coaches a comfort zone where they know they can speak their minds. This meeting with your coaches is to make sure everybody is on the same page, because you do not want coaches to contradict one another—players will become confused, not knowing which coach to believe.

Prior to the training camp, you get the assistant coaches to outline the specific skills they are going to teach that the players need to be successful. Then you get them to document the practice drills they will use to develop these skills, stating the amount of time devoted to these individual skills. After the meeting, your responsibility is to make a task-priority checklist, prioritizing how best to spend your time and energy in practice.

Task-priority checklist for training camp

> Pre-season talk to team
> Physical checkups: team physician checks players out
> Battery of tests to measure speed, quickness, strength, flexibility, and endurance:
>   • Two-mile run timed, twelve-minute run, or Beep (fitness tests)
>   • Some teams require players to run a six-minute mile before they are allowed to practise
>   • Run a distance of the length of arena or field ten times (test speed, 400 yards, partners)
>   • Flexibility tests
>   • Five-minute strength test
>   • "Defensive square drill" to work on lateral motion and quickness of feet
> Hand out practice uniforms: shorts, t-shirts
> Goals of pre-season practices:
>   • Pick team.
>   • Avoid losing any players through injuries. Conditioning goal is to get the team ready for the first game. To teach players how to run properly, bring in track coach.
>   • Improve fundamental skills.

- • Teach basic team systems.
- • Build confidence.
- › Make sure players stretch together fifteen minutes before every practice.

In every practice, the players should work on the fundamentals of their sport. In lacrosse these would be:

- › Passing
- › Form shooting—work on shooting technique by shooting at "shooting boards"
- › One-on-one offence
- › One-on-one defence
- › Loose balls
- › Four-on-four defensive shell drill

Coach should also have a list of things he wants to cover over the length of the pre-season.

Guidelines for training camp practices

- › You figure out how many weeks or pre-season practices you have from training camp to the first league game.
- › You should know what you want to install before the first league game. For example:
  - • First week—install man-to-man offence, man-to-man defence, and fast-break systems
  - • Second week—install specialty teams: Power Play and Man Short
  - • Third week—install zone offence and zone defence
- › You have to be aware that from the very beginning of training camp, the good team starts to become a physical team and to receive leadership from the better or experienced players.
- › You also have to be aware that training camp tells a lot about your team, about its spirit, its toughness, its camaraderie, and its desire to win. On a good team, the competition for positions is fierce. You see players shouting and motivating each other, players trying to cheat in a drill to get a head start, everyone fighting for a job, and players loud-mouthing each other; and because of the physical contact, there are some fights and a lot of pushing and shoving, players making threats and refusing to talk to each other for a while.

    It might be insignificant, but it seems that on a losing team, there aren't many fights in training camp; there is no pushing, fighting, or shoving. There aren't enough players with mean streaks; there aren't enough players hitting other guys hard.

> You want competition at every position. You tell some players that they have the starting position and it is their position to lose. You tell other players that the position is wide open for anybody to take.

> Remember, the first day of training camp for a rookie is the most important day for him. So, how rookies are treated on the first day means a lot. You should make them feel wanted, as their confidence may be lacking.

> The practice time for the first day of training camp is four hours.

> The team practises twice a day, once in equipment and once without equipment. There is a "no equipment" practice for two hours in the morning, including a walk-through of the systems and basic fundamentals, and an equipment practice for two hours in the afternoon, including a scrimmage. In the evening, the team has a one-hour team meeting.
>   **Note:** Something to think about: There is no evidence that double daily, hard training sessions enhance fitness and performance more than single daily sessions.

> At the very beginning of the pre-season training camp, you want it to be like a marine basic training camp with all-out warfare. You want to make it as difficult as possible, so as to test character and mental toughness. You need to see if the players are tough enough to survive the fatigue, the physical hitting, the all-out running, the aggressiveness on loose balls, and the pain. You do not want a "walk-in-the-park" attitude. You want the pre-season practices to set high standards by being much tougher than any game the team is likely to play during the season. You may have to tell players that they are not good enough to play— not because of lack of talent, but because of lack of effort.

> The first practice is the most important practice of the year, as you set the tone for the season; you have as many players trying out as possible because with the large number of potential players, they all know they will have to work hard to make the team; and you can set the tone on how tough it is going to be. If players slack off, you can get rid of them right away.

> You also want to test the players' fitness level (sprint drills, agility drills) and, at the same time, get them in shape.

> You do a lot of teaching of basic fundamentals and your systems. The slogan for pre-season camp is: "Those who remain will be champions."
>   **Note:** At the beginning of the season, Coach should stress defence more than offence so that when practising offence, it will be harder against a good defence.

> Over a long period of time during training camp, you should have a

"routine-buster"; i.e., taking a break from practice and at the same time do some team building. You can take the team bowling, golfing, to a paintball park, or a water park. Just make sure the activity builds closeness and a bond.

ON A GOOD TEAM, THE COMPETITION FOR POSITIONS IS FIERCE

Team meeting

After the team has been picked, you set up a team meeting. At this first team meeting, you work with the players to devise a long-term season outcome goal—where they think the team should realistically end up in the standings. You talk about your philosophy of coaching and the type of playing systems you want the players to play. You then go over a basic list of behaviour and performance goals with the players and have them come up with their own list. The group discusses and establishes the team rules and practice rules, and the consequences if they are broken. You can influence or guide the team with regard to the goals and rules by stating what last year's team did or what successful teams do. Next, with your help, the players come up with a theme for the season.

Pre-season or exhibition games

Pre-season games are used to evaluate and learn about your team's strengths and weaknesses. In pre-season games, you can either gain or lose confidence. So, you should pick exhibition games that are big enough to be a good battle, but provide a good possibility for your team to win, thereby building confidence. In the pre-season, if you play against a good team, you have to remind your team that if they want to be a contender for the championship, this is the type of team they have to be competitive with. You are hoping to build the character of the team by the third pre-season game.

The pre-season speech

At the beginning of the pre-season talk, you must show the team you mean business. When speaking, you should raise your voice, lower it, or pause to let the message sink in. You should be passionate about the team when speaking, using words that come from the heart. You must make sure all the players are listening and looking at you when you speak. Use the "we-form" instead of the "I-form" when you talk to the team; you are talking on behalf of everybody in the organization—yourself, the assistant coaches, the training staff, and the manager. To sell the program, in your talk you must be totally prepared with notes or three to five major points of your message. But remember: "selling the program and the season" most often comes down to listening to the players' concerns or identifying their priorities.

Your first talk at training camp is about family and you use the term "family," because it gives the players a sense of belonging to a special group who will give support, love, and encouragement. You want to make players feel they are a part of the team right away.

Tell them to call you "Coach," or by your first name, or Mr. So-and-so, depending on the age group.

> ***The season will be like climbing a mountain***
>> You talk about the season being like climbing a mountain to plant a flag on the summit. Of course with mountain climbing, the higher you go, the more treacherous and dangerous it gets, so you have to be even more focused as you climb the mountain. If you lose your focus for even a second, it could cost you your life. Even focusing on the summit (future) and not focusing on the next step (present) can be devastating. It's the ability to focus on the precious present moment that is critical.

> ***Coach believes the season will be won in training camp***
>> You believe the season will be won before it even begins, in training camp, where coaches and players set the tone for the season through their hard work and commitment.

> ***The intermediate goal of winning the league***
>> You don't have to start out talking about winning the championship, but it could be implied. You talk about attaining the intermediate goal of winning their league or making the playoffs, which will put them in a position of going after and playing for the championship.

> ***"We will treat everybody honestly"***
>> Our main principle as a team is "we will treat everybody honestly"; and in return, we expect everyone to be honest with us.

> ***What to expect from the coach—his philosophy***
>> You should tell the team what to expect from you—your philosophy, such as "We are not going to yell at you, we are not going to rant and rave, because that is not our style. But we will be hard on you, pushing you and challenging you."

> ***Respect***
>> You ask the players the question: "How do you get respect?" You get respect by treating others the way you want to be treated; by being honest; by showing kindness and consideration; and by accepting others for who they are. The coach tells the players, "Respect is a two-way street. While I am trying to earn your respect, you also have to work to earn my respect."

> ***Coach will look after players***

You will try to keep the players happy as much as possible, within limits.

> ### *Players must give the team first priority for the season*
> You expect players to sacrifice themselves for the team and give total dedication. They must make some sacrifices by giving up individual goals in order to reach a much bigger team goal.

> ### *Coach will treat players fairly*
> You must make no promises you cannot keep. Players have to know they have to earn a spot on the team and earn playing time, and that not everybody will get equal playing time, which is just a fact of life. If a player through his hard work and excellent performance demonstrates he deserves playing time, he will get it. Players must understand that you will probably not treat an experienced player the same way as a rookie. Even though you will treat players differently, you will treat them fairly.

TRYING TO PLEASE EVERYONE IS A FORMULA FOR FAILURE

> ### *"How good do you want to be?"*
> "Do you want to be an average team or do you want to rise above the pack? Do you want to cross the line and become an elite team? That's a decision that you and only you can make. There is a fine line between being good and being great. Are you willing to do what is necessary to be great? Are you willing to work hard and sacrifice for this team?"

> ### *"How committed are you?"*
> There must be "total commitment" from all players to the team. You can ask every player on the team, "Are you committed to the team?" "Are you committed to three practices and two game days per week?" Players must give the team first priority for the season, which means sacrificing themselves for the team and giving total dedication. Commitment is what a player does between games and practices that will tell the difference: good sleep, good nutrition, no drugs, no alcohol, no smoking.

> ### *Tradition*
> "This organization has been built on a successful tradition over the years. Players are coming into a first-class program: best uniforms, best travel, best training staff, best owner, and best coaching. We run a first-class program. We believe in doing the little things perfectly. Therefore, the way you act, the way you dress, the way you present yourself as a team must be professional."

> ***Coach wants players with a positive attitude***
>
> You do not want your players to have a negative or neutral attitude. Neutral is not good. Players with a neutral outlook are complacent and unenthusiastic about playing. Players who are positive get excited, are totally committed and enthusiastic. Your team has to play the game with emotion, passion, and with "fire in its eyes." You want players who hate to lose.

> ***Team meetings***
>
> If this team wants to be successful, it needs goals: a long-term season outcome goal, short-term game performance goals, short-term game behaviour goals and cohesive goals; a theme for the season; practice rules and team rules. The team has got to develop a winning attitude, and that means self-discipline. In order to develop self-discipline, players have to make some rules and be committed to them and to each other. Tell the players if they break the team rules, they will be held accountable and will be dealt a consequence.

> ***This is going to be a very "special" team***
>
> "This team is going on a journey in pursuit of winning the championship and this is how we are going to do it. This team is going to be successful because it has got the talent; it has a great mix of youth and experienced players; it has players that have special gifts; it has players who were born to be great players; it has many players coming from a winning program; it is going to grow as a team; and it is going to have a lot of fun this year. And with the right game plan and attitude, there is no reason why this team cannot win a championship. We are going to give you our best, 100 percent, and in return, we expect you to give your best, 100 percent, back. This team is not going to be ordinary, it is not going to be average, it is going to be something special."

Pre-season formal interview questions

Ask the players:

> What they liked about last year's team

> What things bothered them the most about the team last year

> What are some things they would do to improve this team from last year

> What we can do to have an advantage over all the rest of the teams this year

> What they think should be the team goals for this year

> How they see their role on this team

> What their personal goals for the season are

> What they think is their biggest weakness

> What they think is their biggest strength

> ❯ What are some things they can do to improve themselves
> ❯ What Coach can do to make them happy
> ❯ What Coach can say or do that will help motivate them
> ❯ How Coach did things last year

◼ HOW A COACH ORGANIZES THE SEASON

Season Plan

The season plan starts with having the right long-term season outcome goal and then laying out a plan on how to get there. The season plan is connected with the behaviour goals, which give hope through the rough times, and the performance goals, which give measurement feedback for motivation.

To make up a season plan, you first make a calendar of league games and key dates as reference points. Then you add practice-time dates to the schedule. Finally, you put all deadlines and important dates or problem dates on the calendar, such as holidays, long weekends, or special events, such as school formals and graduation. Big calendars help you see the big picture: where to add or delete practices; where to give time off for rest; and where to anticipate scheduling problems. Remember, the season is a long haul, so you should take the pulse of the team to see if they need a rest or need to be pushed more.

Lists for the Season

> ❯ A prioritized list of positive team performance goals
> ❯ A prioritized list of positive team behaviour goals
> ❯ A list of why a team reaches its potential
> ❯ A list of "whatever it takes" to be successful
> ❯ A list of keys to victory
> ❯ A list of philosophy of coaching
> ❯ A list of Coach's game plan, including a list of fears of certain opponents
> ❯ A list of principles in running a good practice
> ❯ A list of Coach's fundamentals: 1) passing; 2) catching; 3) one-on-one offence; 4) one-on-one defence; 5) shooting; 6) loose balls
> ❯ A list of Coach's systems: offensive strategy, defensive strategy, fast-break strategy, power play, man short
> ❯ A list of components that make a good pre-game talk, between-period talk, post-game talk
> ❯ A list of good, nutritious foods

> ❯ A list of principles for a good weight-training program
> ❯ A list of types of endurance training
> ❯ A list of eight strategies of mental preparation to get a player ready to play
> ❯ A list of things a player can do during a game to help him play to his potential
> ❯ A list of the main rules of the game
> ❯ A list of team rules
> ❯ A list of practice rules
> ❯ A list of things to do when going on the road

Breaking the Season into Steps

To make things even simpler, you can use the principle of "divide and conquer" by breaking up the season into steps, such as knowing the number of games from training camp until the first league game; number of days from the beginning of the season to the championship game; when you reach the quarter-mark of the season, the half-way mark, the three-quarter-mark of the season, and the playoffs. Even going into the playoffs, you can break them down into one-game segments rather than looking at all the games to get to the championship game. By breaking the big picture into manageable steps, it becomes less intimidating and this helps the team to focus on immediate goals and gives them a better sense of control—and therefore less pressure.

Monthly or weekly plan

You can use the monthly calendar system to check the progress of the team to see if it is headed in the right direction. Some coaches divide the season into a specific number of games, such as ten-game segments, or into a weekly schedule, or into quarter, half, three-quarters of the season schedule.

Another idea is using the number of days, rather than number of games or months, before the championship game. You can talk to the team about giving a commitment for the next ninety days leading up to the championship game. Later in the season, you can point out that there are only thirty days left before the championship game. And finally . . . zero days left.

Practice plan

The practice plan is a daily list of things to do in practice. You should use the 80/20 rule here, to make sure you spend most of your practice time working on the drills that give you the greatest return for your time. You set a time schedule for all drills; and use your statistics from the last game to plan practices, because game statistics will reflect what your team has to work on to become better. You should have a few specific goals for each practice, such as a specific skill development, loose balls, fun, conditioning, or strategy. The practice should also reinforce your style of team play. When the practice is over, you should write up an evaluation of the practice for future reference.

Game Plan

A game plan involves specific strategies for dealing with specific opponents.

Note: Why do some teams consistently win more games than others? Is it good luck (possibly); leadership (definitely); great players (absolutely); or preparation (absolutely)?

How a coach prepares a strong game plan

A good game plan keeps the team organized and prepared for each game. As a successful coach, you motivate your team for the game by having them prepared not just on game day, but the twenty-four hours preceding the game.

Here are two sayings to remember: "If you fail to prepare, you are preparing to fail," and, "The coach who is prepared has the battle half fought." You might be out-coached or outworked now and then, but you should never be out-prepared. Games are won and lost in preparation—no team can perform under pressure without preparation.

It takes an enormous amount of organization and time to put a game plan together, but you simply have to be organized and prepared for everything.

A good game plan is "the reduction of uncertainty," which is the absolute essence of coaching. When players know what they have to do and what the opposition is going to do, they will be more relaxed. It's like knowing the answers to a test before writing it. A well-prepared team will approach every game in a state of total confidence and will feel it has a great chance of being successful as long as it plays hard, plays together, plays smart, and has fun. A team will not need much coaching during the game if it is totally prepared. What the team does during the game is what you prepared them for in practice.

The team's game plan becomes almost like a routine or ritual where players have a pre-planned set of steps. It makes much more sense to plan ahead than to wait until the heat of the battle to devise a strategy. For a team to be successful, talent alone is not enough; hard work is not enough; strategy is not enough; and emotion is not enough; preparation and execution are two of the primary factors in a team's success.

Create "good pressure"

It might appear that pressure is a bad thing: racing heart, sweaty palms, tight muscles, and "butterflies" in the stomach, but pressure is necessary for players to play their best, as it is preparing them for the "fight." "Good pressure" occurs when a team is prepared—and being prepared is one way to combat stress as it reduces uncertainty.

"Good pressure" is what players feel when they know what to expect and what to do. "Bad pressure" or stress is something a team feels when it is not prepared.

Pay complete attention to the last detail

The best coaches are masters of detail. As a regular part of your game plan, you must learn to pay attention to the small details that other coaches might neglect. You and your staff have to know exactly what you want to do and how to get it done. You also want every player to understand the game plan and be able to execute it so there is no second-guessing about what everybody has to do. You take nothing for granted, you leave nothing to chance; you are prepared down to the last detail for everything and anything. So check and recheck the game plan and reinforce it to the players.

Prepare for the unexpected

Good coaches stick to their organized game plan. You must believe in your game plan, seldom doubt it, and never panic. It is your responsibility to lower the impact of unexpected situations, surprises, and distractions on the team during the game. You definitely do not want any surprises during the game so you are always anticipating the worst things that can happen and you develop a plan for them. You should have a planned set of steps for unexpected situations; in other words, you expect the best, but you are prepared for the worst.

In your game plan, you should have a list of questions to ask the players to prepare them for every "what if" situation there is and how they are going to react to each one. A well-coached team is never surprised and is ready to adapt to anything it sees. You should know what your players are afraid of and be prepared for it. The more planning you do, the more confidence your team will have going into the game. You expect the unexpected by out-preparing the opposition coach and planning for everything that could go wrong. Then in the actual game you must be willing to throw the whole game plan out the window and wing it, or at least change it or adjust to unexpected problems. Always have a backup plan.

IF YOU FAIL TO PREPARE, YOU ARE PREPARING TO FAIL

Talk about the opposition's strengths and weaknesses

The better your players are prepared, the better they can anticipate what is going to happen. You cannot control what the opposition is going to do, but you can make sure that your team has the "edge" by being fully prepared for their opponent for every game. Knowing what the opposition is thinking, their tendencies, or what they are about to do gives a team a tremendous advantage. By finding out as much as you can about the opposition, your players are able to anticipate what is going to happen before it happens.

Knowing about the opposition gives the team confidence. It's the "knowing"—knowing exactly what you're going to do to "stop" or "score" against the opposition that helps build the team's confidence. In essence, when the players totally understand the opposition, they can confidently focus on themselves. If you know your opponents' past performances, you can predict to a certain degree their future performance.

You should use as many strategies as possible to give your team an advantage in knowing as much about the opponent as possible. You can get all the facts about the opposition through statistical analysis; through scouting reports (best scorers, best passers, weakness of goalie); through watching game films or videos (seeing opponents in action gives the players a better understanding of them); by asking players who played with or against them; and by observing them during warm-ups (seeing where the shooters are shooting and where the goalie appears weak).

Talk about the team's strengths

Your focus in the game plan is only on what you can control. You need a plan of attack based on your own team's strengths to be successful. You should be more concerned with what your team can do offensively, defensively, and on special teams than with what the opposition does. Remember it is bad news to overestimate your own players' abilities or to underestimate the opposition.

14 BEING A GOOD TEACHER OF FUNDAMENTALS AND LIFE VALUES

■ TEACHING FUNDAMENTAL SKILLS

The successful coach has to have the great skill of plain old teaching to make his players better. There is no question that good coaching is good teaching, and learning improves if you use the basic teaching principles. The learning process is also influenced by what you do: What types of standards you set; how patient you are; how you react to mistakes; how enthusiastic you are; and how you give feedback. If you can't teach, you can't motivate, and therefore, you can't lead.

Good Teaching Principles

> You explain or give instructions in a skill
> You or player demonstrates a skill
> Player executes or practises the skill
> Player talks out loud during drills
> You watch, analyze, and give verbal feedback
> You ask questions to correct mistakes
> You use visual feedback from videos to teach

Coach Is Patient in Teaching Fundamentals

You understand that learning a skill is a slow and laborious process, and that it takes time to learn and grow. In teaching a skill, it helps if you have a tremendous amount of patience as players go through their growing pains. You cannot expect players to learn the correct way immediately.

The problem with young people is inconsistency. One day, they look great, the next day they stink. Inconsistencies drive coaches crazy. You must understand that young players need time to develop into the accomplished players they are going to be. It's as much about maturing as a person as it is about maturing as a player.

You may lose control and get angry or upset now and then, but do not give in to it on a daily basis. You know that different players learn in different ways and at different rates. Some players will pick up the skill immediately, while others will have a tougher time.

You have to understand that there are different ways of executing a technique—different ways of passing, of shooting, etc. There might be a certain technique a coach likes to teach, but if a player can execute the skill a little differently and get good results, do not change his technique. Do not be a coach that says, "Do it my way or else." In teaching techniques, you have to be a little more flexible as there isn't just isn't one way to do things. Even with great players, you have to let them do what comes naturally to them. Coaching or teaching great players is more like a partnership than a teacher-student relationship.

Coach Transmits Knowledge Successfully

There is no question: As a coach you have to be able to teach the game. You can have plenty of knowledge of your sport, but your teaching ability will be judged by what your players know. The most important aspect of teaching is being able to translate knowledge into action. You may be the most knowledgeable coach in the world, but if the players on your team cannot translate that knowledge into action, your expertise means nothing. So, to be a good teacher you have to be able to present what you know in an informative, enthusiastic, and interesting way so players can understand what you are talking about.

> ## IT'S NOT HOW MUCH YOU KNOW; IT'S WHAT YOUR PLAYERS CAN DO

Coach Is Tolerant of Mistakes

You can also create a learning environment of support and security by your attitude toward mistakes. When teaching skills, you strive for perfect execution through repetition, concentration, and high intensity; but mistakes are a big part of the learning process. How you respond to mistakes when players are learning a skill is important: If you get upset over mistakes, players will find it difficult to understand and learn because your negative emotion adds pressure to them. When teaching a skill, you must expect some failure at the beginning. You know that making mistakes is the only way to make progress, so you cannot get upset over them. Mistakes give the players feedback that they have to do something differently. Trial and error is one of the most common ways to learn a skill. In turn, with your positive attitude about mistakes, players will not be afraid to make mistakes and in return they will become risk-takers.

Note: A good coach compares her players only with themselves. She does not compare players with other players.

Coach Believes in His Players

You have to believe in and see potential in players and be willing to suffer through players' growing pains. This belief makes players confident about themselves and in turn motivates them to become better. A good coach can take a bunch of unathletic guys and, by believing in them, seeing potential in them, teaching the skills of the game, and helping them understand the game, make them play it better, faster, and quicker.

Coach Sets High Standards
When Teaching Fundamentals

You have to set high playing standards and have high behaviour expectations; in other words, you expect a lot from your players. It's not so much what a player does, but how he does it.

Coach Gives His Players Confidence

Is the fundamental skill problem one of technique or of confidence? You should teach skills as a confidence issue rather than a technical one. Your job is to give your players confidence in executing a skill. The problem could look like one of technique, but it might be a confidence issue. When dealing with skill problems or mistakes, you should follow the 90/10 rule: If there is a problem, and 90 percent of the problem is technique and 10 percent is with the player, then *find out what is preventing a player from performing the skill by working on his personal problem or confidence problem first*, and you will find that most of the problems with technique will go away.

■ THE FIVE STYLES OF LEARNING

Teaching fundamentals does not come under the heading, "one size fits all." Players learn by different teaching styles, so it is your job as a coach to find out what teaching style works best for each player. If you have to tell a player over and over again to do something, and he still can't do it, maybe you will have to find a different method to get your message across.

One player might understand better by watching a video; one might learn better when the skill is physically demonstrated to him; and one might remember better if he sees it on paper. You must understand that the learning process is influenced by players' different learning styles. By knowing this and by using different methods of teaching, you will be able to help everyone, and all players will learn more quickly.

The Five Learning Styles

> Auditory learners
>> Some players learn better by hearing the explanation of the skill, by hearing verbal correction feedback after making a mistake, and by hearing verbal praise for doing the skill right.

> Visual learners
>> Some players learn better by seeing a demonstration of the skill, or watching videos of the perfect skill, or a video of themselves doing it. They learn by your showing, on the blackboard, a play or how the system works.

> Kinesthetic learners
>> Most players learn best by doing or practising the skill, with high repetition in practice and from playing. They do not learn from listening to you talking. You can explain the drill, laying it out on the blackboard, and then take the players out on the floor and repeat what was on the blackboard over and over again. Doing has a much bigger impact than showing. In fact, the greatest teacher is the game: Players learn through playing experience what works and what doesn't work.

> Verbalizing learners
>> Some players learn better by saying keywords to themselves or out loud as they are doing the skill in practice or in a game.

> Reading learners
>> Some players learn better by reading about the skill from written handouts or a play book.

Players Learn Better By:

> Remembering 20 percent of what they hear (lecture, explanation of skill)

> Remembering 30 percent of what they see (demonstration, audiovisual)

> Remembering 50 percent of what they see and hear together

> Remembering 60 percent of what they see, hear, and do (practising)

> Remembering 70 percent of what they see, hear, and say (verbalizing keywords for the skill)

> Remembering 90 percent of what they see, hear, say, and do

When players can execute the skill instinctively and without thinking, they have learned the skill.

Notes: Players can also learn by asking questions and watching films on their own.

Sometimes learning becomes more effective if the coach uses the "buddy system," putting weaker-skilled players with stronger-skilled players to teach the skill. Players are sometimes less intimidated working with a teammate than with the coach. In addition, teaching a skill this way helps the teacher-player learn the skill better, too.

■ THE LEARNING PROCESS

When you teach a skill or a play, you sometimes get nothing but blank stares, as though nothing you are saying is registering with the players. So the question is: are they bad students, or are you a bad teacher? Which is it?

Players develop barriers that slow the learning process, such as poor concentration, distractions, not listening or understanding, fear of mistakes, low self-esteem, stress and anxiety, information overload, a low level of willpower, and no will to succeed (motivation).

How the Player Helps the Learning Process

How many times does a player not know what he is doing in a drill or play right after the coach explained it? Is the player listening or hearing? Hearing is just noise passing over the eardrums; hearing is passive; hearing is when the listener doesn't concentrate on or understand what is said.

One of the keys to learning is the ability to listen. When a player listens, he gives total concentration to understand what is being said. He has to "will" himself to hold his focus by thinking of one thing and blocking out everything else. Players have to fight to keep their minds from wandering; from losing their concentration; and from letting distractions interfere with their concentration.

Listening is hard work, because it takes a lot of work to concentrate and understand what a person is saying. If the player listens and still doesn't understand, it is his responsibility to ask questions to learn. It also helps you out, after you explain something, if the players give immediate feedback that they understand by nodding with their heads. Or you can ask if they understood.

Character players are coachable because: they want to learn and work hard to get better; they take advice willingly; they are humble when they are given instructions and don't have the attitude that they think they know it all; they admit when they make an error and correct it without making excuses; and they have the ability to take criticism without looking for an alibi because they realize they have weaknesses.

Although the responsibility for learning lies with the player more than the coach, the coach can certainly help the process.

Note: "There is no such thing as a bad student, only a bad teacher." From the movie *The Karate Kid*.

How Coach Can Help the Learning Process

The key to learning is listening; so first you have to make sure the players are aware of what listening consists of. Listening is giving the speaker total concentration and nothing else. Players have to learn to not only listen, but understand what is said. When teaching, if you feel the players are losing their focus, you can use humour to combat this.

You must have complete knowledge of the sport. This is important to learning, but isn't the secret to it. You must know how to teach and explain the skills. This is also important to learning, but isn't the secret to learning. You must know what special words you can use to help the players learn more quickly. This is also important to learning, but isn't the secret to learning. You must know what drills you can use. This is important to learning, but this also isn't the secret to learning.

One of the main secrets to learning is: You have to know what the standards (quality reps, done perfectly, intensity level) are for the skill and the drills to help teach the skill. The other secret to learning is you have to make the players aware of their own motivation—wanting to better themselves to play the game. Although you have the responsibility to motivate and help players learn, players have to take on more of the responsibility to learn so that they can perform at their peak every game.

Mental Preparation for Learning

You can help players prepare mind and body for learning. There are certain strategies players can use to put their minds in the best possible state for learning —the "zone" (feel confident, relaxed, can anticipate, totally focused, and enjoy playing):

> Deep breathing for maximum efficiency

> Muscle relaxation exercises

> Visualizing past successes or seeing themselves executing the skill perfectly

> Positive self-talk and positive self-affirmations: "I can"; "I will"

■ THE TEACHING PROCESS

We have already stated that good coaches motivate through plain old teaching principles. And teaching is like learning: there isn't just one way to do it. You have to start from scratch when teaching fundamentals and systems and leave nothing to chance. You must assume players know nothing and teach them everything, paying close attention to detail, as there can be no grey areas where players are left confused.

Good coaching is taking something very sophisticated, very complex, and presenting it in a very interesting and simple way to keep the players' attention and to help them *understand!* You should communicate and teach with excitement and enthusiasm because you have to show you love what you are doing and you want to make it fun to learn and inspire players to want to get better. Even when you go over the same things time and time again, you should never lose your enthusiasm or patience. Learning improves if you use these basic teaching principles below. And before teaching a skill, you have to have some sort of vision, idea, or goal of how the skill is performed.

Note: The difference between showing and teaching is that showing is just demonstrating the skill; teaching, however, is explaining the skill, making it interesting, demonstrating it, and giving feedback.

■ EXPLANATION OR INSTRUCTIONS OF A SKILL BY COACH

The Whole-Part-Whole Method of Teaching

As just stated, good teaching is the ability to take something very complicated and make it simple to understand. You do this by breaking down a skill into simple parts for better learning. You present the skill in a step-by-step progression, using the whole-part-whole method: When teaching a skill, let the players practise the whole skill first, then break down the whole skill into simpler parts with a step-by-step progression so that they understand the skill's mechanics. Players must understand the whole picture before they can understand the parts.

Keep Instructions Brief and Clear

Explaining how the skill works is extremely important in the learning process, along with the demonstration. You should have a list of the main points and use them as a checklist for each skill. Explain the list of terminology used in the skill so that everybody will understand the terms used. You should not use jargon that players won't understand or use complicated words to impress them, but don't talk down to them, either. You should talk to players in such a way that they can understand what you are saying.

Also, keep the instructions brief, simple, and clear. Stress only three or four key teaching points, as most people have short attention spans for learning. It is important for you not to give too much information or too many reminders or tips—otherwise known as "paralysis by analysis"—as this will result in players being totally confused by all this information overload.

The lecture or instructional method is the most widely used teaching method, but it is not the most effective in learning. Players are active people and learn best that way, so keep them active by keeping them involved when you explain the skill. When you give instructions, tell the players what you want: "Do this," rather than what you don't want: "Don't do this," as players may end up focusing on the wrong thing.

THE KEY TO LEARNING IS LISTENING

Explain the "Why"

In the old-school of teaching, the coach simply told the players what to do and how to do it and how they were supposed to do it. Today, players want to know the reason they are doing the skill or understand why they are being asked to do something a certain way. By empowering players by letting them in on your thought process—for example, why we are doing this drill—you are including them in on what you are trying to accomplish.

Knowing "why," players also learn faster and retain information longer if they understand how the specific skill being taught relates to the whole playing system; it deepens their determination to do things right, whether it's a drill or a skill.

Encourage Players to Ask Questions

An important part of the learning process is to encourage players to ask questions, especially when they don't totally understand something. The more questions the players ask, the more they clear up any misunderstandings, and the more they will learn and understand.

Ask Questions to Get a Point Across

Coaching in sport is instruction-based. You show and tell players to do something in the way you want it done. But when you tell a player to do something, "I want you to do it this way," and the player doesn't fully accept the way you want him to do it, his skill or performance might not improve. But if you ask, "Will you do it this way?" and the player agrees to do it that way, he then takes on the responsibility of fully doing it.

You can also ask players questions to make sure they understand what you are saying and what is expected of them. Some coaches like to ask questions just to make sure that all the players are paying attention to what she is saying, i.e., to see if they are listening and if they understand the skill.

Look at the Players' Eyes to See if They Understand

You get the players' attention by getting them to look at you while talking. By continually making eye contact, "reading" their eyes, and "reading" their body language, you can tell if each player in the group is comprehending what you are talking about.

Use the Buddy System

When teaching a skill, you can put a senior with a rookie to act like a mentor or teacher to pass on his knowledge and experience. "You push your buddy, he pushes you." Buddies help each other out and challenge one another in practice. Also, using the buddy system develops the team faster by utilizing the talents of the more experienced players. You should feel that leadership is everyone's role on the team.

■ DEMONSTRATION OF A SKILL BY COACH OR PLAYER

Coach Demonstrates the Whole Skill So Players See It

Actually, it is better if the coach can show the players what to do rather than just telling them what to do, as it sometimes falls on deaf ears. It is so much more inspiring to the players when the coach can himself do what he wants them to do. Players would rather be inspired by the coach showing them how it is done than being corrected by the coach all the time.

First, demonstrate or show the whole skill a player will do in a game. You can explain some of the major points of the skill as the skill is being demonstrated, but remember to talk less and demonstrate more. The demonstrator can start with a slow demonstration then follow it by a full-speed demonstration.

Make Sure the Technique Is Demonstrated Correctly

You should show the correct technique then let the players copy or imitate it. Players can learn through observation and imitation. By watching a skill being demonstrated, players learn without knowing they are learning.

A coach should not demonstrate the skill unless he can do it perfectly. You want the players to get a perfect picture in their minds of how the skill is performed.

Using Videos as a Training Tool

You can even make up individual videos of each player so they can see themselves through the eyes of the coach. During the season, make videotapes that include mistakes you think players can improve on—for example, weak passing or good execution of the skill you are trying to teach. The best way to get a point across is to show a video of the player doing the skill incorrectly or correctly on the floor. A video is worth a thousand words.

Note: Watching game film on their own is one of the best ways for players to learn.

■ EXECUTION OR PRACTISING THE SKILL

Use Visualization

Have the skill demonstrated; then, ask the players to close their eyes and "picture" and "feel" themselves executing the skill perfectly. They can pretend they are watching a videotape of themselves, "from the outside," or they can imagine how the skill actually feels "from the inside."

Practise to Get the Feel of the Skill

Getting a "feel" for the skill is a type of feedback. Once a player understands what they have to do to execute the skill, they then have to physically practise it. In the practice stage, the player gets a "feel" of what it's like to throw a ball or to shoot a puck correctly. Another form of feedback is to see the result of a pass or a shot—that is, whether it goes where the players want it to go. If it goes where they want it to go, then they get the feeling of how it feels to throw or shoot with good results.

Stress Technique over Results at First When Practising

You should first stress the correct *technique* of shooting over the end *result*—hitting the target—for a beginning player to start to learn the skill. Here, the players might do the shooting skill slowly, at first, to get the correct shooting form.

Once the shooting technique is correct, the next progression is the feedback of seeing the result of the shot—that is, whether it goes where the player wants it to go: accuracy. If the shot goes where the player wants it to go, then he gets the feeling of how it feels to shoot with good results.

You should use drills that are not only challenging to players, but also allow them to experience success.

PERFECT PRACTICE MAKES PERFECT

Repetition Is a Key to Learning

Skills cannot be performed correctly without practising. So, repetition is a key to learning. Players learn by lots of repetition in practice. You know the more number of touches a player gets in practice, the more he will improve doing the skill right.

Repetition also builds good habits and confidence. Players learn by doing rather than standing around listening to you. Coaches have a tendency to talk too much, so they should be silent for a while and let the players do the skill, complemented by verbal feedback. There are no shortcuts in the development of skills.

Use Intuition and Science

Good coaching is both artistic and scientific. The scientific part of coaching involves making decisions based on what has worked before. These decisions come from your experience of knowing that certain progressions and certain principles help a player learn better and faster. The artistic part of coaching can kick in when you have tried every scientific principle to teach a skill but with poor results; sometimes you have to rely on intuition to figure out how to get a point across.

Use Progression in Practising the Skill

Develop a progression for practising the skill. For example, the progression for shooting might go something like this:

1. Form or proper technique first: Forget whether the player scores or hits the net.

2. Next, accuracy: Do not worry about the hardness—the intensity—of a shot until the player can hit the target. Here, the player learns what a good shot feels like.

3. Next is power: Work on getting power into the shot. Player can increase the hardness and speed of the shot until he starts to lose his accuracy; but never sacrifice accuracy for hardness. End up practising the shot at game speed, but if he is doing it wrong, have him slow down.

4. Finally, the last stage of learning occurs when the player does not think about technique. He just does it unconsciously and shoots: the result is that the ball goes where it is supposed to go.

    Note: Skills should be executed in a smooth, effortless fashion. If a skill is executed in a jerky manner, find the cause and correct it.

Have Players Talk Out Loud

As players do the skill, you can give them key words to say out loud to help them remember a certain point in executing the skill. For example, while doing a defensive drill, the players can say out loud, "Down, down" to remind them to stay down while in the defensive stance.

■ WATCHING, ANALYZING, AND GIVING VERBAL FEEDBACK

To correct what a player is doing wrong or to reinforce what a player is doing right, you must understand the mechanics of the skill yourself, from your experience gained by being involved in the sport. You should know exactly what a perfectly executed skill looks like. The better you understand the mechanics of a skill, the better you can analyze and thereby correct or suggest. Once you know the problem, it is easy to find the solution.

Learning is 70 percent feedback. How you teach a skill affects the learning of the skill by as much as 30 percent. But giving feedback to a player executing the skill affects the learning of the skill much more—by as much as 70 percent. Having a goal for how to do a skill right points players in the right direction, but it's the coaching, the watching, the analyzing, and the correcting every day that makes the difference. To get better at a skill, you have to teach and teach, and give continuous feedback and reinforcement.

In the old method of giving feedback, the coach just gave the players his opinion about the mistake so as to be in control of the situation or to display his superior knowledge. This technique produced minimal improvement.

Note: Learning works best by praise and repetition. After a mistake, players do not learn as well through criticism as they do through positive reinforcement.

Remember: In learning a skill, correcting the mistake is more important than focusing on the mistake itself.

Common Causes of Mistakes in Skills

> Player has bad form or mechanical problems; this is the most common cause.

> Player has poor timing; the player's mind and body are totally out of sync.

> Player has poor concentration and lets distractions get to him.

> Player didn't understand the instructions, or misunderstood or forgot them.

> Player received too much information and got confused.

> Player is nervous.

> Player tries too hard and ends up practising "tight."

> Player does not try hard enough.

> Player is afraid of making a mistake.

> Player is tired.

> Player is not developed mentally.

> Player puts constant pressure on himself to perform well.

You Must Give Verbal Feedback

Verbal feedback occurs when you tell a player whether he is doing the skill right or wrong. Feedback refers to anything you do to increase the chance of the player's repeating the skill properly or decreasing the chance of his repeating the skill incorrectly. Feedback is where the real coaching is done. It is the most important step in teaching, yet the step most often forgotten.

You have to be realistic and honest in giving feedback. You don't tell players what you think they want to hear; you tell them whether they are doing the skill right or not. If they are doing the skill incorrectly or poorly, the skill needs to be fine-tuned or changed completely. And for this, you need patience. You might lose control and get upset now and then, but you shouldn't make it a regular occurrence. Ranting and raving about a dropped pass is not good coaching—it just makes things worse. You can demand the best from players, but not by screaming, ridicule, or demeaning remarks. To be effective, use a soft voice.

Note: The amount of individual attention given to an individual player will vary depending on whether the player is a starter or an experienced player, versus a substitute player or a rookie; and whether he is highly skilled versus poorly skilled.

Remember: If you never provide your players with any feedback—either positive or negative—how will they know if they are developing or improving?

Types of Feedback

To change a bad technique, such as doing a skill wrong, you should give 60 percent of your feedback as correction or instruction feedback. To reinforce a good technique, such as doing a skill right, you should give 30 percent of your feedback as praise, encouragement, or compliments. To change a bad technique, such as doing a skill wrong, you should give 10 percent of your feedback as "criticism."

So: The ratio of praise and encouragement to criticism is 3 to 1. You should praise (30 percent) three times more than you criticize (10 percent); and you should correct twice as much (60 percent) as you praise (30 percent).

Remember: With regard to feedback, some players respond best to praise, while others need to be pushed harder. So, as a coach you have to figure out whom you can yell at and to whom you can talk calmly to get your message across.

Correction feedback after a mistake is made

The goal of coaching is to get players to perform in a certain way, while building their confidence. As a coach, you are always looking to correct: correcting techniques and fundamentals; correcting getting to spots and timing with regard to executing plays; and correcting behaviour on the floor. You cannot allow mistakes to go uncorrected. You have to point out in a warm, friendly manner how to correct these mistakes, making sure you point out to the players what they did wrong and tell them how you want them to do it the next time. "Bobby, I want you to follow through more." Players should want you to correct their mistakes, because this will make them better players. The real power in coaching comes when you partner up with the player to work together to correct the mistake, versus just criticizing him.

LEARNING A SKILL IS GREATLY INFLUENCED BY FEEDBACK

Some things you can do to help correct mistakes:

> Follow some sort of a checklist as a guideline when analyzing and correcting the player's mechanics.

> Keep things simple when correcting. The mistake is often a minor problem and might need only a small adjustment. You should not panic and try to change the player's whole technique.

> If a player is doing the skill wrong or making a mistake, stop practising the skill immediately and correct the mistake by giving correction feedback—telling her how to do it right.

> *How* you say it when correcting a mistake is sometimes more important than what you say. You should try not to yell, or otherwise show you are upset, when giving corrective instructions to a player. Rather, you should talk to the player in a normal, supportive, friendly voice so he can listen and learn. A lot of the message comes from the tone of your voice and your body language. Negative criticism is sometimes useful, but not during drills when a player is making a sincere effort to improve. You may end up frustrating him and making things worse.

> Remind the player not to try to force the skill; trying too hard to make it happen makes it worse—she should just relax and concentrate.

> Sometimes give advice or make suggestions rather than telling the player what to do; e.g., "Why don't you try it this way?" rather than "Do it this way."

> Show and explain specifically how to do the skill right, such as, when throwing a low pass, say, "Release the ball farther behind your head" rather than telling a player to do the skill better in a general way by

saying simply, "Get your pass up."

> Have the player work on the skill alone after practice. If the technical problem is catching, for instance, after practice you can work with the player's mechanics while he practises catching an extra hundred passes.

> If a player has a mechanical problem, it might arise from worrying about a particular aspect of the skill. In these cases, get the player to focus on a different aspect of the skill rather than worrying about making the mistake. For instance, if the skill is receiving the ball, the problem may arise from the player's fear of failing to catch the ball. The player might be dropping the ball because he is focusing too much on the results. Getting the player to concentrate on the ball by focusing on the number of times the ball rotates relaxes him, and he'll forget to worry about catching it.

> If the mistake happens on the practice floor, stop the action—never play through a mistake. Pull the player aside, get her to explain what she thinks she did wrong; or explain the mistake to her and then move on.

> Focus on what *you* have to do to help the player do the skill right rather than blaming the player for not doing it right.

Note: What about players who practise conservatively and never make mistakes in practices? You have to encourage them to play aggressively without worrying about making mistakes. You can also help this situation by telling players that you want them to make mistakes every day in practice so they can figure out how to handle them in an actual game situation.

The "sandwich" approach to correction feedback

First, you give one positive comment, complimenting the player's performance or what he did well: "Bob, that was a good pass."

Next, give corrective information by telling the player specifically how to fix the mistake or problem: "And if you follow through straight ahead, you will be even more accurate." Remember, when correcting, to tell the player what you want him to do, not what you don't want him to do.

Then finish with a word of encouragement or another compliment: "Bob, that was much better, keep it up!"

When using the "sandwich approach," you should stay away from the word "but" after giving the first compliment. Why? Because the only thing the player will hear is the criticism after the "but." So, replace the word "but" with the word "and," and the player will hear both the compliment for his effort *and* the corrective information on how to improve his mistake. "But" usually precedes negative news and cancels out what is said before it, whereas "and" encourages co-operation.

Remember: If the last thought you give a player is negative, negative things happen. If the last thing you say to a player is positive, positive thoughts happen.

Give positive reinforcement or praise

Positive feedback or reinforcement is verbal approval, praise, recognition, encouragement, or compliments from you to a player for doing something right. It is the most powerful way you can reinforce the proper execution of a skill if you want to see it repeated. Examples of words and phrases to use: "Way to go," "Great job," "Well done," "Outstanding," "Excellent," "Fantastic," "Awesome," "Not bad," "Terrific," "You worked hard," "Keep working," "I knew you could do it," "I'm proud of you."

Positive reinforcement also includes non-verbal reinforcements such as pats on the back, smiles, touches, attention, nods, thumbs-up, fists, winks, applause, or hugs.

You should build on players' strengths, not on their weaknesses; and build on good execution, not poor execution. Positive feedback—praise—is a powerful tool for motivating players to try harder, learn faster, and improve. You make players feel appreciated and valued by praising them. Everyone loves to hear compliments that they are doing well.

However, it is human nature to be more critical than positive. You have to learn to catch yourself when you start criticizing your players too often, because this will certainly destroy their self-confidence. You avoid getting upset or critical when a player cannot execute the skill. You just have to do a better job of teaching. But you can get upset or critical when players lose their focus (not paying attention or fooling around) and when they practise the skill with no effort (lackadaisical, not serious).

How to give positive reinforcement or praise for good skill execution:

> Praise immediately, in front of the team, and make it personal by calling the player by his first name. The rule of thumb is to praise in public and criticize in private.

> Follow the rules of effective praising—be specific, be sincere, and give the praise as soon as possible after the desired skill occurs.

> When giving praise, try to also provide players with useful and meaningful information, as players want to know how they're doing.

> Try to "catch" a player doing the skill right and reward him rather than looking for mistakes all the time; don't wait for the player to execute the skill *perfectly* to give praise. *Any time you see improvement or progress in a skill, you should give praise right away.* Coaches find that telling players "what they are doing right" does make a positive difference in their learning curve.

> Communicate praise and criticism in the same respectful way and do not focus on one more than the other.

> Use a mixture of positive and negative reinforcement, but praise should outweigh criticism by a three-to-one ratio. Too much praise loses its effectiveness; too much criticism destroys players' confidence.

> Help players focus on improving rather than dwelling on what they did wrong. You should work the "Five-minute drill": For five minutes, you will force yourself to only tell or praise players for what they are doing right. You will give no correction or criticism feedback for mistakes.

> Be careful not to over-praise; it might wear out its effectiveness. You should not praise players if they didn't do anything to earn it. Give praise only when there's a good reason for it to make it meaningful. Be sincere with your praise or keep quiet.

> When giving praise, focus as much on effort and hard work as much as the right skill execution to make players feel good! When players are rewarded for good effort, they feel good.

> You can even write words of encouragement on a card and leave it in his dressing stall—or, in this day and age, send an email or a text message—to let a player know he is doing a good job and is appreciated for his effort. This helps the player's confidence level rise and inspires him to do more.

THE BOTTOM LINE FOR A COACH IS TO BUILD CONFIDENCE, NOT TEAR IT DOWN

Negative feedback or criticism

You must give negative reinforcement or criticism only periodically after a player makes a mistake in doing a skill.

Negative verbal feedback occurs when you criticize, yell, or use a harsh tone with a player for making a technical mistake mainly due to lack of effort or focus. Remember, we are building confidence as we teach skills. And if you are hard on players, you might destroy confidence rather than build it.

Obviously, you have to be able to tell a player who executes a skill wrong that it is wrong. You cannot beat around the bush or sugarcoat criticism—you have to give honest, constructive criticism, no matter how uncomfortable it is, by telling the player what he needs to hear. But criticism can be delivered in a positive manner by letting a player know that you believe in her and you are here to help her improve. And remember: Both *what* you say and *how* you say it are very important.

Criticism is used in an attempt to correct or point out mistakes or weaknesses. Remember, you don't want to destroy a player's confidence—you just want to give him an objective assessment of his problem. It seems coaches are always looking for mistakes. Constant emphasis on the negative over a long period of time is the least effective way to motivate players, as it creates a pessimistic environment that douses the fire of enthusiasm. Besides, negative criticism can cause negative thoughts, which creates fear. Eventually, all you become is a "loud radio" that players want to turn off.

But negative feedback can be useful sometimes if done infrequently for impact. If you are going to criticize or yell at a player, you must make sure the player understands that you are criticizing the skill (e.g., poor shooting), not him personally ("lazy," "stupid"). You must make the player realize that you are criticizing only the execution of the skill.

When you do give negative reinforcement, there is no room for excuses by the player. For him, it is a wake-up call.

> Use the "sandwich approach." When you give criticism feedback, be sure to use "the sandwich approach"—you begin with a positive comment, follow it with the criticism for making the mistake, and then finish with a word of encouragement.

> Explain why you are hard on players. If you are "hard" on certain players because you want to help them become better, you should take the time to first build a relationship and then explain why you are being hard on them. You must make it clear that if you yell at them, it doesn't mean you are angry at them or dislike them; you are just trying to help them by correcting their mechanics. So the players shouldn't take the yelling personally.

> Sometimes when you give lots of technical and negative feedback to some players, those players feel they are being "picked on," even if you are doing it in a kind way. They still might not readily accept the criticism, even though they know you care. Again, you must explain: "The reason a player is criticized more than others is because you care about him." That is why you are hard on everybody on the team: you care for everybody. If you don't say anything to players, the players could take it to mean you don't care about them and they should worry.

When you feel there is a need to be extremely hard on a player, the best way to do it is face-to-face and in private.

Results of criticism or negative feedback

> Yelling and criticizing can motivate players in the short run if done sparingly.

> You have to know how your players react to criticism. You can be hard on some players all day and it won't bother them a bit, while with other players you have to be careful with what and how you say it, as it will bother them.

> Yelling and criticizing over a long period of time will make players mentally tired. Before long they "tune you out" or just become numb.

> Yelling and criticizing can be devastating to certain players, especially those who are hard on themselves, those who are just learning the

sport, and those who do not have mental toughness.

> In general, yelling and screaming makes players tense and angry, and makes them feel stupid. They usually end up no longer trying.

> Yelling and criticizing creates a fear of failure and decreases the enjoyment of practising the skill. The player who practises with a high fear of failure is motivated to have a successful practice, not by a positive desire to enjoy the practice, but from fear of the coach's criticism. The fear of failure is a player's worst enemy.

> By criticizing poor skills all the time, coaches will put so much pressure on the players not to make a mistake that they will practise "tight" or will always be worrying about making mistakes. The result is they will not practise with the risk-taking attitude they need. When players fear making mistakes, they will play it safe and end up making mistakes. They need the freedom to make mistakes in order to learn.

> Criticism causes negative thoughts, which create fear; fear causes tension; and tension produces mistakes. It is also important to know how much criticism each player can take.

PRAISE IN PUBLIC, CRITICIZE IN PRIVATE

Types of feedback that hurt the learning process

> Wrong feedback. Some coaches give the wrong information to correct a mistake. This definitely hurts learning more than anything else. Coaches who pat players on the back or give praise for executing the skill wrong or making a mistake sends the wrong message.

> No-response feedback. There are coaches who don't say anything; delay their feedback for a long period of time; or miss the mistake. If it was a poorly done skill, it will continue because it wasn't corrected, or the player didn't know he had done badly. If the skill was executed perfectly, it might not happen again because he might not know it was done perfectly.

> Too much feedback. Some coaches give too much information, called "paralysis by analysis," which also hurts the learning process.

You Ask Questions to Correct a Mistake

Telling players to do something in a certain way does not always cause them to do it. For example, when correcting a player who has a hard time catching the ball you can command him to just "Watch the ball" to help him catch it. Does this actually help a player to do so? If not, what does?

You could ask the player to "Give" with his stick to cushion the impact of the ball, or, "Count the number of times the ball revolves"; these specific instructions might remind him to watch the ball more carefully, which will help him to catch the ball better.

Or when a player takes a bad shot, you try to deal with this problem by giving a technical correction or telling him what he did wrong. If you tell the player what he did wrong, you are blaming the player for making the mistake. You are tackling the symptom, the mistake, and not the cause, the correction. The best way to correct the problem is to ask the player questions, because now you present yourself as a partner in correcting the mistake: "What do we have to do to get you a better shot?" "How far did you miss the open spot?" "How was the defender playing you?" By asking questions, you get your player to think about the problem herself and to perform above what she is capable of performing.

The most effective type of feedback is when the question is subjective. You ask questions to get the defensive player's point of view: "Why did you do it that way?" "By doing it that way, what does it achieve?" "What are some major points you should stress on defending a shooter?" These types of questions promote learning, and a player's performance improves, as he has to think before he can answer. When you are asking questions, you should seek facts as input to make players think. So players' answers should be descriptive and ideally should set you up to ask another question.

Use Visual Feedback from Videos

Analyze the opposition

Another use of videos is analyzing the opposition. Here the team watches and studies the opposition and relates it to their own team's performance. Players watch to see how to beat or stop an opponent. By showing the team everything the opposition does takes the mystery away from the opposition and answers questions on why they are so good at what they do.

A VIDEO IS WORTH A THOUSAND WORDS

Players analyze their own performance

You can use video to instill discipline and teach by analyzing what a player does. You can make up individual videos of each player so he sees himself through the eyes of the coach. During the season, you can make videotapes that include mistakes you think a player can improve on; for example, weak passing. Here, the player watches himself perform and actually *sees for himself* the mistakes he made during the game. This is a great opportunity for self-evaluation, as videos don't lie.

Another approach of using a video is to let a player see himself doing good things on tape: big plays, great shots, great defence, and fighting for loose balls. This video is shown when the player is not playing well; or just before the play-offs when he needs a boost to make him feel good about himself. You, through this highlight video, can remind the player how well he has played before. The idea is to put the player in a confident and positive frame of mind so he will play better and make him feel he can be one of the best players in the league.

Show special movies to motivate the team

You can show all the different sports triumphs: the U.S. Olympic basketball team winning gold; the Boston Celtics winning the NBA championship; the Green Bay Packers winning the Super Bowl; the Chicago Bulls with Michael Jordan winning the NBA championship; and so on.

Once in a while, before a big game, coaches have been known to show videos with a message from movies, such as *Gladiator* and *Braveheart*, to get their team fired up.

■ TEACHING VALUES AND LIFE SKILLS

One of the pleasures of coaching is the opportunity to have a positive influence on players' lives beyond the playing floor/field. The positive habits players develop in learning a sport and playing with a team will stand them in good stead in other aspects of their lives. You can use sports to teach the lessons of life.

In a coaching career, you are bound to experience the thorny question of whether or not to keep badly behaved players on your team. If you keep them on the team, you can at least try to work with them to mend their ways. But if you kick a player off the team for poor behaviour, this player may not have another chance to learn these valuable life values or lessons. Rather than get rid of a bad player, you should use this opportunity to help him or her become a better person.

You have to look at the big picture. What can kids take away from sports to help them become successful and fulfilled in life? Some such qualities would be: remaining physically active throughout life; learning to bounce back from difficulties; discovering how to support other people within a team concept; learning to be honest and trustworthy.

The Problems of Today's Players

In North America today, sports are given a lot of attention, even at the children's level. Gifted athletes get awards, scholarships, huge salaries, multi-million-dollar advertising contracts. They become celebrities. Many young, talented players grow up pampered by society and get special treatment. They are protected and cared for by coaches and parents. Conversely, all this emphasis on athletic achievement can put an unbearable amount of pressure on young athletes, causing psychological problems and vulnerability. Without proper guidance, they can become very self-centred and start to believe that the rules of society and common courtesy are meant for everyone else but them. Self-destructive behaviour such as substance abuse is an extreme consequence. You have a big responsibility not only to assist players to perform at their best, but also to help them avoid these negative consequences.

The Best Way to Teach Life Values

One of the best ways you can teach life values is by being a good role model. Players imitate their coaches and parents. They may inherit talent, but character must be learned by example. You motivate by teaching your players how to be successful through your own hard work and perseverance.

Here are some other ways you can teach life values:

› Through positive reinforcement of good behaviour

› By talking about life skills and how to be a good person

› By sharing life situations from articles in magazines and newspapers to illustrate how ordinary people overcome obstacles and disasters to become successful

› By bringing role models to practices to talk about how to be successful. These role models can be people whom the players look up to; people who had adversity in their lives and became successful; people from whom they can learn. You can use successful people as both an educational and a motivational tool for your players by getting players to look at specific traits that made them successful. How hard did they work? What did they have to do to overcome adversity? How much persistence did they show? These role models motivate by illustrating that it was their choice to be successful.

15 RUNNING A GOOD PRACTICE

■ COACH'S PRACTICE GOALS

The main focus of a successful practice is players hustling with intensity and concentration, exactly as they would in a game. The goals:

> ❯ To develop a positive practice environment that fosters learning and develops confidence

> ❯ To teach and improve fundamentals and skill development; you must stress the correct technique

> ❯ To establish a team system on offence and defence that is coordinated: You must stress execution and timing on offence and positioning on defence.

> ❯ To get players in shape by using good training habits and good physical conditioning drills. A good team goal is "to be the best conditioned team in the country." At the end of practice, the team should be near exhaustion.

> ❯ To make practices fun

> ❯ To increase speed. You run fast drills, with players running from one drill to the next quickly, to get players thinking quickly and to help them improve in speedy movement. The ratio of mental quickness to physical quickness is 4 to 1.

> ❯ To create mental and physical discipline in practice

> ❯ To encourage players to set three personal goals to work on for each practice

■ COACH'S PRACTICE PHILOSOPHY

Written Practice Plan

The written practice plan is a list of things to cover in practice. You set an exact time schedule for all drills, moving quickly from drill to drill. This plan is like a "security blanket," as it keeps you on track with regard to time and what to cover in the practice.

Players Need to Focus in Practice

Your main agenda in practice is intensity and staying focused on the present moment. You want players to put total pressure on every shot, every loose ball—just as though it were a game. To be a serious playoff contender, a player needs to play as well in practice as she would in a game.

You should never allow a carelessly thrown pass or a dropped ball that's a mental mistake.

You don't want players to just show up for practice and neglect the little things.

You want your players to have their mind on business—staying focused in sports is an ability; it is not easy to stay focused, because there are so many distractions.

Be Enthusiastic and Optimistic in Practice

It is the coach's energy and passion that make the difference between a dynamic practice and an ordinary practice. The players will feed off the excitement and energy of the coach. The coach, through her enthusiasm, energy, passion, and excitement, will generate a great practice atmosphere; the result is that the players will enjoy practices. This high level of energy about the team, for the game, and about the practice will be contagious; the players will pick up on this enthusiasm and they will practise full of motivation and energy.

Note: Remember to smile more in practice, show a sense of humour, and joke around with your players.

Better and Better Every Day

You always expect more from your team because you know teams never play a perfect game. There is always something they can improve on. In practices, you should always demand quality execution, because there is always some slippage in games due to the pressure of the game.

You must strive for continual daily improvement. A skill is never perfect—there is always something a player can do to improve to make it a little bit better. The successful teams do things a little bit better every day because they follow the "little bit more" principle. During the season, you must continue to teach and work on the little things, the little basics that people neglect and slowly get away from as the season progresses. You don't want sloppily executed fundamentals and drills. To get this quality, you have to make sure every detail is carried out properly, moving at the right speed so that the players can handle the fundamentals and team systems to build their confidence. If you move too fast, the players will get frustrated and lose their confidence. It's not so much what you do, but how you do it!

You also must keep the plays simple so you have more time to rep them in practice, which in turn gives your players better execution. Even though the opposition knows what you are trying to do, you can still out-execute them because of these high repetitions.

WANTING TO WIN AND PREPARING TO WIN ARE TWO DIFFERENT THINGS

Practice Determines the Way the Team Plays the Game

Your practices must reinforce the philosophy that "the way a team practises is the way it plays"; or, "a team practises to be the best," because the way you conduct your practices determines how your players will play in a game. You must conduct quality practices, ensuring that your team practises hard and plays hard. Your team must believe its practices are harder than those of any other team in the country. You want to get across the idea to your players that "they have to work for everything."

Explain to your players that the reason you are hard on them is to make them better players and to develop mental toughness. You do a lot of talking during practice to push your players. You do whatever it takes to ready your players for combat and to win the war. Because you are hard on your players, you must make it clear to them that you care about them.

You have to tell players what your expectations are in practice, and if the players constantly do otherwise, they will have to sit out the practice. If you set practice rules, you have to back them up with consequences. You cannot waste your time by threatening players in practices. Sometimes it is necessary to yell, just to get a point across. However, make sure you have your emotions under control.

Note: Tell the players that if they are tough on themselves in practice, the game will be much easier.

Note: Give frequent water breaks to the whole team. Players are allowed to drink as much as they want, but together. Plenty of liquid prevents fatigue and dehydration. Players will not get "waterlogged" by drinking a lot.

Explain Your Playing Philosophy

During practice, give your players your offensive and defensive philosophy and tell them that you want it done your way. Explain to them why you want it done this way. You can't expect players to do it simply because you've told them; you must explain the purpose of your systems.

Create a Good Learning Environment

A good coach creates a good learning environment in his practices that allows players to succeed. You have to make sure there are no distractions, there is good lighting, and that all the necessary equipment is ready for practice. You also must be aware of people in the stands who are distracting your players. And you must come to practice in your coaching gear rather than your regular street clothes. This creates a professional environment where players feel this is serious business.

Expect Problems Every Day in Practice

It is a good idea to expect three to four problems every practice, so that when they happen, you don't overreact. You face the problems calmly and confidently.

How Coach Turns a Bad Practice into a Good Practice

> When players have a bad practice, it is usually because you have had a bad practice. It is your fault. You have to go on the floor/field with enthusiasm and excitement, the necessary ingredients to get things done at a high intensity. It is your job to fire up the players at practice to make exhausting hours of practice fun.

> During a bad practice, you have to pull your leaders aside and tell them you are going to need them right now to turn this practice around. Give them the idea that we are "losing" this practice right now and we have to come back stronger in the second half of the practice to "win."

> If having a bad practice, just stop the practice and have a team meeting. You can even go so far as to take the team into the dressing room, just as though they are losing a game and it's the end of the period. In this so-called between-period talk, explain that it is like they are down by a few goals in a real game and they need to get their act together and get control of the game. This is a good time to reinforce how to recover in the middle of a game when playing poorly.

> When practice is going badly, give yourself "five minutes of positive strategy," which means you now look hard for something good happening in practice in the next five minutes. You will go out of your way to notice and comment positively on everything you can and not criticize or correct during that time. This strategy helps you inject a shot of positive energy into your practice.

> Just take a simple break: a water break, or a timeout, to get everything together and relax everybody.

> Sometimes you have to yell at and be tough on everybody during a bad practice to wake people up. Some of your tantrums may not be real, but "put on," to get a point across.

> When the energy is down, the best thing you can do to raise morale and freshen up the team is to back off pushing them and shorten the drills.

■ HOW COACH DEALS WITH HIS PLAYERS IN PRACTICE

> You should greet the players as they come into the locker room or onto the floor.

> During the practice, you should try to mention the players' first names as much as possible. You should always be talking to your players before, during, or after practice, asking them, "How are you doing?" "Don't you just love lacrosse?"

> Treat your players as partners or equals, not as boss and employee.

> Do not allow players to yell at other players.

> Use the "buddy system" in practice. Players help each other out and challenge one another in practice. You should feel that leadership is everyone's role.

> You create integrity and partnership with your players by being honest (keeping promises), having an open-door policy, and leading by example (on time, get things done).

How to Treat Your Players

A coach's general philosophy of treating players is to "treat people the way you would like to be treated." But you can't treat all players the same way because all players aren't the same. You will find that you talk differently to a starting or experienced player (ask) than you do to a rookie (tell). You might find yourself giving special privileges to experienced players who have dedicated their lives and proven themselves in the league, whereas other players (rookies) may have to still earn their stripes to get special privileges. You have to remember that the stars are the "thoroughbreds" on your team, and because they bring something special to the floor/field, you have to handle them the right way.

What You Emphasize in Practice Is Important

Players have to know what is important to you. The kind of players you want them to be has to be stressed in practice. The practice has to reinforce your system, your style of play, your philosophy; and your personality has to inspire your players.

Spend More Time with Your Better Players

It is the better players who are going to carry your team, so they should receive a lot of your attention. Some coaches spend more time with the weaker players to improve their skill level. This does not mean you do not help the weaker players, but often we seem to spend too much time working with the lesser lights trying to elevate their game and forget about the talented players just because we don't think they need as much time.

Players Do Not Have to Be Afraid to Make Mistakes

You do not want your team to practise or play conservatively, afraid to make mistakes. You have to encourage your team to practise and play with reckless abandon and aggressively, knowing that mistakes are a natural part of the learning process. You may even tell a certain player not to make just one mistake — he should make five mistakes every day in practice so he can learn to relax and figure out how to handle them.

Verbal Feedback

During a practice, don't forget to constantly give feedback: correcting, teaching, telling players how to do things right. You must give lots of verbal praise and pat players on the back when the skill or drill is done properly. Some coaches do not tell their players how great they are, as they think this might make them soft.

How to Communicate with Players during Practice

> You should always be asking questions and involving players in decisions about the team. You should get players to always ask "why?" if they don't understand something you said.

> You have to tell players what to do in practice for expediency, but sometimes it is better to turn these commands into requests.

> You communicate best through gentle teaching and constant repetition.

> You communicate through encouraging, praising, and supporting the players.

> You communicate through joking or kidding with your players.

> You have to give players immediate verbal feedback.

> You communicate through persuasion; and the best way to persuade is to ask for help, ask for suggestions, or give reasons why you want something done.

> You communicate by making suggestions rather than bossing players around.

> You challenge your players every day in practice and games by appealing to their pride and competitive spirit: "Is this the best you can do?"

> You have to periodically criticize your players, kick them in the rear, give them no attention at all, and, now and then, yell at them.

> You should talk to each player or at least acknowledge each player, or find one positive thing to say to each one at every practice, even if it's only "Hello!"

> You should call them by their first name. It is important that you mention players' first names as much as possible.

> You should give them reassurance that you care about them by saying a few encouraging words to them or by slapping them on the back.

> You should always be talking to your players before and after practice, such as "How are you doing?" "Do you love it?" "I really like the effort you are putting in."

> You should positively reinforce players, especially when they show self-discipline and self-control on the field/floor. You should be aware that usually the players who get the most recognition on the team are the "stars" or the "troublemakers," not the average guy—and the average player needs attention, too.

How You Make Your Players Feel Special

If you treat your players as if they are special they will become special.

> "Zipper your mouth." Positive reinforcement is your top priority—avoid the negative.

> Find one positive thing to say to each player in practice. When players come and see you to talk informally, you should be uplifting to those players—make them feel good about themselves when they leave.

> Give praise as feedback for good skill execution and doing things right every day. If a player does a good job, tell him, give him praise, be a confidence-builder. But be careful that you do not become just a "cheerleader"—players must earn the praise every day.

> Support, recognize, and reward players for their hard work and effort. You celebrate effort to make players feel great. In fact, you celebrate everything you can. Tell them how proud you are of them, how much you admire them, and how much you appreciate their efforts.

> Praise in public, criticize in private.

> Give players choices, responsibility, and roles.

> Write a word of encouragement on a card and give it to a player; or send a message by email or texting (this can have a tremendous impact).

> Make sure you express to your players what you want, not what you don't want.

Note: A retired player commented that the thing he missed the most were the practices. Games were nice, but he missed the times with the players working together to create a team that executed.

Should Coaches Physically Participate in Practice?

One of the main functions of coaches in practice is to teach, show, explain, supervise, and give feedback to the players, making sure the fundamentals and the drills are done correctly and are completed on time. You have to work through the learning process with the players in practice because you don't expect to simply tell players what to do and then have them do it. You lead best by being on the field/floor; doing hands-on coaching with the players; and being involved with the players by talking to them and giving them feedback. As a coach, you are a role model and should get down and dirty with your players to show or demonstrate to them exactly what you want them to do. This will inspire and motivate your players.

But you do not actually participate in drills, as it interferes with your main task, which is to watch the players, analyze them, and give them feedback on how they are doing in the drill. You are also taking away practice time from a player. By participating in drills, you may think you are getting credibility by showing players you know how to play the game, but actually, the best way for you to gain credibility with your players is by verbally passing on your know-ledge of the game to them. You set the standards of hard work not by physically working hard in drills, but by demanding it in drills and having an organized practice. A work ethic is not established by your setting an example physically in practice, but by doing it in other ways: running a good practice, running good drills, showing enthusiasm and emotion in practice, and by being totally involved in the practice.

■ THE PRE-PRACTICE TALK

Just start with a short team meeting on the practice floor to get the players focused and to set the tone for the practice. You can mention a player's birthday, talk about current events around the world, talk about life, about the next opponent, pick one behaviour goal to talk about, or the breakdown of the last game. From the beginning of the season, talk about the season outcome goal (winning the championships, making the playoffs) to raise the players' expectations and get everyone excited about the game and to raise the focus and intensity in your practices.

Just to change things up, to get the team's attention, you can take them into the visiting team's locker room to give them a different setting for your pre-game talk.

Sometimes you might have team meetings in the dressing room before practice. In certain situations, these meetings become more important than the practices — "clearing the air," removing misunderstandings, goal-setting; defensive meetings, offensive meetings.

You can talk about how special this team is, how proud you are of them, how you admire them, and how much you appreciate their efforts. "Thanks for giving me your best." You can say something like, "I want to thank John for his sacrifices to this team by driving such a long distance and changing his job schedule. It is greatly appreciated."

Or, "I believe in us as a team; we are battled tested, we have faced tremendous adversity and survived. I think you are doing a great job, keep up the good work."

You can talk to the core leaders before every practice to get their feelings about how things are going. And then the player/leaders can talk to the group now and then to get the team excited about their progress as a team.

You should have one specific thought or saying for each practice, such as: "One more"; "One more sprint, one more shot."

Coach Gives a Wrap-up Talk at End of Practice

At the end of practice, you can talk about how you felt about the practice, or you can talk about the upcoming game, or about a certain player who has sacrificed for the team, or about a person in the real world who has overcome some obstacle and succeeded. Finally, end the practice with a good laugh or "cheer."

■ BREAK THE PRACTICE INTO FOUR PARTS

Because there are four parts or areas of performance for a player, break the practices into those areas: (1) the physical: strength, agility, speed, flexibility, endurance; (2) the technical: skill execution; (3) the tactical, strategic, or team skills: knowing what to do and making the right decisions; and (4) the mental: ability to concentrate, handle pressure, rebound from mistakes.

1. Physical Conditioning

Especially at the beginning of the season, the team needs a strong fitness level, so you should work on an aerobic base. Aerobic fitness is the foundation that gives players tremendous energy to work on their skills and systems without experiencing fatigue and injuries during a game. Run the players 1.5 to two miles, timed with certain time objectives. Push the players to their limit to get them in top physical condition for playing at a high intensity. These aerobic runs also test the mental toughness of players to see if they can hang in tough and not quit when they experience fatigue and pain. The team also does a lot of calisthenics, such as push-ups and sit-ups, to keep arms and stomach strong. In the regular-season practices, you mainly get players in shape through the conditioning drills.

Remember: Practice philosophy is to play harder in practice than in a game.

2. The Technical

The team should work on fundamentals every day. A team has to master the basic skills of the game to execute the basic plays of the game. You should be constantly striving for perfection by constantly breaking down the players' skills to improve their technique. In teaching skills, insist on doing the skill with a high number of repetitions at high intensity and doing everything at full speed so the learning curve increases quickly.

Remember: If the players form bad habits, you have to rebuild their skill. This is harder to do than teaching a new skill.

3. The Tactical

Team drills are to teach skills, systems, and strategy. You run game-like drills from a breakdown of your system and what happens a lot in a game. Types of progressive offensive team drills: first do a walk-through 5-on-0 drill; then do teaching breakdown drills where you stop the drill to give feedback 2-on-2, 3-on-3, 4-on-4, 5-on-5; next do defensive progressive drills 5-on-3, 5-on-4, 5-on-5, 5-on-6, 5-on-7; then do 5-on-5 competitive team drills that create stress to put the team under pressure; finally do 5-on-5 scrimmages where you use official referees if possible to model an actual game. If you want the players to get the feel of the game, limit your stoppage of play or teaching during the scrimmage.

4. The Mental

> You build mental toughness training through the conditioning drills. Players learn that they can do "one more," no matter how they feel. This creates players with mental toughness so that when they get tired in a game, they know they can go "one more time."

> You create poise in your players through as many pressure situations as possible. You want to train the players to make the right decisions and react the right way in pressure situations.

> Players can work on getting into the "zone" before and during practice. They work at improving their performance through strategies such as self-talk, visualization, concentration, relaxation, and energizing.

Before practice, players can work on visualization, going over every offensive set play in their minds 100 times. Players during practice can use their "cue word" to get re-focused when they become fatigued or upset in a practice. Players during practice can work on their total concentration by giving their full attention to what they are doing and blocking out all distractions.

THE HAPPIER THE PLAYERS ARE, THE MORE PRODUCTIVE THEY ARE

■ PRINCIPLES FOR RUNNING A GOOD PRACTICE

Have a Practice Plan

The practice should be well organized, with all the drills well planned out and with a time frame set for each drill. Practices are everything and are almost as important as games, because from practices players get confidence. Since you definitely motivate your team by running a good practice, the practice plan is very important, as it serves as a guide. It gives you a feeling of being organized, prepared, and confident. You have to make sure you stick to your practice plan.

> ❭ Organization is the key for running an effective practice. You have to be organized in practice because most of your work and teaching is done there. You must go onto the floor with a written plan of what you want to accomplish, or the purpose of the practice; what you want to teach; well-planned-out drills; the time for each drill; and coloured markers or pennies for "lines" or "positions." The practice plan is a "to do" list of things you have to do to make your team better. This prioritized list of drills helps you stay in control of time and helps fight procrastination. It is a good idea to keep notes on past practices for reference for the next year—number the practices or date them and write down after each practice what was good and what was not.

> ❭ For a two-hour practice, you will need to spend at least thirty minutes to an hour planning beforehand. There is definitely a skill in preparing practices.

> ❭ You should have a general framework for all practices and adjust this framework according to what you have to improve on from the last game and the type of team you are going to play next.

> ❭ You have to be prepared down to the smallest detail for each practice and leave nothing to chance. It seems success usually follows coaches who pay attention to exact detail, so make sure everyone does everything right and with enthusiasm. From the first day of practice you must assume players know very little and need to be taught everything.

> ❭ Try not to give too much information in practice. If you try to give too much information rather than keeping it simple, you will lose the players mentally. If you try to put too much into your practice, such as including a bunch of different plays rather than working on a few simple plays, you lose the most important thing: execution. Just run a few plays with simple techniques to get great execution.

> ❭ With drills, time is everything. Every practice is a race against time, so you cannot waste a minute. Good practice depends on the *quality* of the time spent, not the quantity of time.

> You prepare a top-quality practice where no time is wasted, where every minute is fully used; where all drills are related to the playing system or are game-like; where active participation and high repetition are stressed; and where drills cover all the different learning styles—listening, seeing, doing, and saying—so that the players can learn faster. If you try to wing it, you will end up wasting valuable time.

> You should encourage the players to concentrate on the "present moment" because every moment in practice is precious.

> Beware of the time-wasters: inactivity, disorganization, and meaningless "filler" drills—drills that are not game-like or reflect the system.

> You'll want to spend most of your time on drills that will give you the best results. The question is, which drills will give you the best return? You prioritize your list of things to do; lists are extremely important to coaches. By having a list of drills, you focus on the highest-priority drills, the drills that really matter, that bring the greatest results, the best payoff. To figure out the amount of time you should spend on drills, follow the 80/20 rule: 80 percent of learning skills and playing systems come from focusing on the top 20 percent of all the drills. If you focus on the drills that rank in the top 20 percent in terms of importance, you will get 80 percent results from these drills.

> The first ten to fifteen minutes of a practice is the correction period. You can walk through mistakes the team made in the last game or work on basic fundamentals.

> You must make sure the practice begins and ends when it was supposed to. Let the players know that you will not give extra sprints, laps, or conditioning drills, but in return when you say "run" you expect the players to run all-out.

> You can post the practice plan so the players know what to prepare for. By knowing the routine, players can gauge themselves and give maximum effort.

> You can sometimes let the players organize a practice, but only as a break from the regular routine.

> When picking teams in practice, you should switch the coloured shirts now and then and mix everybody up to let the average players play with the better players. You don't have to keep the "starting" players together all the time.

Work Ethic in Practice Drills

You want your practices to be intense, physical, and competitive. To achieve this, every drill has to have a competitive component where there are winners and losers so that the players maintain their focus and intensity throughout the practice.

> Become an uncommon team. Success is uncommon and not to be enjoyed by the common man. So how do you become uncommon? Some players are uncommon because of their God-given talent or natural ability, but most players have a better chance to be uncommon by effort than by natural gifts. Most players have to have a great work ethic by outworking everyone to be uncommon. Remember, you don't need talent to hustle.

> So the question is: "Do you want to be an average or common team or do you want to rise above the pack?" Although it seems like common sense that players have to play hard to be good, some players just don't get it. Some players feel that if it takes pain, hard work, exhaustion, and commitment to win every week, then they don't feel it is worth it.

> You have to remind players that jogging does not pass for running and working hard. Success is practising and playing at an uncomfortable pace.

> Use team affirmations. You want to instill a work ethic in your team through sayings like, "We believe we are the hardest-working team in the league," "We practise hard to play hard," "We feel we deserve success as a team because we work so hard," "We are going to outwork everybody."

> Get players to work hard. You explain to the players that you are going to give them 100 percent today in practice, and in return you expect them to give you 100 percent. You want your players to work hard because they want to get better, not because you are forcing them. You motivate your players to work hard by getting their input in team meetings on what makes a successful team. Once the players decide that to be a good team they have to work hard, the motivation and commitment will come from the players themselves. The bottom line is by players working hard and performing well in practice, they are rewarded with more playing time and getting off the bench.

> Be aware of lazy and selfish players. Players usually want to work at their own pace. They may be lazy, wanting to do the least amount of work to get by, and selfish, wanting to do it all by themselves. You must demand that players function by your standards and principles. You set the tone for the practice by pushing players to their maximum, demanding they do everything right, and demanding they play unselfishly. You should be always challenging your players to get better.

> Have hard practices. In some of the drills, you want the drill to both teach the players the skill and to fatigue them. Although you have to create this work ethic in practice, you can't make it like a punishment. You want to create conditions in practice that are harder *and more demanding* than any game so that when they play the actual game, it will be easier.

> There is no quick fix, no magic wand to getting in shape. You have to force the team to work past exhaustion in practice and then fight through the fatigue and find an inner fortitude to make

them mentally stronger. By having hard, intense practices, the players will feel physically stronger and mentally tougher; they will get used to pressure; they will have more confidence; and they will get comfortable playing at an "uncomfortable pace."

> Insist on full effort. You have to use fear in practice, even though you might not want to, because the team has to know that if they do not put out an effort, the "hammer" is coming down through less playing time, extra physical activity, or even not playing the next game. You cannot accept mediocrity at practice. Players must be disciplined in their conditioning, because if they are not in shape, they will get tired during the game and will start to make mental mistakes.

  Some coaches instill hard work by punishing the violator for not working hard. If a player is not working hard in practice, the violator is punished by running suicides or sprints to get the point across that if you do not work hard, you will suffer consequences. There is no such thing as a "game player" or a "practice player." Players either work hard all the time or they don't. They cannot turn it on and off.

> Have players grade their work ethic. One motivational tool to make your players aware of hard work is to *ask* players how hard they are working. You and the players can rate their effort from ten (very hard) to one (very light), and compare their ratings to yours.

> Spend more time on defensive drills. These take more time, more work, and more concentration to learn. Certainly a tough defence in practice will make the offence better; plus, when players beat up on each other, nothing will bother them in a tough game.

Keep the Practice Active

Since activity is extremely important in practices, your role in practice is to keep all the players active and moving all the time, with no one standing around. Inactivity creates a feeling that time is being wasted.

Forming "good habits" takes time and can become very boring, so it is important to keep players moving in practice. You want practices that are upbeat, loud, intense, active, fast-moving, and filled with enthusiasm. But be careful: just having activity does not necessarily mean the players are learning the skill properly or forming good habits.

Longer practices are not always better, as they could become boring and repetitive. Sometimes, for teaching purposes, practices are more stop-action than continuous.

Vary the Amount of Time Spent on Drills

The time of season determines the amount of time you spend on fundamentals and team drills. Here is a generality of percentage time:

> Beginning of season: 60 percent of time on fundamentals; 25 percent of time on conditioning; 15 percent of time on team strategy

> Middle of season: 40 percent of time on fundamentals; 25 percent of time on conditioning; 35 percent of time on team strategy

> End of season: 25 percent of time on fundamentals; 25 percent of time on conditioning; 50 percent of time on team strategy

> Playoffs: 25 percent of time on fundamentals and 75 percent of time on team strategy

If the practice becomes too long and you have a choice between dropping team strategy drills or fundamental drills, always stay with fundamental drills, because they are the backbone of execution.

Tailor the Length of Practice Time to Team's Needs

> At the beginning of the season, have a very hard and gruelling two- to two-and-a-half-hour practice.

> During the season, the practice could be one-and-a-half to two hours, varying from a "light" workout to a "hard" workout, depending on whether the team has just played the night before, is going to play the next night, or has a few days off. It is better to practise one hour four times a week than to practise for four hours once a week and try to cram everything into the practice. In hot weather, the rule of thumb is less practice time for a healthier and fresher team.

> Close to playoffs, have only one- to one-and-a-half-hour practices.

> If you can get in only a one-hour practice on the floor/field, then have your players arrive an hour-and-a-half earlier, to practise passing and catching and other fundamentals outside in the parking lot or adjacent area, for an hour.

> Teams should never have two hard workouts in a row during the season. During the season, do not run hard practices where the players' character is being tested. These types of practices are run in the pre-season. You want the players to learn something each practice rather than just having their character tested.

> How much practising is too much and how much is not enough? If a team practises and plays seven days a week, it will burn out. If a team practises and plays three days a week, it will not give itself a good enough chance to win. A team might maintain its present playing level, but will not improve. The ideal number of days is five to six per week; usually two games and three practices is good. Again, this depends on the age level and type of league. A team should spend more time in practice—where players develop good habits—than in games.

Types of Practices

To make sure you cover all aspects of the game, alternate the types of practice. For example, first practice could be stressing the offensive part of the game. Next practice could be stressing the defensive part of the game. The next practice could be stressing shooting and specialty teams. Then start all over again with an offensive practice. If you want a fast-breaking running team, these drills should be involved in every practice, including all the fundamentals.

Besides the specific type of practice, if the practice is right after a game, you should address relevant issues:

"What did we do really well?"

"What didn't we do well?"

"What can we learn from this game?"

"Did we attain some of our performance goals?"

Then you make your corrections through drills. If your practice is before a game, you work on your fundamentals and systems and work on getting better.

The Practice before the Next Game

What you do in the practice before the next game will depend on the weaknesses of your team during the last game and what the next opponent likes to do offensively and defensively. You should make up some drills that reflect what the next opponent likes to do and practise how the team is going to counter it. This type of practice gives the players confidence because they know they are prepared. But the main emphasis before the next game is always on your own team getting better.

Remember: To get your team focused, you should mention the team's next opponent right after the last game.

Variety of Drills in Practice

The main stumbling block for unsuccessful coaches is boring practices, because they do the same thing over and over again, with the result that players lose interest. Of course, you have to run the routine drills that are necessary for success, but these same routine drills can become monotonous. To run good practices, you have to be enthusiastic and organized; you have to put lots of variety in the drills; you have to have lots of activity; you have to put in some mini-games to make it fun and competitive; and you have to create high standards or objectives to achieve in the drills to motivate players to attain the objectives and to build players' confidence.

So try not to run the same drills and the same practices every time; change things up a bit, as the human attention span tends to be short. Have the defence play offence and the offence play defence, for example. Take the players out of their comfort zone and keep them on their toes. The key to good practices is not to become so structured and predictable that you take away the fun, the energy, and the creativity of the players.

Evaluating Practices

You should keep notes on all practices so you can improve on them next time. Did the practice run smoothly? Was it organized? Did the players learn the skill or do the drill properly? Did the players improve? Did the players work hard?

Setting Personal Goals in Practice

Players should set three personal goals for each practice:

> "Mental goals" for every practice to work on their mental preparation, such as energizing, mental rehearsal, and positive self-talk

> A "physical goal" to work on, one fundamental skill for every practice

> A "behaviour goal" to improve their behaviour for every practice

If a player reaches her personal daily goal for the day, she rewards herself by going out and eating her favourite food or by shooting after practice. If she doesn't reach her personal goal, she penalizes herself by taking something away that she likes to do; or by running sprints.

Note: Players feel games are nice, but most players like the practices, where they work together as a team and hang out with their teammates.

Optional Practice

Over the season, you can have optional practices where players can work on anything they want on their own time. Or you can use five to ten minutes of free time during your practice, either at the beginning or the end, where players can work on any part of their game.

Scrimmages

The main reason to scrimmage is to help players get a "feel" for the game. Of course there is no sense in scrimmaging if players cannot do the fundamentals nor play their systems, but there are some lessons that can't be taught and must be learned and experienced by playing. Some coaches scrimmage too much because they don't seem to know what to do in practice, or just don't want to spend the time teaching fundamentals. Other coaches do too much drilling of fundamentals and never scrimmage. So a coach has to balance breakdown drills with scrimmaging in his practices.

At the minor/youth level, it probably is more important to work on fundamentals than scrimmage. Often, minor/youth teams that scrimmage a lot are really wasting time, because the better players will dominate the scrimmage, with the weaker players not getting involved at all and therefore not improving.

If a coach is going to scrimmage, it might be better to scrimmage 3-on-3 or 4-on-4, where more players will get involved with the play.

■ PRINCIPLES OF GOOD DRILLS

Fundamental Drills Are the "Heart of Sports"

A good coach has to be a great teacher of fundamentals, the building blocks of a successful team. You know the game is determined by the execution of fundamentals and they should be worked on every day. How a team executes a skill is more important than what type of play it runs. In fact, your system will look after itself if you are able to do the fundamentals. Most team plays that fail do so because of a mental error or lack of fundamental execution. You want good execution of plays, and the only way to get this is with sound fundamentals; that is, do the basics better.

Good habits are the essence of fundamentals—knowing how to do the skill, what to do in a game situation, and doing it quickly. If you need to choose between fundamental drills or team drills in your practice, always go with fundamental drills.

Note: You must realize that you can teach everyone how to play defence as long as they have the desire, but offence is about talent—you can't teach it; a player is born with the necessary abilities that help his offensive skills.

> ## IF A TEAM CAN'T EXECUTE THE BASICS, IT CAN'T EXECUTE GREAT PLAYS

Guidelines for fundamental drills

> You should have a list of individual drills to use in practice. Prioritize the fundamentals that are required most in a game so you don't waste a lot of time on low-priority fundamentals.

> Look at the position and prioritize the skills needed for it.

> You should spend at least half an hour per practice on the basics. The trick is not to let your players get bored while repeating

these drills. There is no quick fix or instant success to be good fundamentally—only hard work, repetition, and enthusiasm. The journey to continual skill improvement takes a long time.

> If you have to shorten your practice for whatever reason, cut out team system drills, never the basics drills. Be aware of getting caught up in team strategy and team adjustments, neglecting the basic fundamentals of execution. Some coaches like to skip the basics and get right into team-play drills because the former takes too long to teach and is boring.

> Keep the fundamentals very simple and master the simple fundamentals. Good coaches do not believe in playing fancy, so the basics are all the more important.

> Failure and slumps lead players to doubt themselves and their abilities. During this time, fundamentals are more important than ever. If players are having problems, go back to the basics. The key to getting out of slumps is to review the mechanics of the skill and repeat the right techniques over and over.

> Stress to players that they should practise the skill in practice, not in a game. The game is the place for performing the skills. In a game you want the players to have only one thought and that is to do their best and not to try too hard to execute the skill.

> It is a good idea to tell your players why they are doing a drill a certain way. You cannot expect today's players to do it just because you tell them to do it.

> There is no sense in criticizing a player for a mistake if he cannot execute the skill. You have to teach the skill. You can increase a player's confidence by putting him in fundamental drills where he can succeed, by being positive in your feedback, and by putting fun into the drills.

> Teach the new skills and the fundamentals early in the practice.

> Remember in executing drills it is much more than simply knowing how to do them, it is also a combination of deciding what to do and doing it quickly. With all drills, do them at game speed and all-out effort.

Note: You have to adjust your philosophy of teaching fundamentals to the type and level of athletes. In minor/youth you can teach all the players the same technique, one-size-fits-all, and if they don't do it the way you want, they might lose playing time or not play. In the adult leagues or pros, where players might be paid, they are going to play, so you have to be more flexible. Here, you have to find a way to highlight your player's talents and find ways to teach a technique that suits him best and allows him to play to his strength.

How to Get Quality in Drills

Avoid too much repetition

Some coaches feel they get quality of execution by practising plays and drills over and over until they get it right or perfect. These coaches have a tendency to stay with a drill too long because the players are not doing it right and they do not want to move on until players get it right. The result is that the drill becomes boring. When things get too tedious, it is best to move on and then come back to the skill later in the practice or the next practice.

Look for quality, not quantity

If a team practises and plays almost every day over a long season, players will become physically and mentally tired. During the long season, it is much better to cut down the number of practices, but expect intense, quality practices. Moderation helps fuel motivation over a long season.

How do you get quality? You get quality from doing a skill over and over again and putting the stress on doing it right the first time. The good coach runs drills that are shorter, that reflect his systems, and that achieve quality by setting high standards (timed, specific numbers) and then letting the players know if they are meeting those high standards.

If you find yourself repeating things verbally over and over again, you should make it into a drill.

Look for excellent execution

You get high standards by expecting players to do the skill right with good execution. Practising the correct technique in practice creates good execution in a game. You have to get excited over good execution because doing the skill correctly develops good habits. You will be successful against other teams because your players will out-think, out-concentrate, and out-execute the opposition.

Stress improvement every day

You always expect more from your team in practice because you know teams never play a perfect game. There is always something they can improve on. In practices, you should always demand perfect execution, because there is always some slippage in games due to the pressure of the game.

You need to strive for continual daily skill improvement. A skill is never perfect—there is always something a player can do to improve to make it a little bit better. The successful teams do things a little bit better every day because they follow the "little bit more" principle. During the season, you must continue to teach and work on the little things, the little basics that people neglect and slowly get away from as the season progresses. You don't want sloppily executed fundamentals and drills. To get this quality, you have to make sure every detail is carried out properly. It's not so much what you do, but how you do it.

Do not allow bad habits

To get excellent execution, you cannot practise bad habits or let sloppy play be acceptable. Bad habits usually result from bad form or lack of concentration.

Do not allow cheating

Nobody cheats in the drills; for example, in the sprint drills, players start the drill touching the lines or the boards; they all start at the same time; nobody leaves early; nobody takes short cuts; nobody gives a half-effort; and all players touch the far end line or boards.

Practise at game speed

You expect your players to practise the way they play: at "full-game-speed" and extremely competitive. As a result, practices are demanding, as the team practises at a high-quality level every day. If players practise half-effort, they are not going to have a true feeling for what it is going to be like on game day. You must insist players practise at top speed and explosion, because speed wins games. And as the season progresses, increase the practice tempo to make it more game-like.

Notes: If the players are enjoying the drill you are running, then the drill is probably too easy for them. So you have to make it tougher.

You can go full-contact in practice; or controlled contact, where players are hit and bumped; or no contact or light practice with no equipment. You should make practices less physical as season progresses.

The NFL 49ers football team practised often without pads because it helped keep the team fresh and healthy and extended the players' careers.

PRACTISE HOW YOU PLAN TO PLAY, AND THEN YOU'LL PLAY AS YOU PRACTISE

In drills, focus as if "in a game"

Before the practice begins, go through various ways, mental preparation, to focus, such as going through the regular routine to increase their focus. Players must learn to focus in practice the same way as they do in a game. This attitude keeps the player's mind in the present moment, which leads to good execution. Players learn to give complete attention, as if they were in a game, to every pass thrown to them, every one-on-one move they make, every loose ball they go after in practice.

Introduce new skills early

You should introduce new skills and team systems at the beginning of the practice while the players are still fresh and mentally alert and you have your highest energy.

Set statistical goals

In your drills, you should set specific standards or reachable goals for drills that can be measured in a certain amount of time, such as in a "one-minute, full-court, lay-up basketball drill," where the team has to do forty lay-ups at both baskets in one minute. You set up a reward-and-penalty system for motivation. This focuses the players' attention better than if they were simply just going through the drill. If they meet the objective or improve on their number from last time, they can be given a tangible reward, such as a shooting drill, a drink, or a fun drill at the end of the practice. If they did not obtain the standard or meet the objective, they could be penalized by running "suicides," doing push-ups, or running sprints at the end of the practice.

Do repetitive drills

Players learn skills and improve performance by doing a skill correctly over and over again. Since repetition is the "mother of fundamentals," fundamentals have to be practised every day.

Players learn a skill by doing it. Learning a skill and executing it do not come from players sitting and listening to you talk. Coaches usually do too much talking during the explanation of a skill or a drill.

How do you correct a bad habit? You correct a bad habit by repetition and giving feedback. If a player repeats a skill correctly enough times, eventually he will do it naturally. Playing sports well is a matter of habits: the less he thinks about what he is doing, the better a player will play. In times of pressure, when a player's skills are really being tested, good habits will come from discipline and concentration. You want your players' skills to be so good that their reaction is instinctive.

It's not just high repetition, but doing the skill *right* that gives it quality. This sometimes means reducing the number of repetitions to take more time teaching, explaining, and practising the technique of the skill.

The major problem of repetitive drills is boredom. To fight boredom and distractions, and to increase motivation, you must make sure you get the players excited about doing these daily drills by giving lots of variety in these drills; by using new drills to teach the same thing; by making the drills short and snappy;

by making the drills competitive and fun; and by giving the players objectives to attain in these drills, such as scoring as a team five out of twenty-five shots (lacrosse).

PLAYERS LEARN BY DOING, NOT BY LISTENING

Present drills in progression

Because "success breeds success," you have to develop drills that tend to favour success rather than failure. For example, in an offensive drill, make sure you set up the drill so that the offence wins. The player who has a good experience in a drill will want to do it again, with the result of getting better, having good feelings, and gaining more confidence. The problem for you is to make the drills difficult enough to be challenging, but also with strong potential for success.

By drills being progressive, the players get the feeling of success. You run these progressive drills step-by-step so that players will be successful; for example, if a 3-on-2 fast-break does not work, run a 3-on-1 or 3-on-0 to invite success and build confidence. You also must relate the specific skill in the drill to "the whole play" and teach this skill through the progressive drills. As the players progress and start to master the skill, you increase pressure in the drills by adding defensive pressure to make the players learn to think and make good decisions under pressure. Confidence in oneself and one's abilities is just as important as the mechanics of the drill.

The progression for drills takes different forms:

> Progression from fundamentals to team concept

> Progression in speed—standing still, walking, running

> Progression in resistance (defence) no defence, playing medium defence, playing "live" defence

> Progression in numbers: 3-on-0, 3-on-1, 3-on-2, 3-on-3

> Progression in artificial situations: defence over-commits, defence tries to stick check

> Progression in pressure: against time, against statistics, against self, against another player

Present drills in the whole-part-whole progression. When teaching and building a team concept, first show the whole concept, 5-on-0, then break it down into parts: 2-on-2, 3-on-3, 4-on-4 drills, and last, run a 5-on-5 (or however many players your sport uses) drill, putting on pressure. Explain how the drill relates to the big picture.

> ❭   Whole: 5-on-0 (no defence)
> ❭   Part: 2-on-0, 2-on-1, 3-on-0, 3-on-1, 3-on-2, 4-on-0, 4-on-1, 4-on-2, 4-on-3, 5-on-0, 5-on-1, 5-on-2, 5-on-3, 5-on-4
> ❭   Part: 2-on-2, 3-on-3, 4-on-4 (defence)
> ❭   Whole: 5-on-5 (defence)
> ❭   Overload: 5-on-6, 5-on-7 (set up conditions by making drills tougher by adding extra defenders than there normally would be in a game situation)

Drills have to reflect the system

You have to design the drills to fit into your playing systems so that the players don't have to think about the system; this would result in a faster transfer of learning, which saves time. You have to explain and show how the drill relates to the big picture. Drills are now just a breakdown of the system. The drills are also related to the skills that are related to the system. Do not run drills for the sake of running drills; or "filler" drills, which are a waste of time.

Drills are game-like

You can also create game-situations in the drills so the learning process is speeded up. You put the players in a learning environment that will condition and prepare them for every possibility that they may face in a game situation. What they do in practice should be exactly what happens during a game. For example, a one-on-one drill where the offensive player can work or try to beat his defender for twenty to thirty seconds is unrealistic in a game. Make the drill realistic by giving the ball carrier one offensive move or a realistic time, such as four seconds, to beat their defender to make the drill more like a game situation.

Pressure in drills

The ability for players to perform under pressure is one of the most critical traits of being successful. Coaches see players execute and perform well in practice, but once they get into a game, they have problems performing. So one of the most important things a drill should teach a player is how to execute a skill under pressure. The best way to prepare for pressure is to practise pressure situations. Once players can do the skill correctly, they then must practice the skill under pressure and with high intensity. You want to build composure so a player doesn't panic, makes the right decisions under pressure, and becomes mentally tougher. As players learn the skill, you can put them under pressure by:

> ❭   Making drills so that there is pressure and consequences in them. If player loses in a drill, he has to do sprints; if he wins, he gets a chance to rest.

> Trying to create as much competition as possible in every drill, player against player; trying to create as much competition as possible in every drill, because competition helps the team's performance improve

> Making things tougher than they are in a game

> Going against time

> Going against statistics (number of times): have specific goals or standards to meet or beat in each drill and record them

Length of drill

You should make the drills fairly short so players have a higher focus and a higher intensity. Keep fundamental drills no longer than ten to fifteen minutes and team drills between fifteen and twenty minutes. Long drills create boredom, slow down the effort, and players lose their concentration—so don't stay too long with a drill. Sometimes the length of the shifts in the game will help determine the length of some of the drills. Time the players when they run the length of the floor to provide a gauge to aim for in sprint drills. This standard is good for team morale, especially when the players make the objective in the sprint drill. The players feel better and quicker. Emphasize "less quantity and more quality."

Remember: There is such a varying degree of skills with players, not every player will execute them at the same time.

Follow a hard drill with an easy drill

Alternate a tough drill with an easier drill to give players time to recover. But end practices with intense and hard drills to teach the players to "go the extra mile" and to develop mental toughness.

Feedback in drills

Coach gives feedback. An essential ingredient in "getting better" is players getting feedback on how they are doing. Most coaches think that by running drills, players will learn how to do the skill right by just doing the drill. But the drill alone does not teach the player the skill; rather, you teach the player the skill by giving instructions and proper verbal feedback through the drills. Players learn from their coach's feedback by telling the players if they are doing the skill or drill right or wrong. If players don't know how they are doing, they won't know what to work on.

> Correction or instruction feedback. If a player does the skill wrong or makes a playing mistake, you must inform her of the mistake immediately and give her corrective feedback on how to do it right. Yelling out corrections or instructions during practice to tell a player

what to do is part of coaching; for example, telling a player how to properly grip the stick, how to beat someone offensively, or how to take a certain defensive position. Correction or instruction feedback is the most common feedback given throughout practices. Sometimes when pointing out mistakes, instead of taking a "direct shot" at the player, you might put yourself down by saying, "I wasn't very good at this in the beginning, either."

> Criticism. Players have to know why you are being tough on them by yelling at them. You have to tell the team something like, "The player who is never criticized is the one who should worry. I am hard on certain players because I care about them, I see potential in them, and I want to make them better."

> Make corrections one-on-one. When correcting an individual player, don't keep the rest of the team from doing the drill. Take the player off to the side and explain the mistake to him. However, if the majority of the team is making the same mistake, stop the drill and correct the whole team.

Remember: Feedback should be 90 percent positive and 10 percent negative.

Naming the drills

To get the drills running quickly, give all the drills specific names to identify them. This makes it easier for players to remember and quicker for them to start the drill. You should also explain the terminology of your systems so the players will understand what the words mean when you discuss your system.

Main types of drills:

> Teaching drills

   In teaching drills, you give instruction and feedback to the players throughout the drill. These drills are run at about 60 percent speed.

> Competitive drills

   In the competitive drills, the players compete to be the winner or the best in the drill, so you give very little instruction. These drills are run at full game speed and are battles.

   One-on-one competitive drills among teammates are healthy (competition for playing time, for stats, in drills) and make them tougher as a team. Competition inside a team isn't a negative thing; it can motivate players to work and play harder—as long as they stay focused on team skills and not get so focused on themselves that they fail to work on team skills.

   You have to make your practices competitive because if you do not, you will lose your competitive players. Practices, drills, and games are all about competition, where players are constantly trying to outperform their teammates.

If you are lucky enough to have two good players who are competitive, they will instill toughness in your team. These types of players fight all the time either verbally or physically because they are so competitive. You want your players to push each other so you create as many competitions in every drill. You can even put a weaker player up against a tough opponent in practice, which will make him better.

Rather than just doing drills, you should put competition in as many drills as possible to make "getting better" a game and then record or keep the score of every drill. Now every player has to focus in every drill, as players are now playing for something: there are going to be winners and losers. You set up 1-on-1 competitive drills where players or groups of players compete against each other, against time, or against their previous record at full speed and all-out. You can set up "ladders" for conditioning, for shooting percentages, for 1-on-1 competition. The best way to add pressure is to make the drills competitive and intense. There is no question that competition causes performance, focus, and intensity to increase.

After a competitive drill, give a token exercise, such as running a lap, one push-up, one suicide, to losers to remind them that they lost and that they have to strive to do better next time. Sometimes you can have the winners decide what the losers will do.

> Punishment drills

You give punishment drills to refocus or get an idea across on what you want, such as if a team is outworked in a game, you would run a punishment drill; or when a player violates a team rule, such as being late for practice, you would have the whole team run a punishment drill. Punishment drills might not be the best way to get an idea across, but it sure is the quickest way.

Conditioning, Testing, Training, and Mental Toughness

Players are tested for their conditioning level, but are also being tested for their mental toughness, where players push their bodies to the highest level to make them stronger. They are either going to quit or keep on going. You want to find out who will break and who has the mental toughness to persevere.

Some training or testing exercises

> Outside one-mile run: You want your players to run a mile (four times around a quarter-mile track) in seven minutes and thirty seconds. The guards or speed guys usually finish in six/thirty. The big guys or slower players usually finish the mile run in seven minutes. You record the players' times and keep a record.

Note: Under six minutes (fast); seven minutes (high fitness) (average is seven and a half to eight and a half minutes)

> Outside one and a half mile run: You want your players to run the one-half mile (six times around the track) in roughly nine minutes. You record the players' times.
>   *Note:* 8:45 is superior; 8:45–10:15 is excellent; 10:16–12:00 is good.

> Outside two-mile run or twelve-minute run.
>   *Note:* Twelve minutes is excellent; fourteen minutes is good. You record the players' times.

> Inside 300-yard shuttle: You want the players to run the 300-yard shuttle in roughly sixty to seventy seconds (five sixty-yard shuttles or six twenty-five-yard shuttles).

> Inside 400-yard shuttle:You want the players to run the forty-yard dash in 4.3 seconds (ten forty-yard shuttles).

> Beep test (twenty metres) to test conditioning

> "Eleven": Run the whole team width of floor of basketball court (eleven times in sixty seconds). Have three groups of fast, medium, and slow (work: rest 1:2).

> The Running Test: You want three groups (fast, medium, slow) to run sprints the length of the floor. Each group runs their own time, such as sixteen seconds, eighteen seconds, and twenty seconds, then you give them a thirty-second rest, and they will do it again. You determine how many times they run the sprint (five to ten times). This run tests a combination of sprints and endurance.

> "Sprints" down and back the length of the floor: Have the team broken into three groups—fast, medium, slow. Start with five sprints, add a sprint if one player is over a predetermined set time. Or start with ten sprints, and for every sprint under the designated time, drop one (ratio of one run to three rest).

> Relays down and back the length of the floor: Have three lines run against each other, one stick/group; first player on goal line, run down and touch far end boards with stick, run back and hand stick to next player in line (do not throw stick).

> Suicides down and back on basketball court: Run to first Free Throw line extended and back, then to centre line and back, to far Free Throw line extended and back, and to far end line and back, in under thirty seconds. Have three groups—fast, medium, slow. State number of suicides (reps), add one suicide if one player is over the preset standard time.

> You can also run tough practices with twenty-eight minutes of running and conditioning drills, which will show you what kind of shape the players are in and what players are totally out of shape. The practice itself becomes the conditioner. You want to make your practices worse than any game. A team working hard in practice experiences the best conditioning there is.

You must make most conditioning drills as enjoyable as possible by using relays and games, but you can also use them as a physical punishment now and then. If the team plays with no intensity in the last game, then you can make the conditioning drill a punishment to get the point across that laziness is not acceptable. Players must realize that when they are out of shape, they stop thinking; they revert to old habits; they have a tendency to get upset very easily; and they quit. Lack of conditioning does not just affect the legs; it also affects the brain and heart.

Some points to remember about conditioning in practice

> Any conditioning drill without a ball (or whatever is used in your sport) is a waste of time. Players work harder and enjoy running when a ball is involved in the drill.

> In most of the conditioning drills, the full length of the floor/field/court is used.

> Use preset time standards in conditioning drills. Use a stopwatch to time all conditioning drills.

> Always state the number of times the team is going to run a conditioning drill (suicides, sprints) so the players can gauge themselves and run all-out.

> Playing sports well is a matter of a "change of direction," and forming this habit is important; for example, when the team is working on their half-floor defence, bring in the conversion to the other end of the floor by running the fast-break on any possession of the ball.

> The practice format is essential to creating mental toughness, so you must make practices feel like real games by putting players in real-game situations. The best way to create this atmosphere is to begin and end the practice with the bulk of the running drills so at the end of the practice the players are tired.

> The conditioning drills you perform should be done at high speed to bring in the conditioning factor.

> Kids are out there to have fun, and most conditioning drills are not fun. So make conditioning drills fun through players' competing against each other, relay races, and competitive drills and scrimmages where the coach just lets them play. The worst thing a coach can do is to make conditioning a punishment; keep it fun.

Note: "Fatigue makes cowards of us all." General George Patton.
Remember: To condition oneself, a player must punish himself.

Various Types of Drills

> ❯ *Create persistence:* To make the players persistent, the offensive drills are never ended unless there is a score. You want to condition players never to give up on a miss or saved shot.

> ❯ *Create quickness:* Create drills to make players think and act quickly. In practice, emphasize mental quickness, explosiveness, and quick movement. "Be quick, don't hurry." Haste makes waste of energy and causes needless mistakes.

> ❯ *Create aggressiveness:* Teach players to play physically, aggressively, and with "reckless abandon," but under control. So they practise all-out, yet play with controlled aggression. Players need to play with physical aggressiveness to be successful, but they also need to demonstrate controlled aggression in a game.

> ❯ *Create intensity:* How do you get intensity in practice?

  • Keep the drills short so the players can go all-out — no half-effort.

  • Time the drills and have objectives for the drills (number of shots/time).

  • Demand that players play hard. If a player slacks off in a drill, force the whole team to do the drill again.

  • Demand that the players do the drill at full speed and are extremely competitive.

  • Praise players who practise aggressively and intensely.
     Note: You can challenge the defence to play hard and tough in drills by telling them that the offence is going to get five scoring chances, not goals, out of five possessions and they have to stop them from getting three scoring chances.

> ❯ *Teach co-operation:* You want players to learn that they are helpless without the other members of the team. They have to learn to play together. Co-operation-team drills promote this by having the group compete against some team objective or statistical goal. If the team meets the team objective, they get a reward, such as shooting at the end of practice. If they don't meet the team objective, they get a punishment, such as running sprint drills.

  • Run a lot of team-passing drills to create a habit of giving up the ball unconsciously and, thereby, helping build team morale.

  • Tug-of-war — this is a great drill for teaching co-operation. You put the best ten offensive players against the best ten defensive players. Players learn that the team wins by being connected, everybody pulling in the same direction, and helping each other.

> ***Test character or mental toughness:*** To be mentally tough,
> players need to be physically tough and in great shape. Mental
> toughness drills are done at the beginning of the season to see
> what the players are made of. Usually they are endurance runs,
> sprint drills, or thirty minutes on defensive drills. In fact, every
> tough defensive drill the players hate, you should run two or
> three times in practice. By running physical, tough, exhausting
> drills, players learn to mentally tough it out; learn to encourage
> one another, to struggle together, with the result that cohesiveness
> emerges and they learn who their natural leaders are. By pushing
> players to go beyond their mental and physical limits, you will see
> if they will quit. A player who quits in practice is someone who
> will likely quit in a game.
>
> If a player has many weaknesses, such as not quick enough,
> not athletic enough, and just plain not good enough, what can a
> coach do to make him better? You can make him mentally stronger
> to make up the difference in his athletic ability. How do you do
> that? To make a player tougher, you have to constantly challenge
> him that he is not working as hard as he can; that he is not taking
> his game to the next level; that he is backing down against tougher
> opponents; and that he has to be tougher by making hustling,
> gritty plays under pressure.
>
> ***Note:*** If the players enjoy the drills you ask them to do, then
> maybe they are too easy.
>
> ***Teach self-control:*** To become a top player, he has to learn to
> control his emotions. Through drills, you can help players to
> practise controlling their emotions. During games, there are many
> emotional swings, and a player has to be able to handle these
> swings. One way of doing this is to create drills where there are
> emotional ups and downs. And you can even make bad calls on
> purpose against players to see how they will react.
>
> ***Fun drills and games:*** You have to turn work in practice into play
> so the players keep their spark, enthusiasm, and joy of playing.
> You don't want the practice to become drudgery and boring,
> where players can't wait to get off the floor. Remember the saying,
> "All work and no play makes Jack a dull boy." Any drills that
> contain competition, such as team games, co-operative drills,
> and individual competition, will add fun to the practice. So make
> drills into games where you keep score and have a winner and
> loser. The game itself is now being played for the sheer fun of it.
>
> You should try to end practices on a positive note by having a
> fun competition. You can even put in some background music to
> keep the practice upbeat. Your rule of thumb should be to dedi-
> cate a quarter of the practice to having fun to remind the players
> that playing sports is fun and should not be taken seriously all the
> time. Sometimes, after a bad loss you can just run players through
> a bunch of fun drills in practice.

Players Talking in Drills

One of the biggest problems for you is to get players to talk on the floor. Practices aren't just about playing the way you will in a game, it's about *communicating* the way you will in a game. You must insist that players talk on the floor in drills and games, and if they don't talk, they might not get to play.

Especially in the defensive drills, demand communication on the floor to get rid of any indecision or hesitation. Have players call out "screen" to warn their teammate a screen is coming. You want them to communicate early to give their teammates time to react. Teach defensive players to call out their position, e.g., "I've got your left side," to let their teammate who is checking the ball carrier know they have help. It's important, when players get tired or nervous, to get them to talk more on the floor, as this will help keep them mentally alert. Plus talking on the floor is contagious to other teammates.

IT IS NOT WHAT YOU DO, BUT HOW YOU DO IT

16 PUTTING TOGETHER A GOOD PLAYING SYSTEM

A "system" is a means by which players can maximize their contribution to the team by working together and relying on each other. A system gives you a framework for teaching specific skills and plays that are applied within the system to make it work. A system states this is how we are going to play the game.

A system is also a vehicle to give a team an identity, such as becoming known as a passing team, a running team, a defensive team, etc. The successful coach has a vision of how he wants the game to be played to be successful and has the skill of putting together a successful playing system. Remember, a successful team might use different systems, but the key is the players' willingness to buy into the systems; and the challenge is for the coach to get the players to buy into the systems.

The big coaching question is: *Do you create your system around the players you have, or do you force your players to play your system, no matter what?* If you know what system you want to run, then you will know what type of player—their roles and their talent—you want to complement your system. In other words, you force the players you have to play your particular system.

Or you can adapt your system to your players' talents, strengths, and gifts rather than the other way around. In adapting your system to your players, you have to be flexible and have the ability to put your best players in the best possible position to succeed. Once you find out what your players' strengths are, you then structure the team's system slightly to the strength of the players so they can contribute to its success. You don't worry about what a player can't do; you focus on what he can do. Remember, on putting a team together, building chemistry and picking players that complement each other are important skills to have as a coach.

■ MAKE SURE THE PLAYERS KNOW THEIR ROLE

No matter what philosophy you use, you should give everyone a job description and explain to each player his or her roles, responsibilities, and expectations, and how he or she fits into the large scheme of things. Increasing the role clarity for players—knowing their role on a team—has been shown to have a positive effect on their playing performance. The roles are based on a player's strength, natural abilities, and how he performs. It is important that players accept and embrace their role in the overall system. They have to set aside their individual ego and do what is best for the team.

Once they know exactly what is expected of them and how they can contribute to help the team to achieve success, they will perform that much better. In fact, role players are every bit as essential to the success of a team as the "stars." Some players appreciate being given a role, usually the inexperienced players, because it gives them a clear picture of what is expected of them. This makes things simpler and helps them to relax when playing. Players will either just go through the motions or get totally involved with the team, and by your giving each player a role and responsibility on the team they will become more committed to it.

Role Might Be Too Confining

Sometimes placing a player into a role is like trying to put a square peg into a round hole. The role may be too confining for him. Sometimes players who have great offensive ability may be put into a defensive role, which would underplay their gift but help the team tremendously. Usually, offensive players want freedom to play an open creative style so they can express themselves, but might be given a role that is too controlling for them. Sometimes, for the sake of the team, it's not what a player wants to play, but what he has to play.

Ask Players How They See Themselves Fitting into the System

Usually, you give each player a role on the team according to what each can do well and then you can explain how each one of them fits into the system. One way of finding out a player's role is for you to simply ask her how she sees herself fitting into the system and on the team. It is important to talk to a player about her role so that she accepts it more willingly and ends up totally committed to it.

You can ask players: "What do you do best?" "How can we use you best?" "How can you contribute?" "What is the best position for you?" "Where do you want to play?" "Are you comfortable playing this role?" This way, the player will make a better contribution to the team by playing where he feels most comfortable. By discovering what your players can do and what they cannot do, you then place them in a role and position that invites them to either hide their weakness or to take advantage of their strength.

To help players understand the system, you should always be asking them "what if" questions to see if they understand the system and know their role.

In youth sports, it is a good idea to develop "whole players"—players who can play every position—instead of limiting them into positions, roles, and structured system play.

■ GENERAL PRINCIPLES OF A PLAYING-SYSTEM PHILOSOPHY

Put in a Playing System That You Know Works

The key is for Coach to find a system that he knows works, one that he believes in, and hopefully one that will be successful for him over time. Some coaches can work and rework their systems to death and still might not be doing the right things to be successful.

In a successful system, coaches get everybody thinking the same way and they keep everybody organized. Players can now anticipate the movements of each other more quickly because they know what is going to happen before it happens.

Put a Playing System Together That Is Exact

You must have a vision, an idea of exactly how you want your system to work. You cannot be vague about it. By being exact, your players will then know exactly what they have to do and what is important to you . . . what they have to do in carrying out their assignments, e.g., being in the right place at the right time. There can be no gray areas, because ambiguity and misunderstanding lead to losses.

Note: It is difficult to bring new players onto a team and expect them to help right away, since they won't know the system. A player has to know what position she is playing, what is expected of her, and what her role is. You certainly don't want players to be guessing all the time what to do.

Communication

For players to understand the system and each other, they have to communicate with each other on the floor/field so as to avoid confusion and indecision, and thereby minimize mistakes.

List Rules

You should list the guidelines by priorities on offence and the rules on defence. An exact playing system helps to keep the players organized and playing cohesively. In having a system, you will have some rules or guidelines within that system so everybody knows what to do in certain situations. By listing the playing rules by priorities, the players will come to know what is important to you. You can then reinforce to the players when they are doing the right thing; when they are in the right spot or position; when they get in a good defensive stance.

Patience and Discipline

You have to understand that positional play is a big part of discipline. If players do whatever they want, they will end up playing chaotic "street-ball."

To put a discipline-playing system together requires knowing "what to do"—a system that requires patience and a certain amount of orderliness and thoroughness—is one thing, but the most important thing is knowing "how to do it and doing it right"—execution, which takes patience in teaching and explaining it.

Note: A discipline-system is order, as opposed to lack of discipline, which is chaos.

Keep the Playing System Simple

System coaches have to keep the disciplined-system simple to let the great players have the room to make the great plays within the system with their creative talents. Sometimes the veterans, through their creativity and experience, get the job done even though it is not the way the system was designed. Players playing in simple systems have more freedom to focus and stay in the present moment during the game. And with freedom, players don't become robots—where they have to play a certain way—but have the opportunity to be creative and express themselves. The key is to get everybody playing in a disciplined system and still give them the freedom to be creative with their own talents. It is better to have a system that is 75 percent perfect, but 100 percent executable (simple) than a system that is 100 percent perfect, but only 75 percent executable (complicated).

In a "disciplined simple system" players are where they are supposed to be. It's important to be in the exact place at the exact time and do what they are supposed to do while at the same time still have the freedom to be creative.

Also, when it comes time to change the game plan, you can modify simple plans more quickly and easily than you can modify complicated ones.

Although players work at being consistent, they don't want to be so consistent that they become predictable, which might play right into your opponent's hands. If your opponent knows what you are going to do, they can obviously prepare for you and stop you. But even if your opponent knows what you are going to do, a good executing team will still beat them by having options and counter-options.

Notes: Coach should not be so consumed with strategy and systems that he overlooks the fundamentals of the position. If you execute your fundamentals, the system will take care of itself; but if your technique and fundamentals are not very good, the system won't work.

When putting a successful system together, coaches have to determine one or two things the team can do really well. Then they make sure there is not a team in the league that does these things any better.

Deception

Successful system coaches are strong in basic team play, have solid playing systems, and have solid fundamentals they can depend on. They don't plan to fool or out-scheme their opponents all the time, but they do employ some deception, have some surprises, or introduce trick plays now and then as part of their strategy to catch the opposition off-guard during a game.

Lose by Opposition's Weaknesses, Not by Their Strengths

In a successful system, the team believes that if the opposition is going to beat them, they will beat them with their weaknesses, not their strengths. The players will make the opposition "star" players do what they do not want to do, even to the point of double-teaming them.

Pressure and Fatigue

The two key words for all the playing systems are *pressure* and *fatigue*. On defence, you want to wear the opposition down and force them into mistakes with constant defensive pressure. On your breakout, you want to put constant pressure offensively on the opposition by running the floor. On offence, you want to put constant pressure offensively on the opposition with constant movement on offence and attacking the basket/net.

Special Teams

In most sports, system coaches work especially hard on special teams, as they feel they are the heart of the game and can change the strategy of the game. If the opposition tries to intimidate their team and take penalties and they can score on their power play, the opposition will pay the price. This gives a team the edge.

Their philosophy is also that they want to have as many players as possible who can contribute in more than one way to the team. If a player is a big hitter and can play on defence but can't help on special teams, he might not play a lot.

A Sample of a Successful Man-to-Man Basketball Offensive Philosophy

> In most successful offensive systems, coaches play aggressively and attack the opposition on offence and keep them off balance before they can get a chance to attack them defensively. Their philosophy is they want to score first and keep on scoring. Within this system, the players want to set the tempo and be daring and aggressive. They believe they must control their own destiny by being aggressive, or the opposition will. These coaches are action oriented and are willing to take risks by

moving fast and hard. They believe no great battles were ever won on the defensive; sooner or later, a team must go on the offensive.

> Successful coaches run an offensive system that creates an action to get a reaction so that the defence will end up a split second behind them. Doing something that makes a defender hesitate or be tentative from not knowing what the offence is going to do gives the offence a slight advantage. This hesitation or indecision by the defender makes him play slower rather than quicker by reacting decisively.

> The main goal of the offence is to set up a player to get a good shot that he can make every time he gets the ball.

> Coaches play a combination of a running-game (fast) and pull-the-ball-out game to run a half-court game (slow). They want to control the tempo of the game by playing their style. What's your favourite play? Decide who is your best scorer, and get him the ball and play through him. Coach's job in a game is to get his best player to touch the ball.

> Successful coaches run a simple offensive system. They do not do fancy things or try to do too much in any one play but run simple concepts that do not take much time to set up. The most complicated plan of action becomes simple if you break it down properly. Teams are good at what they practise the most. It is about executing good plays with good fundamental play. Remember, become great at one thing and then work on a couple of other things! You do not want to be average at many things.

> Successful coaches are fundamentally sound. They want good execution, and you get this only with sound fundamentals. They believe that the two best things a player can offer on offence are a perfect pass and helping to set a teammate in the clear with a pick or screen.

> Successful coaches use principles rather than patterns in their offence. They believe in freedom within a structured system. They believe in 50 percent one-on-one and 50 percent team play. They do not want their players to be robotic, but have a "feel" for the game.

> Successful coaches sometimes run a structured offence—set plays—with flexibility and good decision-making. They want their players to make "reads" off set plays; that is, they learn to "read the defence." Coaches teach players how to make plays by stressing to their players to see two or three options to making a play instead of running the same play all the time. There is some structure to set plays, but players can deviate by making "reads." Players yell out the play using one word or numbers to make teammates aware of the play. It forces players to think; players have to be thinking all the time.

> Successful coaches do not believe in equal opportunity on offence. They feel their offensive players have to know their roles. Are they a screener, a picker, a 1-on-1 driver, a shooter, a passer, or a rebounder? If a player wants to shoot in a basketball game, he must prove in

practice that he can shoot at least 60 percent (12/20). Even if the team is an unselfish team that shares the ball, Coach still needs someone to put the team on his back, and if a coach has that someone, the team will be successful.

> Successful coaches tailor their team around their best player or 2–3 players, and everyone else complements them. Coach has to play through her stars—she has to put her better players in prominent positions and put the ball in their hands. You can even ask your best player, "Where do you want the ball?"

> At crunch time, make sure your best players are on the court.

> Even though you play through your better players in the offence, everybody still has to be a constant threat and be able to contribute in the offence. The team needs balance, so that everybody is guarded closely by the defence, giving your better players more room to be effective.

> Successful coaches are always adapting and adjusting to the opposition and making personnel adjustments. Coach has to have enough depth on the team that if someone is not playing well, he can make a change.

> Successful coaches in basketball will spread their offence out if their team is small. They make their weaknesses their strength. They spread the opposition out to bring out their big guys from the basket, and then their players can hit the 3-point shot or drive. If you are small, you must pressure more and always look for mismatches.

Notes: The defensive end of the game is the coach's game, whereas the offensive end of the game is the players' game. Offence is more of a skill thing, so let your offensive players use their talents and be creative.

If a player is not scoring, in most sports it is the result of his moving outside the scoring area and waiting for something to happen versus moving inside the scoring area and making something happen.

A Sample of a Successful Man-to-Man Basketball Defensive Philosophy

> Successful coaches believe the force of their personality determines the quality and intensity of their defence. Principles alone do not get the job done; knowledge alone is not enough; you will get better at whatever it is you emphasize.

> The most successful coaches build up their team on the defence end first. They feel they have a better chance of success if they are strong on the defensive end. They have a defensive mindset of physicality, as they feel defence is the most important part of the game, because if their opponents can't score, they can't lose. Because their defence is always "constant" and consistent, they know they can play and be

competitive in every game. In a "disciplined-defensive system," players are where they are supposed to be, which helps players perform as one, as teammates are able to anticipate the movements of teammates.

> The keys to a successful coach's defence are attitude, intelligence, anticipation, concentration, discipline, and effort. Defensive sayings: "Defence is an attitude"; "Defence is just hard work."

> Successful coaches don't want their defensive players to just think about keeping the opposition from scoring, but to get turnovers and score. They want to score from defensive pressure, defensive steals, defensive rebounds, loose balls, and fast-break.

> The successful coach's type of defence is to attack the offence before it has a chance to attack you. They force or dictate the action, but when going after the offence, they do it under control by "closing-out" (e.g., shuffling out to pressure the ball carrier). They want to force the offence to do something rather than wait for it to do it to them, so they take it to the opposition. They force the ball carrier to do what they want him to do.

> The successful coaches are not going to let the opposition run their plays. They want to force the offence into making plays by putting continuous pressure on the ball carrier, the shooter, and the passer. If the defence can disrupt the opposition's system, it can reduce them to a group of individuals on the court as opposed to a team. This pressure creates interceptions and turnovers. They want to pressure the offence into mistakes and turnovers with aggressive checking. If you don't put pressure on the ball, the opposition will pick you apart.

> In their defensive-systems, successful coaches believe in pressure and therefore they generally look for quick, aggressive, tenacious players, because everything they do on defence is based on speed and movement. Their teams, like a small boxer, are not going to knock out anybody, so they have to keep moving and jabbing to wear the bigger teams down. These pressure-defensive coaches don't try to outsmart the opposition; rather they just go out and play physical. It is not just their systems that make them good, but rather how they play. They play fast, hard, and fundamentally sound.

> These pressure-defensive coaches cast the veteran players as the heart of the defence and let the most physical veteran run the defence. Having these veteran leaders on defence is extremely important.

> Successful coaches play "help" defence, because their players are out of position so often by pressuring that they spend a lot of time covering each other's backs. They are quick to help stop ball penetration and then recover back to their check by "closing out." They are always sacrificing themselves for one another.

> The object in defence is to keep the other team from scoring by using a helping man-to-man defence, where they are almost double-teaming

the ball; helping out on all screens; helping out on cutters; helping out on good scorers; and helping out on big centres. We rotate to help.

> Successful coaches have rules on defence, but against certain teams they make adjustments. They also change and make subtle adjustments during a game. Flexibility is the key to defence. Some coaches make the mistake of doing the same thing all the time, which hurts them. The defensive system is strong in basic team play, but it has some deception or tricks—show one thing and do something else.

THE KEY TO SUCCESS IS DOING THE DIRTY WORK

■ DISCIPLINING PLAYERS TO PLAY WITHIN THE PLAYING SYSTEM

You need discipline within a system to get good (not necessarily perfect) execution. You want players who can think quickly and make good game decisions. You want your players playing out of specific positions, yet using their thinking skills and playing skills, especially when under extreme pressure. The ultimate is for players to make the play unconsciously because they have been exposed to the situation so many times that it has become natural. Some coaches feel discipline in a system makes players act like robots who don't have to think, but this is not true.

However, if you are going to stress a disciplined system, you will sometimes have problems with players not doing what they are supposed to do. How do you get your players to do what you want them to do?

You have to instill the right way of doing things by first verbally praising the player when he does it correctly; or correcting when the player does it the wrong way; and, now and then, even criticizing him when he does it wrong. If the point still hasn't gotten across, you might have to take away playing time.

Getting Players to Buy into the System

The best way for you to get discipline within the playing system is to get the team to "buy into your system," because the team's belief in that system might be more important than the system itself. The system won't work unless the players believe in it and are loyal to the team and to you.

Praising Players for Good Execution

Another good way to get discipline within the playing system is to praise good execution, but you should not wait for "perfect" execution. You should look for any progress or improvement in execution by the players within the playing system and praise it immediately if you want to see it repeated. You should not just look to correct mistakes within the playing system.

Consequences for Breaking System Rules

To instill discipline, you must have consequences for players who continually break the playing system rules. One type of consequence for players not doing what they are supposed to do is to take away playing privileges by benching them. Every coach needs power, and the best "hammer" for not following orders or for breaking playing rules is benching players or at least sitting them out for a shift. Benching players tends to be more effective than physical or verbal punishment.

Another type of consequence for not playing within the system is extra physical activity. You have the players do push-ups, sprints, or some sort of running as punishment. Some coaches do not use extra physical exercise for violations of rules because they believe players will learn to hate the sport. Others believe that coaches should use sprints and other types of physical exercises only as a means of improving their players' conditioning; these are a necessary part of regular training and they don't want their players to equate them with punishment. However, if you need to get an idea across as quickly as possible, this type of physical punishment seems to be one of the best ways.

And, finally, there is verbal punishment: yelling, criticizing, scolding, lecturing, and threatening by you. It can even be demonstrated by the tone of your voice. But you must understand that yelling and screaming at players all the time does not create discipline.

Remember: The best way to teach is to reward players for good execution by praising them or patting them on the back.

PART FOUR

THE ART OF MOTIVATION BY WORKING WITH INDIVIDUAL PLAYERS

17 | COMMUNICATING WITH YOUR PLAYERS

One of the most powerful leadership skills in coaching is communication with your players on a daily basis. Effective communication is one of your most important skills in building a player-coach relationship and in return helping players perform at their best. It is the spark that makes a team rise to another level. Your words will either motivate or demotivate your team. But many coaches make the mistake of thinking good communication is all about talking. Your ability to communicate effectively involves more than just your verbal communication skills; it also involves non-verbal communication and active listening. You must learn to be attuned to non-verbal communication.

Mastering all these facets of communication will make you a better coach.

You motivate by being able to get inside the head of a player to bring out his best performance; you might find some key points that will trigger an emotion in a player that inspires him to go out and play to the best of his abilities. Every player is motivated differently on a team, and it is up to you to know your players well enough to know how to get a positive response from them. And the best way to find what method works best is by two-way communication with your players on a one-on-one basis.

This chapter is on how to communicate: listening and asking questions. But you should also ask yourself these questions:

> With whom are you communicating? You are communicating with your players to find out their goals and needs.

> When do you communicate? Before, during, or after practice.

> Where do you communicate? In a player's comfort area, such as on the field/floor.

> Why do you communicate? You need to get to know your players so as to establish common personal goals; transmit information; express the team's behaviour goals; teach a fundamental or explain the playing system; discipline and encourage; air grievances; review and correct playing mistakes; and to motivate the player to play the game hard.

■ VERBAL COMMUNICATION

The ability to communicate with players as a group or individually is your greatest strength. What you say, how you say it, your body language, and facial expressions—all have an impact on connecting with your players. If you have comfortable and warm conversations with your players throughout the season on both a personal level and around playing matters, and give them a feeling of importance and value as individuals, you will be well on the road to developing a successful team.

The question is: Are you respected as a coach or have you got "position" power? Players that play for the "position-power" coach, who says, "Do it my way or the highway," or "Do it because I said so" become irritated under this tight control and, like everybody else, don't like being told what to do.

Players who play for a coach whom they respect, because they feel encouraged and appreciated by him when he asks for their input and their suggestions, have fun and feel in control. Communication is a huge part of morale. If communication is poor, team morale will suffer. Communication also solves most team problems. If there is no communication, problems worsen. The day the players stop talking to you is the day you are no longer their leader.

Your Voice

How you say something sometimes conveys more meaning than what you are actually saying. The tone of your voice (aggressive, passive) and tempo of your voice (fast, slow speaking) sometimes has more impact than what you say. So focus on your tone, your attitude, and your energy when talking to someone as much as you do on what you have to say to them.

Slow down and think before you speak. Remember, slowing down just means doing things purposefully. If you speak with a low-pitched, calm voice, you are perceived to exemplify calmness, strength, and confidence. If you raise your voice to a high pitch and speak quickly, you are thought to reflect excitement, maybe a sense of panic, and perhaps a lack of control. For a coach to project confidence and calmness, he has to slow down in his actions and speech.

Coach Inspires Her Players

When a coach talks, her words must be passionate and energizing to motivate her players. If what she has to say is important, yet her message lacks inspiration, the team's passion may be lacking. As a coach, you have to inspire your players through your words, your actions, and your energy.

Two-way, Open Conversation

The new style of coaching creates an environment in which players take responsibility for setting their own goals and managing their own behaviours. This new school of coaching is to have "open, two-way" communication that is honest and direct, where players feel they can ask questions, talk about their opinions freely any time, and get plenty of feedback from you; this builds trust. In this face-to-face conversation, where everybody is being honest and trustworthy, players are more likely to be open about their opinions if they disagree with you. With this constant attention given by you, it promotes a clear understanding of the players, and players always know what you are thinking about, because you talk to them and keep them informed.

In this "open-door" policy environment of telling the truth, you must understand that when you seek opinions from players, you will get some great suggestions. Some players will tell you what you *want* to hear; some players will tell you what you need to hear; and some players will tell you what you *don't want* to hear, which is sometimes not too pleasant; so don't get defensive if you hear something you don't like.

When you allow players to come and talk with you, you are empowering them to give their opinions and make decisions. You now know what is going on; you know what everybody is thinking, and you can keep a close pulse on the team's pulse because much of your time in practice is spent walking around talking to your players.

Note: In this open-door policy, make sure your mind is open as well: i.e., listen!

Ask Questions to Motivate Players

You can increase your players' motivation tremendously by simply asking for their input or opinions on team decisions, then listening and learning rather than telling them. You have to be a good role model of open communication by always talking to your players, always asking them how they are doing, asking them what they think, and asking them how they think the team can get better. Asking for players' input is a way of saying "I care what you think"; "I want to know what you think." You don't have to know all the answers, but you had better know how to ask the right questions to get players thinking. Also, you start to develop leaders by asking players questions such as, "What do you think we should do?" or "How do you think we can get better?" Then you have to listen to your players' answers to find out what they really want.

Tell Players What to Do—Sometimes

In certain situations, it is your best choice to tell or give orders to your players on what to do with no discussion: when there is little time for discussion (speak clearly and effectively so players understand); when dealing with rookies; and when explaining a fundamental or a system during a game.

The problems with "direct orders" are: giving orders becomes too easy and could become a bad habit; the coach assumes he is understood, whereas he might not be understood; even if the direct order works, it might not be in the team's best interest and it might provoke a stubborn resistance by the players;

and, generally speaking, people do not like to be told what to do. Therefore, you should use the indirect approach whenever possible by turning commands or direct orders into requests or asking for help for players' co-operation.

LEADERSHIP IS NOT JUST TELLING PEOPLE WHAT TO DO

Be Careful How You Handle Your Players

When you give feedback to a player, it is important to remember that "it is not only what you say, but how you say it." Do you correct the problem in a negative way (yelling at her) or a positive way (explaining to her)? Do you say it with a harsh tone or a gentle tone? You have to know with whom you are communicating. Does she respond to directions given gently, or do you have to be more forceful? You have to be hard on some players who are tough, to push them to work hard; yelling or being angry seems to work best for them. For sensitive players, you need to be nice to them by using a calm, quiet voice, a whisper, or a gentle pat on the back. For a tense player, you have to have a relaxed approach when telling her what to do. For a laid-back player, you might have to be a little more emotional in your tone of voice to get her excited about the game. So how do you handle your players?

Notes: If you tell players they have to "work hard," what does that mean? Explain what hard work consists of. You have to give specific statements, not general statements, so players understand. If you tell players they have to "get loose balls," what does that mean? Be specific on how they can get loose balls.

A coach running around barking orders and everyone obeying is not leadership. Barking orders is the exception, not the rule. A coach who insists on instant obedience in every situation is a bad leader.

Be honest with your players

You have to give your players straight, honest answers. You have to tell them the truth, to tell it like it is, no matter how hard it is on them. You have to be honest by saying things to your players that they really don't want to hear; things they need to hear. You don't have to say things they want to hear.

You may motivate one of your better players by telling him that he might be the backup at his position because of the way he is practising. You can motivate a player who is out of shape by telling him that if he doesn't get into shape, he will not play or even be on the team. You can motivate a player by telling him honestly that if he plays well, he will play a lot, but if he plays poorly, he won't play at all—which is usually the case.

Use temper and anger — periodically

You should be aware that by constantly yelling at players, criticizing them, and being negative can demotivate them. You must understand that you do not get a point across or communicate effectively by screaming and yelling.

It is fine for you to be hard on your players, but you will make them feel worthless by criticizing them all the time; always seeing what they did wrong, and never seeing what they did right; never patting them on the back or praising them. When you tell players, "You are lazy," players will think of themselves that way and behave that way. Negative words create barriers that block trust, confidence, performance, and communication.

But you can use your temper or anger in a positive way when it can accomplish a purpose: to charge up your team or just to scare the hell out of your players. The key to using anger effectively is to be angry at the right time and for the right reason.

Use persuasion

One of the best ways to persuade or influence your players, especially experienced players, to do something is to ask them for their help or opinion because you as a coach don't know how. "I need your help . . ."; "I don't know how to get this team to play harder . . ."

Use suggestions

You can use suggestions to lead, again with experienced players. The key as a coach is to get your players to do things because they, and not you, want to do it. By suggesting to players that they do something, you can influence them to do things without telling them directly.

Challenge your players

Coach has to find ways to challenge his players to motivate them. You can directly challenge your players to be the best they can be; you can directly challenge their pride and ego; you can directly challenge them to go the extra mile; and you can call them out to get their butts moving. "How long are you going to get your butt kicked before you do something?"

You can try to challenge a lazy player; usually you can't change a player's character, but you can make him aware of how champions act. It seems most players don't mind being challenged and they don't mind being asked to do something they might be a bit fearful of.

By questioning or challenging his players' playing ability, Coach is basically asking them to prove him wrong. "I'll show him." If a player goes out and proves the coach wrong, the coach has done what he wanted to accomplish: to motivate him.

Involve players in making decisions

Empowerment means delegating power so that players can make their own decisions. How can you inspire and empower players? Basically, you have to use the service-oriented style of leadership by getting the players involved in decision-making. This in turn helps empower and inspire them. When players are involved in making decisions, the result is they become committed and take on ownership because they provided input. It seems players work, fight, and are inspired much more for things that are their own. If you want to have a "team," you have to learn to pass control to your team; you have to involve your players by delegating power and valuing their input in the decision-making process.

Another way of empowering your players is you need to show them that you are interested in their lives and their playing career by talking to them and truly listening to them, whether you are walking around the floor, in the dressing room, or just sitting down chatting. You will find that your players are the best source of advice for solutions to the team's problems.

Give reasons "why"

Players want to know why they are doing the skill in a particular way or why they are being asked to do something a certain way. It is not enough just to say, "Do the skill this way because I told you to do it." So spend less time telling "how" and spend more time explaining "why."

Praise players every day

A major part of your job is to build confidence and self-esteem, and that is why you should praise and give reassurance to your players every day. Praising and giving approval is powerful in building interpersonal relationships. To build confidence and to help players believe in themselves, you should be positive, enthusiastic, encouraging, and complimentary. You should give pats on the back complemented by words and phrases like, "You're a winner," "Everything is going to be all right," "You can do it," "Excellent job," "Outstanding," "Terrific," "Nice going." This type of positive feedback motivates players and makes them feel good about themselves.

Be aware of tone of voice

You must understand that your voice is the greatest motivational tool you have. When you talk, sometimes you have to raise your voice in a firm, forceful way to suggest you are in control; at other times, you will have to lower your voice to a whisper to let what you have said sink in. Your tone of voice is sometimes more significant than what you say.

■ NON-VERBAL COMMUNICATION

Only 10 percent of your message is conveyed by words; over 90 percent is non-verbal communication conveyed by your body language and extra-verbal cues, such as your voice, vocal tone, vocal pitch, and your eyes.

Your Body Language

You have to be aware that your tone of voice, your facial expressions, and your body language give as much of a message as your words. Therefore, a self-confident coach must exhibit, as he speaks, a body language that reflects an image of being confident, friendly, and approachable. The attitude of the body reflects confidence in the coach by the way he stands, his movements, his walk, and his smile. The body language must give an appearance of being completely unfazed, thoroughly relaxed and at ease, but alert both in mind and body. You have to make sure your body language reinforces what you say.

Reading a Player's Body Language

You have to learn to "read" how your players feel through their body language as expressed by gestures, posture, or facial expressions, knowing that the best form of communication is not always the players' words. Is the body language announcing a "posture of defeat": stooping shoulders, slouching, expressing a lack of confidence? Or is it a "posture of confidence": standing straight, shoulders back, head up?

You must "read" your players' body language, especially before a game, because some players don't talk a lot; they won't come and see you; and they won't admit they need help. So it is their body language that communicates how they are feeling—if they are frustrated; if they are happy; if they are nervous; if they are feeling good about the game.

Active Listening

Some coaches feel that to be a strong leader, they have to do all of the talking, but that is just the *opposite* of what a coach should do. To be a great communicator, you need to *listen*, to allow others to express themselves, and to understand what they are saying. Effective communication is a two-way street. It invites players to express their views with the assurance that they will be heard by you.

You should know when to talk and when to listen. In fact, you have to learn to listen more and talk less. Listening is an important skill because when you listen, you learn more; and if you want to build a relationship of trust, where your players feel it is safe for them to say whatever is on their minds, you have to listen.

LISTENING IS JUST AS IMPORTANT AS TALKING

The Art of Active Listening

› Active listening is when you ask questions for answers to clarify the meaning of what the player is saying. By listening to players' ideas and making a concentrated effort to act on those ideas, you are able to gain the players' trust and, in turn, improve the performance of the team.

› Active listening is asking questions and then being comfortable with the silence that follows while waiting for the person to answer. You are telling the person that his answer is worth waiting for.

› Active listening is letting your players do most of the talking and not interrupting except to ask questions for clarification if you don't understand. Communication is about allowing others to express themselves.

› Active listening is when you listen with the intention of trying to understand what your players are saying and wait for your turn to speak. You should not pretend to listen with the intention of responding. You must really listen and do nothing else, not even think of what you are going to say next.

› Active listening is when you listen twice as much as you speak (maybe that is why you have two ears and one mouth). Some of the best coaches say very little; they just listen to what their players have to say.

› Active listening is when you give total concentration to the player and nothing else, as the player may have a problem that will require time to work out. Listening is hard work because it takes lots of concentration, patience, attention, and time to understand what the speaker is saying.

› Active listening is when you look the player straight in the eye when he speaks, because where your eyes go, your attention will follow. This shows that you will give the communicator your full attention.

› Active listening involves focusing with your eyes to read the speaker's body language, and facial expression, and with your ears picking up the speaker's tone of voice.

› Active listening is based on the emotions that are conveyed through listening and observing—the speaker's tone of voice, body language, and facial expression.

› Active listening is when you nod your head up and down now and then.

Note: Coach's good listening skills help to improve performance, boost morale, enhance co-operation, teach and inform players, make players feel valuable and important, and build trust. Players become motivated because they know that they are being heard.

■ EMPATHIZE WITH YOUR PLAYERS

Empathy is your ability to sense the feelings behind what players say and is another key to effective communication. It is important to feel what people are feeling. When a player speaks, you should listen and make no judgments until he or she is finished. You must listen with your ears and eyes.

You have to have the ability to "read" non-verbal communication: tone of voice, gestures, facial expression, and body language. If you really know your players, you should be able to tell if something is wrong by their actions and body language. For shy, quiet, non-talkative players, it is important to observe their behaviour to understand them.

■ CONFLICT RESOLUTION

When an argument—a conflict or confrontation—between a coach and a player arises, you should be aware that most arguments result from misunderstandings, personality conflicts, or some sort of communication breakdown. A conflict or confrontation can be a positive thing if it is built on trust, loyalty, and open, honest communication.

So sometimes it is more valuable for you to create a crisis with a certain player and then face the confrontation. You might feel that this disagreement or argument with the player could be a healthy debate; an opportunity for growth for the player by his bringing out what is bugging him; or just part of building a player-coach relationship.

You should work out a problem or conflict in a productive way using guidelines or rules, not a hit-and-miss approach.

Note: Coaches have to avoid the temptation to solve players' problems for them. If a player has a problem with another player, he has to know that the coach is not the "go-between" guy. Players have to work on conflict resolution by confronting each other directly, person to person, and working it out.

Rules for Arguing

The classic roadblocks to effective communication are personal attacks, such as finger-pointing, backbiting, and faultfinding; and negative talk such as blaming, name-calling, or put-downs. The most destructive form of conflict is based on selfishness: "I have to win."

So the rules for arguing are: no personal attacks, no finger-pointing, no put-downs, no bad-mouthing, no name-calling, and no talking behind the other's back. If you criticize a player's poor performance or bad behaviour, you must make sure the player understands that you are not attacking her personally, but you are addressing her performance or behaviour.

Get the problem out in the open right away

Healthy relationships are those in which mistakes are allowed and conflicts are openly discussed, so that the two participants can grow together. Progress in tackling a problem requires cutting to the chase and getting to the heart of the issue by finding a solution right away. If you have a problem with a player, you have got to confront it head-on, and get the problem, conflict, or issue out in the open right away and talk directly to the player to solve the problem immediately, or it will grow from a minor problem to a major one. Some players love to complain about most things, including the way the team is run, playing time, the way they practise. When players suppress any kind of confrontation, it becomes more draining on a team than fuelling an exciting team.

THE DOGS BARK, BUT THE CARAVAN MOVES ON

Talk face-to-face to improve understanding

If you have a problem with a player, you have to be proactive and go to him directly to confront him about the problem and try to resolve it quickly and move on.

Because you care about your players, if there is some confusion about the problem on their part, you have to sit down with them and have a face-to-face discussion to explain your actions.

Coach and player must listen to each other

Effective communication is still one of the best problem solvers. Both people confront the problem by listening to, and absorbing, each other's comments and issues.

Coach and player must be honest, positive, and low key

You and the player must deal with the problem or confrontation honestly with each other and not hold things inside. But if the player is angry with you—or vice-versa—both of you must remain calm and talk it out.

Emotional control when angry

Applying the following strategies to calm down gives both you and the player the ability to hear, think, and speak with clarity. Before discussing the problem, you and the player must work on emotional control by:

> Counting to ten slowly while taking three deep breaths; this will help calm you down

> Walking away from a potential confrontation until calm

> Waiting ten seconds before reacting or speaking

> Stopping oneself or pausing immediately to get under control before responding. Neither person should respond immediately; not until they feel they are under control. They should exercise restraint over their impulses, emotions, and desires. It is important that they stay on an even keel.

> Maintaining and exhibiting a sense of humour

Make sure both the player and the coach understand the problem

In many conflict cases and interpersonal problems, the real source of the disagreement is a failure to understand each other. So, you should not start solving the problem until you know and understand what the problem is. Many times, the problem is a misunderstanding or a lack of communication between player and coach. If a player is misunderstood, the most important thing for him to do is to explain himself. You must focus on understanding why the player is acting a certain way. Most good relationships are built on a foundation of understanding and trust. You both have to put forth an effort to understand each other.

CO-OPERATE, COMPROMISE, AND SHARE

Coach and player must co-operate and compromise rather than compete

Arguments and conflicts often make for a competition or contest between the two participants rather than for co-operation. In most arguments, the problem is that the participants are more concerned with who is right or winning the argument rather than what is right. Your job is to find out *what's* right, not *who's* right. You have to move the player from a critical "Whose fault is it?" frame of mind to a constructive "What can we do about it?" frame of mind. The best solution to a conflict, confrontation, or problem is a win-win scenario where both persons have co-operated and compromised rather than competed.

Remember: Coaches have a hard time admitting they are wrong. Sometimes they have to admit that the player is right.

18 BUILDING RELATIONSHIPS

The way you deal with people—how you use your people skills—will determine your success as a coach. Coaches are in the people-development business. A coach has to know his players and what makes them "tick": learning how each of your players is motivated by finding out all about them through building relationships. One important coaching task is establishing and maintaining a connection with your players on an emotional level through effective communication.

If you build a strong coach-player relationship, players will follow you, as it is easier to work with someone with whom you have a relationship . . . have shared the good and bad times with . . . and have developed trust in.

The first step in building strong interpersonal relationships is trust. And trust in the coach starts with your credibility; your reputation; your competence; your ability to coach; your principles and values; and it is increased by your genuine caring for your players. You have to earn trust—you can't demand or ask for it—and it is done on a daily basis through one-on-one spontaneous talks, battling together through wins and losses, and having formal interviews.

These spontaneous individual talks can happen anywhere: in the locker room, in the weight room, in the gym/arena/field; they can happen before, during, or after practice; or before or after a game. It is more relaxing and comfortable if you walk with players in their comfort area, such as on the playing field/floor/arena. Once players buy into you, they will follow your visions, dreams, and goals. Players are more likely to follow great coaches than great visions!

Communication through informal and formal talks is one of the best ways to get information while building relationships with your players. But another method to get to know your players is simply to watch and observe their actions in drills and games. By gaining insight into each player's character and competitiveness, you will learn how to lead and challenge them to be their best.

Negative factors that cause relationship problems on a team are:

> Poor communication, where nobody talks

> Destructive conflicts, where players don't know how to argue or to resolve conflicts properly

> Lack of understanding, where the coach hogs information

> Players who just don't ask questions for clarification

> Players who are disloyal and talk behind the coach's and their teammates' backs

> ❯ Distrust because everybody is lying
> ❯ Hidden agendas and selfishness: players have a personal agenda versus a team agenda

One of the single most important factors in bringing a team together is the formation of relationships. Therefore, building relationships with your players becomes all-important because it is the best way to reach your players. The player-coach relationship is second only to the parent-child relationship.

CREATING GREAT RELATIONSHIPS IS HOW GREAT TEAMS ARE BUILT

■ HOW A COACH BUILDS RELATIONSHIPS

You are responsible for forming relationships or partnerships with your players and exhibiting a passion for the game that keeps them energized. You spend 75 percent of your time on team issues through healthy dialogue. Your role is to be a coordinator of talent, behaviour, and the team's culture, in which players feel free to express themselves, even in the midst of negative conflicts. By forming these relationships, you can work on developing the "whole person," not just "players."

Be Approachable

Players approach coach

You start to build relationships with an "open-door policy" or open line of communication where you are available at all times. You have to create an approachable environment in which your players feel comfortable about coming to you or your office with their problems and team concerns. Players respond better to coaches who are open to suggestions and do not have a "know-it-all" attitude.

Coach approaches players

If you want to be a successful coach, you must always initiate relationships with players, especially the first time you meet. Even where there is an "open door" policy where players can drop in and talk to you any time, you still have to take the first step and go to the players rather than waiting for them to come to you. You have to seek out and talk to each player directly and honestly, as players are sometimes afraid or shy to approach you. Remember, you need to find out everything about everybody.

You must see and be seen; you must keep your eyes and ears open; and you must get around and visit and talk with every player before, during, or after practice. You can defuse hostility situations by providing players with a method of talking to you and being available when they need to talk to you.

Note: A player once told me, "If you have a coach you can talk to, not just about your sport, but about anything, that's all you want."

Share Decision-making (Empowerment)

Empowerment means delegating power so players can make decisions. You build independence in players by giving players a sense of control and encouraging them to provide input into team decisions. To get quality in players, you must allow each player to contribute ideas on how they can improve the team and let them participate in decisions affecting the team. Now players have a feeling of ownership and empowerment and become more committed to the team.

It is a known fact that players will have the strongest belief in their own ideas, and, by your listening to these ideas, you build ownership and loyalty. You must have the courage to allow players to challenge your decisions. It is part of your role as a coach to help players understand the rationale behind decisions and invite them to be involved. You give empowerment to your players so they don't always have to go to you to get permission to make decisions and do certain things.

Note: In this type of open, trusting relationship, players don't tell you what you want to hear; they tell you what you need to hear to help the team.

Ask Players Questions

Success comes when every member of the team takes ownership of the direction the team is going. How do you get your players to work with you as the leader? One way is by asking questions to find out what they think the team needs to do to get better. It is important that you "pump" players for ideas on how to improve the team, because the result is involved, motivated, and energized players.

Also, you ask players questions about themselves for clarification: their interests, successes, strengths and weaknesses, fears, dreams, and goals. Listening to the answers, you not only connect with them, but you help yourself by understanding them better. You first have to understand what your players are thinking before you can understand them. When you understand your players, you can help them accept their strengths and move beyond their weaknesses.

Some thoughts on asking questions

> You ask for suggestions and opinions. True coaches realize that answers are important, but questions are essential. You can ask players questions such as:

"What do you think is important to better the team?"

"What do we have to do to improve the team?"

"If you had a wish list, what would be on it?"

"Is there anything I can do for you?"

"What would you do if you were in my shoes?"

"How are things going?"

"Is there anything you need?"

> You have to be aware that by asking questions, you might not always like what you hear when players gripe and complain.

> By your asking questions, the players see that you value their thoughts and opinions. This builds far greater loyalty and enthusiasm than if you tried to force their commitment through your authority.

> If you ask questions, you must also actively listen. You must let the player say whatever he wants without any interruption. By listening, you communicate how much you truly care far more clearly than any words you could have spoken.

> When you ask questions of your players, rather than telling them what to do, you "empower" them rather than "overpower" them.

> When you ask questions, you increase your players' alertness because you enable them to discover their own solutions instead of merely carrying out your orders.

Note: As a coach, do not be afraid to say, "I don't know."

Take a Personal Interest in Your Players

The only way you can lead people is to understand them; and the best way to understand them is to get to know each one of them as a person. You can't change a player's personality, so you'd better try to understand her or try to get her to work with you and not against you.

Try to spend quality time with your players off the court/floor in a non-sport atmosphere; phone them; or just walk around before or after practice talking to them and trying to get to know them on a personal basis. Invest time in your players, immersing yourself in their lives; get to know everything about them, discussing what they are interested in, their hobbies, what is important to them, and what motivates them.

You can ask: "How are you doing today?" "Is everything going okay with you?" "Where do you live?" "Who lives with you?" "How many are in your family?" "What do you like to do?" "Who do you hang out with?" "How are you doing in class?" "How are your grades?" and "Do you have a girlfriend?"

You have to get to know their families, their hobbies, their friends, their faith, their future goals, their birthdays, their parents' names, their girlfriend, their school, and so on. You really have to make the players feel like you care about them as persons.

When you make an effort to get to know each player as an individual, you find out what makes him tick; you learn what is special about him; you can show him you genuinely care about him as an individual.

So, be concerned about your players first as human beings, second as players. You coach persons, not players. You have to get to know your players beyond the sporting arena. You build character in your players by caring for them, by treating them like people, by showing them that they are more to you than simply bodies that can perform special skills in their sport.

You also get close to your players so you can find out what they expect from you. If players know you care about them as people, they will go the extra mile for you.

IF YOU TAKE CARE OF YOUR PLAYERS, THEY WILL TAKE CARE OF YOU

Show Your Players You Care

Give individual attention

You can be tough on your players as long as they know you care about them. You show players you care by giving individual attention and by showing concern in the good times and the bad times. Players need coaches who will take time to work with them, teach them how to play, give them constructive criticism, and be empathetic by feeling what the player feels.

Spending personal time with players really demonstrates that you care about them and helps form a special bond. You must spend a lot of time in the process of getting to know your players, whether it is about sport or life in general. You should take the time every day to do something or say something that lets your players know you care and are interested in them. Don't forget the little things that show you care, such as sending them birthday cards, or giving them handwritten notes thanking them when they do a good job, and, especially, listening to them. During these talks, you treat players as individuals by calling them by their first name, having fun and kidding with them, playfully "picking" on them, listening to them, hugging them, and developing a love for them.

Note: Unfortunately, it is necessary to caution you here about touching players, especially those who are children or young adults. Many school boards and sports organizations have developed policies regarding teachers and coaches touching students and players. Make sure you know what your organization's policies are. It is a shame that these policies have become necessary, because often the best way to show players you care for them is still by hugging them.

Get to know how every player is motivated

You know each player is motivated differently, so you have to know the players well enough to know what method is the most effective to get a positive response from them. And the best way to find what method works best is by communicating with your players on a one-to-one basis. By building relationships with your players, you can understand the mental make-up of each player; then you will know when to get on someone, when to back off, when to push someone, and when to ease up.

Building relationships and developing players as people takes time and effort for you. To do this, you have to get involved with your players' lives to get to know them. Players are different, so you can't treat everyone the same. Are they introverted or extroverted? Are they emotional or low key? Are they loud or quiet? Are they sensitive or tough-minded? Some players need to be calmed down; others need to be pumped up. Some need to be talked to softly; others need to be yelled at.

Note: Ask players to write down positive and negative characteristics about themselves.

Ways to show you care

The most important thing in building a successful relationship is the players' knowing you care about them as persons. How do you show you care?

> ❯ By acting in the players' best interests
> ❯ By always standing up for your players; "As a player, you want the coach to fight for you, and in return you will fight for him!"
> ❯ By being demanding on the floor and caring off the floor
> ❯ By being willing to talk and listen
> ❯ By following the Golden Rule: "Treat others the way you want to be treated."
> ❯ By trying to understand your players—you know what motivates them and you know how to get along with them
> ❯ By being sensitive to the feelings of your players
> ❯ By being understanding; everyone makes mistakes, so you must be constructive, patient, and tactful when offering feedback
> ❯ By being impartial; you do not treat all the players alike, but you treat them all fairly and honestly. Players don't all deserve the same treatment. You give each player the treatment he has earned.

> By believing in your players and supporting them during the rough times. You have to have the ability to feel what the player is feeling so he understands his problem better.

> By always distinguishing between the player and the behaviour or the performance

> By not comparing individual players with other players

> By showing players that you want to help them, thereby earning credibility with them

> By having a pre-game, one-on-one talk with a few players about their play; or to challenge them; or to reinforce to them that they are playing well; or just to get to know them as individuals

Note: Players like to be pushed, because it shows you care. You work them hard, you push them, and you are tough on them. They need that and want that. But you can't be as hard on them as in the old days. Coaching is tougher now, because you have to have more people skills in terms of dealing with players. In the old days, a coach got respect right away through fear and when he said to do something, the players did it. These days you've got to earn respect, not just with the tactics of the game, but by the way you deal with people.

NEVER UNDERESTIMATE THE POWER OF INDIVIDUAL ATTENTION

Share Information with Your Players

In the old school of coaching, coaches felt that the fewer players who knew about what was going on with the team, the better. They acted like meaningful information was top secret.

We know now that the key to effective leadership is the relationship a coach builds with his team. It is also important that a coach foster a culture of information sharing. The modern coach feels that through these one-on-one talks, they should keep their players informed of important information affecting the team. This sharing environment establishes a climate of trust that shows you don't have secrets, and it puts everyone on the same page when you tell players about the game plan; tell them why they are doing certain things; how they fit into the system; where they stand with respect to playing; what their role is; how they can contribute to the team; what is expected of them; and when you ask them if they have any problems.

Being an information-giver builds a player's confidence, which helps him to be relaxed and play with a take-charge attitude.

Be Honest

You must understand that forming a long-term player relationship is about straight talk, looking each other in the eye, and telling each other the truth. Honest communication brings about trust and a good working environment where players feel they have the freedom to be themselves. If your words and actions always seem genuine and sincere, then in return players will always feel they can trust you. Players must feel you always speak from the heart. A damaging lie, a cutting criticism, or an act of unfair favouritism can definitely destroy this trust very quickly.

Make Your Players Feel Good

Every time you talk to players, you should listen carefully and leave them feeling good about themselves and believing in themselves. You can do this by letting the players know the things you admire and appreciate about them; you can tell them how proud you are of them; you can make players feel they are "special" and make them feel important to you and the team.

Many of your players need not only motivation but love. As a coach you should be telling them you love them . . . you love being around them . . . you love the team . . . and, "We are like a family." When the coach shows the parents the love and passion he has for their kids, the parents will feel they are turning their sons or daughters over to someone who really cares.

Note: A good, old-fashioned, handwritten note speaks loudly to players, as it demonstrates that you have taken the time to show you care about them.

Make Players Aware of Internal or Self-motivation

Through relationships, you can figure out what's important to each individual player to help him with his internal motivation. If you help players become aware of what self-motivation is then hopefully they won't rely on just external influences for their spark—they won't wait for you to pump them up. So you make them aware that great players are motivated because they play for the love of the game and want a chance to prove that they can play at this level; but the best motivation is setting a specific personal goal, such as being the best defender in the league.

Build Close Relationships but Keep Your Distance

How close should you get with your players? There must be a line of distinction of how close you get because you are in a position of power over them. You will probably have to make some tough decisions and you don't want any personal feelings to enter into those decisions. You still want to build a close relationship, but you have to maintain a professional distance. You can't cross that fine line where you become their buddies, socialize with them, and go drinking with them, because players could take advantage of you. At the older level, you may allow yourself to become friendlier with your players, but you still need to stand apart as an authority figure.

Have One-on-One Informal Talks

The three key factors in building good relationships are quality time, individual attention, and good communication. One-on-one talks, with open and honest communication, is one of the most powerful ways to build loyalty, dedication, and commitment to the team. These informal talks are where most of the real work of coaching is done. You have a chance to mingle with your players to get to know them and to build a "special" relationship with them. There are some players who will not automatically buy into your philosophy or ideas; you will have to work with them.

By talking one-on-one with your players, you can sell them on your ideas, your philosophy, your systems; you can work on earning their trust; you can compliment them on their play; you can give suggestions about their play; you can discuss their short-term personal goals; you can ask for their opinion about team issues and problems; or you can just use these sessions to ensure that the lines of communication are open. Players don't care how much you know until they know how much you care.

Players need to feel listened to and valued, if they are to excel. You first listen to your players; then you can hand responsibility over to them.

Note: Coaches should definitely have more one-on-one talks with their players than team meetings. But also realize that team meetings before practices are also important in forming relationships.

The quiet players

From these talks, you will find out about those players who are quiet and who you consequently think don't have any problems—but they do. These quiet players are often taken for granted because they give the impression that everything is okay with them. The secret to dealing with quiet players is to talk to them: The best way to find out if anything is wrong is to just ask them.

Coaches tend to focus only on trying to turn around the troublemakers, but they should recognize the well-behaved, quiet players by focusing on something positive they have done or are doing.

Results of one-on-one informal talks

You make players feel you care about them through these one-on-one talks. By "connecting" with players, they feel free to speak up because they know their opinions matter. This connection with you results in players' commitment.

Remember: Players commit themselves to people, not to organizations.

One-on-one informal talks:

> *Motivate players.* The better you understand the players, the better you understand what motivates them; you find out what the players want and what their needs are. You motivate and inspire by forming a good relationship with your players and they in return want to please you and feel bad when they don't play up to their potential.

    Also, from these informal talks, you get a sense of how to talk to your players. Sometimes you are hard on certain players because you know you can yell at them and it won't bother them; whereas with other players, you must always talk in a calm, soothing tone because you know if you yell at them you might destroy their confidence. So you learn to "baby" players who need to be pampered, while being hard on those who can take it.

> *Create loyalty.* If the players get to know you better, they are more likely to enter into a relationship with you and end up wanting to follow you.

> *Get commitment from players.* When you listen to what your players have to say; listen to their input into team decisions; and listen to what they feel like doing, you give them empowerment—which equals commitment.

> *Help you to learn what is going on with the team.* You don't want players snooping for you or "squealing" on their teammates, but you want to know if there are problems brewing on your team. One of the major advantages of spending time with players is that it enables you to detect any team problems and act upon them before they spread and create morale problems.

    Note: Also, if you want to know what is going on, talk to the trainers.

> *Help you to find out about players' personal lives.* In order to lead players, you have to understand them, and the best way to understand them is to get to know them better through these one-on-one informal talks. They give you an opportunity to let players know what is expected of them; bolster their confidence; answer their questions and offer support; and make players feel like they are part of the team.

> *Get players to relax.* You can't just tell somebody to relax and expect them to play that way. You have to create conditions in the team environment, such as open communication, to help players play relaxed.

One-on-One Formal Interviews

This is a private, formal, one-on-one interview with each player in your office. You meet with each player for about ten minutes and talk honestly and openly with him. The primary method of understanding players is to ask questions, but do not make it like an interrogation by asking questions all the time and controlling the conversation. You have to give players time to talk after you ask your questions. By asking questions, you find out what players like to do, what they are good at, and what position they would like to play. From these interviews, players will know better what their role will be and hopefully you will put them in a position on the team to maximize their talents.

The better you know your players, the better you will be able to help them. In these interviews you want to build self-esteem and self-confidence, and motivate your players by listing all their strengths and all their successes. You can also help players understand what their weaknesses are and help them come up with ways to improve themselves.

These sessions are a good opportunity to discuss players' personal goals. In asking players what their goals are, you will find that most of them set their goals too low, or list goals they feel they can easily meet. Surprisingly enough, you will also find that most players don't have a personal dream, such as to be an all-star, but they have general goals, such as "just to become a better player." You have to talk to players about setting specific goals and achieving them. You have to get them to believe they can be better than they think they are.

Formal interview questions to ask players

Sample team questions:
> Are you totally committed to this team?
> What are your team goals? (Regional Championship, City Championship, Provincial / State Championship)
> What can you do to help us work well together as a team?
> What can you do to help create team unity?
> What do we need to do to improve as a team and to become more successful? What can we do more, better, or differently?
> What can you do to make this team better? What can you do to make this team more successful?
> What are all the things we did in a pressure game that helped us work together?
> What can you do to encourage and support your teammates? Do you care about your teammates?
> What would you do if you coached this team?

Sample personal questions:
> What's on your mind?
> What do you want?
> What do you want to be? (Starter, all-star, to be the best, leader . . .)

> What are your personal goals for the season?
> How do you expect to accomplish these personal goals?
> What motivates you?
> How do you expect to accomplish these personal goals?
> How can you give us great leadership?
> What do you see as your role with this team?

19 BUILDING SELF-ESTEEM

When you support and believe in your players and you build self-esteem—make a person feel good about himself, have a sense of self-worth, and believe he is important—you are applying another of the most powerful coaching motivating tools or skills. Self-esteem is a key determinant of performance: Players' enthusiasm picks up, their energy level increases, their learning level increases, and their performance improves. You can't totally motivate players, but you can create an environment where it can happen easily; in fact, players' belief in themselves is a determining factor in shaping their success and happiness in sports.

Make Players Feel Important

This is the most powerful motivator of human behaviour. You have to excel at letting players know that what they do is important and that they do make a difference to the team. To get quality performance, you have to watch for players doing the right things; you have to tell them how good they are every day; and tell them that they are doing a great job. Players want recognition; therefore, giving recognition for players' doing things right helps to build self-esteem. Do not make the mistake of taking players for granted and ignoring them when they are doing a good job.

Make them feel special

Telling players they are "special" satisfies the greatest human need of feeling appreciated. Nobody ever gets tired of hearing how great they are and that they are special. Players need a boost at times; they need to feel like "a somebody"—that is why you make them feel they are the best player at their position in the league.

PLAYERS NEED TO FEEL SPECIAL

Ask them for their opinion

Another way you make players feel important is by sitting down with them and asking them for their opinions about team matters. That you feel what they have to say is important will make them feel valued and needed.

Share information

Another way of making players feel important is by your sharing information with your players about what is going on with the team. You show them that you trust them with the information and that you have no "secrets" from them.

Delegate responsibility

You can make players feel important by delegating personal responsibility. The "new-school" coaches believe that if you want something done right, you must find a way to get your players to do it. The function of the coach today is to delegate more responsibility to players and, by assigning the right players to the right job, they get more things done. Ironically, the more responsibility you give away, the more control you have.

Believe in your players

You build players' self-esteem and confidence level by demonstrating you believe in them and their playing abilities. Your belief and confidence in your players has a direct impact on their performance. If players think you have confidence in them, they will perform at a higher level.

One of the differences between good coaches and average coaches is making players believe they are better than they think they are. It's a fact that players are only as good as you think they are. Telling players you believe in them makes the difference between a fear of failure and the courage to try. You have to see the potential in players and not just see what's happening now; you need to be willing to suffer through their mistakes, knowing they are going to get better with more practice and playing time. You should never put winning—especially at the beginning of the season—over developing players. In fact, when players are in a slump it is the best time to stick with them and support them.

What you can do to help players be the best they can be is to focus on their playing strengths. Never let players' weaknesses get in the way of their strengths. You can build players' self-esteem and confidence by acknowledging their strengths and by reminding them of some of their best performances. You can first build up their strengths, then later on, you can talk to them about improving their weaknesses. In fact, you might find ways to hide their weaknesses in your systems to use their strengths.

YOU BUILD SELF-ESTEEM BY ACCEPTING PLAYERS FOR WHO THEY ARE

Be Positive

The power of positive thinking is very important in a coaching philosophy. Positive coaches make their players feel good about themselves. If you put negative thoughts in your players' minds, you are going to get negative results. If you put positive thoughts in your players' minds, you are going to get positive results. In return, players will have confidence in themselves, in their talent, and in their abilities.

Give praise for doing things right

You make players feel appreciated, valued, and important by praising and complimenting them. You should catch players doing something good or right and then give them praise or positive reinforcement. Your job is to build, not destroy, the player's spirit—so it is important to recognize small successes. If you want to change players' behaviour or performance, you must constantly praise, encourage, and compliment them when they behave or perform correctly; in fact, you should try to pay a compliment to every player every practice.

And you should *praise him immediately* for maximum impact for doing a great job; you should make the praise personal by saying the player's first name as much as possible, as we all love to hear our own name; and you should make sure you compliment or praise him in front of the whole team. You build player loyalty by making them heroes in front of the whole team. "Bob did a great job on getting the most loose balls the last game." Public praise is much more effective than private praise. However, you should never criticize players in front of the team—this should be done in private.

You have to look for and catch your players doing something right, as coaches have a tendency to always look only for mistakes. You should especially be aware of recognizing the accomplishments of your average or role-players, who do not get as much attention on the team as the "stars."

Give positive feedback every day

The magic ratio of positive feedback to criticism is 3:1, but a more reasonable ratio is 2:1. You should be constantly encouraging and complimenting your players; and giving team affirmations in your talks to boost their self-esteem. Therefore, you do not attack your players by judging, ignoring, dismissing, humiliating, ridiculing, criticizing, or embarrassing them.

You can also build players' self-esteem by using positive non-verbal language. You should make it a point every day to give your players some sort of non-verbal recognition with a pat on the back, a handshake, a high five, a hug, a genuine smile, a simple fist tap, eye contact, a thumbs-up, a nod, or an okay sign. You should try to do all you can to build and maintain the self-esteem of your players.

Always stress a positive outlook

You encourage players to make up their minds that they are always going to have a positive attitude and not let anything get them down. Help players to believe they will become what they think they are. Players' increased self-esteem leads to increased performance, and with that increased performance comes a more positive attitude, with the end result that the whole team will start to feel that they are going to be successful. Players' attitudes will determine their success or failure.

Recognize Good Performance by Giving Awards

You can build self-esteem or make players feel important by putting them in the spotlight, giving special awards for outstanding performance. By giving credit to your players, you make them not only feel good but you motivate them to play harder. You build self-esteem by giving out awards immediately after the game for individual outstanding performances, such as the Best Offensive Player Award, the Best Defensive Player Award, the Mr. Hustle Award. You want to make sure that the team celebrates these individual successes. You can use old skates, old gloves, jock straps—anything that is symbolic—to hand out. It is important that you hand out these awards, win or lose. It is a good idea that you keep a record of the awards handed out to each individual player to make sure everybody gets one throughout the season. These rewards are one small piece of the puzzle in your attempt to motivate your team. But remember, these "extrinsic rewards" are strictly for short-term motivation.

Note: Other examples of external material things a coach can use for incentives to get players to perform better: trophies, medallions, ribbons, plaques, jackets, rings, "stars" on helmets, and their name in the newspaper.

Give Individual Attention

One of the best ways to bring out the best in players is through personal contact with them. Giving every player individual attention is one of the keys to building self-esteem. You must show your players you care about them by taking a personal interest in them outside of sports. Let players know you care about them on a personal level every day by telling them and by showing them that you are interested in them as people. They will feel valued as persons as well as players on the team. Showing personal interest in players is one of the most important things you can do to build and maintain loyalty.

Make Players Feel They Belong to the Team

You should be aware of fulfilling players' basic human needs of belonging and feeling safe; players will not grow unless they feel safe. The key element here is to create an environment that makes players feel accepted and safe, especially making rookies or new players feel part of the team. You should encourage and expect all team members to go to the new players and personally welcome them to the team. You should take the time to introduce yourself to the new players, learn their first names immediately, and explain their role on the team. Even giving them a smile will tell them they are accepted, and their self-esteem will increase. Once the players feel they are part of the team, it fulfills their need to be part of something big, and, by being committed to something bigger than themselves, they work harder.

Note: Trainers make sure players' names are over their dressing stall to make them feel needed and important.

Make Players Feel They Are Respected

Honesty is another key to building self-esteem. In other words, if you make a promise, you must follow through. You should never promise playing time and never play mind games with players. You have to let your players know exactly where they stand. Respect is seen as a two-way street, where you have to treat players the way you want to be treated, and vice-versa. Players who feel they are respected by you will give a better performance; and if they get along with you, their performance will be positive.

> ## ALWAYS TREAT YOUR PLAYERS WITH COURTESY, RESPECT, AND CARING

Keep Players Happy

One way is by asking them questions and getting their input. You just ask opinions of your players so they feel valued and needed. If you ask every day what players want, players will eventually tell you exactly what they want (remember, however, that they might not always get what they want); you should never assume you know what the players want.

You also make players happy by giving them the authority to make their own decisions—empowerment. Players love a sense of control over their own destiny; that is why input into team decisions is important. You ask players what they would like as their goals and rules. If you want to be successful, you have to play by the players' goals and rules.

Sweater numbers are important to players because they are very personal, and seen as lucky by superstitious players. So coaches should not hand out numbers casually, thinking players don't care what they get. If two or more players want the same number, have a fair system for deciding who gets the number. (Some coaches flip a coin for sweater selection. Others draw from a hat with players' names written on pieces of paper.) Certainly, returning players should have a choice of keeping their sweater from last year or selecting any new one available. It's the new players with whom this problem will likely arise. Another way of distributing sweaters is to tell all new players that sweaters will be given out as players make or are signed to the team.

> ## YOUR JOB AS A COACH IS TO PUT SMILES ON YOUR PLAYERS' FACES

Be Aware of Your Own Behaviour

You must be aware that what you say or do has a tremendous effect on your players. You must try to display or be a good role model of consistency, patience, and self-control. Today's coaches can't jump all over players and constantly blow up at them and then expect them to follow them. You must be aware that everything you do or say, or don't do or say, has an effect on how your players feel and think about themselves. So consciously do and say things that boost self-esteem in your players.

Note: An insensitive coach will display signs of being aloof, cold, impersonal, and uninterested.

Mistakes

You want to build self-esteem by creating an environment of support in which players are not afraid to make mistakes. When players are having problems, are struggling, or are in a slump, you have to meet with them to build them back up. After a mistake, players have higher self-esteem and confidence with supportive and patient coaches than with coaches who criticize, nag, lecture, or scold.

You can also build self-esteem by providing positive feedback when you correct mistakes and give instructions immediately after them. A positive comment is definitely better than a negative one because positive thoughts will bring positive results. This type of reaction has a profound effect on your players. In fact, to help players learn from their mistakes, you should ask them, "What happened?" rather than always harping on or criticizing the mistake itself. You know that, despite their best efforts, players are always going to make mistakes, so create an attitude of "let's not worry about them when they do happen, let's just correct them, shake them off, and move on."

You can criticize players periodically for dramatic impact because we learn from being criticized. But usually criticism is a confidence destroyer;

it undermines a player's confidence, triggers feelings of failure, and destroys self-esteem. Most times, it is better for you to say nothing rather than to say something negative.

However, players value coaches who give them advice about how to improve for better or worse, and this advice sometimes comes in the form of criticism. You can be harder on players with high self-esteem, because they already feel good about themselves most of the time; but players with low self-esteem tend to be fragile, so you will have to be more gentle with them—they can crumble when criticized.

Note: If a coach is positive all the time, she could lose her credibility.

CORRECT MISTAKES, SHAKE THEM OFF, AND MOVE ON

The major result of high self-esteem is that players play best when they feel good about themselves, and the team is going to be more successful. Players with great self-esteem will do great things by taking risks—such as taking the last shot or wanting the ball in the closing seconds. Players who have low self-esteem do not feel good about themselves; they fear failure; they worry about making mistakes; and they seldom take risks.

20 SELECTING AND CREATING TEAM LEADERS

Although the true leadership of the team comes from you, who are in control of the team, you also need leadership from the players. You may steer the team in the right direction, but the veterans and seniors will have the major impact on the team by driving and inspiring the team and handling things on the floor. One of the keys to being a successful team is strong leadership of the players, where the veterans run the team.

There are players who want to be leaders, but they don't know how. Some coaches just tell their players to prove to them they can lead. One of your main tasks is to use your skill to nurture and build team leaders as they emerge. You can't teach someone to be a leader, but you can help a player-leader become a better leader by telling her what you want from of her.

In fact, you want your players inspiring other players and standing up for each other. So, you work at developing every player on the team into becoming a leader, but there are special players who stand out more. The success of a team depends on a lot on your player-leaders, and the more player-leaders there are, the greater the chance of success for the team.

Notes: It is a very common mistake to suppose that the most talented player on the team is also the most natural leader. This is not always true.

The coaching legacy is when a former coach has had a great influence on you; you are now compelled to do the same for others. Part of a coach's responsibility is developing players as leaders in case they want to go into the coaching fraternity or into a leadership position in life.

Head coaches have to coach coaches. His assistant coaches should know their responsibilities and how the head coach wants the fundamentals taught.

What Makes a Leader?

At some point in the season—preferably at the beginning—your player-leaders emerge naturally, mainly because the players look up to them for one reason or another. They might respect a player's experience or great skills; or the player might simply be someone everybody likes. They are natural leaders because of who they are; they have an inborn quality or skill that makes them leaders. It doesn't matter how good a player is, the question is, "Can he/she lead?"

If they are natural leaders, they will have to learn to accept being a leader, whether they want to be one or not. Their choice is whether they will be an active or passive leader, or a positive or negative leader. Sometimes players have no choice—they just take on leadership. It takes a core of great "natural" player-leaders to show the way for a team to be successful, because so much of sport is confidence and leadership.

DEVELOP A TEAM OF LEADERS, NOT FOLLOWERS

How Does Coach Pick Player-Leaders or Captains?

Rotate captains

Some coaches pick their leaders by rotating the captaincy/leadership through players every game to see how each reacts as a leader. This way, every player has a chance to be captain. Coaches also can provide leadership opportunities by allowing each player to be in charge of something: warm-ups, forming a party, or even acting as team captains in practice or during stretching. But if coaches wait to see who will develop into a leader during the season, it might be too late to influence the team. Sometimes this method is used with youth teams to pacify the parents.

Team vote for captains

Some coaches pick their leaders by having their players vote for their team captain and assistant captains, but this method could become more of a popularity contest and doesn't always result in the most appropriate player becoming captain.

Another good way coaches pick their leaders is to get the team to vote on the captains and assistants with the understanding that the vote will not be decisive, but may help or influence the coaches when they make the final decision. So a coach should talk to the team about the qualities he is looking for in a captain: experience, communication skills, ability to lead by example, and a great work ethic.

Coach picks captains

If coaches don't have any leaders who stand out or who represent the characteristics they want, they have to appoint "special players" to be leaders, who they feel will act appropriately and carry the team on their shoulders.

Let captains emerge

Usually, the best way coaches pick their leaders is by letting the player-leaders emerge or evolve naturally on a team because most of the players look up to them for one reason or another.

But you should try to pick the captain as soon as possible. Selecting a leader can be a challenge, especially when you are working with a new team of players about whom you know very little and whose character or pecking order is yet to be established. You can try to identify the leaders on the first day of camp by noting how they start to take charge of the team; by what they say to you and their teammates; by the way they organize the team into group drills and get things rolling without being told; by the way they perform in practice; and by the way they want to be put in every pressure situation.

How Does Coach Develop His Player-Leaders?

To develop player-leaders, you have to express to your core leaders what you want them to do, what you want out of them, and what they should think about; and then let them go on their own to find their own way.

You will have to invest time in helping players become leaders. Your philosophy should be that you believe everyone is capable of becoming a player-leader on the team, and you express that by giving each one of the players experience in leadership roles.

The best way to develop the core leaders is for you to give them decision-making power and the authority to make team decisions; to give them responsibility to do things on their own without your permission; and to get them involved in team decisions to make them independent. There is no better way to develop confidence and the ability to lead than delegating responsibility. You have to provide players the opportunity to take charge and display their abilities.

To create this empowerment-environment, you have to learn to let go of your control. Some coaches even want to control the emotional impulse of their teams, but it doesn't work. It is much better for you to use your influence via your group of core team-leaders to control the emotional impulse or chemistry of the team. Coach cannot always lead by himself—he has to let others lead as well.

LEADERSHIP IS EVERY PLAYER'S ROLE

Why Do We Need a Core of Player-Leaders?

Core leaders will sell the vision of the team

Having a group of core leaders is part of the process of coming up with a vision of where the team wants to go, the style of play it is going to play, the type of team it would like to be, and the commitment of the team. The core leaders play a vital role in motivating their teammates; they sell the vision and core values in training camp and in the locker room; they create a positive peer pressure to follow the core values; and they become the disciplinarians of the team instead of the coach.

These player-leaders keep you aware of what the players are talking about in the locker room. Be careful here—you don't want these players to be snitches, but just to make you aware of or anticipate any pending problems, or what the players are thinking that could turn into major problems.

Core leaders reinforce core values

You can pick, identify, or develop a core of leaders who represent the team's core values, the team's behaviour goals. This is really important in building a successful team. They will act as informal coaches—an extension of the coach, reinforcing and putting into practice the core values. The core leaders are role models of the behaviour goals, demonstrating how the team should act and play: "Hard work, unselfishness, playing smart, and playing disciplined." The team's behaviour goals help put positive peer pressure on players to act and play a certain way.

Core leaders create team unity

The player-leaders may or may not be the most talented players on the team, but these emerging leaders will have the respect of their teammates and will be able to create team unity and cohesiveness—essential elements for success.

Core leaders make those around them better

Great player-leaders make everyone around them a little bit better, either through their own play or through what they say and do—even to the point that if a teammate makes a mistake out of laziness or lack of concentration, they don't mind getting on his case. These veterans set the standards high for everyone—even in practices—by trying to win every competitive drill and by displaying a great work ethic during and after practices. They feel they are accountable for the way the team plays and are willing to put the responsibility of the team on their shoulders by challenging the rest of the team to play their best. They just have what it takes to be a leader.

Core leaders are great role models and an extension of the coach

Most championship teams have a group of veteran player-leaders who provide leadership and are great role models for the younger players and rookies. They play hard and intense to be an example to the team; they lead; they are the coaches on the floor; they pass on the team's traditions, standards, and values; they take on the responsibility to make sure the younger players are going to class; they are vocal, passionate, and animated to get the players playing hard

(Coach cannot be the only passion-supplier); they tell players what to expect from the coach; they are the disciplinarians of the team rules rather than the coach; they teach players how to win and how to play the game; and they reinforce the identity of the team that it has set. "This is the way we do it here."

It is great motivation and inspiration for the other players to be around great veteran players and see first-hand the way they train, practise, and play. Certainly players look up to veteran players who have played in the league for many years and know the score and can stand up and tell the players how it is. It seems the true leader is the guy with the most "war stories"—stories about the good times and the bad. The core leaders are committed to playing to the best of their ability and to helping mould a collection of players into a team.

You need a core of leaders to go to for their input when needed. "What should we do during this game?" Some coaches show up late for practices just to see if the captain or leaders will take over and start the practice. They are an extension of the coach. The coach depends on them for a lot of things and yet he is harder on them than on the rest of the team.

Notes: "With great power comes great responsibility." (From the movie *Spiderman*.)

If your leaders are not the best players on the floor, you are in trouble.

LEADERSHIP IS NOT SOMETHING YOU OWN AND KEEP FOR YOURSELF

Player-Leaders Need Guidelines

You can't just assign or pick player-leaders and then expect them to do all the things a good leader should do naturally. With some leaders, you don't have to do very much; and then there are other potential leaders you have to work with to help them become good leaders. You have to give them some direction and guidelines so they know what leadership is all about: how to act, the role they would play, and what is expected of them.

Qualities to Look for in Your Leaders

Good leaders have great character

They are someone everybody looks up to. They are quality players with strong personality and character.

Character players are leaders who take charge, take on the responsibility of the team, are not afraid to fail; they put the team on their shoulders, lead by example, encourage others, talk and correct with line-mates on the bench, and set the tone for the rest of the team.

Good leaders emulate the team's behaviour characteristics

Leaders are models of the desired behaviour the coach wants. They must constantly uphold and reinforce the team's principles and behaviour goals:

> ❯ By playing with passion, playing aggressively, playing intensely and hard. Leaders are players who motivate and lead teammates by

- Playing at a higher level than anyone else; by playing harder than everyone else; having the most impact and influence in the game

- Being respected by their teammates for the way they compete in a game every night and how hard they practice

- Having a swagger or an "air" of confidence, almost to the point of cockiness; and they are so passionate about the game they put their heart and soul into playing.
    If your leaders are your hardest workers, you've got a chance or a successful season, because everyone looks up to these guys.
    Great leaders are true warriors who love the battle and who love to compete at the highest level even more than winning. They become the symbol of the team's toughness.

> ❯ By being physically and mentally tough; playing with courage, determination, and persistence. Leaders are mentally tough, as coaches are sometimes hard on them by yelling at them to get a point across to the team, when the team is playing badly, or if they are not giving the leadership the coaches are looking for. Coach sometimes brings the leaders together and asks them, "How could you let your team play the way it did?" Or, when necessary, challenge them to lead the team. They just know how to get the job done.

> ❯ By having a positive attitude and passing it on to their teammates

> ❯ By playing smart and having an unselfish attitude

> ❯ By being encouraging and enthusiastic for their teammates; being supportive of them

> ❯ By loving to play under pressure. They show maturity, emotional control, and stability when under pressure.

Leaders take the responsibility of carrying the team on their shoulders

Leaders become active in leadership, and that means fighting to the end and never giving up. Leaders must know they carry a great deal of responsibility because other players look up to them for scoring production, work ethic, and leadership. They have the ability to lift up and inspire their teammates.

Leaders set high standards

To be known as great player-leaders, the only thing they have to do is play hard. Leaders know they have the power to set the tone for the team by the way they play and practise. They lead by example by working harder than anybody else on the team so that the team will follow them. They do the extras without being told. They arrive early and stay late for practices. They will even stop practices and give the team a talking to if the quality is not up to the team's standards. They have high expectations for themselves and the team and will pressure players to play better and play harder. Leaders think and act like the coaches during a game. Coach wants his players to be thinking what he is thinking. They are almost like player-coaches.

Great leaders are also great role models in speech

Somebody besides the coach has to get after the players. One of the most important things player-leaders have to do is speak to the team on behalf of the coach at team meetings or pre-game talks. Sometimes, during tough times, it's not the coach but the older players who talk to the team to express how they feel and to get the team motivated. They can speak positively, radiating confidence about believing in the team, about all the preparation the team has put in, about the team's work ethic, how hard the team has played, the sacrifices each player has made for the team, why the team is much better than their opponent; and challenge every player in the room to believe they can win. Or they can tell the team they are not happy with the way it is playing.

During the game, player-leaders yell at their teammates to get them into the game. They call their teammates together in a huddle to help calm them down by telling them what needs to be done or by giving orders to make sure everyone is where they are supposed to be and know what to do. In practices, they tell players to work harder, to put more effort into the play, and to put more zip on the pass.

But probably the best way is for great player-leaders to just lead by example.

Player-leaders also have to be able to speak to the coach for the team. They might tell the coach that he is out of line or that he is not being fair with a certain player; or they might question or challenge his opinion on a certain subject. They just tell the coach the way it is.

Player-leaders have to talk to referees to get clarification on a call with "class," self-control, and courtesy, using "Yes, sir," "No, sir."

In timeouts and at half time, leaders have to stand up and take over, saying things such as, "This is how it's going to be." "Here is what we are going to do."

Team leaders help to develop, mould, and create team cohesion

Team leaders run the locker room and set the tone for the team. If somebody gets out of line, the team leaders take care of it by talking to the culprit.

Rather than just expecting them to, they encourage and invite the shy players, the new players, the extras, to partake with the team. The leaders will invite them when the team is going out or hanging around. Good team leaders get rid of any "pecking order" or any cliques on the team and stress team togetherness. Leaders are responsible for getting rid of the disease of selfishness, jealousy, greed, and laziness. Leaders talk to new players and explain what is expected of them and about the team traditions and customs.

Great leaders also have to help create a family environment with family values that consist of caring, trust, love, and believing in each other on the team. They know that a team's personality is based on player-leaders' personalities.

Team leaders can shoulder other responsibilities

They are involved in making decisions on team problems and team rules. They take care of the violators of rules and the bad behaviours by disciplining them. They are the disciplinarians of the team instead of the coach.

They help to pick the three stars after every game: Mr. Defence, Mr. Hustle, and Mr. Offence. They take on the responsibility of planning parties and get-togethers for the team. They may informally have to check curfew when the team is on the road.

PART FIVE

THE ART OF MOTIVATION THROUGH PRE- AND POST-GAME SPEECHES AND GAME COACHING

21 PRESENTATION OF PRE-GAME SPEECHES

The pre-game speech is the same whether you give it before a regular game or a playoff game. You want to relax the players by keeping the same routine. But you can talk firmly to your players, telling them they are prepared and are physically and mentally ready. You don't want to give awkward pep talks and try to force manufactured morale. Over a long season, you cannot deliver the same old presentation—it will become boring and repetitious. Your pre-game speeches have to be interesting, informative, and entertaining.

Besides the actual pre-game speech, you can give out repetitive, constant messages all week at practices before the next game. You can set the tone for the week or before the next game, using anecdotes, stories, and inspirational affirmations to paint a picture of where the team is going this week.

Before the Pre-Game Speech

Time for players to arrive in dressing room

When do you want your young players in the change room to get dressed? If you let them in too soon, there will be too much fooling around. If you let them in too late, they will be rushed to get dressed, and you will have to hurry through your pre-game speech. You want to give the players just enough time to get mentally prepared by themselves, dressed, and ready in time to listen to your pre-game talk. It's a good idea to post a pre-game time schedule on the dressing room wall to let the players know when to get their equipment on, the time for the pre-game stretch and warm-up, and the time for the pre-game speech.

Individual talk with players

Before the pre-game speech, you can have individual pre-game talks with certain players. You can have a brief talk with players before the game about their past play; how they are playing now; to tell them to relax more or work harder; to get them up, or to challenge them: "I want this to be your best game!" You can post the starting lineup, even though the players usually know ahead of time that they are playing. It is important that you do not sit players out without explaining to them why they are sitting out.

Atmosphere in the dressing room

The dressing room just before the game should be fairly quiet. But before this quiet time, as the players are getting dressed, they may be listening to music before the game either on a radio or on their iPods; they may be watching a video of their opponent or of themselves; they may be just talking, kidding around, or indulging in some light humour; or they may be visualizing or doing self-talk. You want to create a businesslike, relaxed atmosphere so your team will approach the game with low intensity. You need to approach all pre-game talks in a businesslike fashion, with controlled passion and, when warranted, emotion.

Note: Some coaches get their team to visualize the opposition coming out pumped-up, emotional, and yelling, and to visualize themselves coming out calm, energized, and confident.

Preparing the Pre-game Speech

You have to spend time preparing your speech because there is an art to giving speeches. You have to know exactly what you want to say, and the better prepared you are, the more confident you will appear. During the pre-game speech, you should have your notes handy to glance at them. You want to remind the players the most important points to be successful. When your pre-game speech is well prepared, you will convey confidence to your players.

Remember: Coaches shouldn't ramble and talk on and on to the team; avoid long, boring speeches, or trying to "wing it."

During the talk, players should be listening

At the beginning of the talk, you must show the team that you mean business by making sure everyone is listening, sitting close together, and looking you straight in the eye; no talking, no fidgeting, no listening to music, no adjusting equipment, no getting dressed. If players are not listening, don't say anything. Just take a few seconds to wait for players to quiet down and give you their complete attention. You can also get players to listen by using humour; by putting players on the spot by asking questions to make sure they are listening; by telling stories about great comebacks and personal experiences. Stories keep players interested. After the story, you can ask the players, "Why am I telling this story?" This can spark some interesting discussion.

How Coach Gets His Message Across

How do you present your message? When you give a pre-game talk, it's about the right presentation. Sometimes it's for showmanship, sometimes it's for a show of confidence, but most times it's to convey information. So how you will best command the attention of the players—or the delivery you choose to use—depends on the situation. Each situation might require a different tone. Most times, your delivery is low key: sometimes you will say nothing at all, which can be very powerful; sometimes it is a humorous delivery;

and sometimes it is a kick-them-in-the-butt delivery. The pre-game talk is about saying the right thing at the right time to get your team to perform at its best.

Entering the dressing room

When you walk into the dressing room, you should walk with purpose, shoulders back, head high, eyes taking in the room. This will project a lot of confidence, poise, and composure. Then, pause for a split second to announce, "I'm here," and give everybody an opportunity to settle down and get serious. When successful coaches walk into the dressing room, they have a certain presence or aura. It seems you either have it or you don't. It is an expression of an inner state of mind.

Start the talk with a show of appreciation

You should try to start every meeting or pre-game talk with "appreciation and triumphs" of certain players or special teams to build self-esteem. You have to constantly remind the players that you believe in them; that they are getting better with each game; that you see immense potential in them; and that you see them as being special. In this appreciation talk, you expand upon how "special" the team is; how each player has contributed; how proud you are of each one of them; how you admire them; and that you will always be there for them. You want the players to feel about ten feet tall walking out of the room, knowing they are going to have a great game.

Read your players' body language

You should make eye contact with everyone in the room so you can see their reaction when you make a statement. Through experience, you get a feel for your team; you learn how to read your players by how they look at you, the expression in their eyes, and their body language. By observing the players' faces as you speak, you can see if they understand what you are saying by their look of excitement and determination, or by nodding their heads. On the other hand, perhaps they are presenting a blank stare that says they don't have a clue, or they have an "I don't care" look, or an "I don't really want to be here" look. By gauging your players' body language, you can adjust your talk accordingly. It's your job to know when your team needs a good pep talk or positive reinforcement, or when it's time for you to back off and say little and give your players some space.

Remember: You have to "read" the mood of the team in the dressing room. Is the team feeling down because it is playing poorly, or is it up because it is playing great? The mood would determine your type of talk.

Let players hear and see your message

The best way to get your message across to your players is to put it on the blackboard, on the overhead projector, or on a basketball/hockey/lacrosse diagram board as you talk.

Keep your talk simple and short

You should make the talk short—five to ten minutes. The best way of getting your message across is by keeping it simple, exact, and to the point—if you talk too much, their minds will wander and you will lose your players. Besides, you don't want to give your players too much information, as they won't remember what you say, and it will just confuse them. You tell the team in a few points specifically how they're going to be successful. Usually, game day is not the time for long, drawn-out speeches. It's a fallacy to believe that the more you talk, the more you get across.

Sometimes you will have to cut your speech short, as you feel they are ready to play; sometimes you might lengthen it to get certain key points across to get the players ready.

When you have to spend some in-depth time discussing the opposition—and even your own team—it might be a good idea to start with the game plan or pre-game talk in the practice before the next game, if you have time. Your dilemma is that you want to keep the pre-game talk short, yet you want your team to be informed of what they have to do, informed about the opposition, and still be prepared, which may take some time.

Remember: The first and last thing you say will be what the players will remember the most.

Speak slowly

The way you sound and what you say when you open your mouth is important. When you speak in front of the whole team, you should make sure you choose your words carefully. Slowing down will buy you time to think things through before you speak so that you don't say something you may regret later. This also gives you the appearance of being relaxed, calm, and confident. Let your players wait a little by throwing in a dramatic pause between key points so that whatever you have said—or are about to say next—will have more of an impact.

This talk has a calming effect on the entire team and gives everyone the impression that things are under control and it is business as usual.

Notes: After the coach's speech, some of the veterans can speak before the game; or just let the players talk it out by themselves.

In the locker room, sometimes you will have nothing to say before or after a game—remaining silent also sends a message. Sometimes, with too many speeches, the players tune you out.

Keep it low key

You don't have to talk down to your young players or yell at them, but speak in a normal, low-key tone to present them with the game plan. You should talk in the first person plural, using "we" and "us," as it says that the coach and players are working together: "When we run, we run hard," as opposed to, "I think you are ready."

You should also talk in the present tense to get the players focusing on the present moment, to get the point across that "all we can control is the very next moment." You should not talk about the past for this particular game—"if we get behind"—or the future, "we should win," "when we get a lead," "we should blow this team out," or "we should beat this opposition team by so many goals." If the players are told they should win, and the team gets behind or it becomes a close game, they might start to panic and push too hard. Once you start talking about winning or losing, the team will be in trouble by losing their focus on the present moment.

Find a phrase, a statement, or a story to inspire your players

Did you know players hear only 10 percent of what you say? Two coaches can give similar pre-game talks; one will put his players to sleep, while the other will inspire them to play energized with a saying, a story, or a team affirmation. So, one of the tricks to get your point or message across is to become a great storyteller in your pre-game talk in such a way that the players can relate to it, visualize it, understand what you are saying, remember it, and be inspired by it.

By your telling an interesting story, your players aren't just hearing what you say; they are seeing it, visualizing it in their minds, and feeling it. The story comes alive and imparts a lesson with word pictures—and "one picture is worth a thousand words." Players become inspired and learn best from analogies and parallels like: "This is like the last stand at the Alamo," or from anecdotes or success stories of ordinary teams or underdogs who overcame tremendous odds to be successful. To teach a point of view, you should also draw lessons from your own experiences and share this knowledge with the team.

Get your message across through humour

Your message can be both informative and entertaining at the same time; but don't tell jokes, one-liners, or hilarious stories unless you are a funny guy. You can insert some humour by picking on a certain player; talking about a moment in the game that the players would find funny; or talking about a funny situation in your own playing experience.

Don't be afraid to laugh at yourself or chuckle when a player says something funny about you. You should join in the fun to show your players that you don't take yourself seriously and that you have a softer side to your personality.

Besides, it is healthy for people to laugh at themselves. But bear in mind that there is a time and place for humour and laughter. Humour is an excellent way to ease the tension of an upcoming game.

Accept some of the blame

In your message, you can accept some of the blame for the way the team is playing and then make your point. This is much better than saying, "You guys aren't doing your job"—this will just create bad feelings. By taking on some of the blame, you can get the team to realize in an indirect way that they are making a mistake. "Let's correct it together and move on."

■ PRE-GAME TALK ROUTINE FOR GAME PLAN

Creating and giving a pre- or post-game talk takes a certain skill not all coaches have or feel comfortable with. Below are some ideas for your pre-game speech to get your team ready for game day. I have listed four parts to the pre-game speech, and a coach can present all four parts or deal with one or two parts, depending on the situation. The pre-game speech or game plan should motivate the players to focus their attention on what has to be done; focus on how to go about it and who will do it; focus on the team's performance goals and behaviour goals; focus on the systems; and focus on how the team is going to approach the game.

When you put the emphasis on these goals and on playing well, you distract the players from their immediate worries, which usually have to do with the skills of the opposing team and whether or not they can win.

It is important to be prepared before giving the pre-game speech so that you will not be distracted by your own worries, which will likely be the same as those of the players. Remember, coaching is saying the right thing at the right time to get the best performance out of your team. So timing and knowing what you are going to say are important when you're delivering your message, whether it is about the opposition, the team's strength, reminding players of their behaviour goals, or giving an emotional talk.

Part 1: The Opposition's Strengths

Knowledge of the opposition is power

You should know that for players to be physically and mentally ready isn't enough; the team has to be prepared for the opposition. You can never be over-prepared. Knowledge of the opposition is power because if you can anticipate what your opponent is going to do before they do it, you will have a slight advantage and play more relaxed. The team's real confidence comes from knowing that they are prepared about the opposition. Most of the preparation—the work and the game planning—is usually done in practices before the game. It is your responsibility to find out as much as you can about the other team.

In this part of the pre-game talk, the team is finding out what to expect from the opposition so there will be no surprises: what defence the opposition will play; whether they are conservative or aggressive on defence; who is playing well; who is their standout player; anything new, or things to watch out for; their tendencies, their strengths and their weaknesses; habits of certain opponents; what plays they like to run on offence; how our defenders can disrupt their offensive flow. From this information on the opposition, you won't change your basic game plan, but you might adjust it. You can even ask the players if they know any players on the opposition.

Do not build up the opposition

There is also a tendency for coaches when playing against good teams to spend all their time on how their team is going to stop them and all the problems they are going to face. In other words, they focus all their time on the opposition, building them up, and do not spend enough time on their own team. Talking too much about the strengths of the opponent is a negative approach, which will put your team in a "defensive mode" rather than simply focusing on what they can do and putting them in an "offensive mode." This negative approach also causes players to play so as to avoid failure, which causes anxiety and doesn't improve performance.

Also, if you worry so much about what the opposition is doing well, you fall into the trap of forgetting what your team is doing well. Your team can't control what the opposition does, but it can control what it does. So do not forget about your own team.

Remember: There should be no reason to fear the challenge of playing a great team. Players should look at playing against a great team as simply an opportunity for a tremendous challenge.

Part 2: Your Team's Strengths

Here, the head coach may share the floor with his assistants or with some of the experienced players.

The defensive coach can talk about the team's special assignments, responsibilities, and adjustments. He reviews the defensive rules the team has to improve upon and the minor adjustments they are going to make against this opponent; what they must be on the alert to defend against. As always, the number one priority is to stop the opposition's best players.

Then the offensive coach can also talk about the team's adjustments and give little reminders the team has to make for better execution.

Each coach presents a theme and gives a few key points for that particular game. Lastly, the head coach delivers a short speech about the three main points for this particular game. For this part of the talk, she makes sure she goes over the team's game plan so as to have the team prepared strategically. She might fine-tune the game plan with last-minute adjustments.

Talk about the team's strengths

The main part of the pre-game talk is to get the players to concentrate on what they are going to do rather than on what the opposition is going to do. You should focus mainly on your team's strategy in your pre-game talk. You reinforce the idea that "we can create the outcome of the game by doing what we do best." You build up your team so the players believe in themselves. Your message is more about competing against yourself than competing against your opponent.

Reinforce and correct the playing system

It is important that you are specific and everybody is clear about what they have to do. You stress certain major points in the playing systems—the offence, the defence, the specialty teams, and the breakouts. You can say to them: "This is what you have to do to be successful"; "Just take care of business, do your job, and look out for each other."

Review the statistics of the previous game

From the statistics of the previous game, you can prepare the next game plan, with slight adjustments for this new opponent. Statistics help you break the last game down. Players want substance in the pre-game talk—cold, hard facts, not generalities. If you want to make a point to the team, use the facts from the statistics; your players can't argue with facts. Remember to also give the positive statistics, things the team has attained, rather than just the negative statistics all the time.

Focus on the performance goals

You talk about improving or attaining the team's specific performance goals. You want to get your players to focus on themselves, to think about the present moment and what they have to do to be successful: that is, attaining their performance goals by winning the one-on-one battles rather than worrying about winning the game or beating the opposition.

You should bear in mind that your approach to the game is never to build the opposition up too much—how good they are—or tear them down—how bad they are. In other words, you do not want your team either fearful of the opposition or overconfident; but you do want your team to respect them.

The short-term performance goals are a big part of the game plan and pre-game speech. If the team attains its performance goals, it will be successful, win or lose!

The idea of beating the best team in the league, the first-place team, the former champion, in a game might make a team feel intimidated and fearful because of the reputation of their opponent. But if you narrow the team's focus to something more realistic and attainable, it won't worry about beating the best team; it will just focus on small steps of achievement such as winning the loose ball battles or keeping the opposition shooting under a certain percentage.

Note: When your players start to get too comfortable, either from winning or staying in a routine too long, complacency starts to set in at which time the team starts to let things slip and take things for granted. You have to keep your team on the edge by changing the routine or challenging them by raising the performance goals.

Go over match-ups

You go over individual match-ups and key assignments. Players like the challenge of being given an assignment: who is going to check their best shooter; what match-up you want. You can sometimes make the game a personal match-up or a personal conflict by telling a player, "Bob thinks he can beat you."

Have three goals for the game

There is no magic speech or formula to be successful. Coaching is reminding, reminding, reminding! "If we do this we will be successful." You can give the team three prioritized goals to be corrected from statistics of the last game. Or say, "We need to focus on these three key things in this game to be successful"—not ten or twenty things. Teams are more effective if they have to concentrate only on a maximum of three things, so give the most important things right away. In fact, research has found that if we want players to remember something important, say it three times; or, even better, have them say it aloud three times. You can give these three quick reminders just before the game starts.

Look for an angle to create a better performance

You should look for some sort of an angle to give your team a psychological edge, to give them a spark, or to get them to focus on a certain aspect of the game that needs improvement. This angle will make this particular game different or unique. You can:

> ❯ Look at the statistics from the previous game to see if there is an angle that you can work on to improve

> ❯ Challenge them in this game to give them a motivation to go to another level

> Challenge them to strive to get a little bit better in a certain area of their game

> Use the underdog angle of "us against the world—going against the first-place team, the referees, and the crowd"

> Even give them a special play, a special defence, a strategy on how to attack the opponent's strength that will give the opponent a surprise and your team an emotional boost. What you want to do is give the team a reason to do something well in this particular game.

> Create a sense of urgency when you know your team is not mentally ready to play. If they have the feeling that they are just happy to be here, they are setting themselves up for a real good butt-kicking. So you must create a crisis by saying "We are not ready to play while our opponent is doing everything in their power to be ready to play."

> Just simply tell them the truth about what got them here for this game—their hard work, their dedication, their unselfishness, and their togetherness.

Get your players in "the zone"

In your talk, you are always looking to get an edge. One way to get players in the zone is by asking them if they have ever played a perfect game. Then you get them to stand up and talk about themselves playing the best game they ever played and how they felt performing at their peak in the zone—they felt that everything happened in slow motion; they felt very powerful; they felt confident, physically relaxed, energized with positive emotions; they anticipated things happening before they happened; they felt everything was effortless, they felt they were ready for fun and enjoyment; and they knew they were going to play their best game ever. By hearing the players telling their experiences and stories of being in the zone, you can feel the energy of the team becoming stronger.

Ask your players questions

Asking questions can be a good way to make sure the players understand what they have to do; to make sure they are paying attention; to actually get input from them regarding the opposition team; or to get them involved in the conversation and get them talking.

> You ask questions about the playing system: "What do you do in a certain play?" "Are you playing a zone or man-to-man defence when in a 10 Orange?"
> **Note:** A lack of understanding of the playing system causes ambiguity and misunderstanding that eventually will lead to losses, and this is an unacceptable reason to fail. You should be asking playing-system questions at any time to make sure the players understand what they have to do in certain situations.

> ❭ You appeal to the players' competitive spirit by asking, "Are you going to let these guys push you around?"

> ❭ You appeal to the teams' pride by asking, "Are we not the best defensive team in the league?" "Is this the best we can do?"

> ❭ You appeal to the players' personal pride by asking: "Can you not stop #24?" "Everybody is watching to see how good you are. Are you going to show them?"

> ❭ You ask questions to question the teams' character: "If this was the last game of the year, is this the way you want to go out?" "If this was our last game of the year, what three things do we have to do right now to be successful?"

> ❭ You appeal to the players' past accomplishments by asking: "Is this the way you played against such-and-such [a great team]?"

> ❭ You give players a direct challenge by asking: "Are we not better than this?" "I am a great admirer of this defence, but we are giving up too many goals." "Do we want to be champions? Then dominate play. Play like champions and don't worry about the consequences."

Part 3: Reminding Players of Their Behaviour Goals

Repeat sayings or self-affirmations

You write one behaviour goal word on the blackboard before a game or practice. Do the players give meaning to, or have an understanding of, this word? You explain the meaning of the word with a personal story of your own experience. You then get the players to picture themselves expressing this word—work ethic, playing together, passion, etc.

Focus on one or two behaviour goals

You mainly stress the team's short-term behaviour goals for the motivational part of your pre-game speech to get the players mentally ready to play. You talk about some of the ideals of the behaviour goals vis-à-vis working hard, making good decisions, playing together, displaying self-discipline, totally concentrating, staying calm and poised, having fun, taking a dirty hit for the team and not retaliating, and playing with self-control.

You might occasionally ask your team, "How badly do you want to win?" Of course all the players will say they want to win, but then again so do all the other teams. One of the differences between being successful and unsuccessful is displaying the behaviour goals, so you have to always be reinforcing them. You can ask the team before the game, between periods, after the game, at the next practice, "Did we behave like and display the characteristics of a successful team?"

Make players aware that they have to work hard

You stress to the players that there is only a small difference between winning and losing so they have to work hard all the time. There is going to be a big play in the game, but nobody knows when it is going to happen. So players have to play like they are going to cause or stop the big play all the time.

Players need to anticipate problems during the game

You can help players anticipate problems by stressing the behaviour goals of self-control and poise. You want your team prepared for anything. You want it to imagine the "perfect game" where all the things that can go wrong will go wrong, such as being on the road, playing in front of a loud, hostile crowd, playing against a team where they are considered the underdogs. You want to prepare the players to shrug off dirty plays and keep playing. You can make up a list of questions to prepare the players to anticipate problems; for example, "What will you do if an opponent gives you a dirty hit?"

Part 4: Emotional or Passionate Talk

Use your voice to express emotion

When you give an emotional speech, the exact words that you use are far less important than the energy, intensity, and conviction of how you say it. So, how you say it is sometimes more important than what you say. You must speak loudly and clearly, with forcefulness, confidence, determination, and from the heart. You have to learn to use your voice to get their attention so you can get your message across. Your tone of voice conveys the real message. Sometimes you allow a pause or a few moments of silence to let them absorb what you have just said; sometimes you raise your voice to stress a point; and sometimes you lower your voice for a different effect.

End the speech at the right time

Timing is extremely important, too. You want to end your talk exactly when the players have to go out on the playing field/floor. You do not want them waiting in the dressing room or on the bench to go on the field/floor. After your talk, you can get everybody in the middle of the dressing room touching hands to get the "magical feeling" of strength and togetherness, and telling them: "We can do this; just go out and play our game."

Plan your emotional talk to get your message across

Sometimes you have to be a good actor: you have to pretend you are upset when you really aren't; you have to act and pretend that you have all the confidence in the world before a game, even when you are scared to death; you have to pretend you are happy when you are angry; and you have to pretend you are slightly concerned about the opposition when in fact you are confident you can beat them.

Whenever you get angry or blow up at the team, you sometimes want it to be a preplanned event to make sure you say the right things. Usually anger is bad, but if you use it right, it can motivate your players. Sometimes you will set the situation up and will warn a player before he goes into the dressing room that you are going to yell at him to get a point across to the whole team, and not to take it personally.

Sometimes a team needs a "wake-up call" to get them out of a daze. It's usually your emotional tone that moves players, not your actual words. Players know you are upset by the way you talk. But also remember that fiery speeches are for an immediate effect only, not for long-term effect. You can't get angry too often. You cannot psyche players up game after game and expect them to perform at their highest level, because your emotional talks will eventually lose their effect.

In this part of the speech, you want to get your message across to your players with more passion, which should have a positive effect. You want to speak in a way that "moves" your players. The key is finding the right time and place to give an emotional speech; sometimes it is just a gut feeling. Now and then, you can get a little excited or a little mad to fire your team up. You might have to look for ways or an angle to get your players fired up at crunch time, or just before they go on the field/floor, as players perform better when they get excited about the game.

Notes: The rule of thumb is, during a long season, you can use your emotional speech more, but during a short season you will have to pick your spots when to be emotional.

Now and then, "Give it to them loud and dirty—that way they will remember it." (George F. Patton)

Poor coaches just seem to lack the energy and passion to arouse the human heart.

Negative results of a too-emotional pre-game talk

The traditional emotional pep talk can do more harm than good most times, especially if the team is already fired up or nervous, as it might increase the players' arousal level, creating even more anxiety before the game. In other words, the players will become like "bulls in a china shop," not thinking straight, just reacting to anything and over-trying, with the result of not performing properly. The traditional emotional pep-talk could also remind players of the importance of the game, which you don't want to do.

Notes: Coaches have found that yelling is pretty ineffective, especially when they yell at older players who really don't need to be yelled at, or when they yell at younger players who will end up just being scared.

Be careful, in your emotional talk, that you don't get so carried away that you can't even remember what you said because you were so mad. Afterwards, when you have settled down, you will feel bad because you didn't take the time to think before you spoke.

In the pre-game speech, you want to usually calm players down rather than fire them up. You have to keep your players' emotions under control, even though emotions and inspirational plays are a big part of a game. It's a fine line to achieve just the right balance.

■ PURPOSE OR RESULT OF THE PRE-GAME SPEECH

You Want the Team to Be Focused on the Job at Hand

The pre-game talk helps the players focus on what they have to do. You want to switch the players' focus from the game outcome goal of winning to the performance and behaviour goals and execution of the systems. By focusing on these goals, players stay aware of things they can control rather than worrying about winning, which they cannot control.

You Want the Team to Be "in the Zone"

The main purpose of the pre-game talk is to help the players get into the "zone." Such as:

> *Feeling prepared.* The pre-game talk gets the players mentally and emotionally prepared for the game.

> *Feeling energized.* The pre-game talk gets the players energized to play at the next level. You can kick-start momentum again, especially after a previous last poor-performance game. The purpose is not to charge the team up too high, but rather to have them ready to play with calm self-assurance. If the team is too hyped up, you might want to calm them down.

> *Believing they will be successful and feeling good about themselves.* The pre-game talk builds a feeling of confidence and hope in all the players going into the game and gets rid of any thoughts of doubt. Confidence and belief always have to be the theme of the talk. When players leave the dressing room, you want them feeling confident and good about themselves; believing they are the better team; and believing they will be successful or victorious.

> *Feeling strong.* The pre-game talk gives the players a feeling of togetherness and strength and that everybody is on the same page. You want the players to leave the dressing room not as a collection of individuals, but as a cohesive unit filled with a feeling of "We can do it!" "We're going to kick some butt!" "We feel stronger and fresher."

> ⟩ *Feeling relaxed*. One purpose of the pre-game talk is to relax the players. You don't want them to get overly excited or too emotional. If you find the team is up-tight, you can say something funny or humorous to break the tension.

> ⟩ *Feeling hopeful.* You want to give the players hope because hope gives them energy and enthusiasm for the game.

> ⟩ **Going out and enjoying the moment.** You tell the players to just go out and have some fun.

■ THE WARM-UP AFTER THE PRE-GAME TALK

Before each game, you try to shake hands with every player, either in the locker room or on the floor during warm-up and say something encouraging to him or her. You want to show unity as the players run onto the floor/field together displaying confidence, togetherness, and a readiness to work. Make sure your players do not look at the opposition during warm-up. During the pre-game warm-up, you want the players to practise everything as if in a game situation, every pass on target and hard. You want to set the tone for the way you are going to play the game.

■ A SAMPLE PRE-GAME TALK

"These are going to be the toughest first five minutes we are going to play all year. They are going to be all over us, they are going to be very emotional, and the crowd will be loud. This is going to be a hard-fought battle, but those are the most satisfying to play in. We have become "battled tested" through all our adversities this year and now we are ready for this game. The pressure of this game will separate the players on both sides—you've got to love the battle and the pressure. You will either rise to the occasion or you won't. The true warrior is someone who knows how to get the job done at the moment of truth."

■ HALF-TIME OR BETWEEN-PERIOD TALKS

Before your half-time talk you must act confidently and keep a positive attitude.

You have ten to fifteen minutes between periods. If, for instance, half time is ten minutes, plan the "timeline" accordingly. You can't just go immediately into the dressing room and talk constantly until the team goes back on the floor.

For the first six minutes between periods, you let the players rest and relax, go to the washroom, have any injuries looked at, talk among themselves, drink, eat oranges, and fix their equipment, while you go over the statistics with the other coaches.

For the next three minutes, you should do most of the talking; do not let any players talk to each other, fix their equipment, or get fixed up while you are speaking. You address the team collectively at half-time and let them know how you feel they are doing.

You should begin your talk by making some positive comment to get the players' attention. You should recognize players or a unit for doing a great job in a certain area. Follow this routine whether winning or losing. Do not focus on the negatives; do not dwell on the past by telling players what they did wrong; do not dwell on the future by telling players that they are going to win; and do not make any major changes to the game plan, although you might want to make some minor adjustments to it.

You give specific information from the game statistics, make minor adjustments, and stress a need for improvement in certain areas of the game. From a priority list, you give three specific corrections or minor adjustments for improvement. Although you make strategic adjustments to the other team, your primary focus should be on your own team. You should know your team's strengths, play to them, and make the opponent beat you doing it.

At Half-Time if Your Team Is Winning

You just stay the course by telling the team to keep on doing what they have been doing. It's when your team is winning the game that you can be tough on them to prevent them from becoming overconfident or complacent. You can be more demanding because the players' confidence is high and they are able to handle criticism better. Usually you don't have to say too much.

If Behind in a Game at Half-Time

You remind the team not to panic, to stick with the game plan, and just pick away at the lead. The only half-time adjustment is to start playing better, running faster, hitting harder, and executing better. Remind the players that somewhere, someplace, sometime they're going to have to plant their feet, take a stand, and fight, and it might as well be now. Point out that regardless of how the game ends, how they conduct themselves in the second half of this game will determine the character and ultimate success of this team.

When your team is doing poorly, it is not a good time to be critical: The team's confidence is low and they need your support so they can feel better about themselves. If you are tough on them when they're down, you might create a very fragile situation. One of the worst things to do is put pressure on the team by stressing that they have to win this game and that they can't make any more mistakes.

But occasionally, if the team is not playing hard or has lost its concentration, you can rip into it by hollering and shouting. Sometimes you can attack the seniors and captains for their poor leadership and example.

In the Last Minute of Intermission

You have your final say and make it the most important point. You make the players feel that they are going to be successful. Look the players in the eye and tell them they are going to have the best period/quarter they have ever had. Again, it's your emotion that moves the players, not your words. You can get angry, but not too often. Sometimes coaches don't even go into the change room at all. They give their captains and assistants the opportunity to use their leadership skills by doing the talking.

It is important that you have an assistant who will tell you how much time is left in the intermission, so that you can time the ending of your talk and still not be late going back out on the field/floor. The team, then, puts their hands together in a circle and leaves the dressing room. You must insist that the team leave the dressing room together rather than straggling.

Note: If the head coach sees a major problem with an individual player, he might delegate an assistant coach to talk to him individually between periods. Some guys have "thin skin" on game day, so they need an individual pep talk. Coach certainly doesn't want to make it worse by screaming at him, but if a guy needs someone in his face to wake him up, Coach will do it.

22 PRESENTATION OF POST-GAME SPEECHES

■ WHAT COACH DOES AFTER A WIN

Try to Keep Excitement Low Key

You cannot let your players get too complacent or too cocky after a win, as some teams, after they are successful, have a tendency to drop off in their play. But of course if a team wins in dramatic style, you want a little celebration. After an easy win, be careful of overconfidence. This would be the best time to mention major mistakes. Right after the game, you should remind the team of the next opponent to get them thinking ahead.

The Thirty-Second Talk

If you are going to go into the change room, you should give the players a few minutes to themselves; the post-game talk should be no more than thirty seconds. You don't have to give a post-game talk every time. You can look at the statistics to give a quick, general summary of the game to the team, but the in-depth, post-game summary should be done later, during a team meeting, or at the next practice after you have analyzed the game from the statistics. Besides, you want to put a lot of thought into what you are going to say to the team.

Right after the game, you shouldn't spend any time going over strategy problems or minor adjustments with the team. This is a waste of time—the players will not likely be paying attention, as they will be too excited over the win. You should try not to over-coach by keeping a young team sitting while you dissect the game! Players are anxious to get out of their uniforms and leave.

Give Some Praise

If you give a post-game talk, you should praise effort and execution. The best thing to talk about is the team's behaviour goals and performance goals and how the team displayed those qualities in the game. Then, you can go over a few key statistics from the performance goals. You can stress how the system and performance stats came through for them. You should recognize individual players or a unit for doing a great job in a certain area. After a win, it is very easy for you to praise everybody, so be careful.

Make Some Suggestions

After a win, you can sometimes be all over the players by telling them some things they are doing wrong because, due to the shock value, they will be more receptive. Sometimes a team wins very easily with no effort; so, to keep the players grounded, you might have to be critical or hard on them for their lack of effort even though they won. As a head coach you give your assistant coaches and players credit when the team wins, but you take the blame when the team loses.

You feel there is always something you can improve upon. You are always thinking how to make the team better. "What can we do better on defence?" "What can we do better against a certain team?"

Awards Ceremony

After you say a few words, the captain and assistants can hand out the awards for the top offensive player of the game, top defensive player, and the Mr. Hustle award. They can use old running shoes, old gloves, jock straps . . . anything that is symbolic.

A Win Sometimes Makes a Team Complacent

Sometimes it is a lot more difficult to handle success than adversity. When a team wins, it sometimes gets complacent and rests on its laurels, which is anti-success. Winning makes players think they are unbeatable and "they can't lose," and when they start thinking they can't lose, they are setting themselves up for an upset.

You have to find just the right balance so the team doesn't get complacent. In other words, your job as a coach is to motivate and challenge your players to continue to practise and play hard, to continue to get better whether they win or lose, and to never be satisfied in their quest of pursuing the championship.

Note: Complacency is a real threat to success. As a coach, do not allow complacency (lack of concentration) and carelessness (not paying attention to detail) creep in.

■ WHAT COACH DOES AFTER A LOSS

The dressing room atmosphere after a lost game is very crucial. After a loss, you definitely cannot go in the dressing room and yell at the players; you can go in and say something positive; you can make a few general comments about the loss; you can take the burden off the team by saying that it was not one person or one thing that lost the game—it was everyone, including you as the coach; or you don't go in the change room at all. Sometimes it is better to leave the players alone, especially if you are upset.

Your Reaction to Losses and Adversity Is Important

You should judge your own feelings after a loss or setback before going into the change room because how you react to losses and adversity is important. It is important for you to stay calm, upbeat, positive, and able to communicate clearly during a crisis. Remember, every player will be hurting, so you had better deal with them first before you deal with yourself.

It is not the adversity but how you and your players react to failures, setbacks, or losses that is important. If you are tense, angry, upset, or stressed out, the players will be tense, angry, upset, and stressed out, which makes them perform worse. You want your players to perform confidently, relaxed, and focused. Adversity is simply part of the game and you have to overcome it to become successful. You have to stand behind your players in success and in front of them in defeat.

Remember, every player will be hurting, so you had better deal with them first before you deal with yourself.

ANYTHING WORTH DOING IS GOING TO BE DIFFICULT

Have a Routine to Calm Down after a Loss

You have to work on controlling your actions, your words, and your emotions. After a loss, you shouldn't go ballistic by ranting and raving; you shouldn't go hollering; you shouldn't change your tone of voice; you shouldn't panic; you shouldn't make the team run laps the following practice for punishment, unless it played poorly; in fact, you shouldn't do anything different.

You have to be your strongest at one of your weakest moments and that's not easy to do. You have to stay calm; you can't let the loss get to you; you can't hit the panic button; you have to keep your negative feelings inside; and you can't lose your sense of humour. You just stay consistent in your behaviour by being calm and supportive. You must look at these problems and crises as opportunities for you and the team to grow and be tested.

It's a good idea for you to have a routine to deal with a loss. Before going into the change room you can go for a walk to unwind, look at the statistics to give the team some positive feedback, or do something else to cheer yourself up. It is a good idea to remind yourself how lucky you are to be coaching this team. You should not be down, be miserable, or feel sorry for yourself after a loss. Just look at the situation you are in: you are coaching a great bunch of kids, you are in a great organization, and you are doing what you love to do. Remind yourself you are living a dream, and it can't get any better than this.

Certainly there is more pressure on the team during a losing streak because the team never knows when it is going to end. Here is where your confidence as a leader must come through in a genuine fashion.

Expect Losses during the Season

As a coach, you should know that your attitude is directly related to your expectations. So you should expect and be prepared for one problem every day and at least three to four setbacks or major crises in a season before they occur, so that when they do happen, you don't overreact, but remain calm, positive, and confident; and begin to think rationally of ways to make the best out of a bad situation. Just like a player who expects a game to be difficult, you must expect the season to be hard. So, planning or anticipating a problem, even one that you don't expect, can avoid negative consequences.

You sometimes have to accept that inconsistency is normal and that your team one night can blow anyone out in the league and next night look like the worst team in the league. So, acknowledge that there will be days when everything goes right and days when nothing goes right.

Get the Players Prepared for Losses before the Season Begins

Losses are not handled in the instant they occur, so you have to have your team prepared for the crisis/loss before it occurs. You have to talk to your players on how they are going to handle a loss/adversity/crisis. And basically how you handle adversity is simple: you either let it beat you or you use it to make you better and to grow as a team. So, you must handle it, learn from it, and grow from it.

A team doesn't have overnight success unless it has had some adversity: It seems success doesn't come without a price. You have to prepare your team for adversity, problems, and losses so it knows they are coming. Then, you need a plan for dealing with adversity for your team because it is inevitable you are going to have adversity at some point in the season. So sit down with your team and talk about all the possible problems the team could have and how you all are going to deal with them. (See below.)

You can come up with many good excuses as to why the team lost the game, which probably are all great excuses, but players have to expect adversities during the season, and this is just one of them. You want your team to respond to adversities or losses like champions by not overreacting and by getting the job done with no excuses.

Sport is like life—unpredictable—and it is your job to teach the team how to handle any unusual situations it might face. One way to do this is to put them into a strict practice schedule, and then create a disruption or crisis just to see how they will respond. Players either adjust or crumble in a crisis.

Remember This Loss

Losses can be a big key to future victories. Frustration, disappointment, and defeat are powerful motivators because they are the result of not achieving what players wanted, worked toward, and hoped for. You can use your team losses as motivators. You remind the players to never forget this defeat and remember how it felt, then put it in the back of their minds. You can use a particular loss as a vehicle to draw strength from or a rallying point throughout the season.

Note: If your team got beaten badly by an opponent, and you know you are going to play this opponent again, you can make up t-shirts with the score on the front; or you can paint the score on the dressing room wall just to remind your team that they had lost badly against this particular opponent.

BEFORE YOU TRULY WIN, YOU HAVE TO GET YOUR BUTT KICKED

Follow the "Twenty-four-hour Rule"

Some coaches have the "twenty-four-hour rule," win or lose. If you don't have anything positive to say after a loss, you wait twenty-four hours after the game, then move on. You don't really evaluate the game with your players after a loss until the next practice. This gives everybody an opportunity to cool off and collect themselves. You want the team to enjoy their successes and learn from their failures and then move forward. You can give the post-game talk at the next practice.

Awards Ceremony

Win or lose, you still need to build team confidence by having a special awards ceremony, with the captains and assistants handing out the awards for the top offensive player of the game, top defensive player of the game, and the Mr. Hustle award. Sometimes you get caught up in the loss after the game and forget about handing out the physical awards or verbal praise because you are so angry that the team lost; but you still have to do it.

Have a Players' Meeting

Sometimes after a loss, the players have a post-game meeting where they can get their feelings made known; they can express their frustrations; they can get rid of any bad taste in their mouths. If they think a certain player is not tough enough, the player should hear this; if they think the offence sucks, they should hear this; if they think the defence is not doing their job, they should hear this. The meeting might start out hot and heavy, but eventually it will calm down after the players have voiced their concerns.

Re-motivate the Team

After a loss, you talk about having dreams, goals, and a plan and then having to go to work on those plans and dreams—all the while handling losses. The real question is not whether you'll face adversity as a team, but how your team will respond to it when it comes.

Staying positive

How do you stay positive after a loss? This is hard to do. You just have to tell yourself that you are going to remain positive and upbeat after the game. You must force out any negative thoughts that enter your mind—because if you think negative thoughts, negative results are sure to follow. As long as you are dreaming about what you want to accomplish, the positives will come easily!

Your confidence as a leader must come through in a genuine fashion after a loss. So, how you and your team react to a loss is important. You cannot expect to have a positive effect on your players tomorrow if you criticize and get upset with them today. A supportive environment for losses is a major motivator for players. You want to create an upbeat, enthusiastic, and fun environment, because your team's environment is everything.

You must take responsibility for overcoming a loss, instead of letting a loss overcome you. During tough times, it's up to you to step up and tell the players that there is no reason to panic or to be fearful. If you react negatively to a loss, you can destroy the team's attitude and energy. If you react positively, you can bring the team's energy back and bring them back together.

You can tell the players how proud you are of them; you can go over things you were pleased with; you can tell them how hard you thought they had played; and you can cover things that you feel the team has to continue to work on.

Re-energize the team

It seems if you lose, you are tired, and if you win, you are never tired. After a loss, you must inspire your players to find the energy to pick themselves up to compete again another day by staying away from being negative. A team after a defeat has a tendency to dwell on the negatives that losing generates and tend to make the situation look bleaker than it really is. Remember: negative thinking breeds negative results.

By dwelling on the positive, you create a positive environment that embraces learning and growing from the loss, which energizes players; by dwelling on the negative, which is easy to do, you create a negative environment that criticizes and blames others for the loss, which hinders development and seems to wear players down.

STAY POSITIVE, WIN OR LOSE

How players feel after a loss

After a loss, doubt starts to creep into the players' minds, and some players lose confidence, feel low, discouraged, disappointed, upset, sad, or angry. You definitely cannot allow your players to sulk after a loss. Everyone will be looking to you for the answers, so you have to provide something constructive to build the team's confidence up and get them ready for the next game.

Build up the players' confidence

After a disappointing loss, you know the players will feel disappointed and upset because they know they could have done better. You must remain calm. Knowing the players will be down, you have to instill confidence and bring them back up for the next game by giving them reassurance that everything is okay, giving them encouragement, sticking by them and believing in them, telling them what a great job they are doing, telling them to relax and just keep on working to improve their game, by going over the good plays, and by recognizing individual players for their effort and enthusiasm. You cannot, however, get through to your players until they begin to take some of the responsibility for the loss and get into a positive frame of mind.

You have to "carry the torch of hope" when everything is falling apart. The more a team loses, the more positive you have to become. Remember, one word of encouragement in tough times is worth a thousand words during good times. You can even challenge the team by asking, "What are we going to do about it?" The answer could be, "Let's stay positive. Let's not panic. Let's find a solution and follow our philosophy: What we start, we finish."

Share stories of how other teams survived after a terrible loss

Another strategy is sharing stories of teams that fought to come back from a bad loss or a losing streak to win. You give the team tangible proof that it can get through this loss and that the experience will eventually make it better.

Storytelling is more than just presenting information and facts. It is giving inspiration and hope so that when the players listen to the story, they get caught up in the emotion. Storytelling can also remind the players of their behaviour goals, who they are, and what their values are.

Players have to find out if they have what it takes to come back from a loss and you help them to do this by telling a story of comebacks by other teams or your own struggles in your coaching career and how you overcame them. You want the story to inspire your team and show them that other teams were in similar situations and were able to do something about it by exceeding their own expectations and beating the odds. Now the players will tell themselves: If other teams can do it, so can they.

You can talk about how other successful teams have suffered through major setbacks and survived—how they just regrouped through hard work; kept believing in themselves; showed a strong character; stayed positive; never gave up; and reminded themselves of their long-term goal. Just as a team must expect a game to be difficult, it must also expect the season to be difficult.

So, planning and anticipating problems, even those that one doesn't expect, can avoid negative consequences. If a team expects things to be difficult, it is at least prepared and ready for any adverse situation. It is not the loss, but how a team reacts to the loss that is important.

Note: Coach is always positive even when losing. The Calgary Flames lost seven games in a row one year and came back to win the Stanley Cup.

On a losing streak

On a losing streak, the toughest thing you have to do is to hold everybody together. You must be a "carrier of hope" who gives hope to your players even when they think there is none. You encourage them not to give up and not to lose faith. You tell them they can weather this storm and to believe they will come out of the streak and survive the season. With hope, players can expect that something great is going to happen.

You have to get the idea across to the players that these tough times are stepping stones to becoming better, and that these tough times can actually push them toward their long-term goal, the championship. The players must realize that the season is a series of ups and downs, peaks and valleys, wins and losses. When the bad times come—and they will come—players have to trust in and hang onto their beliefs in what they stand for—playing hard, playing together, and playing smart.

Note: Just as games don't start before they begin (mental preparation), they don't end when they are over (they linger in the memory); so as a coach you must rebuild.

WHAT YOU BELIEVE WILL HAPPEN
IS USUALLY WHAT YOU GET

Focus on your next opponent

The best medicine after any loss or losing streak is to immediately become absorbed with the challenge of your next opponent. In fact, during the season, you should just prepare for the next game and never look back or down the road.

Focus on the season as a marathon, not a sprint

To keep the loss of a game in proper perspective, you should look at the whole season—the big picture—with the team. You tell them one game is not going to make or break a season. You explain to the team that the season is like a marathon race rather than a sprint. It doesn't matter how you start; it matters that you keep on plugging away to the end, and this one game is just a small piece of the whole puzzle. Whether the team wins or loses the game right now isn't as important as striving to get ready for the final game of the season. So, you are not as concerned about losing as much as how well the team is playing and if they are improving after every game.

To bring everybody back to reality after a loss, you ask the team what it would be like if they had nobody to play next—in other words, if this were the last game of the season and the team would not get a chance to play again. It is not the end of the world; there is always a "tomorrow."

Never accept excuses for losing

Stay loyal; no finger-pointing or blaming. Sometimes after a loss, players feel they have no control and occasionally they lose hope and stop trying. The basic belief that leads to optimism is that losses are due to circumstances the players can control and can change for the better. "We lost because we only got 40 percent of the loose balls." Good teams feel they control what happens to themselves.

Coach can give her players a good list of excuses (we are young, we are small, we are inexperienced, we are slow) as to why they lost, but the bottom line is that the players should take responsibility and ownership of how they played and make no excuses. Also, reinforce that the team lost not because of one play or one player, but because of all the little things the team didn't do.

PERSEVERANCE AND ADVERSITY GO HAND IN HAND

Never give up

In any great endeavour, there will be a bleak point in time where a team is tempted to give up and quit because they're so disappointed and exhausted . . . and that's the exact point in time at which it needs to redouble its efforts to see things through. Many teams stop only steps away from victory because they became discouraged and quit; if they had just intensified their determination and persevered, they would have triumphed.

Another strategy you can use to handle adversities is the philosophy: "If you get knocked down, you just pick yourself up, dust yourself off, and start all over again"; or, "Life knocks you down, it doesn't knock you out." You must remind your team that the great teams always have the ability to bounce back.

Note: Watch for players who don't care or seem unaffected by the loss. This mentality is like a cancer and will spread quickly.

If a team really wants something, it has to work for it. It will run into obstacles, setbacks, and disappointments, but it can refuse to give up. In every team's journey, there are critical moments or turning points where things can go either one way or another. If a team is facing a serious challenge or adversity, it must endure and hang in, as the coach and players are simply paying their dues; paying the price for what it takes to be a great team.

Are you holding the players accountable for the results or accepting excuses? There are two types of teams: those who have learned how to work through a loss, and those who wished they had. There are plenty of talented teams who give up when the going gets tough and there are others who have preserved and triumphed despite incredible adversity. These are the teams that are willing to go the extra mile to be successful. Tenacity is as important as talent.

"Luck" Is the Result of Overcoming Adversity

Certainly to be successful, a team needs to be lucky by staying injury free; avoiding major crises off the floor; getting lucky bounces; and making big plays when it has to. But being lucky is also about being relentless in the pursuit of the performance goals and being resilient in the face of bad luck and adversity. In other words, no matter what is thrown at a team, it has to always find a way to bounce back and overcome adversity.

Remember: As a coach you have to look at the long-term goal, which is getting the team ready for the final game of the season. This takes most of the season. The short-term performance goals help to achieve this final result.

Adversity is just another challenge

There are no great victories in life without tremendous adversity. Before a team can really enjoy success, it must deal with adversity because a team's greatest growth comes from adversity. In fact, dealing with hardship is part of the process of achieving success; it is going to happen. Besides, no team wins every single game in a season. It would be nice to win all the games, but there is something special about a team that gets knocked off course and ends up finding a way to come back on course by doing something outstanding.

Teams persevere when they can look adversity in the eye and see it as a challenge. Adversity gives a team a chance to challenge itself and become stronger. You have to stress to the team that it needs to approach adversity as a challenge—not with concern about the outcome, but with the courage to do its best. Two teams can face the same challenge, but it is the attitude that makes the difference; one team can look at the loss as a challenge, and the other team can see it as an inconvenience or even as a disaster.

The team needs adversity to test its character

After a loss, on an under-achieving team, players act like losers, where everybody gets in everybody's face; turns on each other; argues; criticizes fellow players; blames each other; points fingers; start to feel sorry for themselves; and make excuses for losing. This behaviour is "the kiss of death" and creates a confidence problem, with players ending up playing tight and creating low morale on the team.

How a team reacts or responds to losses, problems, obstacles, and adversity defines it as a team. These losses or problems help build team character. The question is: "Do we dwell on losses or move on?" "Do we give up or keep trying? "Do we meet adversity head on and overcome it or let it overcome us?"

You want to create an attitude that a team develops character only through adversity. It's the ultimate test of a team's character. Without setbacks, adversity, and problems, a team doesn't know whether or not it really is good. So, it is important to see how the team responds to an adversity after a loss.

A team's greatest challenge is after a loss. A loss is the true test of a team's ability. Losses only strengthen the team's mind. Players should give thanks for all the losses they have faced along the season's path, for it is through these that they will grow the most as a team. So, give thanks for the season's toughest losses. When losses occur, the quality and intensity of the team's true character ultimately plays a far greater role than does talent or ability. So, it is your job as a coach to prepare the team to handle any unpredictable situations it might face.

Notes: Here is a coach's talk after a loss: "If we work through this adversity together, we will pull even closer together as a team. Only under pressure and adversity do we really find out what we are made of. This lost game has to be our rallying cry. We just practise and play harder."

Get Ready for the Next Game

"Once it's done, put it behind us." This theme helps the team forget about the loss. After a loss, you reinforce to your players that it's acceptable to be angry, to be upset, to be disappointed, and even cry for a few minutes, but then they must forget about the loss. Some players might need to talk about it to you to get out their anger and frustrations. But the bottom line is that the players have to put the loss behind them and move on to get ready for their next opponent. Players must understand that failure is part of the game and they can't let a loss eat at them and carry over to the next game.

You treat losses just the same way as you treat victories. A coach feels there is always room for improvement, so you try to keep things in perspective whether it is a win or a loss. Win or lose, you always want to get better, you are never satisfied.

Learn from the Loss

You stress that once the game is over, the successful teams handle their loss by not dwelling on it, but learning from it, then forgetting it immediately, and refocusing on the present moment of getting ready to play the next game.

Defeat is a powerful learning experience, as it reveals weaknesses and what the team did wrong and often contributes more to success than wins. It seems you learn more from losing than from winning, and the knowledge you acquire from these losses helps you win more games. "We have been beaten up and battered, but we are getting 'battled tested,' we are learning how to win; we are paying the price for what it takes to be a great team." Losses are seen as an inevitable part of the improvement and learning process.

Focus on Performance Goals and on Why the Team Lost

Two teams can experience the same failure: For one, it builds character and a stepping stone to greater growth; for the other, it is the beginning of progressive conservative play and away from the risk-taking required for growth. What you learn from mistakes is to try not to repeat them and to learn from them.

If a team is going to lose a lot of games, and if winning is the only goal, the players will be constantly frustrated. If, on the other hand, players focus on their behaviour and performance goals, then as these goals either get better or are attained, they will feel a sense of accomplishment.

You always look at the game much more closely when you lose than when you win. You want to know the reasons for the loss. Successful teams learn to cope with the loss, gain from the experience, and correct the mistakes by making minor adjustments.

The team performance goals create a kind of "game-within-a-game" to help break down the loss to understand how the loss happened. For example, the performance goal might be to improve shooting percentage, increase number of loose balls, or reduce the number of turnovers in the next game. This "small step" approach helps a team bounce back. Now the loss isn't so overwhelming, because you have learned why the team lost. You focus on the little things that need improvement to achieve your game outcome goal of winning. Even if the team loses a game, it can still experience some sense of accomplishment by attaining some of these goals.

❯ Evaluate statistics to help understand why the team lost.

A team must be taught how to interpret their losing experience. You can help players learn from a loss by evaluating the game statistics in searching for solutions. A team learns a lot more from a loss than a win because it learns what doesn't work more than what does work; it learns what its weaknesses are and what not to do. You must examine what went wrong by breaking the game down into the simplest of terms and then start to work on what the team has to do to improve. Usually the question is not whether the team won or lost, but whether it attained some of its performance goals. "Basically, for the opposition team to beat us, it was probably because we did not attain our main performance goals; or they played one of their best games ever."

Statistics break the game into simple terms. A team doesn't need a cheerleader or someone who is critical as much as they need someone who's going to give them something tangible, such as statistics or performance goals, to improve themselves. Statistics help analyze the loss, break the game down into simple terms, and tell you where the team's weaknesses and strengths lie for that particular game. The statistics sheets give a more objective analysis or outlook. Team statistics might indicate that the team has to improve its shooting percentage, increase number of loose balls, or reduce the number of turnovers—things it can control—but don't forget to positively reinforce the team when it reaches one of its objectives.

❯ Go over the prioritized list of performance goals for a game.

The team should be going into every game with a prioritized list of team performance goals it wishes to attain. You want to know which performance goals the team did and did not attain.

Even if the team loses a game, it can still experience some sense of accomplishment by attaining some of these performance goals. A team can lose every game and still feel good about itself by feeling it met or improved on certain performance goals. For a team that is going to lose a lot, and if winning is the only goal, the players will be constantly frustrated. The team must focus on the playing systems, the behaviour goals, and the performance goals, and as these goals are attained or improved, a sense of success and confidence is achieved.

❯ Look at the long-term goal, which is getting the team ready for the final game of the season.

Your job is to build team confidence right to the end of the season. So, be less concerned about winning now and be more concerned about how the team is playing and if it is improving with every game, right up to the last game, and hopefully the championship. You have to be constantly searching for ways to improve and understand the lessons from this loss to avoid the next loss.

> Ask, "Did the opposition beat us, or did we beat ourselves?" "Why did we lose?" "Did our team deserve the victory?" Your team needs to do certain things to be successful; it doesn't matter whom it is playing against; it doesn't matter if it is the underdog, the favourite, or if both teams are evenly matched. If your team is going to be successful, it has to attain its performance goals. With these goals, your team feels it is in control of what it can do. There is a fine line between successful and unsuccessful.

WE LEARN FROM EVERY GAME, WIN OR LOSE

Do Not Let Players Change Their Routine or Systems

After a loss, you cannot let your team panic. To change or not to change their routine or playing systems—that is the question. The biggest temptation for players is to think they have to do something different because they lost. Your philosophy is that you do not want your players to make any changes in their routine—in fact, you want them to continue doing what they have been doing because they believe in their routine and in their playing systems.

A good team is not going to change its offensive systems or its defensive systems because it believes they are good. You might adjust or simplify the systems a bit by making one or two key changes or just stress playing faster, harder, and more aggressive, but you are going to stay focused on things that you and the team can control.

Note: Everything you do is with the idea of keeping your players confident, fresh, and healthy throughout the season.

Make Sure the Team's Behaviour Goals Remain the Same

In the post-game talk after a loss, the best thing to do is to talk about the team's performance goals and behaviour goals and how those qualities were displayed in the game. You should be more concerned about the way your team played than whether it won or lost. You can never accept your team being outworked, out-hustled, or losing from a lack of will, discipline, or perseverance. "Is this who we are?" "Is this our standard of excellence?"

You can say: "The behaviour goals—'who we are'—are within the team's control and we are not going to change them even after a loss."

> We have to play and work harder.
> We have to play together more, not selfishly. Players have to bury their egos and do what is best for the team.

> ❯ We have to play smarter on offence with the ball and without the ball. On defence, we have to pressure the ball more, be ready to help more.

> ❯ We have to play with more discipline.

> ❯ We have to play with more passion.

Notes: The U.S. Army's philosophy regarding adversity is "adapt and overcome." You have to get your players to focus on working harder; doing their job; working together; and adjusting to any situation.

After every game, win or lose, you try to leave the team with a lesson with your post-game talk.

Focus on the Team's Philosophy of Success

We are always stressing to our players how important it is to do their best. We believe success is "to go out and do your best, and whatever happens, happens."

"I believe if you give it your all, risk everything, it doesn't matter whether you win or lose." (Kevin Costner from *For the Love of the Game.*)

We believe a team is successful as long as it is improving and getting better as a team; then it is a good season. The question is: "Have we gotten better?" "Are we getting better and improving?"

We believe success is to compete against oneself.

We believe it is the trying that makes the difference, not who is going to win.

SUCCESS IS NOT FOREVER, AND FAILURE IS NOT FATAL

■ POST-GAME QUESTIONS ABOUT THE PERFORMANCE GOALS

You always seem to question yourself about your team's play after a game. As a coach you have to constantly re-evaluate your team's performance. What could it have done differently in the game? It is not about the losses as much as playing at a high standard. Your standards or performance goals define to your team what is acceptable and what is not.

If the performance goals are low, then it will be easy to meet these standards. But if your performance goals are high—to be the best—then your team will have a tough time attaining them. These are the main performance objectives a team tries to attain every game.

These are our prioritized post-game lacrosse questions about our specific performance goals after a win or loss.

Offensive and Defensive Performance Goal No. 1:
We will obtain 60 percent of loose balls and faceoffs.

We want to get 60 percent of all loose balls and 60 percent of all faceoffs. "Did we hustle and get more loose balls and faceoffs than the opposition?" Games are won and lost on loose ball skirmishes. We feel that "He who wants it gets it." Did we fight for all loose balls?

Offensive Performance Goal No. 2:
We will have 25 percent shooting.

We want a shooting percentage over 25 percent. "Did we take good shots? Did we execute on offence, complete passes, set solid picks, and cut through the middle and go one-on-one? Did we move the ball and move ourselves on offence?" "Did we play as individuals?"

Defensive Performance Goal No. 3:
We will keep opposition shooting under 20 percent.

We want to keep the opposition shooting under 20 percent. "Did we play good aggressive defence? Did we put pressure on the ball carrier, on the passer, and on the shooter? Did we hit with solid checks? Did we play intense, solid defence?" The best indicator of our defence is how well the opposition shoots.

Offensive Performance Goal No. 4:
We will keep turnovers under 24.

We want to have 24 or less turnovers. "Did we keep the turnovers down by making good decisions with the ball?" "Did we throw stupid passes, forced passes that ended up on the floor?" We want to throw a high percentage of passes that have a high chance of being caught versus a low percentage of passes such as a spectacular pass, a risky pass, a forced pass, or a pass to a player who is covered.

Defensive Performance Goal No. 5:
We will force opposition over 24 turnovers.

We want to force the opposition into 24 or more turnovers. "Did we force turnovers? Did we put two-hand pressure on the ball carrier to force opposition turnovers?"

Performance Goal No. 6:
We will score one-third of our goals from breakouts and fast-break goals.

"Did we run all-out or jog to create fast-break goals? Did we look to set up our open teammate on an odd-man situation?"

We want our Power Play to score on (4 goals/7 chances) 60 percent of its chances.

We want our Man Short to keep the opposition (3 goals/8 chances) 40 percent and under their scoring chances.

Some other goals to think about: Did we help each other out on defence? Did we physically box out after an opponent's shot? Did we play hard with intensity and outwork our opponent? Did we play aggressive, intense, and physical on defence without taking a penalty? Did we concentrate by anticipating what is going to happen rather than just reacting?

■ POST-GAME QUESTIONS ABOUT THE BEHAVIOUR GOALS

The more well defined your behaviour goals become, the better you will be at attaining your performance and outcome goals.

Did we work hard enough?

> Did we quit? Did we lose because of lack of effort?

> Did we lose fighting and scratching or did we quit and panic when we got behind?

> Did we lose because the other team had better talent?

> Did we lose because of lack of skill?

> Did we lose because the opposition executed better?

> Did we lose because the opposition worked harder and they were hungrier?

> Did we lose because we played poorly, below performance?

Note: Poor performance can be a result of overconfidence, poor play or execution, poor fundamentals, lack of effort, lack of concentration, mental mistakes, or loss of motivation. It is okay to lose as long as we played hard and gave it our best shot.

Did we play together, not selfishly?

Did we bury our egos and do what is best for the team? Losing teams argue on the bench and sulk on the bench. Did we have a "team comes first" attitude? Did we trust our teammates and believe in them? Are we a close team?

Did we make good decisions?

Did we play smart on offence with and without the ball? Did we take good shots with a defensive safety going back?

Did we display discipline?

Did we take a lot of stupid, bad penalties? Did we show our self-control? Did we manage our mistakes and emotions? Did we show any negative emotion in a crisis?

Are we "front runners" or do we have enough character to come from behind?

Did we take pride in our self-discipline? In other words, were we at the right spot at the right time? Were we doing the right thing at the right time? Did we take a dirty hit and not retaliate? Did we keep our mouths shut?

Did we have a good attitude?

Did we display toughness, character, and "fire"? Did we play with passion? Did we have fun when we played?

Did we lose our concentration?

Did we make a lot of mental mistakes? Were we totally focused on staying in the present moment and on our performance?

Did we lose our composure?

Did they beat us or did we beat ourselves? Did we fall apart, panic, play undisciplined, cry, whine, find excuses, argue, blame others, or blame circumstances?

Did we love the pressure situations?

Were we all on the same page?

Did we have a good game plan? Did we adjust during the game? Were we committed to the team? Did we pay the price for success? Did we do the extra things to be successful?

23 GAME COACHING

Coaching basically consists of three elements: recruiting and selecting players for the team; teaching and practising the skills; and game coaching. All three areas are important. But to be successful, you must have the skill of "game coaching." Some coaches can coach well during a practice, but have problems coaching during games. They have problems with different aspects of game coaching, such as analyzing and adjusting to the opposition's strengths, communicating with players during a game, deciding who will play and for how long, dealing with game officials and penalties/fouls, and enforcing good player conduct during a game.

Types of Game Coaching

There are two approaches to game coaching: Some coaches are quiet on the bench and others are loud, constantly shouting instructions. It appears both types of coaches can be successful.

Quiet coaches remain calm during the game to keep their players calm. Plus, being calm keeps their players focused on what they can control, rather than on things beyond their control, such as bad referees' calls. And some coaches feel that as a coach you must be careful not to "over-coach" or overload your players with information, where you are coaching every single play.

On the other hand, some successful coaches never stop coaching and teaching from the beginning of the game to the end, as they look upon every game as just another practice to get better. They never just stand with their arms crossed and watch the game; they are involved vocally, pacing up and down the bench/sidelines and totally absorbed in coaching almost every play of the game. This type of coaching also works, although it is important to concentrate on the playing field/floor and not get too emotionally high, as emotions alone will not help the team win games. Good execution, which they are responsible for, makes the difference. You have to figure out what is the best game-coaching method for you and to coach according to your personality, whether you are quiet and reserved or full of vim, vigour, and vitality.

Sometimes You Have to Tell Players What to Do

There are certain times in a game when, for the sake of expediency, you have to act like a dictator and tell or order players to do something or give blunt commands in a harsh manner, because it is the easiest and quickest way. It is important during the "heat of the action" that players listen and do what they are told without question or hesitation, as there is no time to debate or discuss with them during a game.

■ COACH'S PREPARATION ON GAME DAY

> You can watch videos of your team's last game or watch the opposition for the next game.

> You can work with an individual player on a fundamental.

> You can have a workout yourself.

> You can supervise a one-hour shooting practice for certain players.

> You can get some rest before the game by having an afternoon nap.

Some other game day rituals to control your nerves are: go for a run; have some quiet time to think; visualize bad situations and how you will control your emotions around bad penalties, bad goals, and players' mistakes; and practise a relaxation technique.

Your best time to reinforce your game plan is just before you go into the dressing room to give your pre-game speech. Hopefully, you have already reviewed the whole game plan to the team at the last practice.

During pre-game warm-up, you can watch the other team to see where the shooters are shooting at and where the opposition goalie appears weak.

■ COACHING DURING A GAME

Analyze and Adjust

The key to coaching during a game is the ability to see something, analyze it, and then make game adjustments. You must see opportunities in a game; you must see the fears and threats to your team; you must know what is happening in a game and be able quickly to make adjustments and necessary changes to the game plan at the right time; you must see what is going to happen before it happens, so you are always thinking one shift ahead; you must know what the score is and the time remaining in the period/quarter/game.

You have to be able to recognize and analyze: "Are they running a specific play every time against our defence?" "Are we running the right play and formation against their type of defence?" "Are they playing man or zone defence?" "Is their defence a blitzing or protecting defence?"

Make sure you do not get caught up in watching the game like a spectator—you must stay focused on what is happening on the floor/field.

Look for good plays

A lot of times when analyzing the game, you don't see the good plays as much as the "bonehead" plays. You shouldn't always have to be looking to find fault with your players, even though you should be interested in correcting their mistakes and getting better. You should be looking for the good plays to recognize and praise them.

Focus on the opposition team

Game coaching is the ability to concentrate on not only what your team is doing, but also on what the opposition team is doing; and to make necessary adjustments. It involves watching for the opponent's weaknesses and attacking them aggressively and knowing that certain teams and coaches have certain tendencies.

You want to impose your style of play on your opponents, but you also want to find out what the opposing team does best and maybe turn it against them by making a running team a half-court team or making a half-court team a running team. The bottom line is that you want to know what sort of team you're playing and what you have to do to take advantage of them.

Adjust your game plan

There are games where everything happens the way you planned it, and then there are others where nothing goes as you planned. In the latter case, you do not make wholesale changes, but might adjust your game plan slightly to fit the circumstances.

Who adapts the quickest during the game?

The coach who adapts the quickest and makes split-second decisions during the game has a better chance of winning. Even if you are prepared for your opponent with a solid game plan for every situation, you have to be willing to throw the game plan out the window during the game and ad lib it if necessary. This is where the ability to anticipate knowing what is going to happen before it happens is critical to coaching. Anticipating is more of an art form where you use your intuition and past experiences.

Stay with what works

It is a good idea to keep looking at the big picture by having the right group of players, the stars, the workers, on the floor for the right situation. Do not get away from doing what works.

Take notes during the game

You should keep a pen and paper with you so you can take notes during the game so you don't forget how the opposition is scoring, how your team is scoring, any great plays a player might have made, or any glaring mistakes you might want to mention later. Also, keeping notes helps you pay attention to the details, gives you something concrete to say to your team in between periods, and gives you a feel for the game.

Check the statistics during the game

You should keep quality control by analyzing the statistical data during the game, as it might give you an edge by giving you a good idea of the tendency of the opposition coach.

Give Decision-Making Power to the Players

Getting players to think and make the right decisions during the game is one of the toughest things you have to do. Sometimes, depending on the age group, you will likely have a tendency to "over-coach" by commenting on or adjusting every single play rather than just letting the players play. The foundation of good coaching is giving the game to the players: letting them play; giving them the power, the responsibility, and the freedom to do whatever they want during the game; giving the players the authority to make their own decisions on the floor and the freedom to be creative.

While you give the players this freedom to think on their own and play their game, you still must lead the team by maintaining some semblance of order and discipline. This sharing approach is the most effective way to create a team in which players know more, play with more confidence, are more energized, make better decisions, perform better, and care more about the team.

The players are the ones in the trenches and can give you the most accurate outlook on what is happening on the floor. So you should get input during the game from the players by asking them what they think the team should do in a certain situation; and what they want to do. You should spend more time teaching players to think and make game decisions rather than simply telling them what to do all the time.

Notes: If you are lucky enough to get a team with a lot of talent, the best thing to do is give them more freedom in their play and do less coaching.

Listen to Players' Ideas

Many players come up with good ideas in the "heat of the action" for some type of adjustment, or to take away the opposition's strength. You should listen to your players before, during, and after the game. You should encourage players to think for themselves, so when the time comes for them to make some decisions on their own in the game, hopefully they will make the right ones. Players should also feel that they can share in game decisions about the team with you. Getting players' input about the team makes them take on more responsibility and become more involved in the team.

You should not let your ego prevent you from listening to your players' ideas. The people who know best how the game should be played are the ones playing it. During the game you should not be afraid to ask players what they think is happening and if they have any ideas on how to deal with the problem. You can even let your players diagram plays and dictate strategies during timeouts. This type of environment of "player-input" gives players a feeling of ownership of the team and thereby more of a commitment to it.

"Run" the Bench/Sidelines during the Game

Bench coaching is making decisions for the team first

The decisions a successful coach makes during the game are all based on how they will help the team. The team always comes first before individual players. You have to coach to be successful for the team or else you are cheating it.

To "bench coach," you must give the game total concentration

To make good decisions, you must tune out any distractions, such as fans, opposition players yelling at you, opposing coaches yelling at you, and bad calls by referees. You must be totally absorbed in the game while on the bench/sidelines. You cannot get wrapped up in the action nor can you be a spectator by just watching the game and forgetting your bench responsibilities. As a good coach, you must out-think and out-strategize your opposition coach, and you can only do this with total concentration.

Bench coaching is being aware of the tempo and flow of the game

"Are we playing our game of attacking on offence as well as on defence?" "Are we playing our slow-game and our fast-game on offence?" There is never a perfect game, but a team could play a solid game where players are in sync with each other and they just seem to know where their teammates are. When this happens, just let go and let the players play. With game coaching, when it feels right, then do it.

Bench coaching is controlling the bench/sidelines

Bench coaching is having the players organized on who is going out the door or onto the field, who is coming off the floor/field, and who is sitting out this particular shift.

Bench coaching is changing players

Bench coaching is basically putting the right players in the right place at the right time. It is matching lines against lines, matching certain players against others, looking for mismatches, changing lines after a certain amount of time, putting better players on the field/floor at the right time, and making sure at the end of the game the best players are on the field/floor. You have some, not total, control of the game—by putting in players, putting in plays, and substituting or adjusting the game plan. You certainly have an impact on the outcome of the game because you are constantly moving players in and out of the game. So, substitute wisely and develop a pattern for substitution. But remember not to sit your good players too long. You have to work around your good players by extending their shifts and putting them on special teams.

The team's change rule for players is: When players play all-out, they are allowed to pull themselves out of a game to take a breather and then substitute themselves back in on their own rather than your doing the substitution. Because you stress a work ethic, you would rather see a player play forty-five seconds all-out and then rest rather than play a slow-paced two minutes just to get longer playing time.

A PLAYER'S ROUTINE DURING THE GAME IS PLAY, REST, REFOCUS, AND PLAY

Notes: Coaches have found that players playing together over a long period of time is an accurate predictor of improved performance and execution; so try to keep "lines" or groups of players together longer.

Bench coaching is not just rotating line after line no matter what the situation. This is "house-league" coaching, where players get equal time no matter what the score or the situation.

Bench coaching is to know your players

Discipline and trust come into play when you are "game coaching" because you have to know your players and trust them to do a job. Once players prove themselves in tough situations by making things happen, responding the right way, and making the play work, a relationship of trust in their playing ability begins. You then put these players in pressure situations and on specialty teams because you know they have the discipline for getting the job done. If players don't do what they are told or what is expected of them, you will lose faith in them and not put them in a pressure situation or on a specialty team.

You rely heavily on self-disciplined players because they have developed a mental toughness to get the job done in tight situations.

PLAYERS WIN GAMES – NOT COACHES, AND NOT PLAYS

Bench coaching is knowing the opposition offensive players

You must be aware of the better offensive players on the other team when they are on the floor, and match them up with your own team's better defensive players. These match-ups are among the most critical decisions you make: Putting the best defender on the opposition's best scorer and trying to take away what he likes to do best. You have to decide whether to play their best scorer straight-up, double-team him, or find one good defender to completely deny him from getting the ball. You definitely will not let the opposition's best players beat you. You will force, if anything, one of their "lesser-light" players to beat you.

Bench coaching is making the opposition play your way

You control the game and its tempo by forcing your team's style of play on the opposition. If your team is one that runs, then force the opposition to run. If your team is one that likes to slow the game down, then force the opposition to do so by hanging onto the ball longer and jogging the ball up the floor.

Note: Certainly, if your team is over-matched, you must shorten the game: by not shooting quickly, by not running the floor, and by hanging onto the ball longer on offence ("milking the clock").

Bench coaching involves defence

It is not wise to do exactly the same thing defensively all the time against every team. You have your defensive rules, but against certain teams you will make minor adjustments to take away the strength of the opponent. In most games, during the course of action you have to be flexible; you have to change and make subtle adjustments. The defensive system has to be very strong in basic team play, but you have to have some deceptions or tricks where you make the opposition think you are doing one thing defensively while you are actually doing something else, to create confusion and indecision in the opposition. Because the success of the team depends so much on how the defence plays, you must reinforce the defence by physically rewarding players for playing well on defence (Defensive Award); by playing your best defenders; and by verbally complimenting and praising players on defence for their hustle and hard work.

Expectation of team bench behaviour during a game

Do you want everybody on the bench yelling at their own players, the opposition, and the referee, or do you want to hear one voice: yours? You want your players on the bench to be cheerleaders—enthusiastic, supportive, encouraging teammates, and getting charged up. But you do not want players yelling negative comments. Players should be taking deep breaths, doing self-talk for the next shift, or totally concentrating on the game. If you change a player on the field/floor for another player, and the former displays a negative emotion by dropping his shoulders or banging his stick because he has to come off the floor/field, you tell him that you are giving him "one last chance" of displaying any further negative emotions or you will bench him for the rest of the game.

Coach's Emotion during a Game

Especially in a big game, you shouldn't want to win the game too much, because your emotions will take over your reasoning. You want to be able to think, stay alert, and remain calm during the game to make adjustments. If you get too emotionally high you may lose your cool and not be able to think clearly. You need to coach with both your head and your gut, but mainly with your head, especially in tight situations or during adversity.

Learn to keep your cool

You have to work hard at keeping your composure by remaining cool in a crisis, by controlling your emotions, and by staying calm, especially when it seems like everybody else is losing their composure and everything is falling apart—which is hard for some coaches. The crazier the game gets, the calmer and quieter you must be, as this calmness will rub off on your players. If you get angry and lose your temper, your team might do the same thing. Players look to you to see what "acceptable behaviour" is and what isn't. To control your negative emotions, take deep breaths, stay focused on what is happening, "bite your tongue" on confrontations, and forget or ignore the bad calls and the cheap shots—just as you expect your players to do.

Note: You want your players to show only positive emotions on the floor. Players should not show negative emotions, such as getting upset or putting their heads down when things go wrong.

You can use a planned outburst

Sometimes during the game, it might be a good idea for you to show a preplanned emotional outburst to "fire up" your players. This planned outburst can help you to maintain your ability to think rationally.

You must see the big picture

You must look at this particular game as part of the big picture—the long-range view of the end of the season, versus the short-range view of the actual game itself—to keep winning and losing in perspective. Whether a team wins or loses a game right now really isn't that important. The team plays to strive to get better for the end of the season, not necessarily to win this particular game.

Playing Time

How you manage and control playing time with your players is important. Whom you give the playing-time to and at what time is an art. Of course, if you have great players, you have to use them a lot. You have to play through these great players by extending their shifts and putting them on the special teams.

If a player is not performing well, do you not play him? Or do you stick with him and let him play through this bad stretch? The answer to this is seeing potential in your player. If you think he is going to get better from this bad experience, you keep playing him. But there is a point where you have to decide not to play him, "bench him," or even not dress him for a game to "wake him up" if he is continually hurting the team by not playing well. Basically, you reinforce good performance by playing the player more and with poor performance by playing him less or skipping a shift. It is important for a coach to acknowledge and reward a player for a good performance.

Do not make promises

At the beginning of the season, you should not make promises to players about things such as playing time; that they are starting; that they are on a specialty team; or that they are going to be the team captain, because you will get yourself in a lot of trouble if you can't live up to them. It is best not to guarantee anything, not to make any promises, and not to make any deals with players. Stress that players have to earn everything they get, and the bottom line is, players will not dress for a game or get playing time if they are not getting the job done. But if you must bench a player, take the time to explain the reason for it to the player: not playing well; taking too many bad penalties; or another player is being given a chance to perform—rather than just benching him and not telling him why. Besides telling him why he is not playing, tell him what he needs to improve on and how he can do it; then leave him with some positive comments, such as his great effort in practice is noticed, and to keep up his positive attitude.

How much playing time do you give rookies?

At the beginning of the season, rookie players and superstars should play almost the same amount of time. Some coaches will not play their weaker players until they come up to the level of the better players. But this is a "Catch-22": how can they get better if they don't play? You must decide to play your younger or weaker-skilled players no matter what happens. By playing, rookies and new players will improve their game and will begin to understand the playing system. You might lose some games early doing it this way, but later in the season you will win with the same players. Generally speaking, rookies do not win games—experienced players and "stars" do. When you reach the point when you know the game is won, this is the time to play your "lesser lights" more and to put them on the specialty teams to give them more confidence.

Substitute players who don't play

Do they pout or are they ready to play?

When players are extras on the bench or sidelines, they have a chance to learn a valuable life lesson. Of course all players want to play, so being on the team yet not playing regularly is a difficult position to be in. They have a choice on their outlook: they can sit patiently, work hard in practice, persevere through this rough stretch, keep a positive attitude by being a cheerleader for their teammates, and wait their turn to prove that they can perform when given the chance. Or they can sit and pout and complain about not playing and upset the whole team. If they choose the latter, you have to do something about it. Being a substitute is tough to handle, but a substitute player is expected to be a cheerleader, be positive, enthusiastic, and supportive of her teammates.

Your coaching philosophy should be if players dress for the game, you will try to play them, but for them to play, they must play good defence. Players do not go on the field/floor if they hurt the team defensively.

■ MOTIVATING THE TEAM DURING A GAME

Yell Praise from the Bench/Sidelines

You yell praise or encouragement to reinforce good plays, good skill execution, or proper behaviour. You must make sure you give encouragement for effort as much as for results. When giving encouragement, say the player's first name: "Nice pass, Bob," as this helps the player to remember you gave him praise. You should not wait for perfect execution to give praise. As long as there is improvement: the right idea, or good—not perfect—execution, you should give encouragement.

You should not always look for mistakes, as most coaches do, but you should look for players doing things right, such as any sign of progress in the execution of the playing system. If you praise good execution and good plays immediately, you will likely see them repeated, and players will play at a higher intensity.

Remember, "What gets rewarded, gets done." You should always be positive and enthusiastic on the bench, but at some point in time during the game, you might even have to act like a cheerleader to create positive emotion. When a team gets behind, players normally lose their enthusiasm, become quiet on the bench, and put their heads down. You want your players to be enthusiastic and yelling encouragement to teammates, no matter what the score.

But players do not want you to tell them what they think they want to hear. You should not pat players on the back when they made a mistake or a sloppy play. You should not praise someone who doesn't deserve it, since this type of praise does not help a player and gives him a sense of false confidence. Players want you to tell them what is in their best interest to make them better players.

Note: With some coaches, players really have to work for praise, so when these coaches do give praise, players know they really earned it and the coach means it.

Shout or Yell Playing Instructions from the Bench

Playing-instruction feedback

Instruction feedback should be the most common type of feedback given during a game. You yell instructions to the players from the bench during a game to help players perform better; telling them what to do, to get to the right spot, how to play the ball carrier a certain way, is all part of game coaching. Game coaching is not so much correcting fundamental mistakes, but giving the players instructions so they don't make playing mistakes. Game coaching is constantly reminding the players, teaching them, informing them, praising them, encouraging them, challenging them, and pushing them.

Yelling instructions is not criticism

If you yell out playing instructions or behaviour instructions to the players, is that criticism? It depends on how you say it, what you say, whether it is a personal attack on the player or whether it embarrasses the player. You should explain to your players that when you yell instructions at them to help their performance or behaviour during a game, it doesn't mean you are angry with or dislike them.

Correcting a Mistake on the Bench/Sidelines

The only thing you should remember is not to embarrass players in front of their teammates and fans. If you want to correct a playing mistake a player has made, you should wait until the player comes off the field/floor. If a player makes a mistake during the game, wait until after the shift before explaining to the player on the bench/sidelines what happened or ask her what she thinks she did wrong. Be aware of focusing on the player personally by giving her negative feedback, such as yelling at her, rather than focusing on her performance or the mistake by giving her technical feedback.

When something does go wrong on the floor, our tendency as a coach is to criticize the player who made the mistake, but if you do that, the player doesn't learn from his mistake. To say that "mistakes are the key component to success" sounds contradictory, but it's not. Mistakes help players become successful because they not only learn from them, correct them, and end up getting better, but they also learn how to respond to them.

You certainly have to totally understand your playing system so that if the players do something wrong within that system, you can point out the mistake to them right away. For example, telling your players where to play on defence because of wrong positioning; or how to play someone to force the play a certain way; or to look for the open man on the fast-break. You have to be constantly correcting your players, and sometimes criticizing them for mistakes, but you can do this mainly on the bench, or from the bench, depending on the situation.

Give specific instructions to correct

Here are some general instructions that seem meaningless when you are trying to correct mistakes: "If you don't win this faceoff, you won't take the next one"; "Pass the ball"; "Can't you catch the ball?" "If you are going to shoot, score!" "Stop him!"

You have to tell the player something specific on the bench/sidelines: to correct his technique, to stop the opponent, on how to pass, on how to shoot, and so on. To give good correction feedback regarding bad mechanics of a skill, you must first see the mistake. Then, you have to analyze the mechanics of the skill and tell the player what he did wrong. You might remind a player about a slight correction in the fundamental during a game, but most skill correction is done in practice. If it is a technical mistake during the game, it is your fault for not showing the player the right way in practice. If it is a positional mistake in the system, the player has to take responsibility for not understanding what to do, but you still have to explain during the game what he did wrong.

Talk to a player about his mistake

You give criticism on the bench to correct a playing mistake or bad behaviour, but only periodically for impact. If players are angry with themselves for making a mistake, let them cool off first before talking to them. Next, ask them what they thought they did wrong. Then, you will know if they understood their mistake; if not, you can explain what happened and what the player can do to fix it. If you yell at and criticize players all the time, the players eventually will become tired of it and tune you out.

When you talk to a player on the bench you want the player to first look you in the eye and acknowledge that he understands what you want him to do. If the player doesn't understand what he is being asked to do, he should ask questions to clarify. In certain situations, you should spend some time explaining to the player why he is being asked to do something during the game — rather than just ordering him to do it. If you "shorten" the bench in a crucial game or a crucial time in a game, you should tell the players involved that they are sitting out to give the better players more playing time. Just be honest. You don't have to lie and say you are benching them because they were playing poorly. But if you do bench players for a particular reason, tell them specifically why they are not playing.

Challenge players during a game

You should challenge your players during a game, asking them questions such as, "Is that the best you can do?" "Bob, you are going against the best scorer in the league. Can you stop him?" When you challenge someone, you are saying, "Prove me wrong."

Encourage Players to Talk on the Playing Field/Floor

One of the toughest things you have to do is to teach players to talk on the playing field/court/ice/floor during the game to get rid of any indecision or misunderstanding. The best way to do this is to keep reminding players to talk to one another all the time — players on the floor talk to teammates on the floor, players during a time out talk about adjustments to make, players on the bench talk to players on the floor giving encouragement and sometimes instructions. You can teach players to talk on the floor through constant repetition in practice, just as when practising physical skills. Another way to get players to talk is to tell them to think out loud while playing.

■ TIME OUTS DURING A GAME

When a time out is called, you want your players to sprint to the bench/sidelines and sit down, or stand close to each other, depending on the sport. Players on the bench will stand and cheer and let the players from the floor sit on the bench.

You want your players to look at you when you are talking. If everything is falling apart, you have to act confidently, keep your poise, and keep a positive attitude to make these important strategy points in a split second. You have to speak clearly, slowly, confidently, calmly, and positively. Your emotions will move the players more than your words.

Reasons for Time Out

If it is permitted in your sport, here are some reasons for calling a time out:

> ❯ You are losing
> ❯ The team is starting to fall apart and lose its composure
> ❯ Your opponent is on a scoring spree
> ❯ You have lost the tempo of the game
> ❯ You want to take the crowd out of the game
> ❯ You want to go through some strategy options to counter the opposition
> ❯ You want to give your players a rest

What to Say in Time Out

You can review what you are going to do, reinforce a certain point, give a few specific instructions or reminders, make a few minor adjustments or changes, stress some key points about what the team needs to do, or say nothing at all. You should make the players feel they are going to be successful by doing what you suggest.

> ❯ Ask the players: "What are we going to do?" "What play are we running?" "What defence are we in?" "Who on the opposition has the 'hot' hand?"

> ❯ Ask the players what word (a behaviour goal) did you write on the blackboard during the pre-game talk? Then ask them, "Is this the way we are playing?"

> ❯ If your team is behind in a game, you can direct them to keep doing what they are doing well and not to panic; to stick with the game plan and just pick away at the lead.

> ❯ Sometimes you have to tell it the way it is: "You are playing sloppy and you are not playing like a team. This has to change."

> ❯ Encourage players to talk during time outs so that you can get their opinions or a feel for what is happening; you might ask the players for their advice, as the players might see something different from what you see; or you might ask the players questions to clarify that they know what you are saying.

> ❯ Look players in the eye to see what "feelings" they are expressing: a look of excitement, alertness, and confidence with "fire in their eyes"; or a downcast look of doubt and defeat. If the players have a look of defeat, tell them: "This is what we are going to do to get the job done."

■ PROTECTING A LEAD DURING A GAME

One of the most difficult decisions you have to make during a game is whether to sit on a lead or to hold the tempo that you have built up to get the lead in the first place. The bottom line is that you have to play to win rather than to not lose. By playing not to lose or sitting on a lead, a team plays cautiously and conservatively; a team tries to take time off the clock by hanging onto the ball longer, called "milking the clock"; and a team relies heavily on their defence to hold onto the lead. All these will give their opponent a chance to come back and beat them. You do not want your team to end up playing "not to lose" instead of playing "to win" because if you think you will lose, you will lose—a "self-fulfilling prophecy."

You have to learn to win when you are ahead. So, if your team is ahead in a close game, you should play to win, by playing aggressively, by urging your players to keep on attacking, to keep on playing hard and enjoying the moment, and to keep on playing the same way that got you where you are right to the end, no matter what the score.

But there will be a certain "time and score" in a game, during the last few minutes, when the team is ahead and you have to make a decision to protect the lead by "milking the clock."

IT IS EASIER EMOTIONALLY TO CHASE A LEAD THAN TO PROTECT ONE

■ HOW A COACH MAKES A COMEBACK IN A GAME WHEN BEHIND

The toughest challenge for you as a coach is to stay positive, patient, and optimistic when losing.

You Need a Strategy or Game Plan to Get Back in the Game

> You stress to look to double-team the ball carrier on defence by forcing the ball to the corners and double-teaming it with the off-ball defenders sagging down-and-in to protect the net.

> You stress that you have to win every loose ball and faceoff.

> You stress that you have to fast-break or run even to the point of cheating your two top defenders on the opponent's shot. "We try to switch and keep the breaking defenders at the top of the defence. Our defensive rule is usually the team has to play honest defence, and nobody breaks until the shot is taken and we get possession of the ball. But here we make an exception."

> ❯ If down by two or three goals, you stress running a "hot" offence or a "three-second" offence, which involves moving the ball quickly to get shots off quicker.

> ❯ Stressing you have to full-floor/court press to cause havoc and turnovers.

> ❯ You might have to pull your goalie, if acceptable in your sport, to put an extra attacker on the floor for a six-on-five situation.

> ❯ Bottom line: You have to stress to your players to do a better job than their opponent is doing.

Play Your Best Players Constantly or Until They Are Exhausted

In critical situations, you don't think of plays, you think of players. It is players who make things work or make things fail. Players win games—not plays, not coaches. So you have to work around your better players by extending their shifts and playing them more on the specialty teams.

You can explain the substitution rule that if players are playing all-out, they are allowed to pull themselves out of the game to take breathers and put themselves back in when they are ready to go again.

Stress That Players Must Believe They Can Do It

When the chances of pulling out a win seem pretty slim, that's when belief and hope can rally the troops. A comeback is an attitude that starts in the hearts and minds of the players, where they believe they can do it. If the players believe they are capable of coming from behind, then *believing it is possible makes it possible.* It's the job of the coach to make players believers by using blunt commands such as, "We can do this"; by motivating players to keep on going; and by keeping a positive attitude.

You can ask your team: "Do you believe in miracles?" "Do you believe in the human will?" You can tell them that no one believes we can come from behind, but we can because we believe in miracles. "We believe in the power of the human spirit." "We believe that wars are won on 'will' power." "We believe we can 'will' ourselves to win." "We believe nothing is impossible."

Push Your Players to Play Hard

You have to stress to your players that they will need to redouble their efforts and make super-hustle plays. They have to step it up. And remind the players that they need to play with total concentration. If a team can achieve a championship without a struggle, it's not going to be very satisfying.

Set Short-term Goals for Players

You are always setting some short-term performance goals to attain for every game, such as, in the next shift: "We are going to get more loose balls than the opposition"; "We are going to keep our turnovers down"; "We are going to force the opposition into turnovers"; "We are going to stop the opposition from scoring."

Or you can set some short-term goals for a specific period of time, for example, "In the next five minutes, we are going to outwork our opponent." Or in the next shift: "We are going to outplay our opponents." So even if the team loses the game, it can go away feeling that it had won a few small one-on-one battles; played hard in that five minutes; or attained a few performance goals.

Encourage Your Players to Play Together

Losing causes players to think and act as individuals rather than as part of a team. Your role is to focus the players' attention on the team concept and play together rather than everyone trying to win the game by themselves, going one-on-one. Players, when behind, try to do more than they can do and end up losing their natural playing instincts. They must come together to find a way to win. You have to stress that players need each other more than ever to come from behind. You do not want players pointing fingers at teammates and blaming; it is the loyalty and caring for one another that will get the team through this adversity.

Remind Your Players: They Never Quit

You stress to players that they never give up; they never quit; they never stop believing they will be successful. They become determined not to lose by "thinking of a comeback." In fact, the team should play the same whether winning or losing.

Some teams give in when the game starts to go downhill, and that is when they lose. Your team refuses to give in even if the game starts to go downhill, as they know how to get back into the game. Losing tests their character, gives them an opportunity to shine, and gives them a chance to show that this team has character and that they do have the capability of coming from behind.

Remind Your Players to Play with Poise

Because playing sports is a game of emotions—at least 50 percent emotion—it is therefore a game of momentum, a game of tempo, a game of confidence. If a team gets behind by three or four goals, players shouldn't panic because if they can get one goal, they can get three or four goals back.

Panic will make players do things they will regret. Players who get too excited usually act before they think. Losing causes players to overplay by trying too hard, and that's when they come apart. When players are aggressive (trying too hard) and confused (not thinking) at the same time, mistakes happen. Order (disciplined system) now gives way to chaos (street-ball system).

Good habits and discipline are the best defence against panic. Playing sports is usually a marathon race, not a sprint. In other words, players have to realize that they do not have to get back in the game all at once (panic or sprint). They just keep "pecking away" at the lead, one goal at a time (marathon), with patience and poise, playing their game and staying in the team concept.

For the comeback, you, as the coach, must stay calm, focused, positive and confident; and utilize your best players. You have to stay the same whether losing or winning.

Make Sure Your Players Want to Be There

When things are going wrong, you just state to your players, "Where else would you want to be than right here playing? Everything we have worked for, everything we are about is on display right here, right now. You've got to love this!"

Remind your players that they compete for the sheer enjoyment and love of the competition and the game. So, regardless of the score, the mere testing of their abilities in these dire moments is the measure of the team.

■ NEGATIVE REACTION BY PLAYERS WHEN BEHIND IN A GAME

If a team's main objective of playing is "winning" and it gets behind in a game or things aren't going right, it overreacts like an average or normal team. Average teams look good only when they are winning; called "front-runners," they do all the normal things an average team would do when losing: they fall apart. There are certain typical behaviours that occur when a team falls behind in a game. Watch for these danger signs:

> Players get frustrated and hit the panic button. Their shooting becomes automatic, resulting in "bombing" their shots. They lack the patience to wait for a good shot.

> Ball carrier goes one-on-one a lot. The players stop working together; each player tries to win the game by him/herself.

> Players will hurry to correct being behind, and the more they hurry, the more careless they become.

> Players on the bench and on the floor display no enthusiasm and put their heads down in a "posture of defeat."

> Players will harp on the bench and on the floor; blame and criticize each other; and argue among themselves.

> Players display negative emotions; they get upset with the referee, with coaches, with their teammates, with the opposition; they overreact and throw their sticks or punch the air with their fists.

> Players lose discipline and end up taking bad penalties.

> Players have a tendency to look to you for reassurance and thereby lose their concentration.

■ HOW TO DEAL WITH REFEREES DURING THE GAME

Berating officials definitely works against you. Besides, you are focusing on something that has already happened—the past—and you can't change it, which is counter-productive, as you want your team to focus on the present. You have to concentrate mainly on your team during a game. You can't think about the referee or the opposition players, even though you are analyzing their systems. It's easy to get caught up with the refereeing, but it's best to ignore it. Officials are going to make some bad calls and some good calls.

You want to get every edge you can by making the referees your friends. How? By everybody calling the referees "sir" or "ma'am"; by players handing them the ball/puck; by players not questioning or arguing with every call they make. You can control how you want the referees to perceive your team: as a team that just plays and keeps its mouth shut. Referees are human and they will talk among themselves; and they might regard a team with a bad reputation differently than one with a good reputation. Here are some ideas regarding bad calls by referees:

Do Not Argue with Referees

One team rule should be that nobody argues with the referee or other officials. In fact, nobody should even talk to them except you, the coach; the team captain; and the assistants. You can't let everyone on the bench yell, complain, "nitpick," or "cry" about every call made by the referees. If any voice is heard from the bench, it should be yours alone talking to the referee. You must make it clear that you are the only one on the team who will question a referee's call and perhaps even argue to get a certain point across. Players should not respond to a referee's or official's poor call; they should keep quiet, keep their cool, and show proper respect.

Coach has to be a role model by not yelling at the referees all the time. A coach who knows he might not get any breaks in a game because of this particular referee can explain to his players that "We are going to get terrible refereeing and we have to accept it."

Complaining Can Hurt the Team

To the referees, you are either a good guy or a bad guy, good team or a bad team. If coaches and players bitch at referees, they will become the bad guys, and on a close or questionable call, the bad guy will get the bad call.

When you complain to the referee on every call or embarrass the referee, it hurts the team, and the referee will eventually give you a bad call as payback on a questionable call; whereas, if you treat officials with respect, they might give you the benefit of the doubt on a questionable call.

Also, if you start blaming the referees when a game goes badly, you will be giving your players permission to do the same. It becomes easy for players to blame the officials for their own mistakes. Also, by complaining to the referee on every call, you focus the players' concentration on the referee rather than on the game. They start watching the referee for questionable calls.

You can also find ways of getting the referee to work for you. You can put a "seed" or idea in the referee's mind; e.g., by calmly asking, "Did you miss that hit from behind?"

Note: Part of game coaching is getting players to adjust to a referee's calls by playing smart and according to the way he is refereeing. If a referee is calling every infraction there is, the team has to adapt to his calls.

■ HOW TO DEAL WITH PENALTIES/FOULS

Players have to learn to "take it" as well as "dish it out." A hard-nosed, tough player is someone who has enough grit to take a dirty check or foul and maybe return the favour later in the game, rather than retaliating immediately with the result of receiving a penalty/foul.

To stress discipline, ask the players, "How badly do you want to be successful?" "Are you willing to take a dirty hit for the team and not retaliate to be successful?" If a team wants to be successful, it needs to be disciplined: no "stupid" penalties, no "mouthing off" at the referees; and walking away from any confrontations. You must stress to players that they have to remain focused on their performance. Players must have the ability to keep their poise when everybody else is losing theirs. A disciplined team can still be a physical team without taking bad penalties. It plays physical and aggressive but within the rules of the game. It seems that teams that play on the edge and try to make things happen by playing overly aggressively are going to get aggressive penalties. Eliminating penalties/fouls is a high priority for most teams.

Notes: There are two thoughts about penalties. One is: the least penalized teams in most leagues are the top teams, as it reflects self-discipline. The other thought is that sometimes the bottom teams in the league are also the least penalized because they play conservatively rather than playing aggressively.

A few coaches want to intimidate the other team by not playing within or on the edge of the rules and end up taking a lot of bad penalties. Then they wonder why they are not successful. The biggest problem for coaches is teaching discipline, which is so important in being a successful team. Besides, most good teams cannot be intimidated; that is why they are good.

Penalties/Fouls Happen Usually for One of These Five Reasons:

1. *Lack of discipline*—stupid penalty, poor judgment penalty, uncontrolled aggression penalty. You must explain the difference between being "smart tough"—taking a dirty hit; and "stupid tough"—giving a dirty hit.

2. *Lack of technique*—you have to teach the proper way to check. Teach players to hit hard but clean.

3. *Lack of concentration*—mental errors, player "falls asleep" on the floor.

4. *Lack of self-control*—player gets upset from a bad call and "mouths off" at the referee or receives a dirty hit and takes a retaliatory penalty.

5. *Lack of work ethic*—because of laziness, players won't work for loose balls. Instead of fighting for a loose ball, they just hit the opponent from behind to prevent the opponent from picking it up, with the result of a penalty.

■ EXPECTED PLAYER CONDUCT DURING A GAME

You expect your players to play in a first-class manner: displaying self-control and self-discipline; showing only positive emotions on the playing field/floor; and showing no negative emotions, such as putting their head down and overreacting when things go wrong.

Rules for Players' Behaviour during Games

> Players are to be courteous to referees; to be quick and not sarcastic with "yes, sirs" and "no, sirs."

> Players are not to make comments to the referees about refereeing. No "mouthing off" to referees.

> The scorer points at the passer or makes contact with the passer.

> Teammates touch hands on a good play, but are not to be too showy, with hand slaps or other gestures.

> The bench must be alert, involved, enthusiastic, positive, and active.

> Players must show a great attitude by displaying positive body language.

> Players should compliment each other. Give positive encouragement to teammates, especially after a mistake.

> Players are not to make any criticisms or put-downs about teammates; they are to be positive and enthusiastic.

> Players are to be polite to other coaches and to their opponents.

> Players are not to make any comments about opponents; no "mouthing off" to opponents. When the opposition is trash-talking, they do not respond; they just let their opponents talk and they keep playing.

> Players are to stay focused on the game and be ready for the next play, no matter what has just happened.

> No retaliatory penalties.

> Players are to walk away from any confrontation.

> No profanity.

> After the game, when you give the traditional congratulatory handshakes: each player is to be professional and display sportsmanship; to look her opponent in the eye, give her a solid handshake, and congratulate her, win or lose.

■ PLAYERS' APPROACH TO THE "BIG GAME"

A long time ago, players thought that being in the right frame of mind was a matter of chance. Some days players were on, some days they were not. We now know that thoughts and emotions help players play their best when in the "zone," so it is important that players choose or control how they think and feel to get into the "zone." The way players enter the "zone" is being prepared and having a plan of mental preparation.

The term "in the zone" is when everything comes together; when your performance is automatic and effortless; when you become one with the environment; when everything seems to be happening in slow motion.

Although every single game should be a big game, a particular challenge for you as a coach is how you get your players to approach the "Big Game"—a big league game, against the top team, playoff game, or championship game. Big games magnify everything; they can rattle players' nerves and throw off their concentration; and they certainly offer many more distractions than an ordinary game. It could be the game where all the team's work over the season comes to an end and its long-term outcome goal for the season has approached. It's difficult not to treat these games as something special and to get nervous or fearful about them. Here are some ways to keep your team positive and confident when it comes time to play the "Big Game":

Mindset

The first and most important step toward the big game is the feeling that your players can succeed. The winner's mindset or approach comes first before the winning, so how players approach the game will make all the difference in the world. How they view the game is crucial because they know that their attitude affects their behaviour and performance. Players have to realize that they build these positive attitudes from their habits of positive thoughts; and build positive thoughts from their positive self-talk.

Self-talk

Players have a choice about how they view the pressure of the big game. Before the game, they either force themselves to concentrate on the positives or they let the negatives take over.

The great players control their thinking patterns because they know their inner positive thoughts affect their feelings, which in turn determine their performance. The great players know if they don't learn to control their thoughts, their thoughts will control them. So in order to control their thoughts, they first have to become aware of what they are thinking. So players consciously do positive self-talk over and over again to encourage positive feelings.

A player can talk himself into or out of anything. Before most games, players are going to hear two inner voices in their heads: a positive voice saying: "This is just another game"; "I am relaxed and confident"; "I can do it"; "I am ready and focused"; "I am energized." This voice will make them feel more relaxed and confident. Or a negative voice saying: "This is it! It's now or never!"; "This is a do-or-die situation"; or "I don't feel good." This voice will make them feel nervous.

One of the main goals of self-talk is to lower or eliminate negative thoughts. On a bad game day, a player will have negative feelings. As a result, he isn't relaxed, he isn't confident, and he can't focus properly. He cannot give in to these negative feelings, as they reduce his energy. Negative feelings can and should be stopped by just saying "Stop!" out loud and changing his self-talk to positive thoughts.

Think positive

Players must understand that they cannot play sports without making mistakes, getting upset, losing their concentration, having negative self-talk, and feeling tired and in pain. A team's positive outlook is the most important prerequisite for a successful game. Having the right mindset or approach toward the big game makes a big difference for players. What affects the outcome of a game more than anything else is your players' effort and attitude.

"What you expect to happen will happen!" It's amazing how "positive thinking" impacts on a team's performance. Players have to understand that positive thoughts are a powerful "self-fulfilling prophecy." If players think good thoughts, good things will happen. If a team thinks it is going to be successful in a game, it will be successful.

Think the impossible

A question to put to the players is, "Do you believe in the impossible?" Players have to understand that the game might be difficult, but it is not impossible. Remember, at one time these events were believed to be impossible: to climb Mount Everest; to run the mile in under four minutes; or to high-jump seven feet, and all these myths of impossibility were shattered. There are tons of stories of magnificent human achievement that no one believed possible until they happened. History has proven that feats that seemed impossible became possible through amazing efforts. As a coach, you can tell stories to illustrate, to inspire, to encourage, to inform, and to educate your players that what was once thought impossible became possible.

COACH CAN GIVE THE GIFT OF BELIEF AND HOPE

Project an attitude of confidence

There is a thin line between talents on all teams in most leagues. Therefore, the separation between the teams comes from their attitude, the mental aspect of the game. In fact, there is always a different attitude between the best teams and the average teams, where players are just going through the motions.

With the top teams, there is an aura of confidence, and there is so much cockiness and swagger that it's mind-blowing. The top teams always think positive and they always find a way to win close games. There are games where the elite teams have no business winning but they do even though they didn't play well and should have lost. The opposition played better, were more talented, but the elite team won because they were expected to win.

Notes: Lou Holtz once said that the difference between Notre Dame and South Carolina football is they both play and behave the same as anybody else; the difference is in the way Notre Dame thinks—their approach to the game.

Tell the players that they are getting better every game.

This game is an opportunity for success

You encourage your team to approach the big game as just another opportunity to "challenge" itself and to enjoy, rather than as something to fear. "What a great opportunity for us!" "What a great challenge for us!" It is just another obstacle, another adventure it has to face on its journey to the championship. But the team also knows that the greater the obstacle, the more satisfying the victory. As the Big Game approaches, everyone now has a sense of anticipation rather than of fear.

You want your players to value the competition, enjoy the challenge, and enjoy playing the game without the fear and worry of making mistakes or losing. "Let's have fun and let's go out and show what we can do."

Remember: The better the competition, the better the team is going to perform. Good competition forces players to elevate their performance to levels they thought unattainable.

THE GREATEST THRILL IN SPORTS IS CHALLENGING THE BEST

"We are ready to face our fears"

You remind your players that the best way to deal with fear of or intimidation by a superior team is to go right into its face. You tell them that being afraid is normal, and fear is part of any challenge. You overcome your fears by controlling your fears. You don't worry about the other team. You focus on what you have to do. All teams will hit a moment when they have their backs against the wall and it is their choice whether to be weak or strong when facing fear. They can show their courage by planting their feet, standing firm, and fighting.

You have to get up one more time

The great teams get themselves up to play every game, especially after a big win. It is not easy to get oneself up emotionally to play at high intensity game after game, but winning a championship is not supposed to be easy. If players want to be a championship team, they have to play when they are hurt, play when fatigued, and keep on playing when they get hit dirty. It seems the great teams play the hardest when they feel the worst.

Be Prepared for a Tough Battle

You can tell your players that "This is going to be the toughest game you are going to play all year. The opposition is going to be all over us, they are going to be very emotional, and the crowd will be loud. This is going to be a hard, tough-fought battle, but they are the most satisfying to play in. Our team has become 'battled tested' through all our adversities this year and now we are ready for this game. At some point in the game, somebody's going to give in, and it won't be us."

You approach every big game with the attitude that the game won't be handed to them—they have to earn their success. Players must understand that they are going to be tired because they are going to work hard, and to get to the next level, fatigue is inevitable.

Expect a Close Game

You can remind the players that this particular game is going to be a one-goal game, so everything they do is going to be important. Everything in the big game is magnified: one loose ball, one stop on defence, one good pass, etc. This game is going to be a close game; so if each player does "one more" thing than his opponent does, the team will be successful. If players win the one-on-one battles, they'll win the war.

Believe You Are Well Prepared

Your team has to believe that it is better prepared than the opposition team because it has worked so hard to get ready for this game. It knows it is in excellent shape, both physically and mentally, and is totally prepared for this game. Everybody knows they have a job to do, so they just go out and do it by "taking care of business." A key difference between a coach who is successful and a coach who isn't is not talent; it is about preparation. Good preparation and a good game plan give a team a quiet, confident manner.

Notes: Tell the players: "This game is the reason you ran those suicides and ran the track, worked out in the weight room, and practised so hard."

The team's confidence, leadership, and preparation infect both players and coaches alike.

Follow Your Normal Routine in Getting Ready

Although it's an important game, players get ready for the big game the same as they normally would for any regular-season game. Players develop their own pre-game routine that works for them and then stick to it, no matter the game. They do not do anything different. It is just another game. This preferred approach will help control the nervousness and "butterflies."

Note: Researchers have found that altering routines is one of the major causes of failure or not reaching one's potential at the Olympics.

Show Players How to Overcome Nervousness and "Butterflies"

Players must realize that they will be nervous before a game and must understand that being nervous or having "butterflies" is a good sign, as it prepares the body for competition. If players are not nervous before a game, this is when they should worry.

The problem is that players get too "keyed-up," too nervous, too worried, and think negative thoughts before a game; all this excessive energy creates tension, and tension tightens muscles, which interferes with their performance, erodes their confidence, and speeds up their breathing. No player, when tense or stressed, performs well. Players perform better when they are relaxed and focused.

The great players feel the same way as the average player does before a game. But how do these great players transform their feelings of fear into confidence; of tiredness into energy; of panic into poise? They learn to induce feelings of confidence, high energy, relaxation, fun, and challenge by mental preparation strategies. They move themselves from their "real selves" who show doubt, tiredness, and nervousness to "performer selves" who exhibit these positive feelings of energy, confidence, relaxation, allowing them to focus to get into the zone.

Coaches tell their players before a game to relax, stay loose, and enjoy the game, but the question is, how do they do this? The real opponent is within himself; the player has to win the battle of fear, anxiety, worry, game pressure, negative thinking, fatigue, pain, and tiredness. Here are a few strategies to help a player relax.

Self-talk

A good technique to build confidence and stay focused before the big game is players write down a positive, descriptive statement of how they want to play, such as, "I am going to attack every loose ball; I am going to take only good shots; I am going to play a pressure defence." These performance affirmations remind the players of their strengths and what to say when they do their self-talk.

Deep breathing and relaxing

One of the best ways to relax or calm down is to learn to control one's breathing. By being conscious of her breathing, it helps to relax the player because it takes her mind away from the worrisome thoughts that are causing the tension problem.

> ❯ **Just close the eyes and focus on breathing in slowly until the lungs are full; it is the in-breath that draws in the energy and generates power. Then, focus on letting the air out slowly; it is the exhale that relaxes. This proper deep breathing connects the mind and body by helping a player relax, focus, and energize.**

Muscle relaxation

Another way to relax or calm oneself down is by muscle relaxation:

> **Consciously tighten and then loosen the muscles, starting with the feet and ending with all the small muscles in the face.**

Note: Before the big game, stretch, try to relax, stay focused, and enjoy yourself.

Energizing

To energize players who are feeling sluggish or low on energy, have them do some physical exercises to get "pumped-up," such as push-ups or jumping jacks. Remember, a player gets energy by being energetic and doing aggressive physical activities.

> **Other methods of energizing:**

Taking a cold shower before the game

Stretching

Deep breathing

Making loud noises

Listening to loud music

Visualizing themselves as aggressive, powerful animals

Doing positive self-talk

Acting "as if" they have lots of energy

Taking a posture of confidence

Having fun by getting their teammates laughing

Visualization

Visualization is a mental rehearsal of how a player wants to play in the upcoming game. He can go through his best game in his mind, feeling the way he would like to feel.

> **Find a quiet, secluded spot. Sit down, close the eyes, and see and feel yourself playing: You might see bright colours; smell the air; hear the sounds; feel the touch of the floor on your running shoes. Feel the body movement of executing your skills; and feel the emotions of playing your best game. Envision yourself in the upcoming game against a specific opponent; see what to anticipate from him and what to expect from him. The more "real" the experience, the more effective the performance will be. You will end up feeling thoroughly prepared for the game.**

Visualizing himself performing his best performance will build the player's self-confidence and manage the pressure of the game.

Players Are Prepared to Control the Game

It doesn't matter how big, how tall, or how quick the other team is.

> ❭ If we play great defence, we will control the game.
> ❭ If we execute on offence, we will control the game.
> ❭ If we take good shots, we will control the game.
> ❭ If we make good passes, we will control the game.
> ❭ If we make good decisions with and without the ball, we will control the game.
> ❭ If we make passes against pressure, we will control the game.
> ❭ If we win the loose balls, we will control the game.
> ❭ If we can control the way we play and act, we will control the game.

We make the decisions whether to shoot or not, pass or not, play defence or not, run or not. Upsets occur when teams worry about things they can't control versus worrying about what they can control.

Players Are Prepared to Have Fun

You tell the players to enjoy the moment, to play for the joy of the game. You know fun will keep them loose. To relieve pressure, just remind your players that they are playing for the love of playing so they don't have to worry about winning or losing—just go out and have fun playing.

Players Get a Boost
from a "New Wrinkle," a "Secret Weapon"

Although your focus is on your own team and always on your team, you find that what really boosts the players' confidence is to add a "little wrinkle" to what they are going to do against a strong team. That "little wrinkle" represents "the ace in the hole," "the secret weapon" that will give your team an edge. This confidence allows for a more complete focus by the players on the performance goals. What is the secret weapon? It could be a little wrinkle on the defence, running a new offensive play, something that gives the team a competitive edge, something that they can do better than the opposition.

You can remind your team that their secret weapon is called the *"Fourth Quarter Domination."* Players know that when playing in the fourth quarter, it belonged to them. Why? They played hard over three quarters because of their great conditioning and they played ten players rather than five or six players by their opposition.

Some other wrinkles, especially against a good team, is to keep to a simple game plan that your players can execute; try to mix the tempo up with a slow game to a fast game to keep them off balance; go after them with the best stuff you have right away rather than waiting until the end of the game; and start the game with a play, offensively or defensively, that you can execute really well that will settle your players down. Stress to the team that if it can withstand the initial onslaught at the beginning of the game, it will have a good chance of staying close to them at the end of the game—which is all you want.

Players Are Prepared for Mistakes

What type of player do you want playing for you, especially in the big game: a player who plays conservatively so he doesn't make a mistake or a player who plays aggressively and doesn't worry about making mistakes? Aggressive players know they are going to make mistakes and they must have a plan to deal with them—they must have the mental toughness to overcome mistakes, and it is this toughness that comes from the belief that mistakes are part of the game; that mistakes will be made, and that each mistake is one step closer to success; that they view mistakes as opportunities to learn, so they look for the lesson in all mistakes; that they cannot let mistakes get them upset or angry; and that they must have an attitude of "what's done is done" and move on.

Players Expect to Be an Average-Size Team

You can tell your team to expect to be an average-size team (height, weight, size, speed) against this superior team so they shouldn't have to worry about how the other team looks. You never want your team to look at the other team and say, "Boy, are they big!" or "Look how fast they are!" or "Do they ever look good!"

■ COACH'S APPROACH TO THE BIG GAME

You approach every big game in a low-key fashion to prevent players from feeling they must win. The worst thing you can do before a big game is to overemphasize its importance by telling the players how important it is to win the game. But there is a fine line here because every player knows the truth about how important the game is or about how good the opposition is. In these situations, more than ever, your attitude has a powerful impact on the players' attitude. So you should put a big game in proper perspective by saying something like, "It's just like any other game, so let's take care of business and do what we have been doing." You can coach with intensity and enthusiasm, but you must stay under control and stay focused on your team so the players can enjoy themselves. You can remind the players that this particular game is just like a practice, and that they just play like they do in practice. It is important to be more concerned about the process of getting better than the outcome.

You Want Your Players to Dominate Their Opponent

These traits make a team dominant: competitive spirit, "willpower," persistence, relentlessness, physical and aggressive play, and physical toughness. There is a certain aura, a swagger, a confidence about a "dominant team." It often wins the battle before it begins. It's amazing how "positive thinking" impacts on a performance. "If a team believes it is going to win and believes it is going to crush its opponent, the chances are good it will." You develop an attitude that your team simply cannot be beaten—that it is an overpowering force.

Note: Coach wants the first game of the year to set the tone for the whole season!

You take risks

You create this feeling of domination by having your team taking it to the opposition right away, rather than watching them and saying, "Look how good they are" or "Look how big they are" or "Let's feel them out to see how they react." You don't want your players to be afraid of taking chances. They need to take risks—not recklessly, but with calculated boldness. Lots of teams change the way they normally play in the big game by playing it safe, being cautious or conservative, but not your team. When your team steps on the floor/field to play, their intention is not to beat the competition, but to attack and dominate them. Some of the greatest achievements in sports have come when coaches have taken the most risks.

You play aggressive

One of the team's behaviour goals is to play aggressively all the time. So you must approach every big game telling your team, "We go for it. We hold nothing back." "We attack every chance we get." "We make things happen." "We are going to take it right to them." "We will never have enough goals." "We will never ease up." "We will bury the other team." "We never sit on a lead." "We never play just to hold on."

You know that with your team's "A" game, it can beat anybody; anything less, and the opposition can beat them. In most leagues, anybody can beat any other team on any given night—there are usually no "give-me" games.

When ahead in a game, never let up

You never look back and relax when you are ahead in a game. You want your team to dominate their opponent and to play hard and aggressively for sixty minutes in every phase of the game, right to the end, no matter what the score. If you want to be a "dominant team": you push harder when you get a lead and you never have enough goals. If ahead, you still try to continue to score more goals; if behind, you know you can catch up.

One of the most difficult decisions for you to make in a close game is whether to sit on a lead or to hold the tempo that has built up the lead in the first place. By sitting on a lead, too many teams will allow the opposition to come back. You do not want to start playing conservatively and rely on your defence to protect the lead. If your team is ahead in a close game, you urge your team to keep on scoring, keep on being aggressive, and keep on enjoying the moment. You have to learn to win when you are ahead.

You remind your players of this attitude toward all games, but especially in the Big Game or the ones against superior teams.

BELIEVE YOU ARE GOING TO WIN

Focus more than ever

> Focus on the present moment. You have to have your team approach every big game by concentrating strictly on what it is going to do—the job at hand. In particular, you don't want the team to think about how it is doing, looking behind at mistakes, or looking down the road toward the end of the game. You don't want anything to distract the team from achieving its immediate objective. You want your team to approach every game planning to play "one shift at a time"—to stay in the present moment. So, in reality you don't care what the score is and you really don't want your players looking at the scoreboard.

> Players focus on things they can control. To perform at their peak, players must close their minds and block everything out except on the process, the journey, the moment, their performance of playing hard and smart. With this approach, players feel these are things they can control and therefore this creates relaxation and confidence.

Coach's Outlook for the Playoffs

Coach focuses on the playoffs. You want to stress to your team to play their last five games of the season as if they were playoff games so that they will peak at the right time and have momentum going into the playoffs. In playoffs, everything is magnified because of the pressure.

So, when the playoffs occur, you focus on reviewing everything; on getting a new outlook for the playoffs; and on your team becoming excited and re-energized. During a gruelling playoff series, do everything you can to rest your players; regroup them and go over videos.

If your team is down in the playoff series, it must concentrate in order to avoid getting overwhelmed and anxious. If your team is up in the playoff series, it must concentrate to avoid getting too excited and looking ahead, thinking about winning the playoff series. Your team must just focus on the task at hand, the present moment, playing "one game at a time," and not looking down the road.

Coach's Outlook on the Road for the Big Game

You have to love playing on the road because of the challenge. Your team's attitude has to be that they can beat any opponent, anytime, anywhere. Winning on the road is the most difficult thing to do. It takes extra focus and extra effort to win on the road. Your team must enjoy the challenge of going into someone else's home building or field and overcoming the adversity created by the environment. Some coaches on the road want to attack even more so than in their home space, to shut the fans up and listen to the silence. Other coaches want their team to play at a little slower tempo, play more zone defence, and be more conservative on the road. You as a coach have to decide on what approach you want to take. Good teams win at home; the great teams win on the road.

ABOUT THE AUTHOR

Jim Hinkson played lacrosse for only twelve years—until he was thirty-one years of age—but he felt lucky, because he went to ten national and professional championships and won six.

Jim started playing lacrosse at the ripe old age of nineteen years. He played for the famous Oshawa Green Gaels, where he won two Junior "A" Canadian Champions, in 1963 and 1964. After Junior he played Senior "A" in 1965 for the Brooklin Redmen, and ended up playing in the Canadian Finals again, but lost. In 1968, a professional lacrosse league was formed, and he played for the Detroit Olympics and went to the professional championship, but lost to a team from New Westminster. The following year, in 1969, Peterborough picked Jim up and he again ended up playing in the professional championship, but this time his team defeated New Westminster. From 1970 to 1973, Jim played in Windsor, where he won three Canadian Senior Championships. In 1974, Jim played for the Philadelphia Wings, which went on to the NLL Championship, but lost. During the same year, Jim also played for Canada in the World Field Lacrosse Championship in Melbourne, Australia.

Jim has coached at every level in lacrosse from house league to professional. He spent twelve years coaching pro, major, and junior lacrosse. His first professional coaching assignment was with the Philadelphia Wings of the NLL in 1975. After the league disbanded, he went to junior lacrosse in Toronto to coach the Rexdale Warriors Jr. "A" team from 1976 to 1977. Next, he ended up in Whitby, his hometown, and coached the Jr. "A" team there for three years. He went to two

Canadian Junior "A" Championships in 1978 and 1980 with the Whitby C.B.C. Builders, winning one. One of his big thrills was coaching the Whitby Midget "B" team to the All-Ontario finals in 1998. Since that time, Jim has coached St. Catharines Major Athletics, Akwesasne Major Thunder, New York Saints of the NLL, Toronto Jr. "A" Beaches, and the New Jersey Storm of the NLL.

Besides his involvement in lacrosse, Jim ran one of the most successful basketball programs in Toronto at Stephen Leacock C.I. He coached basketball for thirty-eight years and went to the All-Ontario two times. He has just finished coaching basketball at West Hill C.I. in Toronto for the past nine years.

In the summers, he worked basketball camps at Syracuse University, Michigan University, Penn State University, Olympia Sports Camp in Huntsville, Ontario, All-Pro Basketball Camp at Trent University, and Ridley College in Ontario.

In 1974, J.M. Dent and Son published Jim's first book, *Box Lacrosse: The Fastest Game on Two Feet*.

In 1982, during a "Mr. Mom" stage of his life looking after his children at his cottage, he wrote two more books: *Lacrosse Fundamentals* (1993, 2006) and *Lacrosse Team Strategies* (1996, 2006).

In the spring of 2001, Jim's fourth book, *The Art of Team Coaching*, was published by Warwick Publishing. Then Wiley & Son published *Lacrosse for Dummies* (2003, 2009). Recently, Triumph Books has published *Lacrosse Fundamentals* (2012) and will publish Lacrosse Team Strategies in 2013.

In 2012, Jim was presented with the Queen Elizabeth II Diamond Jubilee medal for his contribution to lacrosse.

Jim has been inducted into the Oshawa Hall of Fame (2009), the Whitby Hall of Fame (2006), the Canadian Lacrosse Hall of Fame (2000), and the Oshawa Hall of Fame (1992).

This was a tough book to write. Jim invites any feedback, good or bad, from his readers about anything regarding the book.

Jim can be reached at **jhinkson@sympatico.ca**. Please contact Jim if you would like him to do a coaching seminar on motivation for sports.